New Directions in Restor

New Directions in Restorative Justice

Issues, practice, evaluation

Edited by

Elizabeth Elliott and Robert M. Gordon

WILLAN
PUBLISHING

Published by

Willan Publishing
Culmcott House
Mill Street, Uffculme
Cullompton, Devon
EX15 3AT, UK
Tel: +44(0)1884 840337
Fax: +44(0)1884 840251
e-mail: info@willanpublishing.co.uk

Published simultaneously in the USA and Canada by

Willan Publishing
c/o ISBS, 920 NE 58th Ave, Suite 300
Portland, Oregon 97213-3786, USA
Tel: +001(0)503 287 3093
Fax: +001(0)503 280 8832
e-mail: info@isbs.com
website: www.isbs.com

First published 2005

ISBN 1-84392-132-4 Paperback
ISBN 1-84392-133-2 Hardback

British Library Cataloguing-in-Publication Data

A catalogue record for this book is available from the British Library

Project management by Deer Park Productions, Tavistock
Typeset by GCS, Leighton Buzzard, Beds
Printed and bound by T.J. International, Padstow, Cornwall

Contents

Notes on the editors and contributors

John Boersig is the Assistant Secretary, Indigenous Law and Justice Branch in the Commonwealth Attorney-General's Department, Canberra. Prior to taking this appointment he was a Senior Lecturer in the Faculty of Law, University of Newcastle, New South Wales. His research work there focused on clinical legal education and indigenous legal aid policy; his current research interest is in the relationship between restorative and indigenous justice. Over the past 20 years he has worked closely with many indigenous organisations, particularly Aboriginal Legal Aid services, as a lawyer and in policy development. Until recently he was also a part-time presiding member of the Guardianship Tribunal of New South Wales.

Serge Charbonneau is the co-ordinator of the Regroupement des organismes de justice alternative du Québec (Courrier électronique: scharbonneau@rojaq.q.c.ca). Holder of a master's degree in Criminology, he is particularly interested in questions related to restorative justice and mediation. He is currently working in developing a program on citizen-driven mediation and conflict resolution, and he is involved in mediations between offenders and victims of serious crimes.

Don Clairmont is Professor Emeritus and Director of the Atlantic Institute of Criminology at Dalhousie University. His research has always focused on social problems and social policy and, more particularly in recent years, on social movements and the justice system. He has published extensively on native justice issues and race/ethnic patterns in the criminal justice system. He has been the official evaluator of the Nova Scotia Restorative Justice Program over the past four years. Current research projects deal with restorative justice, native justice and the problem-solving court, linked by underlying philosophical and organizational commonalities.

Bob Cormier has a PhD in Psychology and has 30 years of experience in the field of criminal justice. He began his career as a psychologist at Kingston Penitentiary, and has occupied various positions in research, program development and policy at Public Safety and Emergency Preparedness Canada (formerly Solicitor-General Canada) since moving to Ottawa in 1982. His current position is Senior Director, Research and Community Development. He was also a member of the Canadian Delegation at the 8th (1990), 9th (1995), and 10th (2000) UN Congresses on the Prevention of Crime and the Treatment of Offenders.

Kathleen Daly is Professor of Criminology and Criminal Justice at Griffith University, Queensland. She writes on gender, race, crime and justice; and on restorative justice and indigenous justice. Her book, *Gender, Crime and Punishment* (1994) received the Michael Hindelang award from the American Society of Criminology. From 1998 to 2004, she received three major Australian Research Council grants to direct a program of research on restorative justice and the race and gender policies of new justice practices in Australia, New Zealand and Canada. She is Vice-president of the Australian and New Zealand Society of Criminology.

Elizabeth Elliott is an Assistant Professor, and Co-Director of the Centre for Restorative Justice, in the School of Criminology at Simon Fraser University, Burnaby, BC, Canada. Her teaching and research interests are primarily in the areas of restorative justice, prisons and criminological theory. She is a former community-based social worker specializing in prison and community reintegration, and taught university courses in Canadian federal prisons.

Dr Robert M. Gordon is a Professor of Criminology and Director of the School of Criminology at Simon Fraser University in Vancouver, BC, Canada. He is the co-founder and Co-Director of the University's Centre for Restorative Justice, and the Chair of the Steering Committee for the University's Gerontology Research Centre.

Arlene Groh (RN, BA) has been a Case Manager for the Home Care Program/Community Care Access Centre since 1990 with experience in both hospital and community settings. She was the Coordinator of the Restorative Justice Approaches to Elder Abuse Project (2000–2004). Currently she is the Elder Abuse/Restorative Justice Resource Consultant for the Elder Abuse Response Team; she is also a board member for Victim Services of Waterloo Region and for Focus for Ethnic Women.

Dave Gustafson (MA, RCC) is the founding and Co-Director of Fraser Region Community Justice Initiatives Association (CJI) in Langley, BC. CJI specializes in training, program development, conferencing and victim–offender mediation across the spectrum from minor schools conflicts to the most serious offences in the Canadian criminal code. Dave is Adjunct Professor in the School of Criminology at Simon Fraser University, Burnaby, British Columbia, where he teaches upper level courses on peace and justice-making theory, restorative models and practices; he also maintains a small psychotherapeutic private practice specializing in trauma recovery and is a doctoral candidate (KLU, Leuven, Belgium).

Gabrielle Maxwell is currently a Senior Associate in the Institute of Policy Studies and was previously Director of the Crime and Justice Research Centre at Victoria University Wellington, Senior Researcher at the Office of the Commissioner for Children and a Senior Lecturer in Psychology at University of Otago. Her current research focuses on youth justice, restorative justice, and family violence.

Brenda Morrison is a research fellow at the Centre for Restorative Justice, Research School of Social Science, Australian National University. She is currently seconded to the University of Pennsylvania, where she is working on developing restorative justice initiatives in schools in Philadelphia. Her primary interests are the development of restorative justice in schools and the psychology of restorative justice, specifically the process of shame management and identity management.

Melissa Ouellette has experience in the field of restorative justice including a work term in a victim–offender mediation program in Sheffield, England as part of an exchange she participated in while completing her Bachelor's degree at Simon Fraser University in Burnaby, BC. In addition, she co-ordinated a restorative justice program for youth in Vancouver, BC for three years. Most recently she completed a Master of Arts degree in the School of Criminology at Simon Fraser University. She is currently working as a research consultant for Indian Residential Schools Resolution Canada (IRSRC). ISRSC is a federal department that centralizes and focuses federal efforts on resolving claims associated with the legacy of the Indian Residential school system.

Jonathan Rudin is the Program Director at Aboriginal Legal Services of Toronto. He has written widely on restorative justice in general and aboriginal justice in particular. In particular he was commissioned to write for the Commission on Systemic Racism in the Criminal Justice

System, the Ontario Legal Aid Review, the Royal Commission on Aboriginal Peoples and Ipperwash Inquiry into the Death of Dudley George.

Tanya Rugge has a BA in Law and an MA in Psychology. Currently, she is a doctoral candidate in Psychology at Carleton University, examining the impacts of restorative justice processes on participants. She joined the Corrections Research team of Public Safety and Emergency Preparedness Canada (formerly Solicitor-General Canada) in 1997 and is currently a Senior Research Officer. Over the past several years she has interviewed numerous offenders and victims, conducted risk assessments, worked clinically with female offenders and conducted research on recidivism, high-risk offenders, young offenders and Aboriginal corrections.

Josephine Savarese is an Assistant Professor in the Department of Justice Studies at the University of Regina, Saskatchewan, Canada and a practising member of the Saskatchewan Bar. She earned her LL.M from McGill University in Montreal. Her current research interests include the analysis of restorative sentencing from the perspective of gender and the implications of legal reforms on women receiving social assistance on the Canadian prairies.

Inge Vanfraechem is a researcher at the Research Group on Juvenile Criminology, at the Katholieke Universiteit Leuven (Belgium). She is chair of the Research Committee of the European Forum for Victim–Offender Mediation and Restorative Justice. She is a member of the COST-Action A 21 'Restorative Justice in Europe' and was partner in a Grotius project on 'Victim–Offender Mediation for Juveniles in Europe' (2002–2003). She is currently preparing a PhD on conferencing for juvenile delinquents.

Lode Walgrave is Emeritus Professor of Criminology at the Katholieke Universiteit Leuven (Belgium), and Director of the Research Group on Youth Criminology. He has also been the Chair of the International Network for Research on Restorative Justice for Juveniles. He has recently (co)edited or written several volumes, book chapters and articles on restorative justice.

Howard Zehr joined the graduate Centre for Justice and Peacebuilding (formerly the Conflict Transformation Program) at Eastern Mennonite University in 1996 as Professor of Sociology and Restorative Justice and is now Co-Director of the program. Prior to that he served for 19 years as Director of the Mennonite Central Committee US Office on Crime and Justice. He received his BA from Morehouse College (Atlanta, GA), his MA from the University of Chicago and his PhD from Rutgers University.

Acknowledgements

The papers in this collection have been culled from the 6th International Conference on Restorative Justice, held in Vancouver, British Columbia, Canada on June 1–4, 2003. The authors would like to thank a number of people whose work through the Centre for Restorative Justice in the School of Criminology at Simon Fraser University made the conference a successful and useful event for practitioners, academics and government representatives. We first acknowledge the significant contributions of the Centre's coordinator, Meredith Egan, who in addition to the regular responsibilities of developing and operating the Centre, assumed a large bulk of the conference organizing workload. We particularly appreciate the manner in which she maintained a balance or 'head and heart' in all of her work, while modelling the values and principles of restorative justice for everyone involved in the planning and hosting of the conference.

We also recognize the work of the individuals on the conference steering committee, of which the authors were also members. The committee included: Dianne Brown, Ray Corrado, David Gustafson, Margaret Jackson, John Konrad, Neil Madu, Kay Medland, Margit Nance, Andrea Rolls, Penny Southby, Vince Stancato, and Jeff Wiebe. The steering committee members dedicated many hours to the event's planning and fundraising. The conference also benefited from the work of several students in the School of Criminology, who were involved in myriad preparations and provided hands-on support during and after the conference. For their contributions, we thank: Alana Abramson, Hazel Bissky, Bonar Buffam, Robb Chauhan, Lara-Lisa Condello, Tammy Hogan, Christine Lamont, Tim Lee, Scott MacMillan, Melissa Ouellette, Lisa Smith, Nicky Spires, Christy Tisdale, and Trent Van Helvoirt.

Finally, we thank the many institutions that provided financial support towards the development and presentation of the 6th International Conference on Restorative Justice: British Columbia Ministry of Public Safety and Solicitor-General, Correctional Service of Canada, David and Cecilia Ting Forum on Justice Policy, Department of Justice (Canada), Law Commission of Canada, National Crime Prevention Centre (Canada), Simon Fraser University, and the Social Sciences and Humanities Research Council (Canada).

Introduction

Restorative justice and best practices

Elizabeth Elliott and Robert M. Gordon

In the past 30 years, the beliefs and practices that together have become known as 'restorative justice' have re-energised the research and policy dialogues in the fields of criminology and public policy. Understood in various ways and on different terrains, restorative justice is found in practices as diverse as criminal justice system diversion programmes and other alternative measures, and in conflict resolution strategies addressing both school discipline issues and changes in school culture aimed at reducing conflict. Restorative justice has been seen both as a guiding philosophy for the practices of making and keeping peace in communities, and as a set of practices that provoke philosophical reflection about the meaning of key concepts such as 'justice' itself. These variants, among others, mark the journey of exploration that has affected thoughts, beliefs and practices in restorative justice.

Restorative justice has been described as 'one of the few big ideas in criminal justice', 'an important movement with huge benefits' and 'a genuine and powerful new idea about justice and crime'.[1] With only a few years of accumulated history, restorative justice is an idea that has found expression in various practices. Ongoing dialogue about the manner of this expression encompasses a spectrum of perspectives that speak to the relative consonance of practice with restorative justice philosophy. Howard Zehr notes that restorative justice 'is a kind of coherent value system that gives us a vision of the good, how we want to be together' (in Coben and Harley, 2004: 268). Embedded in this description is the reminder that restorative practices will ideally embody and reflect the core values espoused in the ideas that inform them (Elliott, 2002).

Since the first implementation of victim–offender mediation in Elmira, Ontario in 1974,[2] restorative justice has been primarily associated with the realm of criminal justice. In Canada, victim–offender mediation was first characterised as an alternative to incarceration rather than as 'restorative justice',[3] which was then seen as restitution within the existing, formal, criminal justice system. Nils Christie (1977) was to expand this notion of 'restoration' through the idea that conflicts were 'property' stolen from their 'owners' by 'professionals', and that the significant losses incurred by this 'theft' were the learning and human development opportunities afforded to 'property owners' by inclusive conflict resolution practices. This opening of a socio-cultural development dimension to restoration also created interesting questions for 'justice' as an almost exclusively legal concept. The result has been a continuing exploration of the challenges posed by both the coexistence and conflation of restorative justice practices and the criminal justice system, and the potential co-optation of the former by the latter.

In the 1980s, the 'alternatives to incarceration'[4] perspective coincided with the emergence of a victims' rights movement that challenged the capacity of the criminal justice system to respond to the needs of victims. By the end of the 1980s, the concerns of these two groups became, at least in part, conflated in the perspective that came to be known as restorative justice. In New Zealand, in 1989, the passage of the Children, Young Persons and their Families Act marked the first legislative attempt to implement restorative justice practices in child welfare and youth justice policy through family group conferences (Hassall, 1996). Later, in 1991, in Wagga Wagga, Australia, the New South Wales police implemented a variation of the New Zealand model that focused upon 'reintegrative shaming' and used a scripted method (Crawford and Newburn, 2003).

Meanwhile, in Canada, pioneering efforts in British Columbia in the early 1990s were focused upon the use of restorative justice, post-sentence, in cases of serious crime.[5] In the mid-1990s, in Sparwood, BC, the Royal Canadian Mounted Police began to implement conferencing using the Wagga Wagga approach in a model that has become known as 'community justice forums' (Chatterjee and Elliott, 2003). Simultaneously, in the Canadian North, attempts by the formal court system to facilitate justice processes that were more culturally sensitive to Aboriginal communities resulted in a hybrid model known as 'circle sentencing' (Stuart, 1996).

The interest in circles has moved beyond the confines of criminal justice to other areas of peacemaking and dialogue (Elliott, 2004a), both inside and outside Aboriginal communities. In New Zealand, Canada and the United States,[6] Aboriginal perspectives on justice have influenced, to varying degrees, the practices of restorative justice. By the early 2000s, restorative justice philosophy and practice was being referenced in Supreme Court of Canada decisions,[7] and reflected in key provisions of the new, federal Youth Criminal Justice Act 2003 (Elliott, 2004b).

After many years of theorising and practice, several conferences have examined the state of restorative justice and how it has delivered on its promises. In 2003, Simon Fraser University's Centre for Restorative Justice[8] hosted a conference – the 6th International Conference on Restorative Justice – in Vancouver, BC, which brought together practitioners and researchers to engage in dialogue on various themes selected for their resonance and controversy. These themes included youth, Aboriginal justice, victimisation and evaluation, and the chapters in this book are a compendium of ideas and research on these topics.[9]

The authors of the chapters represent a number of approaches to understanding restorative justice and include the views of practitioners, theorists and researchers. In many cases, the authors wear more than one hat. The voices of practitioners offer the wisdom of experience and reveal the subtle nuances of restorative practices, as expressed in the chapters by Serge Charbonneau, Jonathan Rudin, Arlene Groh, Melissa Ouellette and David Gustafson. Theoretical insights are also offered in different topic areas, particularly in the perspectives of Lode Walgrave, John Boersig, Josephine Savarese and Howard Zehr. Evidence from empirical research studies is provided in the chapters by Brenda Morrison, Gabrielle Maxwell, Kathleen Daly, Don Clairmont, Tanya Rugge and Robert Cormier, and Inge Vanfraechem.

The first modern renditions of restorative justice were generated within the realm of child welfare and youth justice. The focus on youth has been particularly profound over the years, notably since the late 1980s. Since youth are generally seen as a more promising group for diversion and for other alternatives to the formal criminal justice system, this is not surprising. It follows that most of the research on restorative practices has also been focused upon youth and Part 1 of this book covers four aspects of restorative justice involving young people.

Lode Walgrave begins with an examination of the potential, and the limitations, of the restorative approach for renovating youth justice in 'Towards restoration as the mainstream in youth justice' (Chapter 1). He describes the pressures on rehabilitative juvenile justice to deliver both punishment and lowered recidivism rates, contrasting this to the potential of restorative justice to meet the needs of both victims and offenders leading to greater satisfaction with justice goals. In line with many practitioners and researchers, Walgrave notes that future challenges lie in the dialectical process of addressing the tensions that are produced when implementing participatory, *informal* dialogical restorative processes within a *formal* legal system. Given this, he notes that the work ahead requires the development of good practice in consonance with sound normative and explanatory theory in restorative justice.

Commonly encountered in the domain of criminal justice, restorative justice has also made significant inroads into the realm of public education. Conventional disciplinary methods, coupled with a trend towards 'zero tolerance' policies on violence in schools, have not yielded the results anticipated in creating safe school environments. Brenda Morrison, in 'Restorative justice in schools' (Chapter 2), presents a framework for developing safe school communities using John Braithwaite's notion of responsive regulation, coupled with a focus on shame and identity management in addressing school bullying. Youth interventions based upon restorative principles are presented in the school context, in the implementation of preventative practices of building inclusive communities, and attending to smaller concerns and conflicts before they mushroom into serious incidents of violence. Morrison then offers a regulatory framework within which to place a range of interventions for youth in the school setting. The significance of this work may well be in the unspoken benefits of shifting the attitudes of youth about both peaceful conflict resolution and ways of being with each other, cultivating a more pervasive, normative awareness of restorative philosophy in the institutions of both schools and criminal justice for future generations.

One of the more seasoned researchers in the area of restorative justice and youth is Gabrielle Maxwell, who offers another significant contribution to the literature in 'Achieving effective outcomes in youth justice: implications of new research for principles, policy and practice' (Chapter 3). This chapter presents the findings of a three-year follow-up study in New Zealand involving 520 interview subjects who had participated in youth conferences between 1998 and 2001/2002. Maxwell notes that the results of this research 'are a strong validation of restorative justice theory; repair, reintegration, fairness and respect, participation and empowerment, and forgiveness are key elements in effective outcomes while punitive and restrictive sanctions and stigmatic shaming are counterproductive.' Her discussion reminds us of the importance of bringing core values of restorative justice to life in the practices employed to address youth offending. The research results also point to the perennially overlooked issue of harm prevention through a supportive and healthy rearing of children, something often missing in the lives of youth who later reoffend as adults.

The last contribution in Part 1 is by Serge Charbonneau. He examines the implications of Canada's new youth justice legislation from the perspective of practitioners in Chapter 4: 'The Canadian Youth Criminal Justice Act 2003: A step forward for advocates of restorative justice?' Charbonneau's analysis elevates concerns often raised about the bureaucratisation and professionalisation of restorative justice when communities and instruments of governance are expected to collaborate on matters of common interest. While restorative justice is not mentioned per se in the Youth Criminal Justice Act, it is clear that the Act is informed by existing restorative principles and practices. However, concerns are raised about other provisions of the Act that contradict the restorative perspective, particularly the raising of youth offenders to adult courts, with the prospect of concomitant adult punishments.

Part 2 of this collection focuses upon Aboriginal justice, another significant and influential stream in restorative justice philosophy and practice. The influence comes from at least two sources. First is the now widespread recognition that Aboriginal peoples around the world are over-represented in the courtrooms and prison populations of retributive justice systems. Second, Aboriginal traditions in peacemaking have much to offer restorative justice, particularly in shifting ways of understanding conflict and community through a deeply rooted orientation to relationships and holistic responses to harm. While Maori and North American Indian observers of restorative justice have many valid criticisms and queries to level at restorative justice for the partial and often distorted appropriations of their cultural traditions, the impact of Aboriginal ways on many renditions of restorative justice is significant.

Jonathan Rudin begins this part with his thoughtful discussion of the need for Aboriginal autonomy in 'Aboriginal justice and restorative justice' (Chapter 5). Here the discussion hinges on the impact of restorative justice on Aboriginal justice in Canada, as part of the continuum of problems generated within Aboriginal communities, post colonialism. Based upon his experiences with Aboriginal Legal Services of Toronto, Rudin notes that the integral component of community building in Aboriginal justice makes it difficult for Aboriginal organisations to respond meaningfully to the demands of criminal justice-based restorative initiatives. Rudin points to the three systemic problems of unrealistic timeframes for the set-up and implementation of programmes, the effects of elite accommodation within criminal justice that work against Aboriginal initiatives, and the difficulty of funding projects with needs that traverse many different government jurisdictions and mandates. The way forward, he argues, is for government funding agencies and justice personnel to relinquish some control over Aboriginal justice programmes and to recognise the need for Aboriginal communities to develop and control their own initiatives.

Writing from an Australian perspective, John Boersig addresses the over-representation of indigenous youth in the formal criminal justice system, a familiar issue in North America. In Chapter 6, 'Indigenous youth and the criminal justice system in Australia', Boersig writes from the basis of postcolonial theory, and highlights the symbiotic relationship between law and colonialism in the disproportionate criminalisation of indigenous peoples. He argues that the orthodox approach of sentencing juvenile offenders has failed to accommodate the holistic, child-centred focus of indigenous cultures, the purpose of which 'is to engender happy children'. The potential of restorative justice to remedy this situation hinges on the ability of restorative processes to alter the relationships of power based upon race. Like Rudin, Boersig concludes 'if restorative justice does provide a pathway to justice then it must be an initiative embraced and controlled by indigenous people.'

The final chapter in Part 2 addresses one of the key Supreme Court of Canada decisions invoking restorative justice in the context of Aboriginal peoples. In *R. v. Gladue*, the court endorsed sentencing alternatives that reflect the unique circumstances of Aboriginal offenders, a decision that has been seen as judicial support for restorative justice generally. Josephine Savarese, however, argues in 'Gladue was a woman: the importance of gender in restorative-based sentencing' (Chapter 7) that since the appellant is a woman the court could have expanded the sentencing directives in the decision to include factors unique to Aboriginal women. Within the formal criminal justice system, Aboriginal women are disadvantaged both as women and Aboriginals. Savarese traces the decisions in other Canadian cases involving race and gender, and argues that for restorative justice to work for Aboriginal women a strong focus on more equitable social policies is necessary.

One of the key strengths of restorative justice is the locating of the victim, at least theoretically, in the centre of justice processes. The ability of restorative processes to remain true to this tenet, however, is challenged and often compromised by the offender-focus of retributive justice systems. In Part 3, the topic of victimisation in restorative justice is raised and the chapters address different aspects of victimisation that are illuminated by the tension between restorative and retributive approaches. Voluntariness and vulnerability are two main themes in this part. Questions still remain about the role of victims in criminal cases where restorative processes are subjugated to the demands of formal justice. Simultaneously, other questions are raised around the vulnerability of both victims and offenders created by dialogical restorative processes where information that is shared might result in legal interventions that are not wanted by the parties involved.

Kathleen Daly begins this part with her examination of two restorative justice studies and the implications for victims. In this comparison, she reveals the complexity of victim involvement and the hazards of a 'one size fits all' expectation of victim satisfaction. 'A tale of two studies: restorative justice from a victim's perspective' (Chapter 8) demonstrates that while the courts have a limited ability to vindicate the concerns of victims, restorative conferencing is limited by the individual victim's capacity to engage in meaningful communication with the offender. In the latter instance, Daly notes that meaningful victim involvement is enhanced when victims are less distressed in the aftermath of the harm they have experienced. In the second study, which focused on sexual assault cases, victims reported more favourable experiences in conferences than in courts. The findings of these studies challenge practitioners and researchers to consider the nuances of human engagement from the victim's perspective in the responses to crime and other harms.

Another aspect of victim voluntariness is considered by Arlene Groh in 'Restorative justice: a healing approach to elder abuse' (Chapter 9). Groh's work with older adults was the experiential foundation for the development of an innovative project in Waterloo, Ontario where restorative justice processes are used to address abuses of the elderly by their caregivers. These cases often fall into the realm of the 'dark figure' of crime: crimes that go unreported to the criminal justice system. Abuses that are reported may be discounted by the authorities, and even if they are not discounted there may be no effective remedies for victims. The chapter highlights the evolution of the project, and how the attention on relationships and justice in circle processes help to meet the needs of elderly victims in a manner that does not cause them further harm.

The topic of restorative justice in cases of serious crime is the focus of Chapter 10, 'Exploring treatment and trauma recovery implications of facilitating victim–offender encounters in crimes of severe violence: lessons from the Canadian experience'. The author, David L. Gustafson, is a practitioner who developed, with a colleague, a restorative process designed to address the needs of victims and offenders in cases of serious violence where both parties wanted to work towards a mediated encounter. In this chapter, the focus is upon the success of this work with victims, which is attributed to the attention paid in the programme to the symptoms of post-traumatic stress syndrome. A case study is presented that illustrates the effects of post-sentence interventions guided by a healing, supportive practice that attends to the participants as survivors of trauma. Evaluations of this approach have demonstrated 'unanimous support' from both victim and offender participants, each of whom have participated on a voluntary basis. The implications of this work for criminal justice as a whole are significant, and suggest many avenues for policy and practice research.

The last chapter in Part 3 offers insight into a dimension of restorative justice processes that is often not considered: the legal claims of indirect victim stakeholders. In 'The involvement of insurance companies in restorative processes' (Chapter 11), Melissa Ouellette examines the involvement of insurance companies as stakeholders in restorative processes, particularly in cases of potential civil litigation. Motor vehicle accidents figure prominently in these cases, along with personal injury claims. As non-legislated restorative processes generally require an accused person to accept some measure of responsibility for the harm caused as a condition of participation, the person is put in a position of culpability and liability when participating in restorative processes. Ouellette considers the options for involving insurance companies in restorative processes, and suggests that this issue provokes questions for restorative justice practitioners about who the stakeholders in restorative processes are and how they should be involved.

Finally, and perhaps appropriately, the theme of evaluation and restorative justice is the focus of Part 4. Many years ago, Thorsten Sellin[10] commented that 'beautiful theories have a way of turning into ugly practices' (in Cullen and Gilbert, 1982: 152). More recently, and specifically on the topic, Crawford (2002) has expressed concern that restorative justice literature is much like 'butterfly collecting', where 'the examples sought are "pretty" or "exotic" ones that seek to illustrate the case for restorative justice, rather than engage with the less attractive aspects of social arrangement and human relations' (Crawford, 2002: 111). If restorative justice is to gain further credibility, especially among the sceptics, it also must be accountable as a theory and as a practice. It must display coherence and demonstrate its effectiveness in achieving its objectives. To this end, a number of authors have offered empirical and theoretical contributions that suggest both ways of evaluating restorative justice and future challenges for the area.

Part 4 begins with Don Clairmont's analysis of the Nova Scotia Restorative Justice Initiative in 'Penetrating the walls: implementing a system-wide restorative justice approach in the justice system' (Chapter 12). This chapter follows the implementation of an ambitious initiative to operationalise restorative justice throughout the justice system of one Canadian province. Initial consultations with non-profit agencies and justice system leaders revealed that despite other best-case scenarios, restorative justice would still encounter two walls of resistance: uncertain collaboration with criminal justice system personnel, and wariness on the part of victims and their advocates. With these walls in mind, Clairmont provides some outcomes of the data analysis generated to date, and highlights several process issues that demonstrate both successes and quandries for restorative justice programmes within a system-wide implementation strategy.

On a smaller scale, an evaluation of one programme – the Collaborative Justice Project (CJP) in Ottawa, Ontario – is the focus of Chapter 13: 'Restorative justice in cases of serious crime: an evaluation'. This chapter, by federal government researchers Tanya Rugge and Robert Cormier, examines the research into the effectiveness of a specific court-based restorative justice programme and provides an analysis of the results of participant interviews together with a one-year follow-up review of the criminal histories of the offenders. The CJP works with cases of serious crime for which a period of incarceration of two years or more is possible, at the post-plea (guilty), pre-sentence stage of the formal criminal justice process. As such, it is a good example of restorative justice at work within the conventional system. Rugge and Cormier conclude that over three-quarters of both victims and offenders indicated that their needs had been met by the project and almost all of them noted that they would choose restorative justice over the more conventional process in the future.

Another single project evaluation addressing serious crime is the focus of Chapter 14: 'Evaluating conferencing for serious juvenile offenders' by Inge Vanfraechem. In this chapter a conferencing project in Belgium is examined to determine the satisfaction levels of participants, the involvement of participant support networks and recidivism rates. The process model of conferencing is reviewed, noting that the presence of criminal justice professionals – particularly police and defence lawyers – is not unusual for the project. Vanfraechem then presents the results of action-research that examined both 58 juvenile files and the views of victims and practitioners. The evidence suggests that only about one half of victims attend these conferences, that only a few of these victims know about victims' assistance services generally, that a single conference for co-offenders is better for process integrity than separate conferences, and that recidivism rates are lower for young offenders who participate in the project.

A fitting conclusion to the book is provided by Howard Zehr, a long-standing and respected contributor to restorative justice theory and practice. Zehr extends his typical curiosity into the realm of evaluation, carrying with him many years of work with both victims and offenders. 'Evaluation and restorative justice principles' (Chapter 15) addresses several general issues and concerns with restorative justice theory and practice, from the perspective that evaluation is an element of restorative justice accountability. Zehr identifies four critical issues that speak to the need for continuing evaluation: formal methods using transformative guidelines; the conscious and structured accountability of board and committee inclusion; regular dialogue with various sectors; and the conscientious checking of restorative processes to ensure principled practice. Consistent with these concerns, he concludes: 'Restorative justice is above all about respect for all, and that such respect requires humility … Only if we are grounded in respect and humility can we prevent the restorative approach to justice that seems so liberating to us from becoming a burden or even a weapon to be used against others, as has happened so often with the reforms of the past.' We could not have said it better.

Notes

1 Taken from Butler (2004a). Respectively, the authors of these statements are David Daubney (Co-ordinator of the sentencing review team at the Department of Justice, Canada), Julian Roberts (Department of Criminology, University of Ottawa) and Kent Roach (Faculty of Law, University of Toronto).

2 The Victim–Offender Reconciliation Program (VORP) was the creation of Mark Yantzi and David Worth of the Mennonite Central Committee in Ontario, Canada. The case that catalysed the development of VORP involved two young men who went on a drunken spree and vandalised 22 properties; they agreed to meet with the property owners to apologise and make reparations. See Zehr (1990) and Butler (2004b).

3 The term 'restorative justice' was first coined by Albert Eglash (Llewellyn and Howse, 1999: 4) in the specific context of restitution (Eglash, 1977).

4 Alternatives to incarceration were motivated not only by a larger de-institutionalisation movement in the 1970s and 1980s, but by a penal abolition initiative that challenged the punitive mandate of formal justice responses to crime.

5 Fraser Region Community Justice Initiatives, in Langley, British Columbia, had been offering the VORP program as an alternative measure since 1982. In the early 1990s, Co-Directors Dave Gustafson and Sandi Bergen began offering similar services post-sentence to people involved in cases of serious harm, such as violent sexual assault, robbery and homicide. See Chapter 10 in this book.

6 In the US, Navajo traditions underpin community peacemaking courts (Navajo Peacemaker Courts) that have been in operation since 1982. See Yazzie and Zion (1996).

7 See, for examples, *R* v. *Gladue* [1999] 1 SCR 688; *R* v. *Proulx* [2000] 1 SCR 61, 2000 SCC 5.

8 Centre for Restorative Justice, School of Criminology, Simon Fraser University, 8888 University Drive, Burnaby, British Columbia, Canada V5A 1S6. Also at www.sfu.ca/crj.

9 The 6th International Conference on Restorative Justice was held in Vancouver, 1–4 June 2003. For further information on the conference check the Centre for Restorative Justice (School of Criminology, Simon Fraser University) website at www.sfu.ca/crj.

10 Sellin is recognised for producing seminal theoretical work on culture conflict: *Culture, Conflict, and Crime* (1938).

References

Butler, Don (2004a) 'Justice for all', *The Ottawa Citizen*, Saturday, 11 September.

Butler, Don (2004b) 'How a Drunken Rampage Changed Legal History', *The Ottawa Citizen*, Saturday, 11 September.

Chatterjee, Jharna and Elliott, Liz (2003) 'Restorative Policing in Canada: The Royal Canadian Mounted Police, Community Justice Forums, and the Youth Criminal Justice Act', *Police Practice and Research*, 4(4): 347–59.

Christie, Nils (1977) 'Conflicts as Property', *British Journal of Criminology*, 17(1): 1–11.

Coben, James and Harley, Penelope (2004) 'Intentional Conversations about Restorative Justice, Mediation and the Practice of Law', *Hamline Journal of Public Law and Policy*, 25(2), Spring: 235–334.

Crawford, Adam (2002) 'The State, Community and Restorative Justice: Heresy, Nostalgia and Butterfly Collecting', in Lode Walgrave (ed.), *Restorative Justice and the Law*. Portland, OR: Willan Publishing.

Crawford, Adam and Newburn, Tim (2003) *Youth Offending and Restorative Justice: Implementing Reform in Youth Justice*. Portland, OR: Willan Publishing.

Cullen, F. T. and Gilbert, K. E. (1982) *Re-affirming Rehabilitation*. Cincinnati, OH: Anderson.

Eglash, Albert (1977) 'Beyond Restitution: Creative Restitution', in Joe Hudson and Burt Galaway (eds), *Restitution in Criminal Justice*. Lexington, MA: Lexington Books.

Elliott, Liz (2002) '*Con Game* and Restorative Justice: Inventing the Truth about Canada's Prisons', *Canadian Journal of Criminology*, 44(4): 459–74.

Elliott, Liz (2004a) 'From Scales to Circles: Restorative Justice as Peacemaking and Social Justice', in Julian V. Roberts and Michelle G. Grossman (eds), *Criminal Justice in Canada: A Reader, 2nd edn*. Scarborough, Ontario: Nelson.

Elliott, Liz (2004b) 'Restorative Justice in Canadian Approaches to Youth Crime: Origins, Practices, and Retributive Frameworks', in Kathryn Campbell (ed.), *Understanding Youth Justice in Canada*. Toronto, Ontario: Pearson Education Canada.

Hassall, Ian (1996) 'Origin and Development of Family Group Conferences', in Joe Hudson, Allison Morris, Gabrielle Maxwell and Burt Galaway (eds), *Family*

Group Conferences: Perspectives on Policy and Practice. Monsey, NY: Criminal Justice Press.

Llewellyn, Jennifer and Howse, Robert (1999) *Restorative Justice – A Conceptual Framework*. Ottawa, Ontario: Law Commission of Canada.

Sellin, Thorsten (1938) *Culture, Conflict and Crime*. New York: Social Science Research Council.

Stuart, Barry (1996) 'Circle Sentencing in Canada: A Partnership of the Community and the Criminal Justice System', *International Journal of Comparative and Applied Criminal Justice*, 20(2): 291–309.

Yazzie, Robert and Zion, James W. (1996) 'Navajo Restorative Justice: The law of equality and justice', in Burt Galaway and Joe Hudson (eds), *Restorative Justice: International Perspectives*. Monsey, NY: Criminal Justice Press, pp. 157–73.

Zehr, Howard (1990) *Changing Lenses*. Waterloo, Ont.: Herald Press.

Part I

Youth and Restorative Justice

Chapter 1

Towards restoration as the mainstream in youth justice

Lode Walgrave

Abstract

Youth justice systems all over the world have been under pressure because of an ongoing debate about balancing treatment and punishment in the response to youth crime. The discussion seemed to be repetitive and dead-locked until the emergence of restorative justice opened new possibilities. Restorative justice increasingly appears to be a source of renovating practices and empirical evaluation, a central issue in theoretical and policy debates, and a ubiquitous theme in juvenile justice and criminal justice reforms worldwide. Restorative practices are being inserted into most crime response systems, especially those aimed at youth crime. In this chapter, both the potential and the limits of restorative justice for renovating juvenile justice are explored. In the first section, the essentials of restorative justice are presented. The second section asks which criticisms make a fundamental reform of juvenile justice systems necessary. The third section combines both issues and examines whether the restorative approach can respond satisfactorily to the criticisms. The final section reflects upon the conditions on which the further incorporation of restorative ideas into juvenile justice systems will depend.

Restorative justice

Restorative justice is rooted in multiple origins, such as victims' movements, communitarianism and critical criminology (Van Ness and Strong, 2002). It now appears as a complex domain covering a wide realm of practices, a challenging subject for legal and normative reflection and debate, and a fruitful field for theorising and empirical research. Restorative justice also is a social movement and a field of social science experimentation. Adding to the confusion are apparently similar visions that appear under banners such as 'transformative justice', 'relational justice', 'community justice' and 'peacemaking justice'. In this chapter, restorative justice is characterised as an option for doing justice that is primarily focused on repairing the harm that has been caused by a crime.

Outcome-based definition

This definition is clearly outcome-based. Probably most 'restorativists' prefer a process-based definition (Zehr, 1990; McCold, 2004). Well-conducted restorative processes indeed offer a powerful sequence of social and moral emotions like shame, guilt, remorse, empathy, compassion, support, apology and forgiveness in the offender, the victim and other participants (Braithwaite and Mugford, 1994; Maxwell and Morris, 1999; Harris, Walgrave and Braithwaite, 2004). Restorative justice may favour a common understanding of the harm and suffering caused, and an agreement on how to make amends; it may enhance the willingness of the offender to fulfil these agreements. It may produce satisfaction on the part of the victim, reintegration of the offender and restored assurances of rights and freedoms in society. Such a sequence is the ideal, which is often far from being fully achieved.

However important such processes may be, associating restorative justice with them is perhaps going one step too far. Why are such processes more restorative: because the expressions of remorse, compassion, apology, and forgiveness promote respect, peace and satisfaction? These feelings are outcomes. Voluntary processes are valued, not because of the process as such, but because of their possible restorative impact on the participants and the reparative outcomes they help to achieve. One cannot evaluate restorative processes without taking account of the restorative outcomes they explicitly or implicitly promote. Process-based definitions confuse the means with the goal and limit the possible means to achieve (partial) restoration.

Arguably, restorative justice must give maximal priority to such voluntary, deliberative processes, but restorative justice does not end when they are not possible. When voluntary processes cannot be achieved or are judged to be insufficient, pressure or force must be considered. These coercive interventions also should serve restoration (Wright, 1996; Walgrave, 2002a; Dignan, 2002). Possible judicial procedures should be oriented to enforce obligations or sanctions in view of (partial) reparation through, for example, material restitution or compensation to the victim, paying a fine to a victims' fund, or community service. Such sanctions can have an explicit reparative meaning, though their restorative impact will be reduced. Restorations are not a black-and-white option. Between fully restorative processes and not-at-all-restorative reactions, degrees of restorativeness exist (Van Ness, 2002; McCold, 2000).

Harm

A focus on repairing harm and not on what should be done to the offender is the key to understand restorative justice and to distinguishing it from both the punitive and the rehabilitative justice responses; that is why it is another paradigm (Zehr, 1990; Bazemore and Walgrave, 1999; McCold, 2000). It offers a distinctive 'lens', to use Zehr's term, to define the crime problem and how to solve it. Crime is defined by the harm it causes and not by its transgression of a legal order. Responses to crime should not, primarily, punish or rehabilitate the offender but set the conditions for repairing as much as possible the harm caused.

The harm considered for reparation includes all prejudices caused by the crime: the material damage; psychological and relational suffering by the victim; social unrest and community indignation; uncertainty about the legal order and about the authorities' capacities to assure public safety; and the social damage the offender causes to himself. The only limitation is that the harm considered by the restorative process must be caused by the particular offence. Social exclusion, for example, or psychological problems in the offender may cause the offending but are not caused by the offence. They should, therefore, not be included as primary objectives in the restorative justice process. However, not everyone accepts this limitation. Some believe that restorative processes must also address the underlying causes of offending as primary objectives. This would, however, risk a shift from a harm-focused to an offender-focused programme, degrading the victim into being a tool in the service of the offender's rehabilitation and not respecting the victim as a party on his own. The problems and needs of the offender need to be addressed, but they are not the primary objective of the restoration.

Restorative justice deals with crimes, which are also public events traditionally dealt with by criminal law. This is one of the difficult issues to be resolved in restorative justice theorising. What makes an offence a collective or a public event? After a burglary, for example, restitution or compensation for the individual victim's losses could be private, to be arranged through the civil law, but there is also a public side. We all are concerned that the authorities intervene and try to make things right. If the authorities did nothing, it would hurt all citizens' trust in their rights to privacy and to property. It has been proposed elsewhere (Walgrave, 2003) that the concept of 'dominion', first introduced by Braithwaite and Pettit (1990), be used to try to grasp the public aspect of crime in restorative terms.

Restoration

Different processes may lead to restorative outcomes, but not all are equally appropriate. As mentioned above, the most suitable processes are those that consist of voluntary deliberation between the main stakeholders. Many deliberative processes are currently available (McCold, 2001; Morris and Maxwell, 2001): mediations between the individual victim and offender, most of which are face-to-face, but some of which are intermediated by a go-between; various forms of conferencing in which the victim and the offender are supported by their communities of care (some also include participation by police or community representatives); and sentencing circles, in which the local, indigenous community as a whole is a part of a meeting on the occasion of a crime in its midst.

Besides a healing impact on the participants, the formal agreement after such processes may include a wide range of actions such as restitution, compensation, reparation, reconciliation and apologies. They may be direct or indirect, concrete or symbolic, and the degree of the offender's willingness to undertake such actions is crucial. It expresses his or her understanding of the wrong committed and his or her willingness to make up for it. For the victim, it means the restoration of his or her citizenship as a bearer of rights, and possibly also a partial material redress. For the larger community, it contributes to assurances that the offender takes rights and freedoms seriously and will respect them in the future.

Deliberative processes hold the highest potential for achieving restoration, but if voluntary agreements cannot be accomplished, coercive obligations in pursuit of (partial) reparation must be included in the restorative justice model. Restorative sanctions, enforced by judicial procedures as a result of assessed accountability for the consequences of offending, seem to leave few or no differences between such sanctions and traditional punishments (Daly, 2000; McCold, 2000). There are, however, some essential differences (Walgrave, 2003).

First, punishment is a means in the eyes of law enforcement and it is morally neutral. It does not include any message about the moral value of the enforced law itself. Some political regimes use punishment to enforce criticisable or even immoral laws. Restoration, on the other hand, is a goal and different means can be chosen to achieve it. The goal of restoration itself expresses an orientation toward the quality of peaceful social life, which is an intrinsic moral orientation.

Second, 'punishing someone consists of visiting a deprivation (hard treatment) on him, because he supposedly has committed a wrong' (Von Hirsch, 1993: 9). The pain is intentionally inflicted. An obligation to repair may be painful but is not inflicted with the intention to cause suffering; it may be a secondary effect only (Wright, 1996). Painfulness in punishment is the primary yardstick, while painfulness in restorative obligations is a secondary consideration only.

Third, the intentional infliction of pain 'involves actions that are generally considered to be morally wrong or evil were they not described and justified as punishments' (de Keijser, 2000: 7). The justifications in penal theories (Von Hirsch, 1998) do not convincingly demonstrate the need for systemic punishment. The a priori position that crime must be punished is itself dubious from an ethical standpoint. Thorough exploration is thus needed on alternative ways to express blame, to favour repentance and to promote social peace and order.

Restorative justice proponents advance their approach as being more promising. Deliberative processes, if possible, or obligations with a view to reparation, if necessary, are socially more constructive: they do not respond to crime-caused harm by inflicting further harm on the offender, but by aiming at the repair of the harm. When 'restorativists' consider imposing restoration this is ethically more acceptable than deliberately inflicting pain.

Doing justice

Restorative justice is also about justice. Justice has two meanings here. On the one hand, justice refers to a feeling of equity, of being dealt with fairly, according to a moral balance of rights and wrongs, benefits and burdens. In retributive justice, this balance is achieved by imposing suffering on the offender that is commensurate with the social harm he or she caused by his or her crime. In restorative justice, the balance is restored by taking away, or compensating, the suffering and harm. Victims feel that their victimisation has been taken seriously and that the compensation and support are reasonably in balance with their sufferings and losses. Offenders feel that their dignity has not unnecessarily been hurt and are given the opportunity to make amends constructively. All participants, including the community, feel reassured that rights and freedoms are taken seriously by their fellow citizens and by the authorities.

The best way to guarantee that the losses are well understood and that the reparation is adequate is to leave the decision to those with a direct stake: victims, offenders and others who are directly affected. 'Justice' is what those concerned experience as such. However, the state cannot withdraw completely; if it did, it would leave the parties alone to find a solution. In a voluntary restorative deliberation, the state must be present at least in the background to ensure that the deliberation takes place and results in an acceptable outcome, to guarantee a power balance in the deliberation, and to provide an opportunity to the parties to leave the deliberative process and turn to the traditional judicial response if one of them feels that their interests are not adequately acknowledged. Authorities then demonstrate that they take the victim's and the offender's rights and freedoms seriously, and safeguard the collectively assured set of rights and freedoms.

Legal justice

Justice also encompasses legality. Restorative justice means that the processes and their outcomes respect legal safeguards (Van Ness, 1996; Walgrave, 2002a; Dignan, 2002). Legal safeguards protect citizens against illegitimate intrusions by fellow citizens and by the state. This is obvious in coerced interventions, but it applies also in voluntary settlements. Participation may not be imposed. Agreements must be accepted by the parties and be reasonable in relation to the seriousness of the harm and to the parties' accountability and capacities. How to make sure rights are observed is a matter of debate among restorative justice proponents. Some rely fully on the potentials of communities. They fear the state's power to invade the process and undo its informal, humane and healing potentials. Others try to find a balanced social and institutional context, which allows maximum space for genuine deliberative processes but also offers full opportunities for all parties to appeal to judicial agencies if they do not feel respected in the process.

In a coercive procedure, all legal guarantees must be observed. A traditional criminal justice procedure offers safeguards such as legality, due process and proportionality, but it is not evident that these legal safeguards also apply unchanged in a system premised on restoration. The main function is different, the actors are partly different, and the social and judicial context is different. Contrary to the top-down approach of the traditional process, a restorative system should allow ample space for a bottom-up approach. Thinking about a legal context that combines maximum space for deliberative conflict resolution with complete legal safeguards is only a beginning (Braithwaite, 2002; Walgrave, 2002b; Von Hirsch et al., 2003). It is a crucial challenge for restorative justice development in the future.

The rehabilitative juvenile justice model under pressure

By the beginning of the twentiety century, most states and countries had developed jurisdictions and laws for children who committed offences (Mehlbye and Walgrave, 1998; Winterdyk, 2002). They focused more upon treatment or re-education of the young offender than on determining appropriate punishments for offences. Juvenile justice systems were seldom challenged until the end of the 1960s. By then, several forms of criticism were being advanced, which can be clustered under the following four headings.

Doubtful effectiveness

In juvenile justice it was believed that treatment-oriented courts could help endangered youths become conforming and useful citizens. Clinical and sociological research was undertaken in order to 'unravel' juvenile delinquency. Social work, educational programmes and clinical treatments sought to correct the deviant development of youthful offenders (Rothman, 1980). In the critical 1960s and 1970s, the courts and treatment programmes appeared to be biased by social and ideological prejudices to the disadvantage of the poor and ethnic minorities (Platt, 1969). Evaluations of treatments did not produce encouraging results (Sechrest, White and Brown, 1979). Indeed, some studies pointed to negative results, which were explained mostly through labelling theory. Diversion, however, led to net-widening and left court interventions untouched (Albrecht and Ludwig-Mayerhofer, 1995; McCord, Spatz Widom and Crowell, 2001).

Pessimism about treatment programmes has become more nuanced in the past two decades. A series of meta-evaluations suggest that under some conditions (notably proper staff training and expertise, and proper implementation and assessment), some programmes work (McGuire and Priestley, 1995; Lipsey and Wilson, 1998). It remains difficult, however, to generalise these conclusions. Firstly, the studies measure only quantifiable aspects of the interventions and seldom include context-oriented interventions, such as community building and its influences on social environment. Secondly, the evaluations mostly explore experiments in exceptionally optimal conditions. The step toward routine practices, in general, seriously reduces the gains of the evaluated programmes. Finally, the 'what works' analyses do not address ethical questions about the acceptability of lengthy and intensive restrictions of liberty, which often seem disproportionate to the modest seriousness of the offences committed, and which are of doubtful effectiveness.

Questions thus remain about the generalisability of treatments, about how far the judicial setting helps or hinders these programmes, and about how programmes can be combined with adequate legal safeguards. That

9

specific treatment programmes work for specific groups does not mean that the rehabilitation-oriented juvenile justice system as a whole is effective.

Ineffective legal safeguards

Under the dominant ideology of child-saving and child-raising, it was believed that legal safeguards could be replaced by clinical diagnoses and the juvenile court judge's adherence to common sense. Critical criminology and anti-psychiatry, however, exposed cultural and socio-economic biases in both clinical evidence and common sense. Children's rights movements launched the '4 Ds': decriminalisation, diversion, due process and de-institutionalisation (Empey, 1976). International organ-isations promoted conventions and advocated basic principles for dealing with children both in general and in court, as in the United Nations Standard Minimum Rules for the Administration of Juvenile Justice (1985).

In reality, however, a basic tension was inevitable primarily because juvenile justice jurisdictions tried to combine what cannot be combined satisfactorily. Basing sentencing upon the needs of the offender rather than on the characteristics of the offence inevitably erases enforceable limits on judicial intervention. The judgment is passed with a view to achieving resocialising aims in the future and is less, or not at all, based upon available and checkable characteristics of the offence committed. This 'prospectiveness' in the reaction to juvenile crime (Feld, 1993) and its extension through 'preventionist' ambitions make the juvenile justice system 'insatiable' (Braithwaite and Pettit, 1990): the needs of both treatment and prevention are infinitely large. Traditional legal safeguards are hard to combine with such a system because they are based upon 'retrospection', looking back at the offence, as a yardstick for measuring the permissible degree of restriction of freedom.

Harsher punishment for serious youth crime

Increasingly, juveniles who commit offences are no longer seen as helpless objects in need of treatment; they are viewed as persons who are accountable for their misbehaviour. This is especially true of patterned and violent juvenile crime. Some media dramatise urban juvenile crime and create an image of 'young predators', dangerous individuals who are uncontrollable threats (Singer, 1996). In such a climate, the need for risk management becomes apparent and is inevitably mixed with a retributive 'just deserts' approach. When added to the perceived (partial) failure of the treatment model, the punitive perspective provides arguments for stricter, harsher, and more incapacitating responses to youth crime (Feld, 1999; McCord, Spatz Widom and Crowell, 2001).

However, no valid empirical evidence supports the belief in the crime prevention effectiveness of harsher punishments. The effectiveness of punishment for improving public safety has never been demonstrated, neither through general deterrence (Sherman, 1993) nor through individual treatment (McGuire and Priestley, 1995). Moreover, the a priori position that crime must be punished is ethically questionable (Fatic, 1995; Walgrave, 2003), because it is increasingly clear that censuring crime may also proceed by using alternative processes and procedures oriented toward reparation. Punishment may incapacitate some violent offenders, but the need for incapacitation applies only to a reduced minority of offenders. Penal procedures may offer decent legal safeguards to arrested juveniles, but they may not be the only way to offer such safeguards.

Neglecting victims' needs and interests

Victims are often (mis)used as witnesses in the criminal investigation process and then left alone with their grievances and losses. Many undergo secondary victimisation by the criminal justice system (Wright, 1999; Shapland, Willmore and Duf, 1985). This is also true in youth courts where the rehabilitative view may be detrimental to victims' interests. To protect the young, judges sometimes screen the offender from the victim's anger and claims for restitution or compensation, based upon a concern that these would be too severe and too hard to fulfil.

Currently, the relation between the victim and criminal justice is under reassessment almost everywhere (Goodey, 2000). One spin-off is increasing experimentation with victim–offender mediation and conferencing, educative programmes with special attention to victimisation and judicial restitution orders. In their limited versions, these experiments remain subordinate to rehabilitation or punishment rationales. These experiments, however, are among the most vigorous foundations for the redevelopment of restorative justice.

Restoring juvenile justice through restorative justice?

This section explores whether the criticisms mentioned above could be responded to by re-orienting the juvenile justice system more towards restoration. Would a restorative system be more effective than existing systems? Are restorative justice principles reconcilable with essential legal safeguards? Do restorative responses offer credible responses to serious youth crime? Can they better meet victims' needs and rights?

Effectiveness

Evaluation research on restorative justice practices so far supports optimism. Several surveys (Schiff, 1999; Latimer, Dowden and Muise, 2001; Braithwaite, 2002; Kurki, 2003; McCold, 2003; Sherman, 2003) certainly show many methodological shortcomings, but the overall conclusions are that restorative justice interventions do work and produce outcomes more satisfying than the outcomes of punitive or purely rehabilitative interventions. They are more satisfying to victims and their communities of care, and there is no evidence to suggest that restorative practices have negative consequences for public safety.

As we are exploring here the restorative justice potentials for juvenile justice, we must pay special attention to the impact on the offender. As argued above, influencing the offender is not the primary aim of restorative interventions, but it is not contrary to it either (Bazemore and O'Brien, 2002). Empirical evidence confirms that restorative actions have positive effects on juvenile offenders and more so than traditional juvenile justice treatment programmes.

Satisfaction rates among offenders are high. Fairness experienced in the process and satisfaction with the outcome vary between 80 and 97 per cent of participant offenders (Braithwaite, 2002). Mediation and conferencing yield no, or only slight decreasing, effects in recidivism but '... even badly managed restorative justice programs are most unlikely to make re-offending worse' (Braithwaite, 2002: 61). Compared with the outcomes of court procedures, conferences appear to lower reoffending most in violent and serious offenders (Sherman, Strang and Woods, 2000; Hayes, 2004). This is paradoxical, because conferences are applied mostly to divert rather benign youthful offending from court appearances. Not all conferences have equal impact, however. Those in which the offender expressed remorse and which reached consensus on the outcomes are more effective (Maxwell and Morris, 1999; Hayes and Daly, 2003). Younger offenders desist more after conferences than older offenders (Hayes and Daly, 2004).

But one should not be naive. One conference of a few hours cannot make up for a life course which sometimes went wrong from birth. General living conditions and perspectives are better predictors for reoffending than a conference or no conference (Maxwell and Morris, 1999; Hayes and Daly, 2004). What we can assume, however, is that a conference, if it is well conducted, may offer a better opportunity for reflection and turning the page than the traditional judicial procedures. But the follow-up after the conference is at least as important as the conference itself.

Community service can be imposed as a punitive sanction with an educative aim or with the goal of achieving some (symbolic) compensation. Schiff concludes that 'when community service is imposed as a restorative sanction ... the possibility that community service will benefit offenders, victims and the community is considerably increased' (Schiff, 1999: 343). Several elements may help to understand these positive results. First, being involved in an action with a view to reparation may appear more reasonable and acceptable to offenders than being submitted to a treatment programme or punishment. Also, the priority for deliberative processes offers more potential for respectful and in-clusionary interactions. All of this may refer to what Tyler has called 'procedural justice' (Tyler, 1990). Being treated with respect and equity, being taken seriously and being listened to are crucial for citizens' perceptions of the justice system's legitimacy. For offenders, these factors affect reoffending rates more than formal punishments (Sherman, 2003).

Second, restoration can mediate the harms that the offender did to him or herself by his or her crime if he or she takes the opportunity to repair the consequences of the offence and expresses a willingness to conform. Mediation and conferencing offer a scene for moral, emotional com-munication and mutual understanding, which provide an opportunity to atone. Reacceptance and reintegration are more probable (Braithwaite and Mugford, 1994; Maxwell and Morris, 2001). By performing a community service, the juvenile can express his or her willingness to cooperate and thereby prevent further social exclusion or stigmatisation.

Third, mediation, conferencing and community service have educative potentials that go beyond traditional treatment or punishment responses. Mediation is set up primarily to benefit the victim, but the process also allows concern for the needs of the offender and for his or her social integration. Community service compensates symbolically for the harm caused, but it offers constructive elements for the offender through, for example, networking, learning experiences and social identity building (Bazemore, 1999).

Finally, restorative justice processes can help the offender (and his or her family) become aware of social, relational and psychological problems. The conversation in the conference may make it clear that, for example, drug use is a serious problem or that family conflicts have been dysfunctional for the education of children, which may lead families to accept or seek voluntary assistance. Many conference agreements include such elements.

Legal safeguards

In practice, mediation or conferencing is often carried out to teach something to the offender, using the victim as a kind of 'educative tool' in a rehabilitative framework. 'Educative' community services may be ordered that are disproportionate to the seriousness of the crime. Such anomalies happen because restorative practices are often isolated from their theoretical foundations, and are simply seen as additional possibilities within the existing system.

Basically, however, restorative justice has a better potential to respect legal safeguards than does rehabilitative justice; the focus on harm, for the latter, is retrospective and thus more appropriate than a focus on the needs of the offender. Harm already caused by the crime is a more controllable yardstick for intervention than are the offender's future needs. This kind of 'retrospectivity' is common to the retributivist approach to crime but, as argued earlier in this chapter, crucial differences between restorative justice and retributive punishment exist. In fact, restorative justice appears as a kind of inversed retribution (Walgrave, 2004b). In retribution, the blameworthiness of the unlawful behaviour is clearly expressed, the responsibility of the offender is indicated, and the imbalance is supposedly repaired by paying back to the offender the suffering he or she caused by the offence. *Retribuere*, in Latin, literally means to pay back.

Restorative justice clearly articulates the limits of social tolerance because disapproval of the act is expressed in the restorative processes. What distinguishes restorative censuring from punitive censuring is that the wrongfulness disapproved of is directly related to the harm to another person and to social life. Restorative censuring does not refer to an abstract ethical or legal rule, but to the obligation to respect the quality of social life.

As in punitive retributivism, restorative justice refers to the responsibility of the offender. Punitive retributivism uses a passive concept of responsibility: the offender is confronted with his responsibility by others, and must submit to the consequences imposed by the criminal justice system. Restorative justice refers to an active responsibility: the offender must take active responsibility by contributing actively to repairing the negative consequences of the offence (Braithwaite and Roche, 2001). Whereas passive responsibility is retrospective only, active responsibility is both retrospective and prospective.

The 'paying back' idea is present in restorative justice, and in a more genuine form than in punitive retributivism. In punitive retributivism, the balance (whatever this balance may be) is restored by paying back, to the offender, the suffering and harm he or she has caused. It is supposed that things are then evened out: both suffer equally as much. The total amount of suffering is doubled, but equally spread. In restorative justice, the offender's 'paying-back' role is reversed from a passive to an active role: he or she must pay back by repairing as much as possible the harm and suffering caused. Instead of restoring the balance by doubling the total amount of suffering, it is now restored by taking suffering away. Thus reversed, restorative retributivism also may include a kind of proportionality that, however, refers not to 'just deserts', but to 'just dues'.

Restorative justice holds the potential to develop the legal standards that allow the checks and balances which are needed in a constitutional, democratic state. These potentials are not always realised, but the retrospective dimension offers the ground for gauging the justification of the intervention and the reasonableness of the reparative obligations that may be imposed. In a rehabilitative approach, this ground is less available, because it refers less to controllable external criteria such as the seriousness of a crime or of harm, and more to the needs of the offender.

Responding to serious offending

Most restorative practices are used for less serious cases. Several reasons are advanced in support of the claim that restorative responses are inappropriate for cases of serious youth crime.

First is the notion that those who commit serious crimes respond only to punishment and deterrence. This reflects a naive view of the aetiology of crime, as if the seriousness of a crime expresses the offender's social callousness. Many very serious offenders are sensitive to social influences, can feel deep remorse and are prepared to work to undo what they have done.

Second is the idea that mild misbehaviour might be acceptable for restorative processes, but serious offences are unforgivable and warrant a proportionately hard treatment. Such offending must, indeed, evince public reaction including, possibly, coercion. As argued earlier, judicial force should also be imposed primarily for restoration and not to make the offender suffer. Whereas most restorative justice proponents accept the use of judicial force at the end of the 'intervention line' (i.e. as a last resort), it is a matter of debate how the voluntary and coercive interventions relate to each other.

Third is the belief that respect for the vicitms' feelings requires that harsh punishment be given. It is not clear that most victims of serious crimes want punitive responses. Experience, as in New Zealand and elsewhere, show that many victims of serious crimes, even the parents of murdered victims, agree to participate in a restorative process when it is proposed realistically. Research shows that victims, including those of serious crimes, are more satisfied and feel more respected after a restorative process than after being involved in a traditional penal justice procedure (Strang, 2002). Finally, the objectives of the judicial processes are broader than satisfying the individual victims and their families.

Finally, there is the notion that fewer risks can be taken with those who commit serious crimes, because their possible reoffending is more likely to involve serious revictimisation. Restorative justice proponents increasingly accept the need for the incapacitation of 'incompetent or irrational actors' who commit serious crimes (Braithwaite, 2002; Dignan, 2002). Sometimes, restorative ambitions must be subordinated to concern for public safety. The opportunities and the quality of possible reparation will be reduced, but restorative justice is not completely ruled out, as is shown by experiments in prisons for example (Umbreit, Bradshaw and Coates, 1999; Hagemann, 2003).

All in all, no principled or empirical arguments seem to justify excluding offenders and victims of serious youth crimes from restorative interventions. On the contrary, if the paradigm shift toward restorative justice is taken seriously, the amount of harm and suffering caused by a crime is a reason to favour restorative actions. Victims of serious crimes are hurt more than by trivial offending and are thus more in need of reparation. It may seem more difficult to achieve effective reparation after a serious crime, but it violates restorative justice philosophy to exclude victims of such crimes, in principle, from the possible benefits.

Victims' interests and needs

It may seem self-evident that restorative justice responses meet victims' needs better than does traditional juvenile justice. It is, however, more complicated than that. For rights-focused victim advocates, for example, the more offenders are approached in a constructive and respectful way, the less respect is shown for the victims. Fortunately, that oppositional approach is losing its impact (Weitekamp, 2001; Strang, 2002). Victims increasingly understand that they have much to lose in an unthoughtful coalition with the criminal justice system.

Despite their contrasting roles and originally contradictory views on the criminal incident, both victims and offenders have a common interest in constructively settling the conflict and in the social peace the settlement may facilitate. Victims are more satisfied if they participate in a restorative dialogue with the offender (Strang, 2002). In mediation or conferencing, the human contact in a secure environment reassures most victims, because of the respect and support they experience, because they observe the offender as a human being who is embarrassed by what he has done, and because apologies and other reparative acts express the offender's understanding of the wrong committed and his or her willingness not to reoffend.

However, some victims' concerns must be taken seriously. Some fear that the victim may lose, and that respect for his or her interests and needs may be subordinated to other interests. This risk is especially acute in the juvenile justice context, where the rehabilitative tradition is strong (Davis et al., 1988; Young, 1989). Pressure is exerted on the victim to participate, to be 'moderate' in his or her claims, or to accept agreements primarily based upon the offender's treatment needs. The victim's story may be used as a 'pedagogical means' to motivate the offender to undergo treatment rather than to understand, genuinely, the suffering with a view to determining appropriate reparative actions. Secondary victimisation may then occur.

Taking these problems seriously is no reason to abandon or delimit the restorative approach. On the contrary, it must be clear that abusing the victim runs counter to restorative principles and such deviations must be prevented by strengthening the links between practices and principles. Restorative justice's purpose is to restore, and secondary victimisation is unacceptable.

All in all, it is appropriate to conclude that restorative justice holds great promise for the future of juvenile justice. It offers benefits such that it can address the criticisms, already mentioned, of the predominately rehabilitative juvenile justice system. Restorative justice is more effective, even for reintegrating offenders. Its clear normative approach and its retrospective aspects provide stronger criteria for developing legal safe-guards. The appeal to the offender's personal responsibility seems more adequate for responding to serious crime, and victims are better off with restorative responses than with rehabilitative or punitive ones. Moreover, so far restorative justice does not provoke destructive consequences for public safety and it has a good intrinsic potential for public law enforcement.

A look to the future

Many countries have turned to restorative schemes in their juvenile justice systems in order to make young offenders accountable, to benefit victims, and to avoid a shift towards purely punitive approaches. How far this development will go is unclear. In the most ambitious visions, restorative justice will replace, within a few decades, the predominant treatment approach and become the mainstream response to youth crime. Others are sceptical, and believe that restorative justice will remain only one of the possible reactions to youth crime. Juvenile justice would then develop as a three-track model. Children and adolescents who, because of their age or obvious incapacity, would be considered to have only slight levels of responsibility, would be referred to welfare institutions operating outside of the judicial system but possibly under judicial supervision. Most children and adolescents would be considered able to take responsibility and would increasingly be invited (albeit under pressure) to cooperate in voluntary restorative processes or be subjected to judicial sanctions with a reparative component. Adolescents who are considered serious offenders and at risk for serious reoffending would receive penal sanctions, with a mixed rationale of incapacitation and punishment. The crucial question is how these three tracks might relate to each other, and especially how far the restorative track might reach.

Finding a balanced relation between restorative justice and the law

In their experimental stage, restorative practices can afford some *flou artistique* with regard to legal safeguards, because they are limited in scope and carried out by reformers whose personal moral authority makes serious violations of participants' legal rights unlikely. The more that restorative justice evolves into a kind of mainstream response, however, the more urgent it is to reflect on how to insert it into an adequate legal frame. Legal formalism must not intrude upon the restorative process, but the process must take place in a legalised context.

An intrinsic tension surfaces because the participatory philosophy of restorative justice, aiming at a maximum margin for informal dialogue and process, is difficult to combine with the need for formalisation and legalisation. How to juxtapose informal processes with formal procedures, how to rely upon communities while living in organised states, how to combine creativity and richness in the bottom-up approach with the clarity and strictness of the top-down approach, and how to complement priority with voluntariness and compliance with possible coercion are significant challenges. If restorative justice is taken seriously, the legal safeguards of the punitive systems cannot just be reproduced. Due process, legality, equality, a right of defence, the presumption of innocence and proportionality may be irrelevant or be applied differently. Perhaps other legal principles must be constructed that are more appropriate for the restorative perspective.

The restorative justice literature on these questions is not large. Sceptics doubt that restorative justice can ever offer decent legal standards and would keep it at the margins of the social response to crime (Ashworth, 1993; Von Hirsch, 1998; Feld, 1999). Among restorative justice proponents, different positions are held by so-called 'diversionists', 'maximalists' and 'purists'. The debate is now getting into its stride (Braithwaite, 2002; Walgrave, 2002b; Van Ness, 2003; Von Hirsch et al., 2003). It is one of the decisive themes for defining the possible scope of restorative justice in the future.

Developing good practice

Conferences and mediation are significantly different, and the differences matter. How victims and offenders are invited, guided and monitored and how community service is monitored make an important difference in victims' satisfaction and offenders' motivations and integration.

The experience with restorative processes and with facilitating compliance with reparative agreements is relatively recent. Many practitioners initially proceeded tentatively, based upon their experience and intuition, ad hoc exchanges with colleagues, a few available guidelines and a belief in restorative principles. They can gradually ground their work in programmatic guides and standards (Wachtel and Wachtel, 1997; Balanced and Restorative Justice Project, 1998; Umbreit, 2001), which are based upon extensive experience.

Restorative practice has improved drastically, leading to greater confidence and broader implementation. This is, paradoxically, a threat, as it may lead to routinised 'fast food' practices (Umbreit, 1999) with weak methodological underpinnings. There is a need for ongoing attention to the quality of what is done under the label of restorative justice, and for further developing practice methods. A good method is not a detailed sequence of 'tricks' but must offer orientations to see possible problems and advice on choosing well-considered options based upon intensive experience and a balanced view of what restorative justice can and cannot achieve. It requires a permanent interaction between reflexive practitioners and evaluative research to improve processes and outcomes. It will lead to more satisfaction among victims, offenders and communities of care, an extension of restorative practices to more difficult and more serious cases and an increasing credibility among professionals and the public.

Developing good normative and explanatory theory

Most restorative practices occur in the context of traditional systems which deliver mainstream responses and act as the gatekeepers to possible restorative practices. The gatekeepers may, for example, value mediation because it may influence offenders, or they may accept conferencing because it may include the family in the re-educative process. Genuine restorative values are neither recognised nor valued. It is difficult for restorative justice practitioners to challenge this view because they depend upon the judicial gatekeepers for the survival of their programmes.

Isolated practices run great risks. Paradoxically, the greatest threat to restorative justice may be the unbridled enthusiasm of policymakers, police, magistrates, judges and social workers for integrating a few techniques into traditional rehabilitative or punitive justice systems. A taste of mediation, a bit of conferencing or a pinch of community service are added to the system without questioning the fundamental principles.

The pioneering spirit risks getting lost and being replaced by routinised but uncommitted attitudes and practices that could deteriorate into 'fast food' restorative practices (Umbreit, 1999) ornamenting systems that would essentially remain unchanged. This could strip restorative justice of its renovating potential, and reduce it to a limited, additional opportunity within the conventional criminal justice system.

Therefore, the *technicité* of restorative justice must not be isolated from its theoretical and socio-ethical foundations. Despite some basic common understandings, there is no generally accepted, basic theory of restorative justice. However, such a theory is not what is needed because rigid definitions and rules could limit developments. It is the reflection and the debate itself that keeps the field sensitive to the essentials that must be preserved in the face of the traditional systems. Together with developing methods, ongoing theoretical and socio-ethical reflection must point to the essentials of restorative justice, bundle and interpret experience, and build reference models to orient practices, which all together form the best possible counterforce to avoid absorption into the traditional modes of responding to crime.

Public acceptance and strategy

In almost all western countries, crime problems are exploited commercially by a dramatising media and boosted through populist rhetoric by some politicians, which together lead to simplistic attitudes among much of the public. Many observers typify the social climate as being intolerant of deviancy and inclined to repressive measures against offending. If that is true, the chances that restorative responses will be generally accepted and promoted are significantly reduced.

However, reality is more nuanced. The media and the public represent different views and opinions. Simplistic repressive outcries may sound the loudest, but it is far from evident that they really are the mainstream (Roberts and Hough, 2002). There is an increasingly widespread understanding that purely repressive responses do not offer satisfying solutions and lead to escalations in problems (Skolnick, 1995; Tonry, 1995). There is a growing awareness that simply boosting repressiveness is leading crime control policy into a dead end, with more imprisonment, greater human and financial costs, less ethics and less public safety. Moreover, research on public attitudes towards crime show that they are not unfavourable to restorative responses (Wright, 1989; Sessar, 1999).

There is no reason to be too pessimistic about the future of restorative justice, particularly in the juvenile justice context. Public opinion is neither monolithic nor deterministic and it can be influenced. Restorative justice advocates have a strong case and they may have a profound influence on future developments, if the case is presented well. This is partly a matter of strategy (Walgrave and Bazemore, 1999: Van Ness and Heetderks Strong, 2002). Besides exploiting the full potential of restorative justice practice and vision, specific efforts must be made to get the story out to policy-makers, professionals, the judiciary and the public. If they are informed realistically about what can be achieved, and what cannot, they will be more open to giving restorative approaches a chance.

References

Albrecht, G. and Ludwig-Mayerhofer, W. (eds) (1995) *Diversion and Informal Social Control.* Berlin: Walter de Gruyter.

Ashworth, A. (1993) 'Some Doubts about Restorative Justice', *Criminal Law Forum,* 4, 277–99.

Balanced and Restorative Justice Project (1998) *Guide for Implementing the Balanced and Restorative Justice Model: Report.* Washington, DC: US Department of Justice, Office of Justice Programs, Office of Juvenile Justice and Delinquency Prevention.

Bazemore, G. (1999) 'After Shaming, Whither Reintegration: Restorative Justice and Relational Rehabilitation', in G. Bazemore and L. Walgrave (eds), *Restorative Juvenile Justice: Repairing the Harm of Youth Crime.* Monsey, NY: Criminal Justice Press, pp. 155–94.

Bazemore, G. and O'Brien, S. (2002) 'The Quest for a Restorative Model of Rehabilitation: Theory for Practice and Practice for Theory', in L. Walgrave (ed.), *Restorative Justice and the Law.* Cullompton: Willan Publishing.

Bazemore, G. and Walgrave, L. (1999) 'Restorative Justice: In Search of Fundamentals and an Outline for Systemic Reform', in G. Bazemore and L. Walgrave (eds), *Restorative Juvenile Justice: Repairing the Harm of Youth Crime.* Monsey, NY: Criminal Justice Press, pp. 45–74.

Braithwaite, J. (2002) *Restorative Justice and Responsive Regulation.* Oxford: Oxford University Press.

Braithwaite, J. and Mugford, S. (1994) 'Conditions of Successful Reintegration Ceremonies: Dealing with Juvenile Offenders', *British Journal of Criminology,* 34, 139–71.

Braithwaite, J. and Pettit, P. (1990) *Not Just Deserts: A Republican Theory of Criminal Justice.* Oxford: Oxford University Press.

Braithwaite, J. and Roche, D. (2001) 'Responsibility and Restorative Justice', in G. Bazemore and M. Schiff (eds), *Restorative Community Justice: Repairing Harm and Transforming Communities.* Cincinnati, OH: Anderson, pp. 63–84.

Daly, K. (2000) 'Revisiting the Relationship between Retributive and Restorative Justice', in H. Strang and J. Braithwaite (eds), *Restorative Justice: Philosophy to Practice,* Aldershot: Ashgate, pp. 33–54.

Davis, G., Boucherat, J. and Watson, D. (1988) 'Reparation in the Service of Diversion: The Subordination of a Good Idea', *Howard Journal,* 27, 127–34.

de Keijser, J. (2000) *Punishment and Purpose: From Moral Theory to Punishment in Action*. Amsterdam: Thela Thesis.

Dignan, J. (2002) 'Restorative Justice and the Law: The Case for an Integrated, Systemic Approach', in L. Walgrave (ed.), *Restorative Justice and the Law: The Case for an Integrated, Systemic Approach*. Cullompton: Willan Publishing, pp. 168–90.

Empey, L. T. (1976) 'The Social Construction of Childhood, Delinquency and Social Reform', in M. Klein (ed.), *The Juvenile Justice System*. Beverly Hills: Sage Publications, pp. 27–54.

Fatic, A. (1995) *Punishment and Restorative Crime-Handling: A Social Theory of Trust*. Aldershot: Avebury.

Feld, B. (1993) 'Criminalizing the American Juvenile Court', in M. Tonry (ed.), *Crime and Justice: A Review of Research*, Vol. 17. Chicago: University of Chicago Press, pp. 197–267.

Feld, B. (1999) 'Rehabilitation, Retribution and Restorative Justice: Alternative Conceptions of Juvenile Justice', in G. Bazemore and L. Walgrave (eds.), *Restorative Juvenile Justice: Repairing the Harm of Youth Crime*. Monsey, NY: Criminal Justice Press, pp. 17–44.

Goodey, J. (2000) 'An Overview of Key Themes', in A. Crawford and J. Goodey (eds), *Integrating a Victim Perspective within Criminal Justice: International Debates*. Aldershot: Ashgate, pp. 13–34.

Hagemann, O. (2003) 'Restorative Justice in Prison?', in L. Walgrave (ed.), *Repositioning Restorative Justice*. Cullompton: Willan Publishing, pp. 221–36.

Harris, N., Walgrave, L. and Braithwaite, J. (2004) 'Emotional dynamics in restorative conferences', *Theoretical Criminology*, 8, 2, 191–210.

Hayes, H. (forthcoming, 2004) 'Assessing Reoffending in Restorative Justice Conferences', *Australian and New Zealand Journal of Criminology*.

Hayes, H. and Daly, K. (2003) 'Youth Justice Conferencing and Reoffending', *Justice Quarterly*, 20, 4, 725–64.

Hayes, H. and Daly, K. (2004) 'Conferencing and Re-offending in Queensland', *Australian and New Zealand Journal of Criminology*, 37, 2, 167–91.

Kurki, L. (2003) ' Evaluating Restorative Practices', in A. von Hirsch, J. Roberts, A. Bottoms, K. Roach and M. Schiff (eds), *Restorative Justice and Criminal Justice: Competing or Reconcilable Paradigms?* Oxford: Hart, pp. 293–314.

Latimer, J., Dowden, C. and Muise, D. (2001) *The Effectiveness of Restorative Justice Practices: a Meta Analysis*. Ottawa: Department of Justice.

Lipsey, M. and Wilson, D. (1998) 'Effective Intervention for Serious Juvenile Offenders', in R. Loeber and D. Farrington (eds), *Serious and Violent Juvenile Offenders: Risk Factors and Successful Interventions*. Thousand Oaks, CA: Sage Publications.

Maxwell, G. and Morris, A. (1999) *Understanding Re-offending: Final Report*. Wellington, New Zealand: Victoria University, Institute of Criminology.

Maxwell, G. and Morris, A. (2001) 'Family Group Conferences and Re-offending', in A. Morris and G. Maxwell (eds), *Restorative Justice for Juveniles: Conferencing, Mediation and Circles*. Oxford: Hart, pp. 243–63.

McCold, P. (2000) 'Towards a Holistic Vision of Restorative Juvenile Justice: A Reply to the Maximalist Model', *Contemporary Justice Review*, 3, 357–414.

McCold, P. (2001) 'Primary Restorative Practices', in A. Morris and G. Maxwell (eds), *Restorative Justice for Juveniles: Conferencing, Mediation and Circles*. Oxford: Hart, pp. 41–58.

McCold, P. (2003) 'A Survey of Assessment Research on Mediation and Conferencing', in L. Walgrave (ed.), *Repositioning Restorative Justice*. Cullompton: Willan Publishing, pp. 67–117.

McCold, P. (2004) 'Paradigm Muddle: The Threat to Restorative Justice Posed by its Merger with Community Justice', *Contemporary Justice Review*, 7, 1, 13–35.

McCord, J., Spatz Widom, C. and Crowell, N. (eds) (2001) *Juvenile Crime, Juvenile Justice*. Washington, DC: National Academy Press.

McGuire, J. and Priestley, P. (1995) 'Reviewing "What Works": Past, Present and Future', in J. McGuire (ed.), *What Works: Reducing Re-offending: Guidelines from Research and Practice*. Chichester, NY: Wiley, pp. 3–34.

Mehlbye, J. and Walgrave, L. (1998) *Confronting Youth in Europe: Juvenile Crime and Juvenile Justice*. Copenhagen: AKF Forlaget.

Morris, A. and Maxwell, G. (eds) (2001) *Restorative Justice for Juveniles: Conferencing, Mediation and Circles*. Oxford: Hart.

Platt, A. (1969) *The Child Savers: The Invention of Delinquency*. Chicago: University of Chicago Press.

Roberts, J. and Hough, M. (eds) (2002) *Changing Attitudes to Punishment: Public Opinion, Crime and Justice*. Cullompton: Willan Publishing.

Rothman, D. (1980) *Conscience and Convenience: The Asylum and Its Alternative in Progressive America*. Boston: Little, Brown.

Schiff, M. (1999) 'The Impact of Restorative Interventions on Juvenile Offenders', in G. Bazemore and L. Walgrave (eds), *Restorative Juvenile Justice: Repairing the Harm of Youth Crime*. Monsey, NY: Criminal Justice Press, pp. 327–56.

Sechrest, L., White, S. and Brown, E. (eds) (1979) *The Rehabilitation of Criminal Offenders: Problems and Prospects*. Washington, DC: National Academy of Sciences.

Sessar, K. (1999) 'Punitive Attitudes of the Public: Reality and Myth', in G. Bazemore and L. Walgrave (eds), *Restorative Juvenile Justice: Repairing the Harm of Youth Crime*. Monsey, NY: Criminal Justice Press, pp. 287–304.

Shapland, J., Willmore, J. and Duf, P. (1985) *Victims in the Criminal Justice System*. Aldershot: Gower.

Sherman, L. (1993) 'Defiance, Deterrence and Irrelevance: A Theory of the Criminal Sanction', *Journal of Research in Crime and Delinquency*, 30, 445–73.

Sherman, L., Strang, H. and Woods, D. (2000) *Recidivism Pattern in the Canberra Reintegrative Shaming Experiments (RISE)*. Canberra: Centre for Restorative Justice, Australian National University.

Singer, S. (1996) *Recriminalizing Delinquency: Violent Juvenile Crime and Juvenile Justice Reform*. Cambridge: Cambridge University Press.

Skolnick, J. (1995) 'What Not to Do about Crime: The American Society of Criminology 1994 Presidential Address', *Criminology*, 33, 1–15.

Strang, H. (2002) *Repair or Revenge: Victims and Restorative Justice*. Oxford: Oxford University Press.

Tonry, M. (1995) *Malign Neglect: Race, Crime, and Punishment in America*. New York: Oxford University Press.

Tyler, T. (1990) *Why People Obey the Law*. New Haven, CT: Yale University Press.

Umbreit, M. (1999) 'Avoiding the "McDonaldization" of Victim–Offender Mediation: A Case Study in Moving Toward the Mainstream', in G. Bazemore and L. Walgrave (eds), *Restorative Juvenile Justice: Repairing the Harm of Youth Crime*. Monsey, NY: Criminal Justice Press, pp. 213–34.

Umbreit, M. (2001) *The Handbook of Victim Offender Mediation: An Essential Guide to Practice and Research*. San Francisco: Jossey-Bass.

Umbreit, M., Bradshaw, W. and Coates, R. (1999) 'Victims of Severe Violence Meet the Offender: Restorative Justice through Dialogue', *International Review of Victimology*, 6, 321–44.

Van Ness, D. (1996) 'Restorative Justice and International Human Rights', in B. Galaway and J. Hudson (eds), *Restorative Justice: International Perspectives*. Monsey, NY: Criminal Justice Press, pp. 17–35.

Van Ness, D. (1999) 'Legal Issues of Restorative Justice', in G. Bazemore and L. Walgrave (eds), *Restorative Juvenile Justice: Repairing the Harm of Youth Crime*. Monsey, NY: Criminal Justice Press, pp. 263–84.

Van Ness, D. (2002) 'The Shape of Things to Come: A Framework for Thinking about a Restorative Justice System', in E. Weitekamp and H. Kerner (eds), *Restorative Justice: Theoretical Foundations*. Cullompton: Willan Publishing, pp. 1–20.

Van Ness, D. (2003) *RJ City*. Online: www.restorativejustice.org.

Van Ness, D. and Heetderks Strong, K. (2002) *Restoring Justice*, 2nd edn. Cincinnati, OH: Anderson.

Von Hirsch, A. (1993) *Censure and Sanctions*. Oxford: Clarendon.

Von Hirsch, A. (1998) 'Penal Theories', in M. Tonry (ed.), *The Handbook of Crime and Punishment*. NewYork: Oxford University Press, pp. 695–82.

Von Hirsch, A., Roberts, J., Bottoms, A., Roach, K. and Schiff, M. (eds) (2003) *Restorative Justice and Criminal Justice: Competing or Reconcilable Paradigms?* Oxford: Hart.

Wachtel, B. and Wachtel, T. (eds) (1997) *Real Justice Training Manual: Coordinating Family Group Conferences*. Pipersville, PA: Piper's Press.

Walgrave, L. (2002) 'Restorative Justice and the Law: Socio-Ethical and Juridical Foundations for a Systemic Approach', in L. Walgrave (ed.), *Restorative Justice and the Law*. Cullompton: Willan Publishing, pp. 168–90.

Walgrave, L. (ed.) (2002b) *Restorative Justice and the Law*. Cullompton: Willan Publishing.

Walgrave, L. (2003) 'Imposing Restoration instead of Inflicting Pain: Reflections on the Judicial Reaction to Crime', in A. Von Hirsch, J. Roberts, A. Bottoms, K. Roach and M. Schiff (eds), *Restorative Justice and Criminal Justice: Competing or Reconcilable Paradigms?* Oxford: Hart, pp. 61–78.

Walgrave, L. (2004a) 'Restoration in Juvenile Justice', in M. Tonry and A. Doob (eds), *Youth Crime and Youth Justice. Comparative and Cross-National Perspectives*, Crime and Justice: A Review of Research, Vol. 31. Chicago: Chicago University Press, pp. 543–97.

Walgrave, L. (2004b) 'Has Restorative Justice Appropriately Responded to Retribution Theory and Impulses?', in H. Zehr and B. Toews (eds), *Critical*

Issues in Restorative Justice. Monsey, NY/Cullompton: Criminal Justice Press/ Willan Publishing, pp. 47–60.

Walgrave, L. and Bazemore, G. (1999) 'Reflections on the Future of Restorative Justice for Juveniles', in G. Bazemore and L. Walgrave (eds), *Restorative Juvenile Justice: Repairing the Harm of Youth Crime*. Monsey, NY: Criminal Justice Press, pp. 359–99.

Weitekamp, E. (2001) *Victim Movement and Restorative Justice*. Keynote address presented at the Fifth International Conference on Restorative Justice for Juveniles, Leuven, Belgium, 16–19 September.

Winterdyk, J. (ed.) (2002) *Juvenile Justice Systems: International Perspectives*. Toronto: Canadian Scholars' Press.

Wright, M. (1989) 'What the Public Wants', in M. Wright and B. Galaway (eds), *Mediation and Criminal Justice: Victims, Offenders, and Community*. London: Sage Publications, pp. 264–9.

Wright, M. (1996) *Justice for Victims and Offenders: A Restorative Response to Crime*, 2nd edn. Winchester: Waterside.

Wright, M. (1999) *Restoring Respect for Justice*. Winchester: Waterside.

Young, R. (1989) 'Reparation as Mitigation', *Criminal Law Review*, 1, 463–72.

Zehr, H. (1990) *Changing Lenses: A New Focus for Crime and Justice*. Scottdale: Herald Press.

Chapter 2

Restorative justice in schools

Brenda Morrison[1]

Abstract

Building upon Braithwaite's notions of restorative justice and responsive regulation, this chapter explores the growing concern for regulating safe school communities so that the needs of all members of the school community are addressed. The chapter touches on the findings of reviews of school violence in the United States, reintegrative shaming theory and procedural justice theory, grounding a responsive and restorative approach to regulating safe school communities, as well as best practice models. Central to these theoretical perspectives and the various practical interventions covered in the chapter is a discussion of the importance of shame management and identity management for students. Finally, the chapter develops a regulatory framework within which to place the range of interventions.

Introduction

At the time that the field of restorative justice was establishing itself in the mid-1990s, the vision for schools was already taking form. In 1994, Margaret Thorsborne, a school guidance officer (i.e. school counsellor) in a large high school (1,600 students), introduced restorative justice to schools in Queensland, Australia. She had heard about a new 'conferencing' approach that New South Wales police were adopting to divert young offenders from court, based on the family group conferencing model that was being developed in New Zealand. This approach drew on traditions within the Maori culture and aimed to address the marginalisation of Maori culture and youth, characterised by increasing social unrest and over-representation within detention facilities (McElrea, 1994). After hearing about the process, Thorsborne ran the first school-based restorative justice conference to address the issues raised by a serious assault at a school dance. The success of the conferencing approach abated her:

> ... search for a non-punitive intervention for serious misconduct ... In particular, an intervention for serious cases of bullying which did not put the victim at further risk and also involved parents of both the offender and the victim... [C]onferencing seemed to fit the bill of the ultimate intervention which increased empathy and lowered impulsivity on the part of the bully (Cameron and Thorsborne, 2001: 181).

Since this time, the use of restorative justice conferencing in schools has developed in many different countries to address a range of different behaviours, including property damage, theft, vandalism, drug-related incidents, truancy, damaging the public image of the school, persistent class disruption, bomb threats, as well as assaults and bullying (see Calhoun, 2000; Cameron and Thorsborne, 2001; Hudson and Pring, 2000; Ierley and Ivker, 2002; Shaw and Wierenga, 2002).

While it is important to study the use of restorative justice in schools across a range of behaviours, the study of bullying makes an interesting and compelling conceptual fit with the study of restorative justice, both in practice and theory. On a practical level, we know from research on the school rampage shootings (Newman, 2004) that bullying can feed the wider cycle of violence in schools; thus, the study of bullying is important to understanding and addressing the escalation of conflict and violence, with restorative justice offering a model of effective intervention (see Morrison, 2003; Morrison, in press – a). Bullying is also one of the most insidious forms of violence in schools and wider society, having widespread effects on those involved (Rigby, 2002). Children who bully in school are more likely to continue to use this form of dominating behaviour in other contexts, such as close relationships and the work place (Pepler and Craig, 1997). Through teaching children alternatives to the use of bullying, we may be able to intervene early and curb this pattern of behaviour. Theoretically, bullying and restorative justice have a seren-dipitous fit, in that bullying is defined as the systematic abuse of power

27

and restorative justice aims to restore the power imbalances that affect our relationships with others. Further, there is an interesting synchronicity to the emergence of these two growing fields of study: both have a recent history, emerging strongly in the 1990s.

Kay Pranis (2001: 7) explains how listening and storytelling, key elements of restorative processes, are important to empowerment:

> Storytelling is fundamental for healthy social relationships. To feel connected and respected we need to tell our own stories and have others listen. For others to feel respected and connected to us, they need to tell their stories and have us listen. Having others listen to your story is a function of power in our culture. The more power you have, the more people will listen respectfully to your story. Consequently, listening to someone's story is a way of empowering them, of validating their intrinsic worth as a human being.

Feeling respected and connected are intrinsic to one's self-worth; they are basic needs of all human beings (Baumeister and Leary, 1995). The reciprocal relation between these two needs, respect from others and connection with others, empowers individuals to act in the interest of the group, as well as their own. In the context of schools, feeling connected to the school community increases pro-social behaviour and decreases anti-social behaviour (McNeely, Nonnemaker and Blum, 2002).

School connectedness and social behaviour

There is building evidence that the need to belong is one of the most basic and fundamental human motivations (Baumeister and Leary, 1995). Given this, being marginalised or excluded from a community could be a potentially powerful blow to one's self-esteem. One experimental study found that social exclusion resulted in self-defeating behaviour, and the relationship was causal, not correlational.

> Apparently the desire for social connection operates at a motivational level that precedes the rational pursuit of enlightened self-interest. At very least, our results suggest that a strong feeling of social inclusion is important for enabling the individual to use the human capacity for self-regulation in ways that will preserve and protect the self and promote the self's best long-term interests of health and well-being (Twenge, Catanese and Baumeister, 2003: 423).

Likewise, further studies have shown that social exclusion reduces intelligent thought (Baumeister, Twenge and Nuss, 2002), increases aggressive behaviour (Twenge et al., 2001) and reduces pro-social behaviour (Twenge et al., 2003). These studies make the basic argument that social exclusion has interfered with optimal self-regulation; in other words, individuals' sense of themselves as a productive, responsible and caring citizen is no longer functioning in the best interests of the self and others.

This bears true in the context of school communities. A national longitudinal study of adolescent health in the United States found that students who feel connected to the school community are less likely to: use alcohol and illegal drugs; become pregnant; engage in violent or deviant behaviour; and experience emotional distress (McNeely, Nonnemaker and Blum, 2002). The inference for restorative justice is that through building the capacity for schools to foster supportive relationships for students, schools can address the feelings of estrangement and hopelessness that some students feel. The evidence suggests that the cornerstone of individual well-being, resilience, social development, and productive citizenship is through fostering positive relationships within the school community and the wider community. Theories supporting the practice of restorative justice, have, in different ways, highlighted the reciprocal influence between individuals and groups in building responsible and caring citizenship.

Theories supporting restorative justice

While there is not a single theoretical model that specifies the mechanism through which restorative justice is meant to work, the practice has strong theoretical connections with a number of theories from a range of disciplines (see Braithwaite, 2002). The two highlighted here, Braithwaite's reintegrative shaming theory (1989) and Tyler's procedural justice theory (see Tyler and Blader, 2000), are important to the analysis of bullying and restorative justice in schools that follows.

Procedural justice theory

Tyler's work on procedural justice is important because he shows that individuals care about justice because of concerns over social status, in that justice communicates a message about social status. Building on his theory of procedural justice, he shows that high levels of cooperative relations within institutions are found when individuals feel a high level of pride in being a member of that institution and a high level of respect within the institution (Tyler and Blader, 2000). Thus status is important to understanding the dynamics and outcomes of social engagement, specifically connection with a social institution and respect within the institution. This is corroborated by the finding of the National Research Council's review of the school rampage shootings of the 1990s (Moore et al., 2002). They conclude that concerns over social status are central to understanding, and preventing, deadly school violence:

> One message that comes through loud and clear in the [deadly school rampage] cases is that adolescents are intensely concerned about their social standing in their school and among their peers. For some, their concern is so great that threats to their status are treated as threats to their very lives and their status as something to be defended at all costs (Moore et al., 2002: 336).

These costs, tragically, often include the shooter's own life, as well as the lives of students, teachers and parents. The National Research Council recommends that:

> It is important for siblings, parents, teachers, guidance counselors, youth workers, and employers to be vigilant in noticing when these threats to an adolescent's status occur and to be active in helping them deal with their status anxieties … Young people need some places where they feel valued and powerful and needed – this is part of the journey from childhood to adulthood. If they cannot find paths that make them feel this way, or they find the paths blocked by major threats, they will either retreat or, in the case of lethal shooting and rampages, strike back against those who seem not to value them, or are threatening them, or are blocking their way. Holding spaces and pathways open for them may be an important way of preventing violence (Moore et al., 2002: 336).

Restorative justice is about creating spaces where the pathway that defines a young person's life can be reopened through addressing the power and status imbalances that affect young people's lives, particularly in the aftermath of harmful behaviours such as bullying and other acts of violence. This resonates with Howard Zehr's (2000) analysis of restorative justice as a journey to belonging, which:

> … implies that alienation as well as its opposite – belonging – are central issues for both those who offend and those who are offended against. The journey metaphor also suggests that the goal –

belonging – requires a search or a process and that belonging is not simply binary – you do or you don't – but rather might fall on a continuum. Paradoxically, perhaps, the journey to belonging often involves a journey to identity – the two are deeply intertwined, like a double helix (Zehr, 2000: 1).

Alienation, and the associated depression, were two of the key findings of the United States' Secret Services analysis of the school rampage shootings (Vossekuil et al., 2002; see also Newman, 2004). The Secret Service interviewed 10 of the boys responsible for the shootings, looking for trends along a number of standard social predictors, such as family life, school achievement and number of friends; none were conclusive, shattering the myth that these boys were poor achieving loners from dysfunctional families. However, besides the fact they were all boys, one factor in particular characterised more boys than not: three-quarters of the shooters 'felt bullied, persecuted or injured by others prior to the attack' (Vossekuil et al., 2002: 30). More recently, Newman's (2004) analysis also bears this out. She finds that while all the shooters were not bullied, in all but one of the cases she reviewed there was evidence of social marginality. In other words, the two basic needs of respect and connectedness within the school community were not fulfilled; the boys' social status had faltered to breaking point. Their aim was to recover lost status, and gain respect, through the only means they thought possible – the barrel of a gun.

Newman (2004: 229) proposes five necessary but not sufficient conditions for school rampage shootings, the first being:

> ... the shooter's perception of himself as extremely marginal in the social worlds that matter to him. Among adolescents, whose identities are closely tied to peer relations and position in the pecking order, bullying and other forms of social exclusion are recipes for marginalisation and isolation, which in turn breed extreme levels of desperation and frustration.

The other necessary conditions specified are: psychosocial problems that magnify the perception of marginality; cultural scripts that legitimise the means of resolving the feelings of desperation and frustration; the failure of surveillance systems to identify these students; and the availability of guns. These rampage school shootings are particularly poignant because they characterise deadly assaults on an institution – the school; that is, while the shooters typically chose some specific target for symbolic reasons, the attack was on the institution that failed to dignify their worth as human beings. Thus, while not always the case, marginality, characterised by the lack of respect and belonging, can have devastating institutional and personal consequences for all members of the school community.

Reintegrative shaming theory

Reintegrative shaming theory (Braithwaite, 1989; Ahmed et al., 2001) argues that shame over wrongdoing is related to an individual's sense of belonging within the relevant institutional group, such as family or school. Shame can become a barrier to the maintenance of healthy social relationships. Shame that is not discharged in healthy ways can lead one to attack self, attack others, avoid or withdraw (Nathanson, 1997). Restorative justice conferencing is used to break the cycle of shame and alienation, through a process of reintegrative shaming from respected others:

> … the discussion of consequences of the crime for victims (or consequences for the offender's family) structures shame into the conference; the support of those who enjoy the strongest relationship of love or respect with the offender structures reintegration into the ritual. It is not the shame of police or judges or newspapers that is most able to get through to us; it is shame in the eyes of those we respect and trust (Braithwaite, 2002: 74).

Ahmed (see Ahmed et al., 2001) has developed Braithwaite's (1989) ideas about shame and reintegration in the context of school bullying. In her survey research of elementary school students in Australia, she looked at common predictors of school bullying within three broad categories: family (e.g. family disharmony), school (e.g. school hassles) and individual (e.g. impulsivity and empathy). While many of these factors proved to be significant predictors of bullying, the shame management factor was an equally strong predictor (and stronger against a number of factors). Shame management also mediated many of the other factors within these three broad categories.

Ahmed (see Ahmed et al., 2001) differentiates between two types of shame management: shame displacement and shame acknowledgment. In reference to school bullying, shame acknowledgment is negatively correlated while shame displacement is positively correlated. Shame acknowledgment is associated with taking responsibility for behaviour and making appropriate amends; shame displacement is associated with retaliatory anger, externalising blame and displaced anger. In a further analysis, social discipline styles (punitive or reintegrative) by parents and schools, were associated with the development of bullying and victimisation in school. Thus there is converging evidence that there is a relationship between institutional disciplinary style and the development of shame management strategies. Interestingly, across the institution of family and school, the analysis showed that parenting disciplinary style carried more weight in classifying bullies, while school variables such as perceived control of bullying carried more weight in classifying victims (Ahmed and Braithwaite, 2004).

Social discipline, shaming and shame management

The social discipline window (Wachtel and McCold, 2001) is a useful model in differentiating restorative justice from other forms of social discipline, or regulation (see Figure 2.1). It also provides a framework for understanding reintegration, shaming and shame management. The punitive approach, high on accountability but low on support, characterises stigmatising shaming; the permissive approach, high on support but low on accountability, aims to reintegrate with no shaming; the neglectful approach, low on accountability and support, offers no re-integration and no shaming; while the restorative approach, high on both accountability and support, is the basis of reintegrative shaming.

Interestingly, Ahmed's (see Ahmed et al., 2001) analysis of shame management strategies over wrongdoing can be mapped onto the social discipline window in terms of the four categories of bullying status: non-bully/non-victim; victim; bully; bully/victim. In terms of accountability, non-bully/non-victims were willing to take responsibility for their behaviour and wanted to make the situation better; in terms of support, they feel others would not reject them following their transgression. Victims, like non-bullies/non-victims, took responsibility and wanted to make amends, but felt others would reject them following wrongdoing, signalling a lack of supportive relationships. For bullies, the inverse

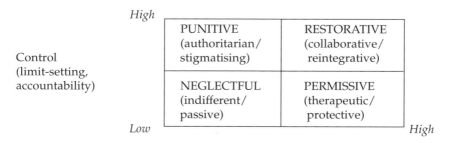

Figure 2.1 Social discipline window (Wachtel and McCold, 2001).

pattern was found: they did not take responsibility for their behaviour, nor want to make amends, feeling no one would reject them following the wrongful deed. Bully/victims captured the worst of this typology: they did not take on responsibility and make amends, but also felt others would reject them following the transgression.

One way to interpret this typology is to argue that victims need more support and bullies need to be more responsible, and accountable, for their behaviour. Indeed, this has been a typical approach to the problem of bullying and wrongdoing: wrongdoers get punished and victims get counselling and assertiveness training. However, this analysis is too simplistic, for we know from the theory and practice of restorative justice that support and accountability must always go hand in hand. Victims and bullies alike require appropriate accountability and support mechanisms. There is evidence that bullies become more accountable when offered the right support mechanisms, and victims, when supported but not held accountable for their behaviour, can fall into distressing cycles of helplessness. Bullies and victims, face to face, with their respective communities of care, increase support and accountability for all involved. The practice of restorative justice builds and supports a normative culture of support and accountability.

This analysis of shame management is corroborated by the clinical literature on shame (see Figure 2.2), drawing on the work of Lewis (1971) and others (see Ahmed et al., 2001). This literature suggests that: victims are caught up in ongoing cycles of persistent shame; bullies bypass shame; bully/victims are caught up in cycles of denied bypass shame; non-bullies/non-victims are able to discharge their shame over wrongdoing. Thus understanding shame management patterns does seem important to understanding bullying and victimisation; further, the relationship between shame management and shaming seems an important regulatory agenda to pursue (see also Ahmed et al., 2001).

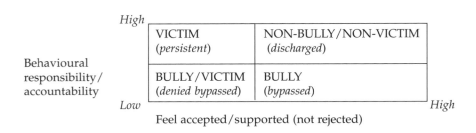

Figure 2.2 Bullying status and shame management

Shame management and identity management

More recently, Morrison (in press – b) integrated Tyler's work on pride and respect as measures of social identification with Ahmed's work on shame management in the context of school bullying. Scheff's (1994) work on shame and pride, following Durkheim's analysis of individuals and groups in society, also supported the analysis, in that he argues that pride builds social bonds while shame threatens to sever them. Based on this integrated analysis a number of hypotheses were tested, with empirical support largely established. In terms of the four bullying status groups, Ahmed's analysis of shame management was replicated, with the measures of pride, respect and identification complementing this analysis. It was found that: non-bullies/non-victims rated highest on both feelings of pride and respect within the school community and identified strongest with the school community; victims rated lower than bullies on the level of respect within the community; while both rated lower on levels of pride. Bully/victims, capturing the worst of both cycles, rated lowest on both pride and respect and identified least with the school community.

This research establishes an empirical association between shame management and identity management, both being indicators of school connectedness. While understanding the specifics of the causal mechanism requires further research, the current evidence supports the suggestion that:

> ... once we have reached the point where a major act of bullying has occurred or a serious crime has been processed by the justice system, shame management is more important than pride management to building a safer community ... Our conclusion is that the key issue with shame management is helping wrongdoers acknowledge and discharge shame rather than displace shame into anger ... Part of the idea of restorative undominated dialogue is that the defendant will jump from an emotionally destructive state of unresolved shame to a sense of moral clarity that what she had done is either right or wrong (Braithwaite, 2001: 17).

This analysis suggests that it is important for communities to create institutional space where harmful behaviour can be addressed through processes that enable shame to be discharged, before anger and other harmful emotions arise, with early intervention being the optimal point of intervention. This conclusion also resonates with Gilligan's (2001: 29) conclusion 'that the basic psychological motive, or cause of violent behavior is the wish to ward off or eliminate the feeling of shame and humiliation.' In other words, pride management not buttressed with shame management offers false hope for building the health and safety of school communities.

Responsive regulation and restorative justice

As the name implies, responsive regulation seeks to be responsive to the needs of those it regulates, scaling up or scaling down regulatory interventions, depending on the concerns of the agents involved and the extent to which the harmful behaviour has affected other members of the community (see Ayres and Braithwaite, 1992). In other words, responsive regulation advocates a continuum of responses rather than prescribed and singular responses. This approach can be contrasted with regulatory formalism, where the problem and the response are predetermined and mandated through codes of conduct, laws and other rules of engagement. Typically, a formalised response involves moral judgment about how evil the action is and a legal judgment about the appropriate punishment (Gilligan, 2001). In the context of schools, behaviour is often regulated through the rules specified in the student code of conduct. Zero tolerance policies, which mandate suspensions for certain rule violations however large or small, are an example of regulatory formalism within school communities. While the aim is to maximise consistency, regulatory formalism often targets those most at risk, through an approach that is high on accountability but low on support (see also Skiba and Noam, 2001).

> Zero tolerance is, intuitively, a reasonable policy – until you look under the veil. Ideologically it is part of a larger political project of 'accountability,' in which youth of color, typically, but not only, the poor and working class, are held 'accountable' for a nation that has placed them 'at risk.' Systematically denied equal developmental opportunities, they are pathologised, placed under surveillance, and increasingly criminalised (Fine and Smith, 2001: 257).

Braithwaite's (2002) ideas of responsive regulation and restorative justice, conceptualised as a regulatory pyramid of responses, offers an alternative to zero tolerance and other formalised approaches. The pyramid model aims to address the issue of when to step up intervention and when to step down intervention. The idea is to establish a strong normative base of informal restorative practices, but when that level of intervention fails, the recommendation is to step up intervention to a more demanding level. This multi-level approach to behaviour management is consistent with recommendations from a number of different sources: the National Research Council's (2002) report, *Deadly Lessons: Understanding Lethal School Violence*; Gilligan's (2001) model of violence prevention based on a healthcare model; and a growing number of approaches reacting to the rise of zero tolerance policies in the United States (see Skiba and Noam, 2001). As Skiba and Noam (2001) conclude:

> ... our best knowledge suggests that there is no single answer to the complex problems of school violence and school discipline. Rather, our efforts must address a variety of levels and include universal interventions that teach all students alternatives to violence, procedures to identify and reintegrate students who may be at risk for violence, and interventions specifically designed for students already exhibiting disruptive or aggressive behavior (p. 4).

They suggest that the most effective strategies: (1) provide instruction on resolving conflict and problems without resorting to violence; and (2) aim to be inclusive not exclusive. This is consistent with responsive regulation based on restorative justice.

Thus the growing consensus is that school safety should be regulated in line with public health regulation, that is along three different levels of preventative efforts that form a continuum of responses, based on common principles, at *primary*, *secondary* and *tertiary* levels. By way of analogy to the healthcare model, the *primary* level of intervention targets all members of the school community through an 'immunisation' strategy such that the community develops a defence mechanism, so that conflict does not escalate into violence when differences first arise. All members of the school community are trained and supported in the development of social and emotional competencies, particularly in the area of conflict resolution, so that members of the school community are enabled to resolve differences in respectful and caring ways that maximise re-integration. Three different universal interventions are outlined below.

The *secondary* and *tertiary* levels target specific individuals and groups within the school community, but still draw on and involve other members of the school community. It is through drawing on other key members of the school community that the intensity of the intervention at the *secondary* level increases. Typically, at this level of intervention, the conflict has become more protracted or involves (and affects) a larger number of people, with a facilitator being required. Peer mediation and problem-solving circles are examples of this level of intervention. The *tertiary* level involves the participation of an even wider cross section of the school community, including parents, guardians, social workers and others who have been affected or need to be involved when serious offences occur within the school. A face-to-face restorative justice conference is a typical example of this level of response.

Taken together, these practices move from proactive to reactive, along a continuum of responses. Movement from one end of the continuum to the other involves widening the circle of care around participants. The emphasis is on early intervention through building a strong base at the primary level, which grounds a normative continuum of responsive regulation across the school community. Across all levels, restorative practices aim to develop inclusive and respectful dialogue that focuses on the health and safety of the whole school community. This is consistent with the conclusion of the National Research Council's (Moore et al., 2002: 8) report which states: 'Specifically, there is a need to develop a strategy for drawing adults and youth closer together in constructing a normative social climate that is committed to keeping the schools safe from lethal incidents.'

This tri-level approach has been described in different ways: the primary (or universal) level targets all members of the school community, with an aim to develop a strong normative climate of respect, a sense of belongingness within the school community and procedural fairness. The secondary, or targeted, level targets a certain percentage of the school community who are becoming at risk for the development of chronic behaviour problems. The tertiary, or intensive, level targets students who have already developed chronic and intense behaviour problems. Within this conceptual model, the students who receive intensive intervention typically also receive targeted intervention, and all students, including those at the targeted and intensive levels, receive the primary intervention.

It also needs to be made clear that while the recommendation is to model violence prevention on a healthcare model, the model proposed is much more dynamic. Instead of a one-shot inoculation at the primary level, the intervention must be reaffirmed in the everyday practice of life at school. At the secondary and tertiary level, while particular students or groups of students are targeted, the inclusive practice of restorative justice necessarily involves students not at a risk. Targeted strategies are about reconnecting students at risk with the school community; thus they necessarily involve students not at risk. The behaviour of some students may keep them at this targeted level for ongoing periods of time, others may drift to this level only a few times, and others not at all. At the tertiary level, these students will have experienced all levels of intervention; however, relationship patterns have faltered to the extent that relationships need to be repaired or rebuilt. In summary, the focus of primary interventions is reaffirming relationships, the focus of secondary interventions is reconnecting relationships, and the focus of tertiary interventions is repairing and rebuilding relationships.

Continuums of response based upon restorative justice

The literature on the practice of restorative justice in schools outlines a number of different continuums of response; no doubt, in practice there are many more. One of the first to be documented was Wachtel and McCold's (2001) continuum of restorative practices that moves from the informal to the formal, with movement along the continuum involving '... more people, more planning, more time, are more complex in dealing with the offence, more structured, and due to all those factors, may have more impact on the offender' (Wachtel and McCold, 2001: 125). Specifically, the continuum of practices (from informal to formal) suggested are affective statements, affective questions, small impromptu conferences, large-group circles, and formal conferences.

Hopkins (2004) sees her whole-school approach to restorative justice as a framework that pieces together the jigsaw of life at school and describes a continuum of restorative processes of increasing complexity, where increasing numbers of people are involved in the process. Specifically, she suggests the following range of responses: restorative enquiry; restorative discussion in challenging situations; mediation; victim/offender mediation; community conferences and problem-solving circles; restorative conferences; and family group conferences.

Thorsborne and Vinegrad (2004) use a multi-level conferencing approach, dividing conferencing processes into two groups: (1) proactive processes which enhance teaching and learning; (2) reactive processes for responding to wrongdoing. Proactive processes are managed through classroom conferences that address a range of issues important to school life. Reactive processes include: individual conferences; small-group conferences; whole-class conferences; and large-group conferences.

Blood (2004) uses a regulatory pyramid approach, describing universal interventions that address the whole school and involve developing social and emotional capacity through: (1) accountability; (2) responsibility for self and others; (3) working together; (4) personal potency. These are put into practice within the school and classroom through policies, curriculum and social skills programmes. Secondary interventions manage difficulties and disruptions in the school and classroom through corridor conferencing, mediation and problem-solving circles. Tertiary interventions aim to restore relationships through the use of restorative conferencing.

These examples highlight the range of responses schools use in establishing a continuum of responsive regulation based on restorative justice. No one continuum has been shown to be more effective than the other; indeed, school communities mix and match these models developing a continuum of response that fits their needs and concerns. Needless to say, there is a strong need for research and development to establish and test different models, and levels, of responsive regulation through a whole-school approach. As a start, a few individual programmes that have been evaluated are outlined below. These are highlighted not because they are definitive programmes that define intervention at the primary, secondary or tertiary level, but because they have been tested against principles or theories of restorative justice.

Primary or universal interventions

A number of different programmes have been used as primary or universal intervention programmes. The three highlighted below emphasise resolving conflict: creatively (Resolving Conflict Creatively Program: Lantieri and Patti, 1996); peacefully (Help Increase the Peace Project: Anderson, 1999) and productively (Responsible Citizenship Program: Morrison, in press – a). Each aims to create a diverse culture of social relationships, which affirms and regulates healthy and responsible behaviour.

Resolving Conflict Creatively Program (RCCP)

This comprehensive K-12 programme supports school communities in the development of social and emotional skills necessary to resolve conflict, decrease violence and prejudice and build strong relationships and healthy lives. The programme aims to develop the skills of active listening, empathy and perspective taking, cooperation, negotiation and the appreciation of diversity. Workshops are targeted to all members of the school community: students, teachers, administrators, support staff and parents. For students, the programme offers 51 different developmentally appropriate lesson plans which are introduced over the course of four years, with schools moving through the following stages of implementation: beginning, consolidation, saturation and full model.

A large evaluation (5,000 students, 300 teachers, 15 public elementary schools) of this programme was carried out in New York City over a two-year period (Aber, Brown and Henrich, 1999). The social and emotional skills developed reduced crime, antisocial behaviour and conduct problems, regardless of gender, grade or risk status, although, there were fewer positive effects for boys, younger students, and students in high-risk classrooms and neighbourhoods. Students who received a higher number of lessons (on average 25 over the course of a school year) benefited the most. Interestingly, the students who received only a few workshops, compared to those who received none at all, had poorer overall outcomes, signalling the importance of consistency. The workshops are often complemented by peer mediation training for a select group of students to enable them to mediate conflict among their peers. Interestingly, the research showed that when there was more emphasis on developing a normative climate through the introduction of more workshops with only a few peer mediators, those classrooms experienced significantly less hostility compared to classrooms that had more peer mediators and fewer workshops. This highlights the importance of building a strong base at the primary, or universal, level of intervention. Further, in addition to curbing antisocial and building pro-social behaviour patterns, students who received substantial RCCP instruction also performed better on standardised academic achievement tests.

Help Increase the Peace Project (HIPP)

The Help Increase the Peace Project was developed in the United States in the 1990s and grew from a concern about the increasing violence in society, particularly in schools. There was a conviction that a school-based non-violent conflict resolution programme could be an effective target. HIPP is based on two assumptions: 'First, that conflict, while natural to all human interaction, does not have to be destructive, but can instead instigate positive change and growth. The second assumption is that societal injustice lies at the root of a great deal of violent conflict' (Anderson, 1999: 11). The aim is to develop a community of care and trust, such that participants feel significant and recognised, with the students' interests becoming the basis for the learning. The process eventually includes role plays to ground the skills they have developed. The programme now has roots in many different countries such as Canada, New Zealand and Australia, where it has been used to complement other restorative practices in schools (see Blood, 1999).

In practice, HIPP brings together a cross-section of the school community or classroom and takes participants through a series of workshops that aim to build skills for responding to conflict without violence, analysing the impact of societal injustice on themselves and others, and working on taking action for positive, non-violent personal and social change. The programme is more about process than content in that it is the process of involving the students in the programme that is the cornerstone of its effectiveness. Further, learning occurs at a process level through active modelling by facilitators and other group members. As the pro-gramme develops the facilitators find that the groups become self-regulating in that the students take on the responsibility of regulating their peers. As such, regulatory 'rules' are not handed down from a higher authority (such as a teacher or principal) but become everyday practice for all members of the school community; the aim is to shift from a paradigm of power and control to a paradigm of mutual respect and understanding.

A pre-post evaluation of HIPP (Woehrle, 2000) was conducted in the United States in the 1998/1999 school year. The results showed that students who completed HIPP workshops were significantly more likely to utilise constructive responses to conflict and to exhibit problem-solving behaviour rather than responding with destructive or conflict-escalating behaviour. Students who participated in a HIPP focus group suggested the programme: (1) broke down student cliques; (2) 'humanised' their relationship with their teachers; and (3) helped them be more proactive in dealing with violence in the school. One inner-city high-school student, after participating in a HIPP group, said:

> With all the high school shootings, I think if it is not required but everybody goes to it, at least one day of it, and open up to people and they don't feel alienated and they feel like they have friends, people they can talk to then we wouldn't have the violence around here … I hate to say it but I'm surprised we haven't had a school shooting already, I mean there are so many people around here that feel like they are left out of everything, and you try your hardest to get them involved but you know they've been outcast so long that they'll just kind of push you away … But I think HIPP would definitely help if everybody goes to it. They can find out they can be friends and don't have to alienate somebody because they're different.

Teachers who participated in a HIPP focus group suggested that the programme: (1) teaches important life skills; (2) changes the student–staff relationship; and (3) changes the school climate. One teacher commented:

> HIPP has allowed me to get much deeper with students – more than can be done in a regular class! The training always gives me a sense of hope and awe as I see students catch the glimmer and spark of positive power and as barriers between students begin to thaw. Working with student trainees as colleagues has helped me let go of 'in-chargeness' and has provided immense growth for the students in their confidence and self-esteem.

Responsible Citizenship Program (RCP)

This programme aims to develop a range of related processes that support the maintenance of healthy relationships: community building, conflict resolution, emotional intelligence and adaptive shame management. The programme is based on a number of principles of restorative justice. One set of principles grounds the community-building process, a second set grounds the conflict resolution process. The first set of principles plays on the programme acronym (RCP): respect (R), consideration (C) and participation (P); in that restorative justice is a *participatory* process that addresses wrongdoing, through offering *respect* to the parties involved and by *consideration* of the story each person tells of how they were affected by the harmful incident. While these core principles remain relevant throughout the programme, a second set of principles is used to develop students' strategies on how to *resolve conflicts productively* (a further play on RCP). These principles are introduced to the students as the REACT keys: Repair the harm done; Expect the best; Acknowledge feelings/harm done; Care for others; Take responsibility for behaviour.

This programme was piloted in an Australian elementary school (age: 10–11 years; n = 30; see Morrison 2001, in press). The pre-post evaluation showed that: (1) students' feeling of safety within the school community increased significantly; and (2) students' use of adaptive shame management strategies (i.e. shame acknowledgment) increased and maladaptive shame management strategies (i.e. shame displacement and internalised feelings of rejection) decreased. In other words, post-intervention, the students' use of strategies became less characteristic of victims who typically feel they would be rejected by others following wrongdoing and less characteristic of offenders who typically displace their shame and anger onto others. The level of respect, consideration and participation reported by the students also increased. The school principal noted the real-life relevance of the programme, as did the classroom teacher who commented that she began noticing the use of particular jargon associated with the programme being used in everyday situations. The students felt the programme taught them to understand how other people felt, what to do if you did hurt someone or someone hurt you, to respect other people, consider them and let them participate proudly. In summary, the most important conclusion to draw from this pilot study is that programmes such as RCP, and no doubt others, are effective in developing students' adaptive shame management strategies and decreasing students' use of maladaptive strategies. This is an important research and development agenda to pursue.

Secondary or targeted interventions

When harmful behaviour escalates causing deeper harm and/or affecting a larger number of the school community, interventions must be stepped up and become more intensive. Given this escalation, this level of intervention typically requires a third person to help shift the level and intensity of dialogue between those affected by the harmful behaviour.

Peer mediation

Mediation has been defined as a 'structured method of conflict resolution in which trained individuals (the mediators) assist people in dispute (the parties) by listening to their concerns and helping them negotiate' (Cohen, 2003: 111). After the mediator clarifies the structure of the process and allows the parties to explain their thoughts and feelings, participants are encouraged to talk directly, develop options and reach a consensual settlement that will accommodate their needs. In the context of peer mediation, the neutral person is a fellow student (or students), who has been trained in mediation. Peer mediation programmes are now an extremely popular means of resolving conflict in schools, with literally thousands of programmes in existence, in many different countries (see Cohen, 2003).

However, while some programmes have been found to be effective, systematic reviews of peer mediation programmes show non-significant or weak effects (Gottfredson, 1997). As Braithwaite (2002: 60) concludes:

> It appears a whole-school approach is needed that not just tackles individual incidents but also links incidents to a change programme for the culture of the school, in particular to how seriously members of the school community take rules about bullying. Put another way, the school not only must resolve the bullying incident; but also must use it as a resource to affirm the disapproval of bullying in the culture of the school.

This analysis complements the evidence cited above in the evaluation of the Resolving Conflict Creatively Program, which showed that, compared to universal interventions, an emphasis on peer mediation was less effective in curbing hostility in the classroom. Thus, at the very least, secondary interventions must be complemented with primary interventions. Other school districts, such as the New South Wales Department of Education and Training in Australia, have complemented peer mediation programmes with tertiary interventions, such as restorative justice conferencing, through their Dispute Resolution and Alternatives to Suspension Projects.

Problem-solving circles

Problem-solving circles can be developed and run in many different ways. The programme developed here aimed to build students' capacity for collective problem-solving through a process that addressed everyday concerns within the classroom and school. This classroom practice built from initial workshops that develop a normative climate of healthy social and emotional skills, but then took the process one step further through introducing the students to the three stages of a restorative justice conference (see below) using role play and discussion. Once the students felt confident with the process, they were encouraged to bring problems and concerns within the classroom to the circle. Circles then became a regular feature of the classroom.

This programme was evaluated in an Australian elementary school (Morrison and Martinez, 2001). All students in three mixed classes (grades of 4, 5 and 6) took part in the study. The intervention was tested in one classroom (n = 12), while the other two classrooms acted as control groups. Problems brought to the circle included annoying behaviour, teasing, feeling left out, aggressive behaviour and stealing. The teacher reported a number of benefits to the classroom, including: the provision of a safe place to share problems face to face; modelling effective conflict resolution; encouraging the open expression of emotion; allowing the class to move beyond niggling behaviours; and contributing to a 'way of being' based upon respect, communication and support. She also reported a number of significant breakthroughs: a boy, who would shut down during conflict at the start of the year, was asking for open communication by the end of the year; another boy evolved naturally from the role of aggressor to supporter; another boy, with extreme learning difficulties, found a voice for his strength in providing positive solutions; another boy's modelling of open expression broke the taboo on shedding tears; a girl, a strong learner, convened two of the circles independently; and a boy integrated from the behaviour support unit, willingly contributed and found another tool for managing his relationships.

This programme was also evaluated using an adaptation of the Life at School Survey (see Ahmed et al., 2001). Compared to the control group, a number of significant differences were found. Students in the intervention class showed higher levels of emotional intelligence, reported greater use of productive conflict resolution techniques, felt that the teacher was more interested in stopping bullying, felt that the teacher held bullies and victims more accountable for behaviour, reported less use of maladaptive shame management strategies and reported less involvement in bullying (Morrison and Martinez, 2001).

Tertiary interventions

This level of intervention aims to be the most intense and the most demanding. The circle of care around the victim and offender is stepped up to include parents, other caregivers and professionals, offering further support, as well as accountability mechanisms. These larger circle processes exist in a variety of forms, each having unique features. These include healing circles, sentencing circles, family group conferences, community conferences and diversionary conferences. A face-to-face victim offender conference is reviewed here, as it is the predominant model used in schools and has been evaluated.

Restorative justice conferencing

Restorative justice conferencing is used to address serious incidents of harm in the school community by gathering the people most affected by the harm or wrongdoing together to talk about: (1) what happened; (2) how the incident has affected them; and (3) how to repair the harm done. Besides the 'offender/s' and the 'victim/s', these individuals also invite a community of support, which typically includes parents, brothers, sisters and grandparents, but can also include aunts, uncles, peers, school personnel and personnel from community agencies. A conference facilitator talks with each of these people to determine who needs to attend and readies the participants for the conferencing process. Once the conference is convened, all participants sit in a circle to listen to the consequences of the incident and what needs to be done to right the wrongs and to get the lives of the 'offenders' and 'victims' back on track. Empowering participants often means developing the level of responsibility (and accountability) for the behaviour of the 'offender/s' and the level of resilience of the 'victim/s', although this dichotomy is crude. The immediate result of the conference, which is typically an emotionally powerful event, is a written agreement about what the offenders will do to repair the harm, signed by the offender and the conference facilitator.

This process has worked under a range names: community accountability conferences (Education Queensland); school forums (New South Wales Department of Education and Training); community group conferencing (Colorado School Mediation Center); community conferencing (Calgary Community Conferencing); and restorative conferencing (Home Office, England). Many of these programmes, across a range of countries, are currently being evaluated or have been evaluated, with results generally replicating those of the initial evaluation of community accountability conferences in Queensland, which remains significant in term of evaluated outcomes and lessons learned (Cameron and Thorsborne, 2000).

A total of 89 school-based conferences were convened in response to serious assaults (43), serious victimisation (25), property damage and theft (12), truanting, class disruption, damage to school reputation and bullying (18), drugs (2) and a bomb threat (1). Overall, outcomes for all participants were positive; they reported that they had a say in the process (96 per cent), were satisfied with the way the agreement was reached (87 per cent), were treated with respect (95 per cent), felt understood by others (99 per cent), and felt the agreement terms were fair (91 per cent). Victims reported that they got what they needed out of the conference (89 per cent) and felt safer (94 per cent). Offenders felt cared about during conference (98 per cent), loved by those closest to them (95 per cent), able to make a fresh start (80 per cent), forgiven (70 per cent) and closer to those involved (87 per cent). Further, offenders complied with most or all of the agreements (84 per cent) and did not reoffend within the trial period (83 per cent). School personnel reported they felt the process reinforced school values (100 per cent) and felt they had changed their thinking about managing behaviour from a punitive to a more restorative approach (92 per cent). As for family members who participated, they expressed positive perceptions of the school and comfort in approaching the school on other matters (94 per cent). These results have, to a large degree, been replicated in a number of other studies in Australia, Canada, England and the United States (see Calhoun, 2000; Hudson and Pring, 2000; Ierley and Ivker, 2002; Shaw and Wierenga, 2002). Further, the Minnesota Department of Children, Family and Learning (2002), which support one of the longest standing projects using restorative justice in schools in the United States, has shown how the use of restorative practices across a range of levels is an effective alternative to the use of suspensions and expulsions.

While these results are encouraging, the evaluation of these trials highlighted tensions between the existing philosophies and practices in controlling behaviour, typically characterised by punitive measures emphasising accountability and restorative interventions such as conferencing. This was particularly problematic when restorative conferencing was implemented as a 'one-off' intervention for serious incidents in isolation of other support mechanisms. For example, there were many incidents that were eligible for a conference but were not put forward, with a variety of reasons given (Cameron and Thorsborne, 2001). Typically, the students most at risk are the ones that do not get it but need it most. These early trials highlighted two points: first, for conferencing to be effective at a secondary and tertiary level it needs to be complemented through proactive measures; and second, all practices need to be framed within a wider framework, substantiated through integrated policy. In other words, restorative justice practices, to be effective, must contribute to all aspects of the school discipline system. The proposed regulatory pyramid of responsive regulation, based upon restorative justice, offers a way forward; yet, shifting the predominant paradigm of social control offers significant challenges. At the same time, there is reason for hope, as education systems in a number of countries are now beginning to heed the lesson of restorative justice and responsive regulation.

The Department of Education and Skills, in England, this past year announced their Safer School Partnership strategy that recognises that schools are at the heart of many communities, and advocates restorative justice as a means of building community relations and offers an alternative to school exclusions. They, together with the Home Office and Youth Justice Boards, are offering funding for training and evaluation of restorative justice initiatives. Likewise, the Department of Education, Science and Training, in Australia, has launched, with initial funding, their National Safe School Framework which incorporates many elements of restorative practices. The hope is that this support and funding will be sustained, for it is essential to the development of life skills and opportunities of our next generation of citizens.

Sustaining safe school communities

While a continuum of responsive and restorative practices is essential to regulating safe school communities, alone they are insufficient to sustaining the practice long term (see Morrison, in press). Managing a safe school climate also requires (1) continuing support to enable school communities to learn and develop these skills and practices, and (2) continuous monitoring which is responsive to the ebb and flow of social life, and behaviour, within the school community. Thus a whole-school approach requires at least three mechanisms of support to be sustainable long term: practices to support behaviour, systems to support practices and data to support decision-making. Building on the continuum of practices outlined above, systems need to be developed that support the practices at all three levels of intervention, and data needs to be collected to support decision-making at all three levels as well. And with these three levels of support comes accountability, for with all areas of restorative and responsive regulation support and accountability work together, each driving the other, hand in hand.

Conclusion

Restorative justice and responsive regulation promotes resilience and responsibility in the school community through the responsive regulation of relationships, by way of shame management and identity management. While shame is a complex emotion, the failure to discharge shame can result in fractured social bonds and social marginalisation. This can feed a cycle of harmful behaviour, not only to others, but to the self as well, as seen in the school rampage shooting that often ended in suicide. Shame and alienation cycles disempower. Restorative justice and responsive regulation aim to empower, through breaking cycles of shame and alienation. The repair of social relationships, through the discharging of shame, must be validated, developed and legitimated through a continuum of practices that addresses harmful behaviour. All members of the school community need to develop the skills to respond effectively when differences first arise; but when this initial intervention fails, resources need to be in place to follow up with more intensive interventions. It is in this sense that restorative justice empowers the school community to be more responsive and more restorative. It is about reaffirming, reconnecting and rebuilding the social and emotional fabric of relationships within the school community. This is the social capital that underlies a civil society – a richly textured fabric that we must continually weave, attend to and mend in our school communities.

Note

1   The author would like to acknowledge the supportive environment of the Regulatory Institutions Network within the Research School of Social Sciences at the Australian National University; particularly, the influence and support of Eliza Ahmed, Valerie Braithwaite and John Braithwaite.

References

Aber, J. L., Brown, J. L. and Henrich, C. C. (1999) *Teaching Conflict Resolution: An Effective School-Based Approach to Violence Prevention*. New York: National Center for Children in Poverty.

Ahmed, E. and Braithwaite, V. (2004) 'Bullying and Victimization: Cause for Concern for Both Families and Schools', *Social Psychology of Education*, 7, 35–54.

Ahmed, E., Harris, N., Braithwaite, J. and Braithwaite, V. (2001) *Shame Management through Reintegration*. Cambridge: Cambridge University Press.

Anderson, M. (1999) *Help Increase the Peace Program Manual*. Baltimore, MD: American Friends Service Committee.

Ayres, I. and Braithwaite, J. (1992) *Responsive Regulation: Transcending the Deregulation Debate*. New York: Oxford University Press.

Baumeister, R. F. and Leary, M. R. (1995) 'The Need to Belong: Desire for Interpersonal Attachments as a Fundamental Human Motivation', *Psychological Bulletin*, 117, 497–529.

Baumeister, R. F., Twenge, J. M. and Nuss, C. K. (2002) 'Effects of Social Exclusion on Cognitive Processes: Anticipated Aloneness Reduces Intelligent Thought', *Journal of Personality and Social Psychology*, 83, 817–27.

Blood, P. (1999) *Good Beginnings: Lewisham Primary School Connect Project*. Sydney: Lewisham Primary School.

Blood, P. (2004) *Restorative Practices: A Whole-School Approach to Building Social Capital*. Manuscript held by Circle Speak, Sydney, Australia.

Braithwaite, J. B. (1989) *Crime, Shame and Reintegration*. Cambridge: Cambridge University Press.

Braithwaite, J. B. (2002) *Restorative Justice and Responsive Regulation*. Oxford: Oxford University Press.

Calhoun, A. (2000) *Calgary Community Conferencing School Component 1999–2000: A Year in Review*. Available online at
http://www.calgarycommunityconferencing.com/r_and_eseptember_report.html.

Cameron, L. and Thorsborne, M. (2000) 'Restorative Justice and School Discipline: Mutually Exclusive?', in H. Strang and J. Braithwaite (eds), *Restorative Justice and Civil Society*. Cambridge: Cambridge University Press, pp. 180–94.

Cohen, R. (2003) 'Students Helping Students', in T. Jones and R. Compton (eds), *Kids Working It Out*. San Francisco: Jossey-Bass, pp. 109–19.

Fine, M. and Smith, K. (2001) 'Zero Tolerance: Reflections on a Failed Policy that Won't Die', in W. Ayers, B. Dohrn and R. Ayers (eds), *Zero Tolerance: Resisting the Drive for Punishment in Our Schools*. New York: New Press, pp. 256–63.

Gilligan, J. (2001) *Preventing Violence*. New York: Thames & Hudson.

Gottfredson, D. (1997) 'School-Based Crime Prevention', in L. Sherman, D. Gottfredson, D. MacKenzie, J. Eck, P. Reuter, and S. Bushway (eds), *Preventing Crime: What Works, What Doesn't, What's Promising. A Report to the United States Congress*. Washington, DC: National Institute of Justice.

Hopkins, B. (2004) *Just Schools: A Whole-School Approach to Restorative Justice*. London and New York: Jessica Kingsley.

Hudson, C. and Pring, R. (2000) 'Banbury Police Schools Project: Report of the Evaluation'. Unpublished manuscript held by the Thames Valley Police.

Ierley, A. and Ivker, C. (2002) 'Restoring School Communities. Restorative Justice in Schools Program: Spring 2002 Report Card'. Unpublished manuscript held by the School Mediation Center, Boulder, Colorado.

Lantieri, L. and Patti, J. (1996) *Waging Peace in Our Schools*. Boston: Beacon Press.

Lewis, H. B. (1971) *Shame and Guilt in Neurosis*. New York: International University Press.

McElrea, F. (1994) 'Justice in the Community: The New Zealand Experience', in J. Burnside and N. Baker (eds), *Relational Justice: Repairing the Breach.* Winchester: Waterside Press, pp. 93–103.

McNeely, C. A., Nonnemaker, J. M. and Blum, R. W. (2002) 'Promoting School Connectedness: Evidence for the National Longitudinal Study of Adolescent Health', *Journal of School Health*, 72, 4, 138–46.

Minnesota Department of Children, Family and Learning (2002) 'In-school Behavior Intervention Grants', in *A Three-Year Evaluation of Alternative Approaches to Suspensions and Expulsions.* Report to the Minnesota Legislature.

Moore, M. H., Petrie, C. V., Braga, A. A. and McLaughlin, B. L. (2002). *Deadly Lessons: Understanding Lethal School Violence.* Washington, DC: National Research Council.

Morrison, B. E. (2001) 'Developing the School's Capacity in the Regulation of Civil Society', in H. Strang and J. Braithwaite (eds), *Restorative Justice and Civil Society.* Cambridge: Cambridge University Press.

Morrison, B. E. (2002) '*Bullying and Victimisation in Schools: A Restorative Justice Approach*', *Trends and Issues in Crime and Criminal Justice*, No. 219 (February). Canberra: Australian Institute of Criminology.

Morrison, B. E. (2003) 'Regulating Safe School Communities: Being Responsive and Restorative', *Journal of Educational Administration*, 41, 6, 689–704.

Morrison, B. E. (in press) *Bullying, violence and alienation: Building safe school communities through restorative justice and responsive regulation.* Sydney: Federation Press.

Morrison, B. E. and Martinez, M. (2001) 'Restorative Justice through Social and Emotional Skills Training: An Evaluation of Primary School Students'. Unpublished honours thesis: Australian National University.

Nathanson, D. L. (1997) 'Affect Theory and the Compass of Shame', in M. R. Lansk (ed.), *The Widening Scope of Shame*. Hillsdale, NJ: Analytic Press, pp. 339–54.

Newman, K. S. (2004) *Rampage: The Social Roots of School Shootings.* New York: Basic Books.

Pepler, D. and Craig, W. (1997) *Bullying: Research and Interventions. Youth Update.* Ontario: Publication of the Institute for the Study of Antisocial Youth.

Pranis, K. (2001) 'Building Justice on a Foundation of Democracy, Caring and Mutual Responsibility'. Unpublished manuscript held by Minnesota Department of Corrections.

Reddy, M., Borum, R., Berglund, J., Bossekuil, B., Fein, R. and Modzeleski, W. (2001) 'Evaluating Risk for Targeted Violence in Schools: Comparing Risk Assessment, Threat Assessment, and Other Approaches', *Psychology in Schools*, 38, 157–72.

Rigby, K. (2002) *New Perspectives on Bullying.* London and Philadelphia: Jessica Kingsley.

Scheff, T. J. (1994) *Bloody revenge: Emotions, Nationalism and War.* Boulder, CO: Westview Press.

Shaw, G. and Wierenga, A. (2002) 'Restorative Practices: Community Conferencing Pilot'. Unpublished manuscript held at the Faculty of Education, University of Melbourne.

Skiba, R. J. and Noam, G. G. (2001) 'Zero Tolerance: Can Suspension and Expulsion Keep Schools Safe?', *New Directions for Youth Development*, 92. Winter.

Thorsborne, M. and Vinegrad, D. (2004) 'Restorative Practices in Classrooms: Rethinking Behaviour Management'. Unpublished manuscript held by Margaret Thorsborne and Associates, Buderim, Queensland, Australia.

Twenge, J. M., Catanese, K. R. and Baumeister, R. F. (2003) 'Social Exclusion and the Deconstructed State: Time Perception, Meaninglessness, Lethargy, Lack of Emotion, and Self-awareness', *Journal of Personality and Social Psychology*, 85, 409–23.

Twenge, J. M., Baumeister, R. F., Tice, D. M. and Stucke, T. S. (2001) 'If You Can't Join Then, Beat Them: Effects of Social Exclusion on Aggressive Behavior', *Journal of Personality and Social Psychology*, 81, 1058–69.

Twenge, J. M., Ciarocco, N. J., Cuervo, D. and Baumeister, R. F. (2003) 'Social Exclusion Reduces Prosocial Behavior'. Unpublished manuscript.

Tyler, T. and Blader, S. (2000) *Cooperation in Groups: Procedural Justice, Social Identity and Behavioral Engagement*. Philadelphia, PA: Psychology Press.

Vossekuil, B., Fein, R. A., Reddy, M., Borum, R. and Modzeleski, W. (2002) *The Final Report and Findings of the Safe School Initiative: Implications for the Prevention of School Attacks in the United States*. Washington, DC: United States Secret Service and US Department of Education.

Wachtel, T. and McCold, T. (2001) 'Restorative Justice in Everyday Life: Beyond the Formal Ritual', in H. Strang and J. Braithwaite (eds), *Restorative Justice and Civil Society*. Cambridge: Cambridge University Press, pp. 114–29.

Woehrle, L. M. (2000) *Summary Evaluation Report: A Study of the Impact of the Help Increase the Peace Project in the Chambersburg Area School District*. Baltimore, MD: American Friends Service Committee.

Zehr, H. (2000) *Journey to Belonging*. Paper delivered at the international conference: Just Peace? Peacemaking and Peacebuilding for the New Millenium, Massey University, Albany, New Zealand, 24–28 April.

Chapter 3

Achieving effective outcomes in youth justice: implications of new research for principles, policy and practice

Gabrielle Maxwell

Abstract

New research from New Zealand follows up the file outcomes over three years for 1,003 young people aged 16 years who had family group conferences in 1998. Five hundred and twenty of them were interviewed. Observational data and interviews were collected from another 115 cases in 2001/2002. The findings are presented on the extent to which restorative goals have been implemented. Critical factors predicting outcomes are identified and the implications of these for policy and practice are discussed. The research demonstrates that the nature of the youth justice system does affect critical outcomes for young people, both in terms of reducing offending and increasing the probability of other positive life outcomes. Restorative practices that include empowerment, the repair of harm and reintegrative outcomes make a positive difference while the extent of embeddedness in the criminal justice system, severe and retributive outcomes and stigmatic shaming have negative effects. There are also important findings for crime prevention that suggest the need to focus on support for families, the importance of educational qualifications and the need to respond effectively when children first come to the attention of the welfare and youth justice systems. Proposals are made for standards against which practice can be assessed.

Introduction

In 1989, new legislation resulted in a new youth justice system for New Zealand that is now recognised as the first formal adoption by the legal system in any country of a system of justice based upon restorative principles and practice. It also introduced the family group conference, which has since become the prototype for the introduction of restorative conferencing processes prior to, or as an alternative to, sentencing in the criminal courts. From 1990 to 1991, Allison Morris and the author were fortunate enough to be able to evaluate the effectiveness of the new system and the results of that research were published in 1993 (Maxwell and Morris, 1993). At that time, the focus of the research was primarily on the extent to which the new legislation achieved its objectives. However, it was too early to collect data on the longer-term outcomes for those children and young people who became involved with it.

Later work on understanding reoffending (Morris and Maxwell, 1997; Maxwell and Morris, 1999) followed up on those who participated in the earlier research. Reconviction records were obtained and, in the 1999 study, interviews were carried out with a sample of approximately 100 young people who had been through a family group conference in 1990–91. These data showed that less reoffending and more positive life outcomes depended, in part, on the extent to which processes were restorative. However, it was not possible to compare the outcomes for experimental and control groups and multivariate analyses from which reliable conclusions can be drawn required larger samples.

In 1999, funding was obtained for a new study on achieving effective outcomes (Maxwell et al., 2004) that was designed to provide more reliable answers to questions about the impact of the key, new restorative youth justice processes and the factors involved in best practice. The goals of this study have been to examine the extent to which the objectives of the youth justice legislation are being met, to examine the extent to which the restorative aspects of the process are achieved and to identify best practices by identifying practice factors associated with reoffending and factors related to positive outcomes.

Methodology

The data: the retrospective study

Twenty-four youth justice coordinators were selected as a sample that varied with respect to age, ethnicity, gender and practice. A sample of

1,003 young people who were at least 15 years and 9 months of age at the time they had a family group conference facilitated by the selected coordinators over a period around the calendar year 1998 was drawn from the files of the Department of Child, Youth and Family Services (CYFS) to provide a retrospective sample. In 2000/01, 520 of these young people were interviewed and data were obtained on their history in the adult justice system, if any, since they reached the age of 17 years. Except with respect to age, this sample was judged to be representative of the 1998 period and comprised over one-third of all the older cases nationwide at that time. Around one-third were Maori, 15 per cent of them were female, and 15 per cent were young people from the Pacific Islands.

The data: the prospective study

A sample of 115 family group conferences was obtained in 2001/02. These comprise a prospective sample that will be followed up in 2003/04. These conferences were facilitated by 18 of the same 24 coordinators whose cases made up the retrospective sample or by an additional Pacific coordinator especially recruited for the prospective study. Interviews were conducted with at least 100 young people, families and victims after the conclusion of the conference and Youth Court, as appropriate. Second follow-up interviews with victims were also conducted at the time by which any actions that the young person had promised to perform for the victim should have been completed.

Police Youth Diversion study

Other data came from a study of 1,794 cases involving young people apprehended in 2000/01, and from CYFS files on the entire 6,309 cases referred for a family group conference in 1998. An initial report describing the processes operated by the New Zealand Police Service has already been published (Maxwell et al., 2002) and further work is currently under-way to relate the experiences of diversion to reoffending data.

Additional sources

The Ministry of Justice, CYFS and the Department for Courts have all supplied additional relevant data from 1987 to the present on young people who have offended.

The youth justice system in New Zealand

Goals and values

The youth justice system in New Zealand is set out in the Children, Young Persons and Their Families Act 1989 (the Act) and the goals and values underpinning the system are explicitly described in its objects and principles. These emphasise a number of established values relating to the protection of rights, welfare and justice considerations:

- *Protection of rights*. Children and young people must be informed of their rights, strict and limited conditions govern police powers of arrest, a parent or nominated person is required to be present at any interview, children and young people are not required to make a statement, they are entitled to legal representation, and they must be fully informed of their rights in language and a manner that they can understand.

- *Welfare*. Rehabilitative options and support for families should be provided, children cannot be prosecuted in the Youth Court until they reach the age of 14 years and time frames for resolving matters must be appropriate to their age.

- *Justice*. Diversion from courts and custody is to be preferred as are least restrictive sanctions. There is an emphasis on accountability and a separation of welfare and justice matters.

There is also an emphasis on newer and restorative values of empowerment of children and families, repair of harm and the reintegration of offenders into society:

- *Repair*. Young offenders are expected to attempt to repair the harm they have done and this may happen through the genuine feelings of remorse, expressions of apology, making restitution or reparation, and undertaking work for the victim or work in the community.

- *Empowerment*. Empowerment of victims, families and offenders is to be achieved through both practice and processes that emphasise the meeting together of those involved in or affected by the offending, participation of them in the process, and their involvement in reaching consensus decisions.

- *Reintegration*. Reintegration can be achieved through forgiveness, restoring connectedness among those involved and putting in place plans for the young person that will be rehabilitative and build skills.

Key innovative processes

The new youth justice system has adopted a number of new processes which are a key to achieving the goals outlined above:

- Police warnings, both informal verbal warnings and more formal written warnings sent to the young person and their family are used to indicate the inappropriateness of the offending behaviour and to warn of the consequences of future offending.[1] About 44 per cent of young offenders are dealt with in this way.

- Police youth diversion (or, as it is sometimes referred to, alternative actions) is used for about one-third of all children and young people who come to the notice of the police. These will involve a police Youth Aid officer developing a plan with the young person and their family (and sometimes in consultation with the victim), which can include actions intended to repair harm and plans to prevent further offending by referring the young person and/or the family to suitable services or negotiating about schooling problems.

- Family group conferences (FGCs) are at the heart of the new system for the more serious offenders. About 8 per cent will be referred to them directly by the police, and the Youth Court will refer the remaining 17 per cent (who have been formally charged) for an FGC before any decision is made about the court's response. FGCs have been described more fully elsewhere (Maxwell and Morris, 1993; Maxwell et al., 2004). They are intended to provide an opportunity to those most affected by the offending (the young person, their family and the victims) to play a full part in the process of discussing possible outcomes and reaching a consensus decision about recommendations and plans for repair of harm and prevention of future reoffending.

- The Youth Court is required to manage matters in ways that enhance the understanding of procedures by participants, involve families and young people, consider the recommendations of the family group conference and follow them unless there is no agreement or there are good reasons under law for modifying them. It, too, is required under the Act to follow principles that are diversionary, involve least restrictive sanctions and minimise the time taken to process cases and complete tasks.

- Youth offending teams are currently being set up throughout the country (Ministry of Justice and Ministry of Social Development, 2002). These teams comprise all the professionals involved in youth justice in each area including youth justice coordinators, youth aid police, youth justice social workers, judges, lawyers, court staff and service providers from the areas of health, education and community services. Their role is to ensure that practice is in line with principles, that day-to-day problems are resolved, that inter-agency cooperation proceeds smoothly and that the needed services and backup are provided to children, young people and families.

• Community response options are the final key to implementing the system. Suitable services and strategies need to be available to ensure that families receive the support they need in caring for their children and young people, and that the needs of the children and young people in the areas of health, education and leisure are provided for.[2] Suitable arrangements also need to be made when the young person is ordered by the court to undertake tasks in the community as an alternative to custody.[3]

Research outcomes

Accountability, repair and well-being

The goal of achieving accountability for young people is being achieved almost universally through the plans agreed at the family group conference (90 per cent of conference plans include measures intended to ensure accountability), and through the orders of the Youth Court. Although there are no data reporting on the outcomes of the monitoring of these orders, information from the young people indicates that in over 80 per cent of cases the required tasks are satisfactorily completed.

When the data on the accountability elements of plans are further broken down, the results show that some form of response intended to repair harm is part of the plans for four out of five of the young people. Elements that are fundamentally restrictive were present for nearly 60 per cent of the plans, although it is doubtful that these will always have been necessary for public safety or consistent with the goals of the Act.

Measures to enhance well-being were included in the plans for about half the young people: 39 per cent had some type of reintegrative element and 31 per cent had a rehabilitative element in their plan. However, the elements of plans intended to promote well-being are not necessarily being fully implemented and this is especially true of the rehabilitative aspects of plans. Both reintegrative and rehabilitative options are too rarely available for the young people and those that are available are not necessarily effective.[4]

Empowerment

The main process goals of the family group conference – ensuring that the appropriate people participate, that victims and families are involved and that there is consensus decision-making – appear to be being largely achieved. Not all victims attended but this was mainly because they did not choose to do so. More young people were reporting feeling involved than in the years immediately after the Act (Maxwell and Morris, 1993) but, as this was still only reported by about half of the young people, there is room for improvement if the FGC is to reach its full potential. Decision-making did not always reflect a true consensus and there was evidence that, at times, professionals dominated decision-making.

Cultural responsiveness

The data on the experiences of Maori and Pacific Island family group conferences shows that they can be successful in engaging families and arriving at successful outcomes. Success appears to be facilitated when the process treats the family members with respect and acknowledges them and their role in a manner which goes beyond token gestures. The participants need to feel validated and central to the process rather than merely being provided with an opportunity to participate. They need to be left to take charge of decisions rather than have professionals suggest or make decisions for them. They need to be spoken to in a language and a manner they understand by people who understand and can respond to them in ways that are affirming and respectful. They may need encouragement to provide their young people in turn with the support, affirmation and forgiveness that the young person will need if they too are to become part of a solution that sets wrongs right and builds towards a constructive future. In addition, speakers of English as a second language must always be enabled to understand the process.

There is clearly room for improvement in the way family group conferences are managed in these respects. Best practice would be for the person convening the conference to ascertain the specific cultural expectations of the participants prior to the conference and to clearly explain the use of any culture-specific processes to all participants at the beginning. In particular, it is important that the person convening the conference ensures that all participants in the family group conference are introduced to each other. When interpreters are not able to be present, any non-English speakers should be identified and encouraged to seek clarification (perhaps from a family translator) throughout the conference.

Time frames

Appropriate time frames in convening and completing family group conferences are, for the most part, being met within CYFS, but time frames for police and the Youth Court in making referrals to a family group conference seem unnecessarily long. Considerable delays can occur in the Youth Court, especially where sittings are infrequent, where administrative problems arise and, less frequently, when there is repeat offending before a case is completed. Other contributing problems appeared at that time to be the lack of monitoring of time frames and of progress towards the completion of plans.

Protecting rights

Information on the extent to which young people's rights were being protected was not available. Procedures for recording the actions of the police in arresting and interviewing young people were in place during the early years of the Act (Maxwell and Morris, 1993) but these appear to have been discontinued. In addition, records have not been kept on whether or not the young person was asked if he or she agreed with the summary of facts and, if not, what processes were followed either to correct the allegations of police or to arrange a defended hearing. All young people who were charged in the Youth Court had a youth advocate appointed to represent them. However, there are no formal arrangements for monitoring the performance of youth advocates.

Diversion and decarceration

Achieving diversion and decarceration are integral objectives of the 1989 Act. The increased use of diversionary practices and the decreased use of incarceration are some of the most dramatic consequences that have occurred with the introduction of the Act and they have continued over recent years. Since 1990/91, the use of police warnings remains much the same; there has been an increased use of police youth diversion with fewer being sent for family group conferences; there has been a slight decline in the numbers of convictions and transfers to the adult courts; and, over recent years, fewer young people have been given prison sentences. Figure 3.1 indicates the decline that has occurred in the number of youth court appearances since prior to the introduction of the Act, and Figure 3.2 indicates the decline in custodial outcomes.

There are, however, two areas where there has been an increase in the use of criminal proceedings in ways that do not appear to be related to the increased seriousness of offending or to the increased severity of the outcomes decided upon. The first is that police are, compared with 1990/

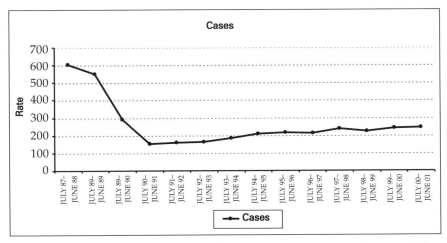

Figure 3.1 Rates per 10,000 distinct cases in the Youth Court aged 10–16: 1987 to 2001.

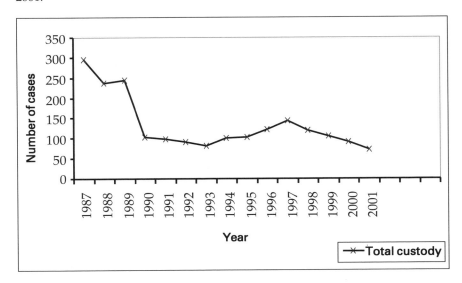

Figure 3.2 Custodial outcomes: 1987 to 2001.

91, referring a greater proportion of cases to the Youth Court (17 per cent in this study compared to 10 per cent reported by Maxwell and Morris in 1993). The second is the somewhat greater use of Youth Court orders, although this may be a consequence of the greater number of referrals for which the police are recommending a court order. These findings may be related, in part, to limited resources for managing family group conferences and, in part, to a lack of commitment to the importance of diversion from the Youth Court among some police officers. Better resources, better training and more consultation among professionals could lead to a reduction in Youth Court loads and in the need for Youth Court appearances for relatively minor matters, without compromising the need to ensure appropriate outcomes. The new Youth Offending Teams may prove to be useful in this respect.

Predicting outcomes

Life outcomes

Since the family group conference, most of the young people were able to develop positive goals and achieve successes. Seventy per cent of those followed up had been constructively employed in the last six months and over 80 per cent reported close personal relationships. About 60 per cent or more do not want any further involvement in crime, feel life has gone well for them and have positive views about the future. Thirty per cent had not been detected in any offending.

However, negative life events and risk factors were also recorded for over 60 per cent. About one-third said that they had been involved in further detected offending and this figure agrees with court records. Data on convictions for offences committed as an adult showed that nearly one half appeared before the courts in the first year after they turned 17 years, and after three years this figure had risen to 69 per cent. Offences most often involved property, followed by traffic and violence. Within three years, 22 per cent had received a prison sentence.

Predicting life outcomes

The results of the analysis undertaken to predict reoffending and positive life outcomes as young adults were clear and consistent, both internally and with previous studies that examined similar issues (Fergusson et al., 1994; Zamble and Quinsey, 1997; Farrington, 1994; Andrews et al., 1999). The data provide strong support for the model described in the full report of this research (Maxwell et al., 2004) that explains both reoffending and positive life outcomes from a variety of earlier life events. Family background factors had an impact on the young people's lives but so too did the responses of the youth justice system, including a restorative family group conference. Events subsequent to the conference also affected young people's future. Phrased like this, the conclusions seem to be common sense. Yet, there is no support for those who call for stronger justice system responses based upon punishment and retribution as methods of protecting communities rather than on repair and re-integration. These data demonstrate that, if reoffending is to be reduced and the breach in the social harmony is to be repaired, diversion and decarceration are critical, and so too are constructive processes and responses. The findings here are a strong validation of restorative justice theory; repair, reintegration, fairness and respect, participation and empowerment, and forgiveness are key elements in effective outcomes while punitive and restrictive sanctions and stigmatic shaming are counterproductive. The analyses reported here validate that:

- early action is important and is likely to be effective in preventing re-offending and ensuring positive life outcomes;

- the focus of early intervention needs to be upon building positive relationships in both the school and the family environment, rather than on simply reacting by denunciation or punishment to early indicators of anti-social behaviour;

- using diversionary strategies, least restrictive sanctions and avoiding charges in the Youth Court wherever possible is likely to lead to more positive outcomes;

- a constructive family group conference can make an important con-tribution to preventing further offending despite negative background factors and irrespective of the nature of the offending; and

- life events subsequent to the conference also matter. Taking advantage of the opportunity to respond to psychological problems, alcohol and drug misuse, educational failure and lack of employment opportunities are all important options that could reduce reoffending and increase positive life outcomes.

The data describe a number of different aspects of the family group con-ference that are important in making reoffending less likely. There should be good preparation before the conference. At the conference, the young person should feel supported, understand what is happening, participate and not feel stigmatised or excluded. A conference that generates feelings of remorse, of being able to repair harm and of feeling forgiven, and of forming the intention not to reoffend, is likely to reduce the chances of further offending. Processes that are diversionary, sanctions that are the least restrictive and outcomes that are constructive are associated with positive life outcomes. These findings provide a validation for the objects and the principles underlying the 1989 Act and the features that those close to the youth justice system in New Zealand have identified as being important to good practice (Levine et al., 1998), and for the main tenets of restorative justice theory.

However, few of the young people in this study appear to have participated in positive and effective programmes. The results of research (Sherman et al., 1997; Farrington, 1994; Andrews and Bonta, 1998; Andrews et al., 1999) would strongly suggest that, if the restorative process were followed up with appropriate programmes of good quality, the outcomes would be even more positive.

The findings also indicate that there are different types of young people. While most either experience positive life outcomes and fail to reoffend, or experience negative life outcomes and reoffend, there is another group who have a more mixed experience as young adults. This group were identified as reporting positive life outcomes but also being involved in further reoffending. Further work needs to be undertaken to describe these differences more fully. There are also puzzles around why it is that having matters resolved in court and relatively severe sanctions are linked to negative adult life outcomes. The direction of causation is by no means clear and further analysis may provide additional information.

Nevertheless, the findings identified clearly the most important precursors of good outcomes in respect of backgrounds and criminal justice events. They also identified critical factors in building upon positive youth justice system experiences by:

- providing appropriate and effective mental health services;
- making employment a realistic possibility; and
- avoiding placing the young people in situations where they form close bonds with others involved in offending.

Further implications for policy and practice

Crime prevention

An analysis of the background factors most likely to be associated with conviction as an adult has a number of implications for crime prevention strategies:

- As in other research, a number of factors can be identified in the family backgrounds of young people which place them at risk. Potentially, these can be addressed by early intervention programmes aimed at such children and young people.

- Early involvement with CYFS, either for reasons of care and protection or because of earlier offending is an important predictor of negative life outcomes. This finding suggests the importance of ensuring the quality and effectiveness of interventions when a child or young person first comes to the notice of CYFS.

- A lack of school qualifications is another major factor in poor outcomes indicating the critical impact of effective management of problems that lead to school drop out and failure.

The level at which a young person is dealt with in the youth justice system emerges as an important factor in life outcomes. This finding underlines the importance of compliance with the diversionary principles of the Act by ensuring that children and young people are always dealt with at the lowest possible level in the youth justice system.

Recording data

Currently there is a lack of consistency in recording systems across agencies that is a major impediment to both research and policy development. In addition, much of the data that is desirable, such as data on residential admissions and lengths of stay and data on re-offending, are not available. If practice is to improve, information on performance needs to be readily accessible from reporting systems based upon a well defined, clear and comprehensive database which has the following features:

- consistent identification numbers for individuals used by police, CYFS and courts;
- a case-based approach to recording rather than an offence- or incident-based approach;
- key data on processes of police warnings and diversion, conferencing and court appearances including dates of referrals and other actions;
- complete data on the outcomes of cases;
- consistent criteria for the performance of key tasks such as time frames for referral, decision-making and the completion of cases;
- data on the monitoring of key elements associated with effective practice;
- information on reoffending;
- standard use of self-reported ethnicity.

Monitoring

A number of key points were identified at which the monitoring of practice is necessary if best practice is to be achieved. These include:

- monitoring the protection of rights when a young person is arrested or interviewed;
- monitoring of police practice in deciding to take no further action, warn, divert, refer to family group conference, or charge in the Youth Court;
- monitoring of young persons' admissions of responsibility and agreement with proposed plans at the family group conference;
- monitoring of the completion of elements of the plan after the family group conference;
- monitoring of programme provision in terms of availability and effectiveness;
- monitoring of follow-up reporting to victims.

Standards

A number of criteria were identified in the research that can be used in setting standards to determine the extent to which optimal outcomes have been achieved (cf. Braithwaite, 2002). Inevitably, achieving such standards will never be possible in all cases. However, designing practice to maximise the chances of optimal outcomes is likely to be helpful providing the indicators selected and the process of assessment do not lead practitioners to achieve positive outcomes through the way they evaluate and record events. Important process features associated with optimal outcomes include whether or not:

- constructive support is provided to the young person both during and following the youth justice process;
- the young person accepts responsibility for wrongdoing;
- the young person genuinely feels remorseful;
- conference outcomes include appropriate restitution and repair of harm to victims;
- a genuine apology is made;
- reintegrative measures are put in place for the young person;
- the young person is forgiven both by the victim and his or her own family or *whänau*;
- stigmatisation and labelling of the young person has been avoided;
- the young person forms an intention not to reoffend.

Effective practice

The analysis of the data has identified a number of best-practice features. In summary, the key features of best practice that have emerged from observations of conferences, a consideration of the views of participants and statistical analyses of outcomes are as follows.

- Ensuring that youth justice coordinators receive professional support and backup in an office where morale is high and their contribution is valued.

- Effective preparation of core professionals. It seems crucial for all professionals who may be called upon to take part in a family group conference to receive training in their roles. Training should include identification of key tasks and knowledge of best-practice guidelines. The use of simulated role play situations involving coordinators and other local professionals under the guidance of a skilled trainer could allow rehearsal and discussion of options that would optimise the chances of constructive and effective outcomes consistent with best practice.

- Ensuring the right participants are invited, including fathers as well as mothers and other people who will be able to support the young person, and ensuring that the numbers of professionals are limited to those who are essential for the process.

- Effective preparation of other participants. For families, young people, victims and professionals unaccustomed to attending conferences, preparation appears to be best achieved at a face-to-face meeting with the coordinator, where information is given on the purposes of a conference, the order in which things are likely to occur, the role that each will be expected to play and possible options for outcomes.

- Consulting participants about preferences with respect to time, place and process. The Act requires that participating families and victims be asked about preferences with respect to process prior to the conference and that these wishes are responded to whenever that is possible and the other key participants agree.

- Greeting participants on arrival, introducing the victim to others, ensuring appropriate seating arrangements and beginning with formal introductions.

- Explaining any culturally responsive processes that may be used, such as *karakia* and prayers, and the language that will be used.

- An early discussion in the conference of the facts of the offence and checking to determine whether or not the young person denies or substantially accepts these facts. It is important that there should be no suggestion of either the family or the professionals coercing the young person into agreeing with the facts set out by the police.

- An opportunity for any victims' views to be fully expressed, elaborated upon and heard with respect and without interruption.

- An opportunity and, if need be, active encouragement for the young person and their family to respond to the victim without interruption or additions by other participants at this time.

- An opportunity for all to be fully involved in a discussion of options for responding to the offending before the family and young people deliberate privately.

- Ensuring that the young person and family are given time to deliberate privately.

- Listening to and considering the proposals of the family and the young person.

- Encouraging an open discussion to ensure that all participants can express their views on the proposals and negotiate modifications where there is agreement.

- Avoiding domination by one or more parties of any part of the proceedings, especially by the professionals.

- Ensuring that all are treated fairly and with respect and encouraged to contribute at all key phases, including prior to the private family time and after the young person and family have made their proposals.

- Ensuring that all are in full agreement with the final plan, but, if this is not the case, recording details of the non-agreement.

The research has focused on identifying a number of desirable outcomes of practice from the perspective of the young person. Many of these have already been noted above. The outcomes include:

- being well prepared for the conference, that is consulted about arrangements and informed about what will happen;
- having people present that support and care about him or her;
- understanding what happened;
- being treated fairly and with respect;
- not being stigmatised and excluded;
- participating fully through presenting views and being involved in decisions;
- feeling remorse, including understanding the victims' views and feeling genuine regret for what happened;
- feeling able to repair the harm that was done;
- feeling that others forgave the young person and gave him or her another chance;
- deciding to keep out of trouble in the future.

When young people responded to the conference in these ways, they were more likely not to reoffend and more likely to experience positive outcomes as young adults. Similarly, family and victims responded positively when they:

- were prepared for what would happen;
- were greeted, introduced and enabled to participate fully;
- understood what was happening;
- were treated with fairness and respect;
- were involved in the decision about outcomes; and
- felt that the young person was genuinely remorseful and had attempted to make up for what he or she had done and made a resolution not to reoffend.

In addition, there will doubtless be aspects of practice that are important but have not been identified here because of the type of data collected and the questions that were asked. For example, the need for professional supervision, regular conferences and meetings with other coordinators in the area and the use of regular team meetings of all local professionals[5] have been identified as important by youth justice coordinators and others in both this and previous research (Levine et al., 1998; Maxwell and Morris, 1993; Maxwell et al., 1997; Morris and Maxwell, 1999). Further information about programmes that are effective in rehabilitating and reintegrating young people is still needed. The hoped for opportunity to undertake an analysis of the impact of programmes on reoffending and reintegration has been limited by the relatively low numbers for whom programmes were provided in the retrospective sample and the limited time frame for data collection in the prospective sample. The impact, on outcomes, of receiving support from effective youth justice social workers has not been assessed because the latter were rarely involved with the young people in the 1998 sample. And only minimal information on Youth Court processes has been collected due to limits on budgets and on the records that are available.

Restorative justice for young offenders in New Zealand

Parallel to the development of the youth justice system in New Zealand has been the development of restorative justice theory and practice in the adult system, here and throughout the world. The New Zealand youth justice system continues to attract great interest because it is the only national system anywhere in the world, and because it has now been in operation nationally for over 12 years; consequently, judgments can be made about its ability to deliver what it promised in its early years. What then is the verdict today?

In some respects, the youth justice system has continued to grow in strength and become more restorative in its philosophy and practice. The sanctions adopted by family group conferences remain at least as restorative in 2002 as they were in 1990. The way in which the police have developed their own diversionary practices reflects restorative philosophies rather than the punitive philosophies that underpin much police action in response to young people in other jurisdictions. The Youth Court appears to have become even more inclusive than it was in 1990/91, if the views of young people and families are to be relied upon. Victims more often appear to feel positively about their experiences than in the early years. Reintegrative and rehabilitative programmes were offered more often in 1998 than in 1990/91 and current policies aim to strengthen this aspect of the youth justice system. Meanwhile, both community- and government-sponsored models of providing restorative justice options in the adult justice system are flourishing.

On the other hand, restrictive sanctions are still being used in cases where these do not appear to be necessary for public safety. And the practice of laying charges in the Youth Court has increased in cases where relatively minor offending is involved and where relatively minimal sanctions are arrived at. Furthermore, there remain areas where improvement in practice is both needed and possible. Enhancing the well-being of the young people remains a major area where their needs are not being met. Victims and young people are not always being effectively included in decision-making at the family group conference. Youth justice co-ordinators and other professionals do not always manage the conference situation in a way that optimises involvement, encourages consensus decisions and provides an opportunity for remorse and healing. The use of the Youth Court for making decisions could be reduced. And improvements in both monitoring and the keeping of records on key processes and outcomes could allow a youth justice system to be built around optimising effective practice that should achieve greater satisfaction for participants, repair harm better and reintegrate more of the young people into the wider society.

Summary of guidelines on best practice and practitioner effectiveness

Effective practice

Effective practice means:

- Treating all young people fairly irrespective of their ethnic group especially when deciding who to prosecute.
- Avoiding bringing matters before the Youth Court when they are unlikely to require Youth Court orders, especially for Maori young people.
- Arranging family group conferences that ensure that:
  - all participants are well prepared and consulted about who will attend, and about the venue, the processes and the time;
  - all who attend are greeted and introduced – victims as well as families;
  - all who attend understand what is happening and have support;
  - victims, families and young people participate fully – they are able to say what they feel and are involved in decisions;
  - professionals do not dominate the conference and the decision-making, and as few professionals are present as is possible;
  - young people are treated with fairness and respect and feelings of stigma and exclusion are avoided;
  - cultural practices used are appropriate to the setting and situation, and decided in consultation with the participants;
  - expressions of remorse, the repair of harm, including the use of restorative sanctions, and the option of forgiveness are facilitated;
  - punitive and restrictive sanctions are avoided whenever possible;
  - reintegrative and rehabilitative options are arranged as appropriate plans are monitored and victims are kept informed.
- Minimizing the delays in processing at all levels and minimizing the use of lengthy remands in custody.
- Ensuring that young people have options for gaining educational qualifications, vocational skills and suitable employment.
- Avoiding arrangements that bring together young offenders and develop friendships that can focus on anti-social activities.
- Providing programmes that respond to psychological problems, and that help them learn how to develop positive relationships with others as well as to deal with issues of anger and drug and alcohol misuse.

Practitioner effectiveness

A number of factors affecting practitioners were identified:

- Youth justice coordinators identified the need for support through professional supervision, backup and training, and for resources to fund conferences, to arrange programmes and to make appropriate placements.
- Good relationships and effective team work among youth justice professionals is necessary and all need more training in relation to the Act and best practice.
- The skills of the coordinator were undoubtedly important. Some co-ordinators related better to some young people than did others but the critical factors have not yet been identified.

Notes

1 There is provision for a formal police caution but, in practice, this is not used.
2 Ideally one would add victim support services to this list. However, while these are increasingly available in New Zealand, the provision for and management of these services has been the responsibility of other players in the justice sector.
3 The top tariffs in the Youth Court are orders for supervision; for supervision with activity (where the young person remains in the community but carries out a plan which involves supervised activities and 24-hours-a-day, seven-days-a-week monitoring); supervision with residence (in a residential youth centre for up to three months followed by six months supervision); and transfer to the District or High Court for sentence (usually this will be followed by a prison sentence or other adult penalty).
4 Some increase in the proportion referred to programmes or training courses was, however, noted for the 2000/01 sample compared to the 1998 sample and since that time additional resources have been made available to improve services.
5 Including Youth Court, Police, CYFS and community agency personnel as currently being set up under the Youth Offending Strategy (Ministry of Justice, 2003).

References

Andrews, D. A. (1994) *An Overview of Treatment Effectiveness: Research and Clinical Principles*. Ottawa: Department of Psychology, Carleton University.
Andrews, D. A. and Bonta, J. (1998) *The Psychology of Criminal Conduct*, 2nd edn. Cincinnati: Anderson Publishing.

Andrews, D. A., Dowden, C. and Gendreau, P. (1999) 'Psychologically Informed Treatment and Clinically Relevant and Psychologically Informed Approaches to Reduced Re-offending: A Meta-analytic Study of Human Service, Risk, Need, Responsivity and Other Concerns in Justice Contexts'. Unpublished paper. Ottawa: Department of Psychology, Carleton University.

Braithwaite, J. (2002) 'Setting standards for restorative justice', *British Journal of Criminology*, 42, 563–77.

Farrington, D. P. (1994) 'Human development and criminal careers', in M. Maguire, R. Morgan and R. Reiner (eds), *The Oxford Handbook of Criminology*. Oxford: Clarendon Press.

Fergusson, D. M., Horwood, L. and Lynskey, M. (1994) 'The childhoods of multiple problem adolescents: a 15-year longitudinal study', *Journal of Child Psychology and Psychiatry and Allied Disciplines*, 35 (6), 1123–40.

Levine, M., Eagle, A., Tuiavi'i, S. and Roseveare, C. (1998) *Creative Youth Justice Practice*. Wellington: Social Policy Agency and Children, Young Persons and Their Family Service.

Maxwell, G. M. and Morris, A. (1993) *Family Victims and Culture: Youth Justice in New Zealand*. Wellington: Social Policy Agency and Institute of Criminology, Victoria University of Wellington.

Maxwell, G. M. and Morris, A. (1999) *Understanding Reoffending. Final Report to Social Policy Agency and the Ministry of Justice*. Wellington: Institute of Criminology, Victoria University of Wellington.

Maxwell, G. M., Morris, A. and Shepherd, P. (1997) *Being a Youth Advocate: An Analysis of Their Role and Responsibilities*. Wellington: Institute of Criminology for Victoria Link.

Maxwell, G. M., Robertson, J. and Anderson, T. (2002) *Police Youth Diversion: Final Report. Prepared for New Zealand Police and Ministry of Justice*. Wellington: Crime and Justice Research Centre, Victoria University of Wellington through Victoria Link.

Maxwell, G. M., Kingi, V., Robertson, J., Morris, A. and Cunningham, C. (2004) *Achieving Effective Outcomes: Youth Justice in New Zealand*. Wellington: Ministry of Social Development.

Ministry of Justice (Te Manatu Ture) and Ministry of Social Development (Te Manatu Whakahiato Ora) (2002) *Youth Offending Strategy: Preventing and Reducing Offending and Re-offending by Children and Young People: Te Haonga*. Wellington: Ministry of Justice (Te Manatu Ture) and Ministry of Social Development (Te Manatu Whakahiato Ora).

Morris A. and Maxwell, G.M. (1997) *Family Group Conferences and Convictions, Occasional Paper No. 5*. Institute of Criminology, Victoria University of Wellington.

Morris, A. and Maxwell, G. (eds) (1999) *Youth Justice in Focus: Proceedings of an Australasian Conference held 27–30 October 1998 at the Michael Fowler Centre, Wellington*. Wellington: Institute of Criminology, Victoria University of Wellington.

Sherman, L. W., Strang, H. and Woods, D. (2000) *Recidivism Patterns in Canberra Reintergrative Shaming Experiment (RISE)*. Canberra: Centre for Restorative Justice, Research School of Social Sciences, Institute of Advanced Studies, Australian National University.

Sherman L., Gottfredson, D., Mackenzie, D., Eck, J., Reuter P. and Bushway, S. (1997) *Preventing Crime: What Works, What Doesn't, What's Promising*. Baltimore, MD: Department of Criminology and Criminal Justice, University of Maryland.

Zamble, E. and Quinsey, V. (1997) *The Criminal Recidivism Process*. Cambridge: Cambridge University Press.

Chapter 4

The Canadian Youth Criminal Justice Act 2003: a step forward for advocates of restorative justice?

Serge Charbonneau

Abstract

The Canadian *Youth Criminal Justice Act*, which came into force in early 2003, contrasts sharply with the orientation of the previous legislation (the Young Offenders Act 2003) in several ways. Among these are the institutionalisation of a police officer's discretionary power, the increased participation of victims and families, the assumption that extra judicial measures are effective in improving the levels of responsibility among youth, and the use of the civil community through justice committees and consultative groups. The purpose of this chapter is to examine the new law while relating it to the concept of restorative justice and other youth justice reforms in western countries. In particular, the chapter examines whether the Act is affected significantly by trends in restorative justice and the consequences for the future of the restorative justice movement, particularly in Canada.

Introduction

From the outset, the *Youth Criminal Justice Act* (hereinafter referred to as the YCJA) does seem to open the door to the development of initiatives generally associated with restorative justice. Yet a number of programmes currently in existence – programmes having certain similarities to the measures put forward by the YCJA – include some unsettling directions, a clear indication of what is at stake in the development of a conceptual framework for restorative justice. The fundamental question remains: 'Is our purpose to increase social control and heighten intolerance, or is it to foster real change in the way we deal with those who do not abide by the law or accepted standards of behaviour?'

The coming into force of the YCJA provides a new opportunity to examine the particular environment resulting from this legislation and to reflect on its directions. The first task will be to situate the restorative justice movement in the broader context of justice. Following is a review of the major trends emerging from this new Canadian legislation and an attempt to identify its perspective(s) on the basis of a typology of social reactions. Finally, a focus is directed to what is at stake and the opportunities provided by this new legal framework.

Restorative justice

Given the profusion of purportedly restorative justice practices, a number of authors have attempted to identify what might distinguish this form of justice from more traditional approaches (Zehr, 1990; Van Ness, 1997; Walgrave, 1993). Simply put, they have tried to answer the following question: 'What are the criteria that would lead one to conclude that a particular initiative truly fits the definition of restorative justice?'

These efforts to develop a conceptual framework follow in the wake of the classification of social controls as drawn up by Horwitz (1990) and Hulsman and de Celis (1982). This classification describes five types of social reactions, including the compensatory and conciliatory types, which very closely embody the features and characteristics now associated with restorative justice. Howard Zehr's work (1990) was one of the first contributions to the definition of restorative justice; it has since become a standard reference work for many practitioners involved in implementing innovative approaches to justice. This was followed by the contribution of Lode Walgrave (1993), whose work on a definition highlights a number of elements that may serve to typify various justice models, such as retributive justice, rehabilitative justice and restorative justice. The Law Commission of Canada also produced a discussion paper (Llewellyn and Howse, 1998) that considered similar models in working towards a conceptual framework for restorative justice.

For these authors, restorative justice represents a new paradigm, a new way of looking at crime and responding to it. One of the fundamental features of restorative justice is that it places the victim at the heart of the process. The proponents of restorative justice argue that retributive and rehabilitative justice show very little concern for the victim, who is more or less excluded from the conflict under consideration as well as from the process leading to its resolution. At best, a victim's participation is limited to testimony that will assist in determining the guilt of an accused. One of the goals of restorative justice is to rectify this problem by fostering the active participation of victims. They also argue that restorative justice sets itself apart from other forms of justice in the way that it deals with offenders. Rather than simply punishing or attempting to rehabilitate offenders, it seeks to involve them in repairing the harm resulting from their behaviour.

For some analysts such as Walgrave (1993), restorative justice has other distinguishing features. Contrary to retributive justice and rehabilitative justice which focus, respectively, on the offence and the offender, restorative justice is concerned first and foremost with the harm done to the victim as a result of a crime. Such a perspective entails an approach quite different from that which calls for specific sanctions for specific crimes or which would have sentences shaped to fit the personality of an offender.

Other authors, such as Jaccoud (1998, 2003), prefer the notion of symmetry. In their view, for justice to be truly 'restorative' both parties need to experience its restorative effects. Hence, there could conceivably exist two forms of restorative justice, one that is symmetric and another form that is asymmetric in which one party experiences reparation to a greater degree.[1] These notions lead us to consider what existing organisations and what actors are best suited to implement such practices. Some organisations would have a hard time adjusting to the changes for which restorative justice calls.

Though painted in broad strokes, the above represent the main features that would allow for a distinction to be made between the processes most akin to traditional justice models and those that could be said to be 'restorative' in nature. Recently, certain authors have attempted to address this issue by suggesting a continuum model of restorative justice practices, categorising the 'restorativeness' to which the system aspires, from minimally, through moderately, to fully restorative systems (Van Ness and Strong, 2001).

Yet those same authors neglect to consider certain elements that, in this writer's view, are essential. In order to properly identify the type of justice that is being offered, one needs to focus not only on the process itself, but also on the outcomes or decisions resulting from that process – in short, to focus on what types of measures are implemented at the end of that process. Further, it is equally important to consider the organisations responsible for establishing the decision-making processes, as well as those responsible for implementing the measures stemming from those decisions. Finally, one also needs to consider the actors involved. For a better understanding of these comments, some of the main processes associated with these various forms of justice are reviewed.

A consideration of processes

Different processes may come into play in dealing with an offence, some more coercive than others. Some, such as trials, are well known because they have been a part of the judicial landscape for a long time. Others have a more recent history and apply to different areas of the law. Such is the case with arbitration, a process often used to resolve labour and commercial disputes.

Some of these processes may be associated more easily with restorative justice, notably mediation, victim/offender meetings, conflict resolution circles, healing circles and family conferencing, to name a few. All of these processes share a common objective: to improve communication between the parties. Most importantly, all can give rise to a series of measures aimed at allowing the offender to repair the harm resulting from his actions. In other cases, both parties commit to a particular process for the sole purpose of putting an end to the conflict that opposes them. Such processes or measures may include restitution (in the case of stolen goods), direct or indirect reparation, an apology, some form of compensation, treatment, training and probation.

Relevant organisations: their missions and the key players

In looking at the various organisations involved in the criminal justice system, one of the first elements to consider may be their mission statements. There have been major changes in the administration of justice over the past few decades, as a greater number of distinct organisations and bodies were allowed to take part in the process. The operation of the criminal justice system now depends on a number of autonomous government organisations; police forces (municipal, provincial or federal), correctional services, public security departments, courts, the bar, are main examples. These have been complemented by several non-governmental organisations, such as John Howard Societies and non-profit youth organisations, that have entered the field with a view to providing various services or programmes; this phenomenon was most prevalent in Canada in the 1970s and 1980s.

Many of these organisations provide services, such as mediation or circles, that are generally associated with restorative justice. In addition, some governmental organisations are also involved in developing programmes based on restorative approaches. As a result, a variety of mediation programmes are now being offered by a number of different organisations whose missions are clearly very different. As an example, Quebec counts several providers of mediation services, such as victim–offender mediation sponsored by either correctional services or alternative justice organisations, and school-based or community-based mediation.

This gives rise to a number of questions. For example, is it appropriate to refer to all these programmes as restorative justice programmes? This question may appear simplistic if all that is taken into consideration is the nature of a process and the type of measures resulting from that process. Yet when one takes a closer look at these organisations and the people involved, it becomes even more difficult to make a determination. The following example will illustrate why that is so.

In 1983, in Finland, a non-governmental agency established a mediation programme based on a collaboration of its practitioners with public agencies (Gronfors, 1992). As this collaboration progressed, a curious phenomenon occurred. The ideology that had motivated the founders of the programme gradually faded and was supplanted by the ideology of its government partners. In concluding his analysis of the agency, Gronfors was forced to recognise that the imbalance in the respective weights of the professional ideologies had had a perverse effect on the work of the practitioners and the fundamental mission being pursued by the founding agency.

As this example suggests, it may be misleading to focus on the process alone in order to make a determination as to whether a particular justice programme is restorative in nature. A more developed way of making that determination would involve an analysis of all the elements that contribute to the process, namely the organisation and its mission, the people involved and their professional ideology, the processes in place and their outcomes. These were the conclusions reached in an analysis of existing mediation practices in Quebec in the 1980s (Charbonneau, 1998). It was observed that mediation was often used as a tool to educate young offenders or to provoke change in them. It was concluded that the professional ideology of mediators and the mission of the organisations were two factors that contributed to the transformation of mediation into a tool to serve the particular purposes of organisations.

The YCJA and restorative justice: yes, but ...

Most authors (Walgrave, 1993; Zehr, 1990; Van Ness, 1997; Jaccoud, 1998) agree that for restorative justice to be possible, an important change needs to occur in our social reactions and that our focus and attention need to shift toward the consequences of an offence. Is this the case in the area of youth justice? Under the *Juvenile Delinquents Act* 1908, intervention was focused upon the individual in a spirit of rehabilitation, reintegration and education, and without too much concern for rights. The *Young Offenders Act* 1984 later attended to the issue of rights.[2] Indeed, greater attention was given to a young person's rights and attempts were made to consider the needs of victims. Yet in the end, the personality of a young offender remained a key factor in determining the type of interventions that took place.

The main focus

In a way, the YCJA seems to offer a different perspective. However, identifying that perspective is a somewhat complex matter as so many aspects do not seem to make sense. This legislation creates new categories of offences that call for special forms of treatment and particular sentences. More specifically, a presumption is built into the legislation that non-violent offences will be dealt with outside of the judicial process, making it likely that violent offences would be directed to the courts. It also includes a presumption that an adult sentence will be imposed on youths found guilty of a presumptive offence (murder, attempt to commit murder, manslaughter and aggravated sexual assault).[3]

In short, non-violent offences would preferably come under the discretionary powers of the police as set out in section 6; slightly more serious offences would be subject to extra-judicial sanctions, while the more serious offences and repeat offenders would be dealt with through the courts. Most offences would be subject to youth sentences, except for those that have already been identified as subject to adult sentences.

Hence, all processes stemming from this legislation are dictated by the nature of the offence, and several of the presumptions that are introduced are predicated upon this limitation. In addition, the YCJA creates two new types of offences: presumptive offences and serious violent offences. For the most part, sentencing is focused on the offence. Certain types of procedures are limited to certain types of offences and some of the more serious offences are subject to somewhat automatic responses. One may legitimately question whether such measures are congruent with a restorative justice approach. As many authors have suggested (Walgrave, 1993; Zehr, 2002; Van Ness and Strong, 2001; Jaccoud, 2003), under a restorative justice model there is a shift in focus toward the consequence of an offence. An analysis of the YCJA leads one to conclude that such a shift has not occurred, suggesting that this legislation moves us further away from the restorative justice model.

However, certain aspects of this legislation leave open the possibility of introducing considerations other than the offence alone. Hence, the Preamble, the Declaration of Principles and General Objectives, the Principles and Objectives of Extra-judicial Measures, and the Purpose and Principles of Sentencing as outlined in section 38 would allow for the consideration of various other elements in line with restorative justice thinking. However, the law never makes a single reference to the notion of restorative justice or how judicial or extra-judicial sanctions should be expressed, and the presumption of adult punishments holds a rather punitive connotation.

Adult sentences?

The presumption that an adult sentence will be imposed is undoubtedly one of the most punitive aspects of this legislation. This provision is based on the belief that adult sentences are effective and it completely disregards the principles and objectives of the YCJA. One could argue that no adult sentence that is imposed can ever be linked to restorative justice. This measure was included in the legislation to appease public opinion and certain provincial jurisdictions calling for harsher sentences for young offenders found guilty of serious crimes, as well as for persistent offenders.

As a result, victims were excluded from the judicial process, as was the case with conferencing. Consultative groups (section 19) are not likely to participate in cases where adult penalties are possible. The provisions of section 39 that limit the circumstances under which a custodial sentence may be imposed are ignored with the presumption of adult punishments. When the possibility of adult punishments is applied, the rules that determine what punishments are reasonable are modified and it is the adult punishment that is applied. The rules on specific punishments are then suspended. In short, a number of positive features of the legislation are circumvented so that sentences acknowledged for their punitive nature may prevail. Once again, one might argue that this provision of the YCJA bears little or no resemblance to restorative justice. Fortunately, the Canadian government has announced its intention to amend this section of the *Act* to comply with the ruling of the Court of Appeal of Quebec, which found this provision to infringe upon the Canadian Charter of Rights and Freedoms.[4] It is principally the dispositions presuming adult penalties and the publication of the identity of the youth accused that were found to be invalid.

Victims

There are several instances in which the YCJA calls for more consideration of victims. But there are concerns that these good intentions could remain unattended.

> According to the intentions expressed by the Canadian Government, victims should be heard, they should play a more important role in court proceedings, if they so desire, and they should have the opportunity to participate in these proceedings. Yet, the process that would allow for this to happen remains rather fuzzy. The only details provided have to do with community-based sanctions – in relation to which victims should have the opportunity to express their views and feelings – and with community-like programmes such as family conferencing and circle sentencing. However, no indication is provided as to what proportion of cases might qualify for such proceedings nor is any indication given as to the degree of seriousness of offences that might be considered. As we noted previously, the Canadian proposals still view the courts as the pivotal element of the justice system, particularly with regard to the most serious offences, which is to say those cases in which victims could benefit the most from another approach. (Maxwell and Morris, 1999: 50)

Indeed, the Act calls for the increased participation of victims, and the principles of sentencing outlined in section 38 speak of harm done and reparation. Moreover, there is no doubt that the provisions relative to extra-judicial measures attach a great deal of importance to the principles of restorative justice.

Will the Youth Justice Committees[5] make recommendations that necessarily favour procedures or outcomes inspired by restorative justice thinking? The frame of mind or the ideology of people responsible for decision-making and extra-judicial measures programmes is an issue that is not without importance. As Shaw and Jané (1998) have pointed out, many factors may interfere with a change in philosophy and police culture could be one of those factors. 'Observers of the police have often identified police culture as one of the main factors impeding change: providing training and issuing directives is simply not sufficient.' Along those same lines, giving new responsibilities to the police offers no guarantee that these will be fulfilled in keeping with a restorative mind-set. The same is true of Youth Justice Committees, for that matter:

> Developing partnerships in restorative projects presents a major challenge for the police and community members ... It will be

difficult for community members not to defer to, or expect the police to take the lead in community committees and partnerships, and difficult for the police to give up some of their power. (Shaw and Jané, 1998: 54)

Clearly, the fact of introducing new provisions or promoting processes that are generally akin to restorative justice will in no way prevent institutions associated with the repressive system of justice from exploiting these activities as a means to their own end.

Bifurcation

In adopting such an approach, the Canadian government has followed in the steps of other countries (such as France, England, Scotland, South Africa, Australia and New Zealand) that have decided to divide the offender population into two groups, to be managed differently. Some criminologists have used the term 'bifurcation' to describe this trend (others refer to a twin-track policy), thereby pointing to a two-tiered system of justice.

In 1977, British criminologist Anthony Bottoms was among the first to touch on this issue in his analysis of the new criminal justice policies of the British government. He observed that the effect of these policies was to reserve diversion mechanisms (i.e. sanctions other than imprisonment) for 'minor' offenders while the more 'serious' offenders would be subject to harsher sentences.[6] As is evident, the spirit of the YCJA is in tune with this trend observable in several western countries.

Practically speaking and in light of the debates internal to the restorative justice movement, one might say that the YCJA qualifies as a minimalist[7] piece of legislation. Indeed, it appears to support the principles of restorative justice in the context of extra-judicial measures. However, the more serious offences will, in all likelihood, be dealt with in keeping with the principles and objectives of the traditional criminal justice system.

Conclusion

Given the concerns outlined to this point, it would seem that the YCJA draws upon a hotchpotch of perspectives from a social reaction point of view. While several of its principles reflect a restorative perspective, its structure is undeniably penal in nature. The terms used in the legislation refer to 'sentences' and one of its very significant provisions would have young offenders found guilty of a serious offence subject to adult sentences, thereby endorsing the notion that harsh sentences are effective. Several of the stated principles and objectives of the YCJA are inspired by the rehabilitative model, thus limiting the restorative approach to less serious offences. Beyond its stated objectives, the YCJA identifies the police as first interveners and gives them the discretion to apply a series of non-judicial measures in the case of minor offences. As a result, the mission of the police and the professional ideology of police officers take on an added importance.

As it has been demonstrated, the YCJA could lead to very diversified practices having nothing in common with a restorative justice approach. Our initial question remains relevant: 'Is the effect of the YCJA to increase social control and heighten intolerance or is it to foster real change in the way we deal with those who do not abide by the law or accepted standards of behaviour?' Chances are that, despite the government's stated intention to reduce the use of formal criminal justice processes, an increasing number of young people will be subject to measures that will be far more punitive than restorative. Many of the dispositions of the YCJA appear to increase formal social control and to widen the criminal justice net.

Two major challenges arise from this legislation. The first will be to ensure that police and citizen participation do not focus only on a quest for public safety and foster zero tolerance policies. This issue is of greater significance in relation to extra-judicial measures and as it pertains to the possible contribution of youth justice committees. As far as the judicial process is concerned, the main challenge will be to make sure that, in determining an appropriate sanction, the focus is on the impact of an offence on the victim rather than on the offence itself, and to make sure also that the recommendations resulting from conferences reflect a restorative frame of mind.

It is a pressing matter that the advocates of restorative justice undertake an analysis of the legislation in force in their own countries. Such an analysis would allow an assessment of whether the laws are truly reflective of the goals and aspirations of the restorative justice movement and whether the legislative process is congruent with the prevailing rhetoric. Referring to the YCJA as legislation inspired by restorative justice thinking might provoke cynicism for many people working from a fully restorative perspective. Yet there are opportunities stemming from this legislation that could be maximised by fostering the use of conferences and striving to ensure that each step of the process is focused on a restorative outcome.

Notes

1 The asymmetrical type of restorative justice is more likely to occur in the penal context, for example, in the case where a victim refuses to engage in a reparative process, or in the case where an offender has not been apprehended.

2 It is worth noting that the adoption of the YOA occurred in a context of the validation of citizens' rights generally, put in force through the invocation of the Canadian Charter of Rights and Freedoms in 1982.

3 As this presentation does not allow for a detailed analysis of the YCJA, comments are limited to its essential provisions.

4 The Court of Appeal of Quebec rendered the opinion that Sections 62, 63, 64(1) and (5), 70, 72(1) and (2) and 73(1) of the YCJA violated Section 7 of the Charter, arguing that in the cases of adolescents having committed certain designated offences, the evidence of justifying factors for the imposition of a specific punishment must be the same as that for punishments applicable to adults.

5 Youth Justice Committees, as described in the YCJA, are to be constituted by groups of citizens 'to assist in any aspect of the administration of this Act or in any programs or services for young persons' (Section 18 (1), YCJA).

6 On this topic, see Dominique Robert (1994). *L'esprit et la lettre: les libérations conditionnelles au Canada de 1956 à 1992.* unpublished Master's thesis, University of Montreal.

7 According to Walgrave (1999), advocates of restorative justice may be divided into two schools of thought: the minimalists who favour negotiated processes that are most often informal, and the maximalists who would like to see the objectives of restorative justice adopted throughout the criminal justice system.

References

Bottoms, A. (1977) 'Reflection on the Renaissance of Dangerousness', *The Howard Journal of Penology and Crime Prevention*, 16(2), pp. 70–95.

Charbonneau, S. (1998) 'Restorative Justice Trajectory in Quebec', in L. Walgrave (ed.), *Restorative Justice for Juveniles: Potentialities, Risks and Problems.* Leuven: Leuven University Press, pp. 229–243.

Gronfors, M. (1992) 'Mediation: A romantic ideal or a workable alternative?', in H. Messmer and H.-U. Otto (eds), *Restorative Justice on Trial.* Netherlands: Klumer Academic Press.

Horwitz, A.V. (1990). *The Logic of Social Control.* New York: Plenum Press, pp. 19–95.

Hulsman, L. and J. Bernat de Celis. (1982) *Peines perdues.* Paris: Éditions du Centurion.

Jaccoud, M. (1998) *La justice réparatrice.* Communication présentée à l'occasion de la rencontre de réflexion intersectorielle en Montérégie (Saint-Hyacinthe).

Jaccoud, M. (2003) *La justice réparatrice et la médiation: convergences ou divergences?* Paris: l'Harmattan.

Llewellyn, J. and Howse, R. (1998) *Restorative Justice – A Conceptual Framework.* Ottawa: Law Commission of Canada.

Maxwell, G. and Morris, A. (1999) 'Perspectives néo-zélandaises sur la justice des mineurs au Canada', *Criminologie*, 32 (2), 37–54.

Robert, Dominique (1994) 'L'esprit et la lettre: les libérations conditionnelles au Canada de 1956 à 1992.' Unpublished Master's Thesis, University of Montreal.

Shaw, M. and F. Jané. (1998). *Restorative Justice and Policing in Canada: Bringing the Community Into Focus.* Final Report Presented to the Royal Canadian Mounted Police and the Ontario Provincial Police.

Van Ness, D. (1997) *Perspectives on Achieving Satisfying Justice: Values and Principles of Restorative Justice.* Paper presented at Achieving Satisfying Justice Symposium, Vancouver, B.C. on March 21, 1997. Available at: http://www.restorativejustice.org/rj3/Full-text/dan/satisfyingjustice.pdf

Van Ness, D. and Strong, K. H. (2001). *Restoring Justice*, 2nd edn. Cincinnati, OH: Anderson Publishing Company.

Walgrave, L. (1993) 'La justice réparatrice et les jeunes',in J. F. Gazeau and V. Peyre (eds), *Au-delà de la rétribution et de la réhabilitation: la réparation comme paradigme dominant dans l'intervention judiciaire contre la délinquance des jeunes.* Neuvième journées internationales de criminologie juvénile, Vaucresson, (juin).

Walgrave, L. (1999) 'La justice restaurative: à la recherche d'une théorie et d'un programme', *Criminologie*, 32 (1), 7–29.

Zehr, H. (1990) *Changing Lenses: A new focus for crime and justice.* Waterloo, Ont.: Herald Press.

Zehr, H. (2002) *The Little Book of Restorative Justice.* Intercourse, PA: Good Books.

Part 2

Aboriginal Justice and Restorative Justice

Chapter 5

Aboriginal justice and restorative justice

Jonathan Rudin

Abstract[1]

Restorative justice initiatives now regularly acknowledge the influence that Aboriginal concepts of justice have had on their development. While there certainly are commonalities between restorative justice and Aboriginal justice projects there are also substantive differences that are not always as readily recognised. This chapter argues that there is a need to expressly recognise the distinct nature of Aboriginal justice programmes in order to ensure their survival as meaningful responses to community needs. The chapter addresses why there is a need for Aboriginal justice programmes at all, examines the types of initiatives that have developed in response to this need and looks at the problems facing the further development and expansion of such programmes. It is argued that Aboriginal agencies and organisations need to be recognised as the only sources for the development and implementation of Aboriginal justice programmes for Aboriginal people, wherever they are found.

Introduction

As restorative justice practices become more accepted and adopted by the mainstream justice system, there is an increased recognition of the contribution made to the development of these practices by Aboriginal peoples. While there is generally no reason to doubt the sincerity of this recognition, the reality is that the mainstreaming of restorative justice threatens the viability and the very existence of Aboriginal justice programmes.

This chapter will argue that it is now time – indeed it is past time – to recognise Aboriginal justice programmes and practices as distinct from restorative justice programmes in general. It is essential that such recognition occur or the future of Aboriginal justice programmes may be in jeopardy. With this recognition, however, must also come the commitment to allow Aboriginal communities and organisations to develop and deliver justice programmes to their constituents, wherever they are located. The chapter begins by discussing why there is a need for Aboriginal justice programmes in Canada. That discussion will look at the crisis of over-representation of Aboriginal people in Canadian prisons and the causes of that over-representation. Following that discussion will be an examination of some of the issues facing Aboriginal communities and organisations as they attempt to develop justice responses that are relevant to the needs of their communities. And, finally, some basic suggestions will be made as to how Aboriginal justice programmes should be recognised and validated. While the discussion will focus on the situation in Canada, many of the points raised may well be relevant for Aboriginal people in other countries; however, it will be for others to draw whatever parallels they think are relevant.

The causes of Aboriginal over-representation in prisons

The most visible and obvious example of the failure of the criminal justice system to deal fairly or adequately with Aboriginal people in Canada is the dramatic over-representation of Aboriginal people in provincial and federal prisons. The phenomenon of over-representation first came to the attention of Canadians with the publication, in 1989, by the Canadian Bar Association of Professor Michael Jackson's report 'Locking up Natives in Canada' (Jackson, 1989). The report's findings were dramatic. Aboriginal people were over-represented in jails across the country in staggering numbers; for example, while Aboriginal people represented only 2 per cent of the population in Canada in 1998, they comprised 10 per cent of those in federal penitentiaries.[2] In Manitoba, Aboriginal people made up 6 per cent of the population but 46 per cent of provincial inmates, while in Saskatchewan, Aboriginal people constituted 7 per cent of the population but 60 per cent of the inmates in provincial prisons (Jackson, 1989).

The report stirred a number of responses and initiatives; it also encouraged the continued collection and examination of data regarding Aboriginal over-representation. Sadly, every year, the problem of Aboriginal over-representation increases. By 2000, 57 per cent of inmates in Manitoba prisons and 75 per cent of inmates in Saskatchewan prisons were Aboriginal. At the federal penitentiary level, Aboriginal people made up 17 per cent of the federal prison population in 2000 (Centre for Justice Statistics, 2000). If looking at the problem could make it go away, then Aboriginal over-representation would have disappeared in Canada; instead, it appears that the more the topic is studied, the more hands are wrung over the issue and the worse the problem becomes.

The issue of over-representation has drawn comment from the Supreme Court of Canada. In the landmark case of *R* v. *Gladue*,[3] the Court spoke about the problem of over-representation in Canada both generally and as it relates specifically to Aboriginal people. At paragraph 58 the court said:

If over-reliance upon incarceration is a problem with the general population, it is of much greater concern in the sentencing of Aboriginal Canadians.

And then, after reviewing many of the studies on Aboriginal over-incarceration, the court, at paragraph 64, reached the following important conclusion:

These findings cry out for recognition of the magnitude and gravity of the problem, and for responses to alleviate it. The figures are stark and reflect what may fairly be termed a crisis in the Canadian criminal justice system. The drastic over-representation of Aboriginal peoples within both the Canadian prison population and the criminal justice system reveals a sad and pressing social problem.

The government of Canada addressed the issue of over-representation in the Speech from the Throne in January 2001 when it pledged to see Aboriginal rates of incarceration drop to at least the same percentage as that of Aboriginal people in the general population, within a generation (House of Commons Debates, 2001).

Addressing the issue of Aboriginal over-incarceration need not necessarily lead to initiatives in Aboriginal justice. There are many possible causes of over-representation and before a solution can be prescribed the reasons must be determined. The Royal Commission on Aboriginal Peoples addressed this issue in their report on criminal justice *Bridging the Cultural Divide* (Royal Commission, 1996). In its discussion of the causes of over-representation, the Commission identified three main theories. While each theory had its merits, the Commission identified what it considered to be the most significant of the three.

The first theory most often advanced to explain over-representation is the 'culture-clash' theory; this theory states that the reason for Aboriginal over-representation is a clash between Aboriginal notions of justice and those of the non-Aboriginal society (see, for example, Sinclair, 1994; Ross, 1992, 1994). Given the allocation of power in society, the result of this clash is that Aboriginal people end up in prison in disproportionate numbers. Examples of a clash of cultures abound. In Aboriginal societies, for example, there is a strong imperative to accept responsibility for one's actions. Acceptance of responsibility and guilt in the legal sense are two very different notions. As has often been noted, many Aboriginal languages have no way of translating the word 'guilty'; instead, people are asked if they take responsibility for what has occurred. It is easy to see how this significant difference could lead to more pleas of guilty from Aboriginal people than would be expected. A number of authors have written in some detail on how the issue of culture clash plays out on a daily basis in the courts in Canada, notably Sinclair (1994) and Ross (1992, 1994).

If the cause of over-representation is culture clash, then one possible solution to the problem is to find ways of bridging the two cultures. Indeed, as noted above, the title of the Royal Commission's study on this topic was 'Bridging the Cultural Divide'. There are many ways to try to accomplish this goal. Among the initiatives that have been underway for 20 years or more is to have Aboriginal courtworkers assist Aboriginal accused persons who are going through the justice system. Court-workers help explain the system to Aboriginal people and their families and also provide cultural interpretation for justice system personnel. Other steps can be taken to make the dominant justice system more receptive to the realities of Aboriginal people. These types of initiatives are often lumped under the rubric of 'indigenisation activities'.

Critics of indigenisation point out that the way to resolve culture clash should not always be to find ways to make Aboriginal people more comfortable with the non-Aboriginal system. Instead, initiatives should be taken to make the non-Aboriginal system more comfortable with Aboriginal people (Sinclair, 1994). As well, consideration should be given to allowing Aboriginal people to address the issue of culture clash by removing the matter from the non-Aboriginal system altogether. If Aboriginal people have their justice issues dealt with by other Aboriginal people in distinct Aboriginal justice programmes, then there is no clash.

While there is a great deal of merit in the culture clash theory and proponents of the theory have helped to elucidate some of the very real problems that Aboriginal people face when enmeshed in the criminal justice system, the theory's great weakness is that it does not really explain why many Aboriginal people find themselves before the courts. If the cause of over-representation is culture-clash, one would assume that those Aboriginal people who would be most enmeshed in the justice system would be those who came from communities where the Aboriginal culture was the strongest. Conversely, one would expect Aboriginal people raised outside of traditional Aboriginal homes to be less likely to come into conflict with the law. This theory, however, does not comport with reality (Rudin, 2000).

While comprehensive demographic data has not been collected on Aboriginal offenders, the data that does exist indicates that there is no reason to think that Aboriginal people who are raised in non-Aboriginal settings have less conflict with the law. Indeed, the data suggests just the opposite. When the Royal Commission on Aboriginal Peoples met with the Native Brotherhood at the Saskatchewan Penitentiary, they asked all of those members of the Brotherhood who had been adopted or placed in foster care to raise their hands; every hand in the room went up (Royal Commission, 1996).

Aboriginal Legal Services of Toronto has compiled data on those individuals who have entered their Community Council programme. The Community Council is a criminal diversion programme that has been operating since 1992. Over the years, the programme has dealt with well over 1,000 different Aboriginal offenders. Given the broad nature of the programme's protocol with the Crown Attorney's Office, many of those who enter the programme would receive a jail sentence if they remained in the system. Data on the programme's participants reveal that approximately 44 per cent of those in the programme were either adopted or in care. In addition, 77 per cent of those diverted indicated that they had little or no contact with the Aboriginal community in Toronto or elsewhere. While family dislocation is generally a predictor of involvement with the criminal justice system, it is a more significant factor with regard to Aboriginal offenders. A study done by the Correctional Service of Canada indicated that Aboriginal people who have been adopted or placed in foster care come into the prison system at a greater rate than non-Aboriginal people who have faced the same circumstances (Trevethan et al., 2001).

It is clear, then, that while there is definitely a culture clash with respect to Aboriginal and non-Aboriginal views of justice, this clash cannot be seen as the reason for Aboriginal over-representation in the criminal justice system.

The second theory examined by the Royal Commission (Royal Commission, 1996) was the 'socio-economic' theory. This theory proceeds from the incontrovertible truth that if you want to know which group of people is at the bottom of the socio-economic ladder in any country, all one need do is see which groups come before the courts in disproportionate numbers. Since Aboriginal people are at the bottom of most socio-economic indicators in Canada, it is not surprising, the theory posits, to find Aboriginal people over-represented in jail.

Proponents of this theory argue that changes to Aboriginal rates of over-representation are not likely to occur until the economic status of Aboriginal people improves. Rather than put energy into developing alternative justice programmes, efforts should be made to improve the material conditions of Aboriginal people. As with the culture-clash theory, there is much to recommend in the socio-economic theory. The relationship between poverty and crime is well-established and there is no reason to believe that this relationship does not exist among Aboriginal people.

While it is true that the poor are generally over-represented in jails, poverty is, for most groups, a somewhat transient experience. Thus, while members of particular ethnic or religious groups might initially be over-represented among the poor and thus among the imprisoned, over time, the economic lot of most groups rises. This has not been the case for Aboriginal people in Canada who have seen members of immigrant communities arrive in the country impoverished but, over time, rise socio-economically. Therefore the problem with this theory is that it does not go far enough – it does not explain why, to use the words of the Royal Commission (1996), 'Aboriginal people are poor beyond poverty.'

The final theory examined by the Royal Commission, and the one that the Commission accepted as the best explanation for the continued over-representation of Aboriginal people in Canadian jails, is the Aboriginal experience of colonialism. Colonialism in Canada had, and has, many faces. Whether through residential schools, the denial of treaty rights, the criminalisation of spiritual practices, the prohibition of gatherings, the mass apprehension of Aboriginal children by child welfare authorities or any of the many other tactics adopted by governments or their surrogates, the overall goal was the same: to destroy Aboriginal people as distinct peoples. Indeed, for a long time this was the government's expressed policy. On one level, the colonial process was a failure. Aboriginal people still are a real and visible presence in Canada. On the other hand, the impact of colonialism on the lives of Aboriginal people is perhaps most graphically seen in the reality of over-representation.

It is in large part due to the impact of colonialism that Aboriginal people find themselves in prisons; it is why Aboriginal people make up an increasing percentage of the prison population, even as that phenomenon is decried by the courts and the government of the day. It is why the non-Aboriginal justice system is unable to meaningfully address the causes of Aboriginal criminality. It is why the Royal Commission (1996) concluded that:

> The Canadian criminal justice system has failed the Aboriginal peoples of Canada ... First Nations, Inuit and Métis people, on-reserve and off-reserve, urban and rural ... in all territorial and governmental jurisdictions.

Significantly, this finding was endorsed by the Supreme Court of Canada in *Gladue*.[4] The court extended that finding by addressing the limited impact of prison on Aboriginal offenders and determining:

> ... as has been emphasized repeatedly in studies and commission reports, aboriginal offenders are, as a result of these unique systemic and background factors, more adversely affected by incarceration and less likely to be 'rehabilitated' thereby, because the internment milieu is often culturally inappropriate and regrettably discrimination towards them is so often rampant in penal institutions.

If the cause of Aboriginal over-representation is colonialism, the solution to the problem will have to be found by Aboriginal communities themselves – it is not possible for colonial structures to remedy the problems that they have created. For this reason, one of the cornerstones to addressing the problem of over-representation must be the development of restorative justice responses to criminal behaviour by Aboriginal people. The impacts of colonialism cannot be remedied by having non-Aboriginal organisations, whether they be government or non-governmental organisations, tell Aboriginal people what they can and cannot do; that process, however well meaning, just perpetuates the colonial experience.

It is for this reason that restorative justice responses have to be seen in a broader perspective. The impact of colonialism was to take away first the right, and then often the ability, of Aboriginal communities to maintain order. Taking away this vital function (along with the other functions essential to governance) the colonial experience told individual Aboriginal people that they were not worthy and they were not capable of looking after themselves. In order to give back to individual Aboriginal people the knowledge and understanding that they do have the ability to take responsibility for their lives, Aboriginal communities need to be given the tools to meaningfully respond to incidents of disorder.

It is this process of community building that distinguishes Aboriginal justice programmes from restorative justice programmes in general. It certainly is true that some restorative justice initiatives result in communities gathering strength and developing new found cohesion. However, that is not generally a requirement or a necessary outcome of a restorative justice process in the non-Aboriginal setting. In the Aboriginal context, this aspect of community building, of decolonisation, is essential to the ultimate success of any restorative justice programme (Proulx, 2003). If the justice programme is not rooted in the community and if the individuals the programme is meant to serve do not take away from the process that the Aboriginal community is directing the enterprise, then the colonial message that Aboriginal people are not capable of determining their own lives is reinforced. It is the reinforcement of that message which undermines whatever other positive aspects come out of the process.

Challenges facing Aboriginal justice programmes in Canada today

Community control or self-determination in the area of justice can take many forms. The Royal Commission, and other studies and reports, concluded that Aboriginal nations currently have the constitutional right to establish and administer their own distinct justice systems, although the Commission recommended that control over justice be negotiated with the relevant levels of government. The Royal Commission reported in 1996, and it is safe to say that there have been no significant steps taken, to date, to vest control over justice matters in any comprehensive manner to any Aboriginal community or nation.

At the same time, the Royal Commission recognised that justice initiatives can take place on two tracks, one track being self-government and the other focusing on changes within the existing system. Looking at this second track, how is the Canadian justice system doing in terms of allowing Aboriginal organisations and communities control over aspects of justice processes that have an impact on their lives? What progress is being made in decolonising the practice of justice in Aboriginal communities?

On one level, Canada is clearly a world leader in encouraging the development of Aboriginal justice programmes at the community level. Most provinces and territories in Canada have a number of Aboriginal justice programmes in operation. Significantly, a number of these pro-grammes are located in urban areas, increasingly the place where

Aboriginal people are living. At the same time, there are problems with these local initiatives. Some of the problems are common to almost any community-based endeavour in the justice field: a lack of consistent funding for programmes; volunteer burn-out and excessive reporting requirements, to name just a few. But there are three distinct challenges that Aboriginal justice programmes currently face in Canada, challenges which, cumulatively, could make the survival of such programmes problematic.

The three challenges can be summarised as follows: (1) confusion about what constitutes an Aboriginal justice programme; (2) reluctance to confront and address the reasons why some Aboriginal justice programmes are no longer operating; and (3) the quest for standardising the delivery of Aboriginal justice programmes.

What is an Aboriginal justice programme?

The popular conception of an Aboriginal justice programme, one that is held outside of Canada perhaps even more than within the country, is of initiatives such as sentencing circles. The belief that sentencing circles are a form of Aboriginal justice displays a serious misunderstanding of the hallmarks of an Aboriginal justice programme. Sentencing circles developed in Canada in the late 1980s and early 1990s. The use of circles was pioneered by judges in the Yukon, particularly Judge Barry Stuart. Judge Stuart laid out the need for innovations in sentencing Aboriginal offenders in the case of R v. Moses.[5] Since the first circles were held, increased use of the circle sentencing process has taken place across the country, although use of this option was always more pronounced in Western Canada. Sentencing circles appear to be falling out of favour with the courts in recent years, for reasons that will be discussed later.

The purpose of a sentencing circle is to provide a judge who is sentencing an Aboriginal offender with more detail regarding the circumstances of the individual's life and also to provide the judge with information about alternatives to incarceration in cases where prison would appear to be the most likely outcome. Sentencing circles also provide an opportunity for the judge to hear from the offender, the offender's family and community, and often the victim, in a setting that is more likely to induce candour and openness. The circle is also an opportunity for the offender to hear from people who care about him or her but are concerned with the person's behaviour, and also to hear directly from the victim (Lilles, 2002).

There is no set format for a sentencing circle although, as the name implies, participants generally sit in a circle for the hearing. The judge leaves the bench and sits as an equal participant in the process. Often the judge will dispense with the wearing of her or his robe and participate in business attire or more casual clothing. Crown and defence counsel also participate in the circle, but generally have no more authority or opportunity to speak than anyone else in the circle. The other members of the circle will often include the offender, of course, his or her family, friends, employer, co-workers, neighbours and community members. If there is a victim to the offence, the victim will also often attend, with support from her or his family and friends. The investigating police officer, probation and parole and other community representatives may also be a part of the circle. The way the circle will be conducted will differ from judge to judge and community to community. Often elders are involved in the setting up of the circle, the saying of prayers and setting the tone for the hearing.

As noted above, the purpose of a sentencing circle is to provide information to the judge as to the best disposition of the matter. While the judge sits in the circle like any other participant, ultimately it is the judge who makes the final determination as to sentence. The members of the circle may reach a consensus as to what they think is the best resolution of the matter but, in the end, it is the judge who has the last word and who will ultimately fix the sentence. Since the sentencing process is part of the judicial hearing into a criminal matter, oversight of the process rests with the judicial appeal process. Decisions of sentencing circles have been appealed to Courts of Appeal which have overturned decisions of judges who were following the suggestions of a circle.[6] The Supreme Court of Canada has yet to hear a case involving a sentencing circle.

After the initial enthusiasm for sentencing circles, particularly in the Western Provinces and in the Far North, the use of circles has diminished. There are likely two main reasons for this. First, Courts of Appeal have set out guidelines regarding the types of offences and offenders that are suitable for sentencing circles. These guidelines may have quashed some of the enthusiasm of a number of parties for the process. The second problem with sentencing circles is that at a time when courts are facing increasing pressure to resolve cases quickly and expeditiously, sentencing circles take a significant amount of court time. A sentencing that might be done in 10 to 20 minutes if done in the traditional court manner might take half a day or longer if done through a sentencing circle. Although the result of the process may well be better for all, institutional pressures, particularly in busy urban courts or in remote fly-in courts where the court party might arrive for a day every two or three months, make reliance on sentencing circles problematic.

As an innovation in the way sentencing is conducted, sentencing circles are clearly beneficial. They have been used in cases involving non-

Aboriginal offenders as well. Sentencing circles are best seen as an example of the desire by courts to arrive at better ways of creating meaningful sentences for offenders, particularly Aboriginal offenders. However, it must always be kept in mind that sentencing circles are not an Aboriginal justice initiative or programme; they are judge-made and judge-led initiatives. This does not diminish their worth, but it is important to be clear about what sentencing circles are and what they are not.

If an Aboriginal community were consulted about how they would like to play a role in the justice process, very few communities would likely say, 'what we would like is for the judge to sit with us and listen to what we have to say and then go away and tell us what the sentence will be.' Some communities might well decide that this is how they would like input into the system but, arguably, most would not. Sentencing circles represent the input the justice system will allow Aboriginal people to have. If sentencing circles are the only option, then some communities will embrace that opportunity, but only because it is the only one being offered. An Aboriginal justice programme is one where Aboriginal people in a community are given some options and opportunities to develop processes that respond to the needs of that community. As we shall see in the discussion of the next two challenges facing such programmes, the failure to give Aboriginal people a meaningful opportunity to embark on that journey is a major problem.

Systemic problems

The development of Aboriginal justice programmes began in earnest in the early 1990s. Over the years, a number of Aboriginal justice programmes that were established have ceased to function. There has not been any detailed analysis of what led to the demise of these programmes. Indeed, there is generally a reluctance to speak about these programmes at all. It is important to try to determine why some programmes no longer exist because lessons can be learned from these experiences.

There is a tendency to attribute the demise of these programmes to internal organisational problems such as too much staff turnover and insufficient or inadequate staff training. There is no question that some programmes have foundered because they were not adequately staffed or because the proper staff were not in place, but why did these developments occur? Are there more systemic problems facing the development and operations of Aboriginal justice programmes? This chapter argues that there are more systemic issues and that it is important to discuss them in order that they might be addressed, and that Aboriginal justice programmes have a better opportunity to survive, and indeed flourish.

The three systemic issues that have proven to be the downfall of a number of Aboriginal justice programmes are: (1) the macho minister problem; (2) elite accommodation; and (3) governmental silos. While the failure of an Aboriginal justice programme is generally laid at the door of the programme itself, these systemic problems arise from outside of Aboriginal communities. Just as the Aboriginal community should take responsibility for a justice programme that it is no longer able to operate, so should the non-Aboriginal actors who play a role in setting the stage for the often predictable and sad ending to such programmes. While post-mortems of programmes may take place, the results of these examinations are rarely made public, and the fact that the same mistakes are made again and again suggests that lessons are not being learned.

The 'macho minister' approach to the development of Aboriginal justice programmes refers to the process by which a Minister of Justice or senior government official will place unrealistic expectations on how quickly a community can get a justice programme up and running. The term 'macho minister' is given to this approach based on a particular and oft-reported occasion when a Minister of Justice who shall remain nameless arrived at a meeting of local First Nations chiefs and said, in effect, 'I've got $50,000; who has the balls to set up a justice programme in the next three months?' Not surprisingly, given the desire by many communities to have some input into the justice system, and even with only a short window within which to receive funding and set up the programme, a local First Nations community accepted the challenge. But developing justice programmes is not a variant of reality TV shows or some display of strength by which one or two individuals bend the will of a community and, by virtue solely of their incredible abilities, get a justice programme up and running in record time.

For justice programmes to succeed in a community there needs to be a period of consultation. The community has to have some input into how they want to deal with justice issues. There is a need to learn about pro-gramme delivery options and determine the capacity of the community to provide justice services. None of this can be done if the requirement for access to funding is to become operational within a few short months in order to fit with government fiscal years or other political priorities.

Dropping a justice programme into a community without adequate time for consultation is a recipe for failure. Working on a tight time line, what is likely to happen is that the justice programme is going to grab a justice approach 'off the shelf'. They might send staff to a training session delivered by an Aboriginal or non-Aboriginal provider and attempt to implement that process immediately in the community. They might also get copies of forms, protocols and procedures used by other Aboriginal justice programmes and attempt to superimpose them on their community. In either case, the odds of survival for the justice programme are slim.

A significant number of studies have recommended that Aboriginal communities receive some funding to allow them to take on community consultations and development prior to establishing a justice programme (Obonsawin-Irwin Consulting, 1992; Moyer and Axon, 1993; Sheila Clark and Associates, 1995; Royal Commission, 1996). Such consultations would look at the readiness of the community to undertake a justice initiative, examine the needs in the community, review possible service delivery options and assess them in light of the community's capacity, ability and desire, and educate the community as to the programme. There would also be time for the recruitment and training of volunteers and the determination of what types of cases the programme should address. None of this is possible in two or three months. When the inevitable failure occurs, the government minister or official usually simply blames the community: 'well they weren't ready' or 'they couldn't handle it' and avoids any hard questions about their role in the process.

The second factor in the demise of some Aboriginal justice programmes is the phenomenon of 'elite accommodation'. Aboriginal justice programmes exist because players in the justice system have discretion and are able to exercise that discretion, if they choose, in ways that can encourage the development and growth of Aboriginal justice programmes. For example, the police have discretion whether to lay a criminal charge, even in circumstances where it is clear that an offence has been committed. Crown attorneys have the discretion as to whether or not to prosecute particular offences or to rely on alternative means to resolve the matter. Judges, as noted above, have discretion as to how information will be gathered for the purposes of sentencing. Those with discretion in the justice system must be concerned with using that discretion fairly. They must also keep in mind that, on occasion, the exercise of discretion could lead to problems for them. Inappropriate use of discretion is a ground for complaints and perhaps discipline.

Those who work within the justice system and who are sympathetic to the failures of that system with respect to Aboriginal people are often inclined to use their discretion in support of Aboriginal justice initiatives. At the same time, it can be seen as professionally risky to be seen to cede authority in particular matters to an Aboriginal community, particularly a community with no history of involvement in this area. One consequence of this dilemma is that justice personnel decide to trust an individual or individuals in a community with the responsibility for dealing with justice matters that the authorities have determined they are willing to allow the community to resolve. Essentially, then, this particular individual becomes the surrogate for the police, Crown prosecutor, judge or whoever in the system is exercising that particular discretion. The justice system actors permit the individual to administer the justice programme because they have personal faith and confidence that the individual can do the job.

The lure of this opportunity, from the perspective of the Aboriginal person who is entrusted with the responsibility, is quite clear. If this person has an interest in justice and in the improvement of the condition of his or her people, then it becomes a difficult offer to refuse. The problem with this approach is that by locating the seat of the justice initiative in one person, the community itself is shut out of the process. The interests of the justice system personnel are to ensure that the exercise of their discretion is carried out properly and that, to them, is best assured by essentially deputising someone in the community to take responsibility for justice matters. The interests of the community, however, may well be located elsewhere.

When problems occur within the justice initiative – and problems will inevitably occur – it is very easy for fingers to be pointed at the Aboriginal person who has been exercising personal authority over the programme. When people are shut out of the process they become suspicious. It is easy to see how charges of favouritism can emerge if the programme is not truly subject to some community control and accountability. Unfortunately, for many justice system personnel, who may not know the particular community very well, their preference is for personal accountability; thus one or two individuals are set up to sit in the crossfire between the desire for community and personal responsibility. The outcome of this crossfire is that often the reputation of the individual is tarnished and, therefore, that of the justice programme. If the allegations against the person are significant enough, the programme's ongoing viability is threatened.

The third systemic problem facing Aboriginal justice programmes is that of the 'silo mentality' of governments. Funding, supervision and responsibility for Aboriginal justice programmes usually fall within the mandate of a specific federal or provincial ministry; in many cases there is both one federal and one provincial ministry involved with a justice programme. In most cases, the ministry charged with this responsibility will be the federal Department of Justice and/or the provincial Ministry of the Attorney General. In order to measure success, the number of cases diverted, or some such measure, is often used. The problem with this approach is that, again, it does not often accord with the needs of the community.

Small communities, such as many reserves, have a significant number of needs. Many of these needs might be met, in part, by a justice programme, depending upon the way in which the programme is structured. When a community identifies its needs, it often does not differentiate between which ministries are responsible for seeing that a particular need is addressed. For example, the goal of the community might be to see healthier individuals in the community on the basis that the healthier the individual, the healthier the community. This might lead the justice programme to look at more systemic issues within their community. There may be a need for new programmes or services. Depending upon the range of programmes and services available in the community, the justice programme might be the locus for these initiatives. But now we have a problem. The justice programme is funded to deliver justice-related programmes not school lunches, or victims' groups or any other programme that might further the overall health of the community. Exerting efforts in this area, and in particular expending funds, could violate the funding agreement between the justice programme and the government.

Government ministries fund programmes that relate to their particular mandates; in the case of justice ministries, that mandate relates to justice-related activities such as the diversion of cases out of the criminal justice system. For an Aboriginal community, particularly a smaller community, matters may be seen in a broader context. Thus if young people are breaking into stores for food the issue of breakfast or lunch programmes properly belongs, from a governmental perspective, to community services not justice. If the justice programme spends justice funds on community services, funds may well be misspent. Fiscal audits of programmes can discover that funds have been used for improper purposes.

But should these developments be surprising? It would be surprising if a small community with a few thousand inhabitants generated enough criminal activity to keep a justice programme fully operational. Should it not be expected that in cases like that, the justice programme would identify some of the more significant systemic issues and attempt to address them? From a holistic perspective, community needs do not come neatly packaged in boxes with labels like 'justice', 'health' and 'social services'.

What about the funding agreements? The argument is often made that if a community does not want to be bound by particular funding strictures they should not sign a funding agreement that binds them to such restrictions. The problem with this argument is that it ignores the reality of the environment in which funding agreements are signed. Increasingly, communities wanting justice programmes have little room to negotiate in the development of their funding agreement. It is, in essence, a take it or leave it proposition. Even if government officials are willing to be more flexible, legal departments within the ministries increasingly are insisting on standardised contracts with identical clauses where the only difference between agreements is the amount being paid out, the budget lines and the names of the contact persons in the community. In such situations, it is not surprising that programmes run afoul of funding rules by spending monies in 'unauthorised' areas.

The quest for standardisation

The issue of standardised contracts is but a small example of the quest for standardisation that is motivating much of government initiatives in the Aboriginal justice area and, as a result, jeopardising creativity, new development and the continuation of Aboriginal justice programmes as vital forces in their communities. When Aboriginal justice programmes began to flourish in Canada in the early 1990s the programmes were all local in nature. Their existence often relied upon relationships between local justice system personnel and Aboriginal people and organisations. The local nature of these programmes provided some strength to them. Because those involved in their creation were living in the communities, be they reserve, rural or urban, there was often recognition of the needs and capacities of the community. At the same time, this structure was also precarious. For one thing, a move out of the community, on the part of the programme's justice system champion threatened the viability of the programme. An additional factor compounding this instability was that such initiatives generally required funding, funding that was not available at the local level and thus required approaches to the provincial or federal governments.

Inevitably, as more and more programmes began to develop, more and more requests were made for funding for these initiatives. The more requests that came in, the more it seemed that governments needed to develop a common response to such requests. One of the overarching rationales for governments as they developed responses to funding requests was the desire to ensure equality: equality in programme delivery, in funding and in expectations.

Equality with respect to programme delivery focused primarily on the types of cases that would be appropriate for Aboriginal justice pro-grammes. In this context, the equality concern was that justice should be the same for everyone. While community capacity could mean that not every community might have a restorative justice programme, the types of cases that such programmes should deal with should generally be the same; after all, justice in Canada does not differ from place to place as there is one Criminal Code for the entire country. It would not be fair or equitable if a person charged with an offence in one jurisdiction could escape all criminal liability by having his or her case diverted to a restorative justice programme while such a programme did not exist elsewhere. This problem would be exacerbated if programmes were open to dealing with more serious offences. As well, there was the concern that standards would ensure that no programme could get too far ahead of the curve and take on matters that perhaps were outside their capacity or might raise difficult questions for politicians.

Standardisation was also seen as beneficial for those government officials who were charged with funding such programmes. Fairness and bureaucratic efficiency would be enhanced the more programmes were alike. It would then become easier to determine funding needs and to assess a programme's ability to meet specific goals and targets in comparison with other programmes in order to measure success.

On a broader level, a more recent rationale for standardisation arose to address definitional issues, in particular what is a restorative justice programme? In order to cope with an ever-increasing number of criminal charges coming before the courts, many jurisdictions have adopted a number of alternative justice responses to move cases, generally minor crimes, out of the system altogether. These types of programmes, as important as they are to the administration of justice, are not truly restorative justice programmes as they have considerably different goals (Hughes and Mossman, 2001).[7] Defining the hallmarks of restorative justice programmes would therefore assist in determining the nature of a programme, the expectations for it, and perhaps, funding levels as well. The federal government has developed a response in this regard by drafting a set of guidelines for restorative justice programmes based upon the model guidelines developed by the United Nations but tailored to address Canadian concerns.[8] These guidelines are meant to encompass Aboriginal justice programmes, even though the programmes are not specifically referenced.

What can be wrong with these rationales for more standardisation of restorative justice programmes? Who is not in favour of treating people equally? The first rationale – that everyone should be treated the same when coming before the courts – suffers from two problems. The first is that it compares an idealised version of the justice system with the practical realities of restorative justice programmes. A better comparison would be with the actual reality of justice as it is practised on the ground, as compared to the actual practice of restorative justice. On this basis, the argument collapses at the outset. Despite the fact that criminal law is the same across the country, there is no uniformity in sentencing. Within provinces there is great discrepancy in the way certain offences are handled. In some cases, those discrepancies emerge when comparing even neighbouring judicial districts. More broadly, for example, crime tends to be treated with longer jail sentences in smaller communities than in big cities. Offences that might result in suspended sentences, discharges or terms of probation in a city such as Vancouver regularly result in jail sentences in smaller towns. This problem is even more pronounced when the sentencing practices are examined on a province-by-province basis. It is clear when looking at such figures that some provinces are, for example, more likely to use prison as a sanction than other provinces. All of this puts a lie to the claim that, in a practical sense, there is any real equality of treatment of offenders across geographic borders, whether municipal or provincial, within Canada.

The second problem with the 'equality' argument is that it advocates a model of equality that is at odds with the prevailing view of equality held by the courts. The idea that equality is achieved by making sure everyone receives a similar sentence for a similar crime is an argument for formal equality: equality of treatment. With the introduction of the Canadian Charter of Rights and Freedoms in 1982, the country has moved to a vision of substantive equality, where the focus is on equality of outcome. Substantive equality means that sometimes we must treat people differently in order to achieve the same result. If the result we wish to achieve through the sentencing process is to deter offenders from committing offences, as well as keeping communities safe, then we must recognise that there are many ways to accomplish this goal within the sentencing process. The Supreme Court of Canada has explicitly recommended that courts adopt a more restorative, and thus a more individualised, approach to sentencing (Rudin, 2003).[9]

The bureaucratic impetus for standardisation, although understandable, has two regrettable and related difficulties. The first is that by centralising what can be funded, the amounts of funds available, and often the types of offences amenable to Aboriginal justice programmes, local creativity and responsiveness is choked off and the scope for such programmes is pushed to the lowest common denominator. The second is that the quest for a standard definition of what constitutes a restorative justice programme might make it difficult for Aboriginal programmes to develop and respond to the needs in their communities.

Restorative justice programmes develop in response to local needs and as a result of collaboration among a variety of actors at the local level. These creative and innovative responses then form the basis for more communities wishing to undertake such projects. Ironically, this growth then spurs the need for 'standards' choking off the very factors that made the programmes such a success in the beginning. The result of this aspect of the push for standardisation means that two of the longest running and most studied Aboriginal justice programmes in Canada would likely have difficulty getting off the ground if they were launched today.

In Manitoba, in the late 1980s, the Hollow Water Community Holistic Circle Healing initiative developed to address a particular need in the four communities around Hollow Water, Manitoba. The need in those communities was for a response to the high rate of sexual abuse, particularly child sexual abuse. Studies in the communities found that a large number of people living in the area had been sexually abused as children and were now sexually abusing children (Royal Commission, 1996). The justice system dealt with the issue by imprisoning the offender for a number of years and then returning him to the community after sentence no better able to deal with the issues that led to the commission of the offence than before conviction. Dissatisfaction with this approach to the problem led to the creation of Community Holistic Circle Healing. There is not the space here to discuss this process in any detail. What is relevant for this discussion is that these communities identified their justice concern as the sexual abuse of children. In response to this concern, the community developed a remarkable process that worked with the existing criminal justice system so that victimisers were not sent to jail but, instead, remained in the community to work on their healing.

While Hollow Water is often lauded as a visionary and successful way of dealing with one of the more seemingly intractable forms of criminal behaviour, the continuation of the programme has always been in jeopardy. The comprehensive nature of the programme has meant that it does not fall easily into the specific funding bailiwick of any particular ministry. Thus it has been particularly vulnerable to the problem of silos. More relevant to the discussion of standardisation, as justice officials work to develop standard protocols for Aboriginal justice programmes in provinces, cases like the sexual abuse of children are automatically put off-limits for such programmes. While there are obviously good reasons to think that most Aboriginal justice programmes could be way over their heads when dealing with such offences, the blanket prohibition on dealing with such offences could mean that programmes building on the work in Hollow Water would not be able to get started.

In Toronto, Aboriginal Legal Services of Toronto's (ALST) Community Council Programme was the first urban Aboriginal justice programme in Canada and is one of the longest running Aboriginal justice programmes in the country. The protocol that the programme signed with the Toronto Crown Attorney's Office in 1991 is significant for the flexibility it gives to the programme. In a nutshell, no offences or offenders are inherently ineligible for the programme.[10] In addition, once a client attends their Community Council hearing, the matter cannot go back to court even if the client does not complete his or her Community Council decision.

The longevity of the programme is one immediate indicator of its success. As a result, many Aboriginal justice programmes from across the country are encouraged to visit ALST to see how the programme operates. At the same time, no other Aboriginal justice programme has been able to operate with a protocol as open-ended as the one used by the Community Council. Concerns about standardising programmes, and ensuring equality among programmes, has severely limited the abilities of many Aboriginal justice programmes to take on a significant range of cases and/ or offenders. As with Hollow Water, had the Community Council come into existence today, it is unlikely that it would be able to operate under its current protocol.

It is difficult to embrace the call for the standardisation of Aboriginal justice programmes if two of the more celebrated and successful examples of community development and initiative in creating such programmes cannot be replicated today due to the tight grip of standardisation. It is understandable why government officials would want to impose some measures on Aboriginal justice programmes. Accountability is a vital aspect for any programme that receives funding from any source. However, if the drive for standardisation is not really about accountability but is actually about making it easier for government officials to administer programmes, then the development is problematic. To the extent that this desire frustrates the will of the Aboriginal community and gets in the way of the community's ability to deal with the real justice issues that confront it, we return to a more contemporary form of colonialism – bureaucratic colonialism. Regardless of the rationale, colonialism is still colonialism and the more Aboriginal communities are restrained and restricted from taking real control over justice issues, the less the programmes that are developed will be able to meaningfully respond to the needs of the Aboriginal community.

One of the unfortunate consequences of the standardisation process is that some Aboriginal justice programmes may begin to operate in a clandestine manner. Local justice officials and Aboriginal justice programme staff and volunteers continue to do what they have always done, but they simply neglect to tell senior government officials of their activities. These officials then may collaborate with this approach by accepting reports and not asking any probing questions. This 'don't ask – don't tell' way to deliver Aboriginal justice has its appeal as a short-term solution, but ultimately can only lead to more problems. At some point, the practices in the community will become known, often as the result of a particularly difficult or controversial case. While government officials will maintain that they had no idea what was going on, the Aboriginal justice programme may be shut down or severely scaled back and justice personnel who assisted the programme may be reprimanded. The only lessons learned will be either 'follow all the rules' or 'do a better job of keeping things secret'.

The proposed adoption, by the Canadian government, of a statement of principles of restorative justice based on similar discussions by the United Nations is also problematic. The biggest problem with the Canadian and UN initiatives is that rather than describing restorative justice in terms of what such processes are expected to accomplish, the guidelines explicitly come out in favour of one particular model of restorative justice: victim–offender reconciliation.[11] For victim–offender programmes, the guidelines have some utility, but equating restorative justice with victim–offender reconciliation does a great disservice to the range and scope of restorative justice programmes, particularly in Aboriginal communities.

The difficulty with a definition of restorative justice that is tied to one particular method is if that definition is linked with bureaucratic desires to standardise programmes, there is a great danger that all programmes that do not fit within the victim–offender paradigm will find it difficult to obtain funding. Even if current programmes are exempt from such a response, this development might well make it difficult for new pro-grammes to develop. All of these issues are particularly significant for Aboriginal justice programmes. While the draft guidelines at the UN and the Canadian level explicitly credit the development of restorative justice programmes to Aboriginal justice concepts, the guidelines do not recognise that Aboriginal justice initiatives are not historic relics from which lessons can be drawn, but rather vital contemporary projects which have their own distinct needs that must be acknowledged and addressed.[12]

The way forward

Many of the challenges facing Aboriginal justice programmes in Canada described in this chapter can be attributed, in large part, to the fact that there has not been explicit recognition that restorative justice programmes in Aboriginal communities must be delivered by Aboriginal organisations. In order for justice programmes in Aboriginal communities to be success-ful, Aboriginal people must control the alternative justice processes.

There is now widespread recognition that traditional non-Aboriginal justice responses have not served the Aboriginal community well; indeed, there is a general dissatisfaction in the way that the justice system responds to criminal acts committed by anyone. This dissatisfaction has meant that many organisations have looked to restorative justice approaches for a better way to provide justice to communities. The range of organisations that now provide such programmes is surprising and include police services, community organisations, religious groups, large metropolitan or provincially based non-profit organisations and international organisations with local branches promoting particular restorative justice approaches.

The motivation for these groups to move into the area of restorative justice is multi-faceted. Certainly, almost all organisations involved in this work are committed to seeing a change, of some sort, in the system. For police, there is likely also recognition that restorative justice approaches are going to be used; therefore, the more the police are embedded in these processes the more they will remain relevant and be able to maintain current funding and staffing levels. The same mixture of commitment to social change and awareness that restorative justice is a place where money is being spent also motivates most of the other organisations and groups involved in this area. Aboriginal communities are particularly fertile ground for restorative justice providers. For one thing, there is the widespread recognition that the non-Aboriginal justice system in its current guise has not worked. Secondly, there is a feeling that there are funds available for organisations wishing to provide such services – and, indeed, there are. And this is where we run into difficulties and challenges.

Recognising that Aboriginal communities should control the develop-ment of justice initiatives also means recognising that there is a need for community consultation and development and that the justice pro-grammes that emerge from such processes might differ from one another both in their focus and their funding needs. These sorts of programmes are more costly and more difficult to administer than some of the more off-the-shelf approaches offered by other providers.

Without an explicit recognition that justice in Aboriginal communities should be under the control of those communities and that such control must include deciding how restorative justice approaches will be delivered and administered, the door is open for other justice providers to enter. Most Aboriginal communities rely upon government funding to develop and implement justice programmes. However, despite govern-ment commitments for new programmes in this area, there is little new money available for communities that do not yet have programmes in place. This means that Aboriginal communities dissatisfied with the current status quo may have to look to non-Aboriginal justice providers to develop alternatives. The sad problem with such outside sources is that importing justice solutions does not build community capacity and challenge colonial assumptions. Rather, it may well reinforce these notions.

What is to be done? There is a strong need for two initiatives to be implemented immediately. The first is for government funders and justice system personnel to let go of some of the control they exercise over Aboriginal justice programmes. Rather than move to create universal protocols for use by all Aboriginal justice programmes, governments should realise that community needs must dictate the way in which justice programmes develop. It is, therefore, vital that communities be given the time, opportunity and funding to determine how they wish to approach justice issues. That exploration should not begin with a list setting out where the community cannot go; instead, the community should be encouraged to look at whatever responses they feel that they can realistically meet. Letting go of control does not mean removing any accountability. Governments, indeed all funders, are more than justified in requiring that those who receive funds account for those funds. Such accounting should not be merely financial but should also set out the particular activities in which the community is engaged. But letting go should mean that communities are not punished for being innovative and for looking at justice as part of a holistic approach to the community, one that may well cross a number of government ministries.

The second measure, and perhaps the most important, is for governments, and all justice providers, to recognise and affirm that Aboriginal justice programmes must be developed and controlled by Aboriginal organisations and communities. This must be a first principle and should animate all discussion in this area. Aboriginal justice programmes should be recognised as distinct endeavours from other restorative justice programmes. The importance of developing community responses in Aboriginal communities – urban, rural and reserve – must be central to the process. These initiatives are as important for their contribution to combating the impact of colonialism as for their ability to better respond to criminal activity in the community; in fact, without the former objective, it will be difficult for the projects to achieve the latter.

In this regard, everyone with an interest in restorative justice generally, and Aboriginal justice in particular, has a role to play. Academics, community organisers and volunteers, restorative justice practitioners, etc., would do well to remember the words of Karl Marx (not a person often quoted in restorative justice circles) who said, in his *11th Thesis on Feuerbach*, '… philosophers have merely interpreted the world in different ways; the point is, to change it.' Everyone involved in the restorative justice movement is doing this work because they want change. They are interested in studying new developments and they want to learn how to do their work better, but everyone, in their own way, wants to change the world for the better.

One way to work towards this change is by saying, whenever the opportunity presents itself, that Aboriginal justice programmes belong to Aboriginal people, that Aboriginal justice programmes must be developed by Aboriginal people and Aboriginal organisations, and that Aboriginal justice programmes are a unique and distinct initiative apart from other restorative justice programmes. If that is said, and if that is lived in the work that is done, then while it does not guarantee success for Aboriginal justice programmes – for after all that is up to each programme in each community – it might at least guarantee survival for the programmes that, without that assurance, face challenges that could seriously undermine their very existence.

Notes

1 The opinions expressed in this paper are those of the author and do not necessarily represent those held by Aboriginal Legal Services of Toronto.

2 Inmates serving sentences of two years or more serve those sentences in federal penitentiaries; those serving sentences of less than two years serve them in provincial correction centres.

3 *R* v. *Gladue* [1999] 1 SCR 688.

4 Ibid.

5 *R* v. *Moses* 71 CCC (3d) 347 (1992).

6 For an example, see the Saskatchewan Court of Appeal's decision in *R* v. *Morin* 101 CCC (3d) 124 (1995).

7 For example, programmes developed across the country in the early 1990s to deal with matters such as first-offender shoplifting cases have expanded their mandates over time. Any restorative aspects of such programmes are largely incidental.

8 The Draft Values and Principles of Restorative Justice in Criminal Matters and be found at: http://www.restorativejustice.ca/NationalConsultation/ValuesandPrinciplesdraf.htm.

9 The Supreme Court of Canada in *R* v. *Gladue* (see note 3) at paragraphs 71 and 72 stated:

> In general terms, restorative justice may be described as an approach to remedying crime in which it is understood that all things are interrelated and that crime disrupts the harmony which existed prior to its occurrence, or at least which is felt should exist. The appropriateness of a particular sanction is largely determined by the needs of the victims, and the community, as well as the offender. The focus is on the human beings closely affected by the crime ... The existing

overemphasis on incarceration in Canada may be partly due to the perception that a restorative approach is a more lenient approach to crime and that imprisonment constitutes the ultimate punishment. Yet in our view a sentence focussed on restorative justice is not necessarily a 'lighter' punishment. Some proponents of restorative justice argue that when it is combined with probationary conditions it may in some circumstances impose a greater burden on the offender than a custodial sentence.

10   As a result of Crown guidelines for diversion programmes generally, developed after the Community Council protocol, cases of domestic violence or sexual assault are not diverted to the programme. In practice, impaired driving charges or charges where a conviction is required in order to request a firearms prohibition, are also not diverted.

11   While the preamble to the principles sets matters out in a general sense, the first enumerated principle states: 'Participation of a victim and offender in a restorative justice process should be based on their free, voluntary and informed consent ... Consent to participate may be withdrawn at any stage.' The rest of the principles proceed along this victim–offender reconciliation line.

12   The preamble states

that, based on traditional communal culture and values, Aboriginal people historically utilised a concept of justice akin to what we now refer to as Restorative Justice, and the fact that the evolution of their experience will continue to shape Restorative Justice in both Aboriginal and other communities.

References

House of Commons Debates (2001) Vol. 1, No. 2 (30 January), 14–15.

Hughes, P. and Mossman, M. J. (2001) *Re-Thinking Access to Criminal Justice in Canada: A Critical Review of Needs, Responses and Restorative Justice Initiatives.* Ottawa: Department of Justice. Available at: http://canada.justice.gc.ca/en/ps/rs/rep/rr03_2a.html.

Jackson, M. (1989) 'Locking up Natives in Canada: Report of the Canadian Bar Association Committee on Imprisonment and Release', *University of British Columbia Law Review*, 23, 215–300.

Lilles, H. (2002) *Circle Sentencing: Part of the Restorative Justice Continuum.* International Institute for Restorative Practices. Available at: http://www.iirp.org/library/mn02/mn02_lilles.html.

Moyer, S. and Axon, L. (1993) *An Implementation Evaluation of the Native Community Council Project of Aboriginal Legal Services of Toronto.* Toronto: Ministry of the Attorney General.

Obonsawin-Irwin Consulting (1992) *Future Aboriginal Community Justice Project Development Needs: An Addendum to the Sandy Lake and Attawapiskat First Nations*

Justice Pilot Project Evaluation Report. Toronto: Ministry of the Attorney General.

Proulx, C. (2003) *Reclaiming Aboriginal Justice, Identity, and Community.* Saskatoon: Purich Publications.

Ross, R. (1992) *Dancing With a Ghost.* Markham: Octopus Publishing.

Ross, R. (1994) 'Duelling Paradigms? Western Criminal Justice Versus Aboriginal Community Healing', in R. Gosse, J. Y. Henderson and R. Carter (eds), *Continuing Poundmaker and Riel's Quest: Presentations Made at a Conference on Aboriginal Peoples and Justice.* Saskatoon: Purich Publications, pp. 241–68.

Royal Commission on Aboriginal Peoples (1996) *Bridging the Cultural Divide.* Ottawa: Minister of Supply and Services.

Rudin, J. (2000) 'Aboriginal Self-Government and Justice', in J. Hylton (ed.), *Aboriginal Self-Government in Canada*, 2nd edn. Saskatoon: Purich Publications, pp. 205–27.

Rudin, J. (2003) 'Pushing Back – A Response to the Drive for the Standardization of Restorative Justice Programs in Canada'. Unpublished paper, 6th International Conference on Restorative Justice. Available at: http://www.sfu.ca/cfrj/fulltext/rudin.pdf.

Sheila Clark & Associates (1995) *Building the Bridge, A Review of the South Vancouver Island Justice Education Project.* Vancouver: Sheila Clark & Associates.

Sinclair, M. (1994) 'Aboriginal Peoples, Justice and the Law', in R. Gosse, J. Y. Henderson and R. Carter (eds), *Continuing Poundmaker and Riel's Quest: Presentations Made at a Conference on Aboriginal Peoples and Justice.* Saskatoon: Purich Publications, pp. 178–84.

Statistics Canada, Canadian Centre for Justice Statistics (2000) *Adult Correctional Services in Canada, 1999–2000.* Ottawa: Canadian Centre for Justice Statistics.

Trevethan, S., Auger, S., Moore, J.-P., MacDonald, M. and Sinclair, J. (2001) *The Effect of Family Disruption on Aboriginal and Non-Aboriginal Inmates.* Ottawa: Correctional Service of Canada. Available at: http://www.csc-scc.gc.ca/text/rsrch/reports/r113/r113_e.pdf.

Chapter 6

Indigenous youth and the criminal justice system in Australia

John Boersig

Abstract

The over-representation of Indigenous children in the criminal justice system is well documented. One of the most important outcomes of the Australian Royal Commission into Aboriginal Deaths in Custody, finalised in 1991, was to highlight the difficulties faced by Indigenous people within the criminal justice system, particularly in the area of Indigenous juvenile incarceration. The orthodox response by one State within the federation, New South Wales, as expressed in legislation and court sentencing practice, is marked by a failure to stem the ever-increasing rates of Indigenous incarceration. Focusing upon court practice and case law, this chapter critiques the orthodox responses by government over the past ten years to the problem of Indigenous juvenile incarceration. Criticism of the government's inability to address this problem is long-standing and damning, and underscores the inadequacy of various strategies used to address this issue. Drawing from a postcolonial theoretical framework, the chapter questions the orthodox response by the government to this problem. It is suggested that the failure of government calls for a rethinking of law reform, and that 'restorative justice' may provide a pathway forward.

Introduction

More than a decade has passed since the Royal Commission into Aboriginal Deaths in Custody highlighted the difficulties faced by Indigenous people. It is apparent that one of the major 'problems' – Indigenous youth incarceration – remains unsolved. Moreover, it has been accepted by successive New South Wales (NSW) governments that this is a 'problem' that society must address[1] and that the 'problem' is getting worse.[2] A review of the literature discussing this issue reveals that there has been an ongoing dialogue among researchers, at a popular level in the press and between other stakeholders in the criminal justice sector.[3] The sentencing of Indigenous people remains an urgent and important issue (Cunneen, 2001; Sarre and Wilson, 1998). Criticism of the government's inability to get results is longstanding and damning, and underscores the inadequacy of the government response (ADICWC, 1992; Dodson, 1996), the lack of 'will' to implement the recommendations of the Royal Commission into Aboriginal Deaths in Custody (Cunneen, 1997) and the failure to recognise and respect Indigenous rights (Jonas, 2001).

Orthodox solutions

The solutions to the over-representation of Indigenous youth in the criminal justice system traditionally put forward by government in NSW over the past 10 years (as elsewhere in Australia) locate strategies in two major forms of governance – public policy and judicial governance through the courts. While these strategies of state governance are certainly of a broad circumference, this chapter is concerned with the management, by the state, of criminal offending by Indigenous youth in court: one 'site' of governance.[4] It is at this site that the judge or magistrate is expected to apply the orthodox 'principles of sentencing' in accord with the notion that 'equality' and 'justice' are provided for all who come before the court;[5] this is a predominant orthodox discourse. Although this chapter is primarily concerned with governance through the courts at the *moment* of sentencing Indigenous youth, it should be noted that criminal justice practices and policies are complementary and form part of a 'whole of government' response to offending.[6]

Statistics

The over-representation of Indigenous youth in the criminal justice system is well documented. NSW statistics reveal that 2 per cent of juveniles aged 10 to 18 years of age are Indigenous. It is reported that in 1999/2000, on average, 355 juveniles were held in custody each day; 123 (35 per cent) were of Indigenous background. Between 1996/1997 and 1999/2000 the general juvenile detainee population decreased but the number of Indigenous offenders increased from 30 per cent to 35 per cent (DJJ, 2001: 17–18).

Statistics clearly show that the over-representation of Indigenous juveniles continues to remain at a high level (Cunneen and White, 1995; Luke and Lind, 2002), as it has for adults, particularly young adults between 18 and 25 years of age (Carcach et al., 1999; Baker, 2001). The Aboriginal and Torres Strait Islander Social Justice Commissioner recently pointed out that the numbers of Indigenous prisoners had increased by 8 per cent each year since 1991 (compared with 3 per cent for non-Indigenous people) and now form 20 per cent of the prison population (14 per cent in 1991), while Indigenous people constitute just over 2 per cent of the Australian population. The incarceration rate moved from 13 to 15.5 times that of non-Indigenous juveniles, and 'consistently made up approximately 42 per cent of the total juvenile detention population' (Jonas, 2001: 2).

Postcolonial theory[7]

This chapter adopts a postcolonial reading of the culture and history of Indigenous people because, arguably, it decisively explains the current situation of Indigenous people in Australia.[8] By its nature, postcolonial theory confronts an imperialist or coloniser's reading of history (Adams, 1995). In this sense, postcolonial theory lays bare its own assumptions about power and imperialism, stating clearly that it is a critique of the colonial and neo-colonial society from the perspective of the colonised (Culhane, 1998). Neo-colonialism can be defined as a reinscription of colonisation practices in contemporary society. In other words, the oppression of Indigenous (colonised) society continues while the 'people who colonised those countries run them, effectively excluding the first inhabitants' (Yazzie, 2000: 43).[9] This impact is keenly felt in the legal field: in the incarceration of Indigenous people in jails and in their appearance before courts (Cunneen and McDonald, 1997; RCAP, 1996), in the operation of the legal system (see Hanks and Keon-Cohen, 1988; Bird, 1996) and in their need for legal services (HRSCAA, 1980).

Law and colonialism have a symbiotic relationship, imperative to the maintenance of the social order. Law, it is suggested, is a primary acculturating institution in colonisation, and continues in this role in neo-colonial society. Colonial authority was always ultimately justified by recourse to the law as an act of domination (Merry, 1991). Explicit in the act of colonisation is the import of state authority and, in practice, a colonising power was immediately faced with questions of how to import this authority. On the one hand, the colonial power needed to retain authority over its own citizens and, on the other, it needed ways to regulate the relationship between colonial government, its citizens and the Indigenous people already inhabiting the land (Woodman, 1988).

It is argued that a postcolonialist paradigm is crucial to both under-standing contemporary society and plotting change to neo-colonial structures and systems. In a similar and linked way, the drive to self-determination by Indigenous people expresses a sense of agency and ability to effect change, which is apparent in the 'resistance' to colonisation. This position is strongly argued by Indigenous people who pursue and articulate strategies of decolonisation (see, for example, Battiste, 2000; Behrendt, 1995; Borrows, 1996; Langton, 1993; Stevens, 1997; Watson, 1996; Youngblood and Henderson, 1996).

Sentencing – an orthodox response to juvenile offending

Courts differentiate between juvenile and adult offenders.[10] Yet, while there will be some quite pointed differences that arise as a child moves to become an adult at 18 years of age (such as the loss of access to specialist youth facilities or particular privileges against self-incrimination), the notion of a concession to 'youth' within adult sentencing blurs this line, extending and mitigating responsibility along a continuum that extends from 10 to around 25 years of age. As a consequence, an examination of sentencing in this field must generally be undertaken in terms of looking at the way courts consider the implications of youth, not simply of childhood.[11]

Youth as mitigation

The sentencing of Indigenous children is considered a sub-set of 'mitigation'. Mitigation, the lessening of the seriousness of circumstances or an offence, may arise in a sentencing process from the fact of an offender's 'youth'. In NSW the 'youth' of an offender may be a mitigating factor in sentencing, and greater concern is expressed for the prospects of rehabilitation (Potas, 2001). Where the courts are dealing with a person who is also a child, further weight is generally given to issues of reform/rehabilitation (see, for example, the New South Wales cases of GDP[12] and XYJ[13]). Yet, 'youth' cannot be used as an excuse that allows exculpation from responsibility.[14]

In the case of GDP the court made what might be said to be a definitive distinction between adult and child offenders. In this case, there was an appeal against a decision of a District Court Judge who had found that the young offender had 'extraordinary prospects of rehabilitation', but determined that 'the ordinary principles of sentencing applied ... in exactly the same way as they applied to adult offenders' (at p. 114). The judge imposed a period of incarceration. This raised an immediate tension between the principles of punishment, highlighting the relative importance of the sentencing principles of rehabilitation, as against deterrence and retribution. The Court of Criminal Appeal rejected the assessment of the lower court, indicating that the true position was that a different *emphasis* of the sentencing principles applied to young offenders. The appellate court stated:

> Had it been an adult who had committed these offences, then the principles of retribution and, more importantly, general deterrence, would have demanded a custodial sentence of considerable length. But rehabilitation must be the primary aim in relation to an offender as young as this applicant (*GDP*, at p. 116).

Limits to the special consideration due to youth

It seems, following *GDP*, that the court accepts that it must, to some extent, deal with juveniles in a 'special' way, and this has meant providing particular sentencing mechanisms for juvenile offenders; but there are limits. The key phrase arising from this case, it is suggested, is 'that a different emphasis' is given to the interpretation of sentencing purposes, principles and rules when applied to juvenile offenders; but they are by no means overturned by the fact that the court may be dealing with either a child or a young adult. The court in *R* v. *FQ*,[15] when increasing a sentence on a 14-year-old juvenile convicted of armed robbery, said

> For present purposes it is necessary to note that general deterrence still retains a place in the sentencing of young offenders. The extent to which regard will be paid to general deterrence depends on the particular circumstance of each case ... despite his youth the respondent had demonstrated a continued contempt for the law and regrettably very uncertain prospect as to their rehabilitation ... the very serious objective circumstances of the subject offence are aggravated (at p. 5).

In other words, the same principles and methodology are used in sentencing children and adults and the general sentencing legislation applies (Blackmore, 1992). The mitigation arising from the youth of an offender, in that sense, remains one factor to be taken into account and is to be balanced with all the other purposes and principles of sentencing.

The real question at the *moment* of sentence, it is suggested, is most likely to be 'how much' sentence to pass rather than the more reflective question of 'why?' In this sense, the 'how much' decision made when sentencing a juvenile sits comfortably within the orthodox traditions; in asking 'why?', however, more fundamental and critical questions about the nature of crime and punishment arise (see Von Hirsch, 1998). Nonetheless, the orthodox traditions indicate that the court should weigh *all* the principles and factors associated with the sentencing process, including the sentencing options available, when coming to a conclusion about the length of a sentence.

Dealing with a juvenile as an adult 'according to law'

The sentencing of juveniles, it is argued, occurs not in contra-distinction to adults but rather as a point on a sentencing continuum that covers all criminal offending. In this context, 'youth' is a factor at the moment of sentence. The point of intersection is marked when the court exercises a sentencing discretion in a particular case.

The sentencing task is further underlined when a court comes to consider whether or not to deal with a juvenile 'according to law'. In the normal course, any person 18 years of age or older who commits an offence is dealt with as an adult; that is, in accordance with the law and punished without the benefit of being considered a child. In *Nichols*,[16] the court said there is a line over which the serious nature of a crime means the benefits of youth must give way to the gravity of an offence. Likewise in *SDM*,[17] where the actions of a young offender were equated with the commission of a serious offence by an adult, the leniency they would otherwise attract may well be lost.[18]

Discretionary application of principles

In *R* v. *R*,[19] the court determined that there are a number of matters to be taken into account when assessing whether or not to sentence a juvenile offender 'according to law'. These include the gravity of the offence, the age of the child and the kinds of penalties that may be meted out, particularly in relation to serious offences. The court further indicated that where a custodial sentence is likely to be served in prison rather than in a detention centre and there is a need for a supervised period of parole, then the child should be dealt with 'according to law'. Yet the resonance of these considerations seems remarkably similar to the usual considerations raised whenever an adult is to be sentenced. There is, it is suggested, an elusive quality about the decision to sentence 'according to law' that allows for no definitive statement of position and it must be couched in fundamental notions of judicial sentencing discretion.

The tension between sentencing principles is activated because it is otherwise said that in relation to children, 'rehabilitation' should take on a more *predominant* aspect in the process. Thus in *XYJ*,[20] the court affirmed a 'statement of principle' that had been applied 'many times' (*XYJ*, at p. 6; see also *GDP*) as set down in *Smith*.[21] In *Smith*, a case heard in 1964, the court perceived a congruence between the private interests of a juvenile offender and the public interest of society at large, because the court said that its aim in sentencing was to engender an understanding of citizenship in the offender.

The limitations of statutory guidance

The orthodox view is one that reflects, as commentators have pointed out, the concern that the rehabilitative principles entrenched in legislated principles, such as section 6 of the New South Wales Children (Criminal Proceedings) Act 1987, operate against the imposition of an appropriate punishment by demoting the importance of deterrence (see, for example, Fox and Freiberg, 1999).[22] This view is amply characterised in the judgment in *Pham*.[23] In that case, the court acknowledged that the reticence to send young persons to prison may be overcome by the gravity and frequency of the offence, thereby diminishing the court's 'protective aspect' over juveniles.

Nevertheless, even when a child is dealt with 'according to law' regard must be had to the section 6 principles set out in the Children (Criminal Proceedings) Act 1987 (*GDP*, at p. 116). The application of law and principles remain, significantly, a matter of judicial discretion. The point also remains moot, however, as to the extent that the court takes 'regard' of youth when considering the answer to the 'how much?' question. In the light of other case law, 'youth' is simply one factor among many taken into account at the moment of sentence.

Youth and sentencing guidelines

Sentencing guidelines are said to assist the court to balance judicial discretion with consistency of sentences, both in terms of length and as between co-offenders (see Spigelman, 1999). Where the balancing of all 'factors' comes into play, the individual discretion of the court will determine the weight attached to each factor and, in the context of the present discussion, 'youth' will not attach an automatic predominant mitigating force to the penalty.[24] Again, this may really be another question of 'how much?' rather than 'why?' The approach taken by the Court of Criminal Appeal in *R v. Wong and Leung*,[25] a drug dealing case, articulates this view:

> There is a significant body of authority for the proposition that appellate courts may lay down guidelines for the exercise of discretion, both statutory and non-statutory ... The step of promulgating a guideline in quantitative terms is a logical development of what such courts have long done (at para. 16).

Consequently, and notwithstanding the sentencing principles established in children's court legislation in NSW, it follows that common law principles are still applicable when a court is expected to follow a guideline judgment; the courts are seeking to apply general principles to particular offences. Thus the guidelines set out in adult armed robbery cases such as *Henry*[26] (heard in 1999 by the CCA) may well be relevant to the imposition of a penalty upon a juvenile who commits armed robberies. The issue, of course, will be whether or not the age of a juvenile will, in itself, mean that the case becomes 'exceptional' and therefore outside the sentencing pattern expected in *Henry*, that is incarceration for four to five years.

The interface between these factors may well be crucial, not only for the length of a sentence, but as to the place where the sentence is served. Issues of youth and rehabilitation may carry more weight when the court looks at the practical implications of the sentence, such as should an 18-year-old youth go to an adult prison or into a juvenile detention centre? In *R v. SDM*, heard in 2001, the sentencing perspective in *Henry* was applied in a case where the young offender received a four-and-a-half-year sentence. However, the court directed, pursuant to section 19 of the Children (Criminal Proceedings) Act 1987, that the sentence be served in a detention centre rather than in a prison. It was accepted that *Henry* did apply to juvenile offenders, although an 'allowance' must be made for youth:

> If the effect of these decisions was to construe *Henry* in a way that would entirely exclude its application to juvenile offenders, ie those who qualify as 'child' within the meaning of the *Children (Criminal Proceedings) Act, 1987*, section 3(1), then that approach would, in my view, have been inappropriate, having regard to the nature and purpose of a guideline judgment (*SDM*, at para. 6).

The application of sentencing guidelines to juveniles

The import of decisions such as *SDM* is that sentencing guidelines will apply to juveniles. In that sense, the mitigating factors of youth (and also those connected statutorily to the principles in section 6 of the Children (Criminal Proceedings) Act 1987) must be read together with the import of the guideline judgments. This means that, on the principles of parity, juveniles who commit a similar offence to an adult can expect a similar type of sentence, although at least some of the sentence may be served in a juvenile detention centre. This conservative position is affirmed in the approach taken in *R* v. *LBK*[27] and in *Blackman and Walters*,[28] both cases that were heard in 2001.

It can be concluded that youth offenders, whether they be Indigenous or non-Indigenous people, given the demonstrable continuum of the sentencing regime, remain subject to orthodox sentencing principles in the same way as an adult. More specifically, in serious offences, the courts are inclined to deal with juvenile offenders as they would adults, and this leads to incarceration. The practical consequences, it will be argued, is an over-incarceration of Indigenous youth. The orthodox approach to sentencing leaves little room for alternative approaches and retains a primary place in the administration of justice. As a consequence, the implication for Indigenous youth offenders is that the orthodox approach to sentencing would seem to hold little prospect of redressing high incarceration rates.

The failure of the orthodox approach

The over-representation of Indigenous children in the criminal justice system and concomitant high level of incarceration pose a clear problem for the government. Indeed the neo-colonial discourse of governance expects that the *state* will identify and deal with social problems: the crime problem; the juvenile problem; the aboriginal problem; and so on and so forth. At the foundation of this chapter it is posited that no solution offered by the state ultimately countenances the handing over of the state's authority and power. All solutions remain tied to the field of state governance as articulated, for example, in juvenile justice policy that promotes indigenisation of state bureaucracy and diversion systems (such as youth conferencing), while sentencing practice and procedure remain tied to the criminal justice system (as in circle sentencing).

Race and juvenile sentencing

The implications of orthodox sentencing practices are no more harshly felt than by Indigenous youth offenders. This general pressure on the state to address offending can be seen in the statistics that mark Indigenous youth offending. It starts with an 'extremely high apprehension rate', is reinforced by a 'compounding bias in the exercise of police discretion' and occurs in a 'court sentencing structure which, while apparently equitable, reinforces and magnifies previous systemic effects' (Luke and Cunneen, 1995: 81). It has been argued that problems exist because the traditional mode of considering the operation of the law pretends to have 'color blindness' (White, 1986). Is this what is occurring within the orthodox sentencing process?

The court as an 'inter-racial' site of conflict

It is suggested that the orthodox explanation of the prerogatives of punish-ment clashing with the principles of reform at the moment of sentencing has a deeper significance: the court becomes the *inter-racial* site of conflict and rationalisation. The fundamental question arising from the imposition of penalty is really *how* to deal with an Indigenous juvenile offender; however, the penultimate outcome turns on the nature of an offence and the expectations of society. It has been argued that there is an expectation inculcated into the court system that draws from the complex relationship between offending, parental responsibility and notions of child welfare and which raises questions about the place of an Indigenous youth offender within society. Thus in the background material tendered in a sentencing process the 'relevance of these developmental and environ-mental factors was *assumed rather than becoming the subject of analysis*' (Brady, 1985: 122, emphasis added).

It is further suggested that when the court makes a determination of sentence it considers whether the offender can be redeemed to become a 'good' citizen; in this case it occurs at a site, the court, where the state provides the definition of morality, ethics and community, not the offender or the Indigenous community. This is not a process, then, where the court questions its ability to refine the law and implement order. Racist assumptions and substructures are not open to examination, nor is a link made between racial difference and the provision of justice, where '[T]hose who define, administer and enforce criminal justice are over-whelmingly white, while the 'subjects' of their attention ... are dis-proportionately black' (Goldson and Chiwada-Bailey, 2000: 52). The result for Indigenous youth, it is suggested, is that the benefits that arise from 'youth' are abrogated by the operation of sentencing guidelines and in the delimitation of dealing with a child as an adult 'according to law'.

Consequently, the sentencing process must be re-constructed to admit discussion that reveals the rationale for Indigenous child offending: the questions that need to be asked are those that address the relationships that arise from *racial* difference. The orthodox sentencing regime does not admit or encompass an a priori challenge to authority and power that, it is argued, arise from the historical consequences of colonialism. Consequently, the state, caught in a shallow debate, fails to address the fundamental socially based flaws that arise from marginalisation and exclusion from power, and the 'problem' of Indigenous youth offending remains perennial.

Re-addressing the 'problem' of indigenous youth offending

Indigenous youth offending is recognised as an issue throughout western countries; the concern is not unique to NSW.[29] A non-orthodox perspective may also allow fresh insight on the issues. For instance, one Indigenous commentator, speaking in the context of the experience of the Amerindians (but reflecting more broadly on society), cuts to the core of the matter when he says the 'purpose of any society ... is to engender happy children. The extent to which we are able to do that is the extent to which we are successful as a group or as a culture' (Cajete, 2002: 186). The way that society asks questions about the Indigenous youth offenders is, in this sense, as important as the issue itself. This is certainly not the question asked by the court when determining sentence. Rather, as has already been shown, the sentencing process is about balancing 'principles' and weighing the particular facts of each case; hence, the application of adult sentencing guidelines to juvenile offenders. The gravity of an offence will outweigh the mitigating factor of 'youth'.

The need for a new approach

A new approach is needed to attempt to break through the restrictions imposed by an orthodox discourse about sentencing. The discourse itself provides the language that frames perspective and insight (or lack of it); that is, the way the issue is *seen*. Is the problem 'seen' as that of the individual transgressor, or is Indigenous youth offending allowed a more systemic description? It is argued, in this chapter, that unless the discourse facilitates solutions that challenge the dominant frameworks of power, Indigenous people will be unable to participate in the resolution of youth offending. At base perhaps the real test, as suggested by Cajete (2002), is whether the criminal justice system seeks to 'engender happy children'.

This is demonstrably not the way the orthodox court appears to articulate the sentencing process. The discourse that carries the discussion about Indigenous child-offenders, whether arising from criticism or accommodation, must move beyond questions about dealing with a youth 'according to law'. The present engagement between sentencing principles and praxis that one sees in the orthodox rendition of mitigation due to 'youth' may well be better understood by considering the tenor of the debate in the light of a postcolonial analysis. The domain of the court is likewise moribund in finding a solution, as cases such as *SDM* illustrate, as it does not seem that the orthodox sentencing process is able to develop solutions that are inconsistent with the historical Anglo-Australian nature of its operation. The management of Indigenous youth offenders in court appears to oscillate around an orthodox appreciation of the problem and its resolution as a matter of individual responsibility alone (*Jap*, 1998), rather than a corporate acknowledgment of historical oppression.

A solution found in 'restorative justice'?

One answer that may attempt to challenge the hegemony of orthodox sentencing discourse is the so-called redemptive notion of 'restorative justice'. In a certain form – as youth conferencing and circle sentencing – it has recently found some favour with the state (Braithwaite, 1998; Fattah, 1998). This notion calls forth a number of strategies, and turns on the belief that criminal offending is a breach of faith with the community. Consequently, a process of sanctioning involves bringing an offender back into harmony with the community. It has been identified as a strategy that, although not a panacea, may be particularly effective in dealing with juvenile offending (Sarre, 1999a).

Could 'restorative justice' provide the paradigm shift with which to reinvigorate the potential for resolution of Indigenous youth offending? Contemporary thought seems to be looking hopefully at this notion, both in Australia (Daly and Hayes, 2001; Bargen, 1999) and in other countries (Johnstone, 2002; Walgrave, 1998; Morris and Maxwell, 1998). The 'conferencing' movement, seen as Family Group Conferencing in New Zealand and a variant of circle sentencing in Canada, claims to use a 'restorative justice' method. Both ideas have recently been imported into Australia and, significantly, the origin of the approach is said to lie in the need to address the problem of *Indigenous* offending.

A pathway for indigenous solutions

Many in the Indigenous communities, both in Australia and elsewhere, support the idea of restorative justice, although the process is not without critics.[30] It is often linked to a resurgence of 'traditional' culture and values, and seen as a mechanism for Indigenous involvement in the administration of criminal justice (Behrendt, 1995; Green, 1998). In NSW, the idea has generated significant state support, particularly in the discussion of solutions to Indigenous youth offending where the major innovations of conferencing and circle sentencing are situated.

If there are links between restorative justice and the orthodox administration of criminal justice they need to be critically examined. It is suggested that an 'add-on' or 'one size fits all' system such as 'conferencing' may be convenient, but if it fails to alter relationships of power based upon race then it cannot be said to be *restorative*. In short, if restorative justice does provide a pathway to justice then it must be an initiative embraced and controlled by Indigenous people. The subtext of this analysis, then, is one that also embraces notions of Indigenous sovereignty and self-determination as the foundation and core for any initiative.

Indigenous sovereignty is not a notion that sits well in the criminal justice system. Yet, as the over-representation of Indigenous youth in the criminal justice system illustrates, Indigenous people feel the impact of state sovereignty at alarming rates. It is incumbent, therefore, to look more closely at the orthodox solution to Indigenous youth offending that is attempted in the courts at the moment of sentencing.

Conclusion

The argument in this chapter turns on a theoretical framework that seeks to reposition the way questions are asked about the gross incarceration rates of Indigenous youth. The argument moves from the acknowledgment by the state that, notwithstanding the implementation of *orthodox* solutions over many years, there remains an Indigenous youth offending problem, and towards a position that places resolution in a new field of discourse. This approach moves Indigenous youth offenders from the margins to the centre of the discourse.

The neutrality of the legal system should not be assumed (White and Perrine, 2001). Indeed, the change needed is one that does not articulate the issue as an *Indigenous* problem at all, but rather posits that Indigenous youth offenders are 'problematised' by the dominate discourse about offending, both in the courts and generally. The shift is one of perspective in which a new paradigm is sought. A critical analysis of orthodox sentencing shows that by purporting to focus on the individual case, so-called notions of parity and proportionality operate to ensure harsh sentences are imposed on Indigenous youth.

This paradigm is located in an Indigenous-based theoretical framework. The new discourse should be one that connotes a shift of power and authority in the context of Indigenous self-determination and sovereignty. A non-impartial process within a value-charged environment grounded in a reinscription of colonial race relations is assumed. In this way, the 'facts and statistics' move beyond the limitations and staleness of the current discourse into a field where new answers are possible.

Notes

1 Government has acknowledged the 'problem' and made recommendations. In NSW the 1992 Legislative Council Standing Committee on Social Issues recognised that Indigenous child-offenders had 'special needs' by making four recommendations: community-based sentencing options; elder involvement in the sentencing process; supervision of community-based orders in 'local Aboriginal communities'; and that incarcerated children be given 'adequate contact' with Aboriginal organisations and culturally relevant programs (NSW LCSCSI, 1992: xxx–xxi).

2 For example, the need to reduce high incarceration rates of Indigenous people was identified in the Annual Report of the NSW Department of Corrective Services (NSW DCS, 2000/2001: 74). The number of deaths in custody remains high (Collins and Mouzos, 2001).

3 For example, 'Scaring up the votes' (Sydney Morning Herald 27/1/2003), 'Sentencing innovation breaking vicious circle of jail terms' (SMH 15/5/2003).

4 The notion of 'governance' is inherently problematic. It is used here to acknowledge, as Penrose and Jackson have ably shown, that government (and the law) form part of a hegemonic system (Jackson and Penrose, 1993).

5 These principles are well established in NSW through a long line of cases (Potas, 2001; see also Fox and Freiberg, 1999, and Manson, 2001).

6 The NSW Premier, Bob Carr, makes this point: 'I want to talk about how we are being tough on the causes of crime … in talking about how to reduce crime, we are talking about the kind of society we want. Leadership must come not only from the government and police but from the whole community' (SMH 24/10/2002).

7 While the notion of postcolonialism is not unproblematic (Slemon, 1995; Loomba, 1998: 245; Battiste, 2000: xix) the value of its critique of colonial and postcolonial culture is well founded (see Ashcroft et al., 1995).

8 The development of postcolonial theory has hinged on an acceptance that the colonial state will oppress the pre-colonial peoples. Loomba, for example, defines 'colonialism' as '… the conquest and control of other people's land and goods' (Loomba, 1998: 2). This process is one which involves physical invasion of another's land, the destruction of pre-existing social and cultural structures, an assumption of political and economic control, the establishment of social relations based on racial inferiority, and the weakening of resistance to allow control of society (Frideres, 1983: 295–320). In this manner, therefore, colonialism can be seen as insinuating imperial control throughout every aspect of society and culture.

9   The 'very notion of a "post-colonial past" may be most misleading' (Miege, 1980: 35) or, as Perrin argues, this is a condition that exists as much from an inertia and paralysis, and '[I]n these senses, the persistence of a present which, by rights, ought to have passed – an insistence of the past in the present' (Perrin, 1999: 19).

10 It is a 'widespread communal belief that juveniles are not to be equated with adults' (Fox and Freiberg, 1999: 828), and as in Victorian state legislation, the 1987 NSW legislation accepts this opposition as its underpinning.

11 There are shifting sands in the definitions of 'child' and 'youth'. Strictly, childhood ceases after a person reaches 18 years of age; a 'youth' is someone between the mid-teens and 25 years of age.

12 *R* v. *GDP* (1991) NSW CCA, 53 A Crim R 112.

13 *R* v. *XYJ, NSW CCA*, unreported, 15 June 1992.

14 *R* v. *Jap* NSW CCA, unreported, 20 July 1998.

15 *R* v. *FQ* NSW CCA, unreported, 17 June 1998.

16 *Nichols* (1991) 57 A Crim R 391.

17 *R* v. *SDM* 2001 NSW CCA, unreported, 8 May 2001.

18 *Contra*, considerations such as the closer the youth is to 18 years of age the more relevant will be notions of rehabilitation over deterrence or punishment (*Nguyen* NSW CCA, 14 April 1994, see also *Biggs* NSW CCA, unreported, 5 March 1987).

19 *R* v. *R* (1993) A Crim R 95.

20 *XYJ* NSW CCA, unreported, 15 June 1992.

21 *Smith* (1964) Crim LR 70.

22 These principles stress notions of 'the best interests' of a child, the importance of rehabilitation and the protection of 'due process' and must be taken into account by a sentencing court (Blackmore, 1989: 54–5).

23 *R* v. *Pham* (1991) 55 A Crim R 128.

24 'To a considerable degree section 6 reflects general sentencing principles applicable to young offenders, e.g. in relation to the subordination, in general, of punishment and general deterrence to need to foster rehabilitation: Wilkie NSW CCA 2 July 1992, and *GDP*' (*SDM* 2001, at para. 19).

25 *R* v. *Wong and Leung* 1999 NSW CCA, unreported, 16 December 1999.

26 *R* v. *Henry* (1999) 46 NSWLR 346.

27 *R* v. *LBK* 2001 NSW CCA, unreported, 4 July 2001.

28 *Blackman and Walters* 2001 NSW CCA, unreported, 8 May 2001.

29 In Canada, aboriginal youth represent 4 per cent of that population but constitute 12 per cent of alternative measures cases, 15 per cent of open custody facilities, 16 per cent of secure facilities and 15 per cent of probationers (Kowalski, 1999: 7). Issues of race are often considered as one factor in assessments or even ignored (see, for example, in the United States, Towberman, 1992, and Snyder and Sickmund, 1996).

30 The issues of 'occidentalism' and 'netwidening' are acknowledged (Blagg, 1997).

References

Aboriginal Deaths in Custody Watch Committee (1992) 'What the White Paper Ignored: Submission on Future Directions for Juvenile Justice in New South Wales', in I. Moores (ed.), *Voices of Aboriginal Australia: Past Present Future*. Springwood: Butterfly Books, pp. 240–50.

Adams, M. (1995) *A Tortured People: The Politics of Colonization*. Penticton: Theytus Books.

Anaya, S. J. (1996) *Indigenous Peoples in International Law*. New York: Oxford University Press.

Ashcroft, B., Griffiths, G. and Tiffin, H. (eds) (1995) *The Post Colonial Studies Reader*. New York: Routledge.

Baker, J. (2001) 'The Scope for Reducing Indigenous Imprisonment Rates' No. 55 March, *Crime and Justice Bulletin Contemporary Issues in Crime and Justice*, NSW Bureau of Crime Statistics and Research, Sydney.

Bargen, J. (1999) 'Youth Justice Conferencing in New South Wales: A Personal View of the Practicalities and Politics of Introducing the Young Offenders Act 1997 (NSW)'. Unpublished paper presented to the Legal Aid Commission Juvenile Justice Conference, 15 May, Sydney.

Battiste, N. (2000) *Colonial Indigenous Voice and Vision*. Vancouver: University of British Columbia Press.

Behrendt, L. (1995) *Aboriginal Dispute Resolution*. Sydney: Federation Press.

Bird, G. (1996) 'Koori Cultural Heritage: Reclaiming the Past?', in G. Bird, G. Martine and J. Neilsen (eds), *MAJAH Indigenous Peoples and the Law*. Sydney: Federation Press, pp. 100–128.

Blackmore, R. (1989) *The Children's Court and Community Welfare in New South Wales*. Melbourne: Longman Professional Press.

Blackmore, R. (1992) 'The Sentencing Act and the Children's Court', *Current Issues in Criminal Justice*, 3(3), 335–8.

Blagg, H. (1997) ' "A Measure of Shame?": Aboriginal Children and Conferencing in Australia', *British Journal of Criminology*, 37(4), 481–501.

Borrows, J. (1996) 'With or Without You: First Nations Law (In Canada)', *McGill Law Journal*, 41(3–4), 629–65.

Brady, M. (1985) 'Aboriginal Youth and the Juvenile Justice System', in A. Borowski and J. Murray (eds), *Juvenile Delinquency in Australia*. Sydney: Methuen, pp. 112–25.

Braithwaite, J. (1998) 'Restorative Justice', in M. Tonry (ed.), *The Handbook of Crime and Punishment*. New York: Oxford University Press, pp. 323–44.

Cajete, G. (2002) 'Indigenous Knowledge', in M. Battiste (ed.), *Reclaiming Indigenous Voice and Vision*. Vancouver: University of British Columbia Press, pp. 181–91.

Carcach, C., Grant, A. and Conroy, R. (1999) 'Australian Corrections: the Imprisonment of Indigenous People', *Trends and Issues in Crime and Criminal Justice*. Canberra: Australian Institute of Criminology, No. 137, pp. 1–6.

Collins, L. and Mouzos, J. (2001) 'Australian Deaths in Custody and Custody-Related Police Operations 2000', *Trends and Issues in Crime and Criminal Justice*. Canberra: Australian Institute of Criminology, No. 217, pp. 1–6.

Crime Prevention Division (2000) 'Juvenile Crime in New South Wales Report: Statistical Profile of Juvenile Offenders'. Available at: www.lawlink.nsw.gov.au/cpd.nsf/pages/JJRCHP3.

Culhane, D. (1998) *The Pleasure of the Crown: Anthropology, Law and First Nations.* Burnaby, BC: Talon Books.

Cunneen, C. (1997) *The Royal Commission into Aboriginal Deaths in Custody: An Overview of its Establishment, Findings and Outcomes.* Canberra: Monitoring and Report Section, Aboriginal and Torres Strait Islanders Commission.

Cunneen, C. (2001a) *Conflict, Politics and Crime.* Crown's Nest: Allen & Unwin.

Cunneen, C. (2001b) *The Impact of Crime Prevention on Aboriginal Communities,* Aboriginal Justice Advisory Council, Sydney in J. Baker, 2001, 'The Scope for Reducing Indigenous Imprisonment Rates' No. 55 March *Crime and Justice Bulletin Contemporary Issues in Crime and Justice,* NSW Bureau of Crime Statistics and Research, Sydney, 3(2), 90–110.

Cunneen, C. and MacDonald, D. (1997) 'Indigenous Imprisonment in Australia: An Unresolved Human Rights Issue', *Australian Journal of Human Rights,* 3(2), 90–110.

Cunneen C. and White, R. (1999) *Juvenile Justice: An Australian Perspective.* Melbourne: Oxford University Press.

Cunneen, C. and White, R. (2002) *Juvenile Justice Youth and Crime in Australia.* Melbourne: Oxford University Press.

Daly, K. and Hayes, H. (2001) 'Restorative Justice and Conferencing in Australia', *Trends and Issues in Crime and Criminal Justice.* Canberra: Australian Institute of Criminology, pp. 1–11.

Department of Juvenile Justice (2001) *Aboriginal Over-Representation Strategic Plan.* Sydney: NSW Department of Juvenile Justice.

Dodson, M. (1996) *Indigenous Deaths in Custody 1989–1996.* Canberra: The Office of the Aboriginal and Torres Strait Islander Social Justice Commission.

Fattah, E. (1998) 'Some Reflections on the Paradigm of Restorative Justice and its Viability for Juvenile Justice', in L. Walgrave (ed.), *Restorative Justice for Juveniles: Potentialities, Risks and Problems.* Leuven: Leuven University Press, pp. 389–401.

Fox, R. and Freiberg, A. (1999) *Sentencing State and Federal Law in Victoria,* 2nd edn. Melbourne: Oxford University Press.

Frideres, J. A. (1983) 'New Perspective on an Old Problem: The Macro–Model', in J. Frideres (ed.), *Native People in Canada: The Contemporary Conflicts.* Scarborough: Prentice Hall, pp. 294–323.

Goldson, B. and Chigwada-Bailey, R. (2000) '(What) Justice for Black Children and Young People?', in B. Goldson (ed.), *Youth Justice: Contemporary Policy and Practice.* London: Ashgate, p. 52.

Green, R. (1998) *Justice in Aboriginal Communities: Sentencing Alternatives.* Toronto: Purich Publishing.

Hanks, P. and Keon-Cohen, B. (1988) *Aborigines and the Law.* Sydney: Allen & Unwin.

House of Representatives Standing Committee on Aboriginal Affairs (1980) *Aboriginal Legal Aid.* Canberra: Australian Government Publishing Service.

Jackson, P. and Penrose, J. (eds) (1993) *Constructions of Race, Place and Nation*. London: UCL Press.

Johnstone, G. (2002) *Restorative Justice: Ideas, Values, Debates*. Cullumpton: Willan Publishing.

Jonas, W. (2001) *Social Justice Report*, Report NA.2002. Canberra: Aboriginal and Torres Strait Islander Social Justice Commission.

Kowalski, M. (1999) 'Alternative Measures for Youth in Canada', *Juristat*, 19(8), 8.

Langton, M. (1993) *Well I Heard It on the Radio and I Saw It on the Television ... An Essay for the Australian Film Commission on the Politics and Aesthetics of Filmmaking by and about Aboriginal People and Things*. Sydney. Australian Film Commission.

Loomba, A. (1998) *Colonialism/Post Colonialism: The New Critical Idiom*. New York: Routledge.

Luke, G. and Cunneen, C. (1995) *Aboriginal Over-Representation and Discretionary Decisions in the NSW Juvenile Justice System*. Sydney: Juvenile Justice Advisory Council of NSW, www.lawlink.nsw.gov.au.

Luke, G. and Lind, B. (2002) *Reducing Juvenile Crime: Conferencing Versus Court*. Available at: www.lawlink.nsw.gov.au, accessed April 2002.

Manson, A. (2001) *The Law of Sentencing*. Toronto: Irwin Law.

Merry, S. (1991) 'Law and Colonialism', *Law and Society Review*, 25(4), 889–920.

Miege, J.-L. (1980) 'The Colonial Past in The Present', in W. Morris-Jones and B. Austin (eds), *De-Colonization and After*. London:, Frank Cass, pp. 35–47.

Morris, A. and Maxwell, G. (1998) 'Restorative Justice in New Zealand: Family Group Conferences as a Case Study', *Western Criminology Review*, 1(1), online at: http://wcr.sonma.edu/v1n1/morris.html.

New South Wales Department of Corrective Services (2000/2001) 'Ten Years on – The Department's Response to the Royal Commission into Aboriginal Deaths in Custody', in *Annual Report NSW Department of Corrective Services*. Sydney: NSW DCS.

New South Wales Legislative Council Standing Committee on Social Issues (1992) *Juvenile Justice in New South Wales*, Report No. 4. Sydney: NSW LCSCSI.

Perrin, C. (1999) 'Approaching Anxiety: The Insistence of the Postcolonial in the Declaration on the Rights of Indigenous Peoples', in E. Darien-Smith and P. Fitzpatrick (eds), *Laws of the Postcolonial*. Ann Arbor, MI: University of Michigan Press, pp. 55–74.

Potas, I. (2001) *Sentencing Manual: Law, Principles and Practice in New South Wales*. Sydney: Law Book Company.

Royal Commission on Aboriginal Peoples (1996) *Bridging the Cultural Divide: A Report on Aboriginal People and Criminal Justice in Canada*. Ottawa: Ministry of Supply.

Sarre, R. (1999) 'Family Conferencing as a Juvenile Justice Strategy', *Justice Professional*, 11, 259–71.

Sarre, R. and Wilson, D. (1998) *Sentencing and Indigenous Peoples: The Proceedings of Roundtable on Sentencing and Indigenous People*. Canberra: Australian Institute of Criminology Research and Public Policy Series.

Slemon, S. (1995) 'The Scramble for Post-Colonialism', in V. Ashcroft, G. Griffiths and H. Tiffen (eds), *The Post Colonial Studies Reader*. New York: Routledge, pp. 45–52.

Snyder, H. and Sickmund, M. (1996) *Juvenile Offenders and Victims: A National Report*. National Centre for Juvenile Justice.

Spigelman, J. (1999) 'Sentencing Guideline Judgments', *Current Issues in Criminal Justice*, 11(1), 5–16.

Stevens, S. (1997) 'Native Self-Determination and Justice', in A. Morrison (ed.), *Justice for Natives Searching for Common Ground*. Montreal: McGill-Queens University Press, pp. 28–33.

Towberman, D. (1992) 'National Survey of Juvenile Needs Assessment,' *Crime and Delinquency*, 38(2), 230–8.

Von Hirsch, A. (1998) 'Penal Theories', in M. Tonry (ed.), *The Handbook of Crime and Punishment*. New York: Oxford University Press, pp. 659–82.

Walgrave, L. (1998) *Restorative Justice for Juveniles: Potentialities, Risks and Problems*. Leuven: Leuven University Press.

Watson, I. (1996) 'Law and Indigenous Peoples: The Impact of Colonialism on Indigenous Cultures', *Law in Context*, 14(1), 107–19.

White, J. (1986) 'Introduction: Is Cultural Criticism Possible?', *Michigan Law Review*, 84, 1373–87.

White, R. and Perrine, S. (2001) *Crime and Social Control: An Introduction*. Melbourne: Oxford University Press.

Woodman, G. (1998) 'Part II. Urban Normative Fields: Concepts, Theories and Critiques, Ideological Combat and Social Observation. Recent Debates about Legal Pluralism', *Journal of Legal Pluralism and Unofficial Law*, 42, 21–55.

Yazzie, R. (2000) 'Indigenous Peoples and Post Colonialism', in N. Battiste (ed.), *Colonial Indigenous Voice and Vision*. Vancouver: University of British Columbia Press, pp. 39–49.

Youngblood and Henderson, J. (1996) 'First Nations Legal Inheritance', *Manitoba Law Journal*, 23, 1–29.

Chapter 7

Gladue was a woman: the importance of gender in restorative-based sentencing

Josephine Savarese

Abstract[1]

In 1999, the Supreme Court of Canada released its decision in *R* v. *Gladue*. The decision is praised for endorsing sentencing alternatives that reflect the unique circumstances of Aboriginal offenders. A fact that is generally overlooked is that the accused, Tanis Gladue, was female as well as Aboriginal. This chapter argues that *Gladue* should also be interpreted with a feminist lens that would illustrate the necessity of linking gender and race in the restorative sentencing process. It explores the potential for racialised and gendered social relations to be taken into account in the determination of criminal sanctions. Decisions like *Gladue* and others have expanded restorative possibilities. The criminal justice system could enhance its ability to acknowledge the social inequalities that inform the system's operations with the aid of feminist critiques.

Introduction

A great deal has been written about the Supreme Court of Canada's ruling in *R* v. *Gladue*.[2] The case interprets section 718.2(e) of the Criminal Code of Canada that requires judges to consider the 'circumstances' of Aboriginal offenders on sentencing.[3] Some commentators hold that the decision will not lessen the over-representation of Aboriginal offenders in Canadian prisons and jails.[4] Others take a more hopeful stance, asserting that restorative-based sentencing will counter the punitive tendencies of the contemporary system. According to this perspective, section 718.2(e) will initiate changes, even if they are modest ones.[5]

The rich debate fostered by *Gladue* has prompted awareness of the strengths and limitations of section 718.2(e) as a tool for addressing inequity in the justice system. An aspect of the decision that has not been analysed is its potential impact on Aboriginal women. The literature assesses the case in gender-neutral terms, failing to acknowledge that the subject of the case, Tanis Gladue, was a woman, as well as an Aboriginal person.

In this chapter, an argument is made for an expansion of the *Gladue* sentencing directives to include factors that are unique to Aboriginal women. It is also argued that Tanis Gladue and other Aboriginal women involved in the criminal justice system encounter circumstances particular to their gender as well as their race. To achieve restorative aims, sentencing must consider both.[6]

Section 718.2(e) and the *Gladue* decision – an overview

In 1996, the Canadian Parliament amended the Criminal Code of Canada to include section 718.2(e);[7] it moved sentencing away from a retributive focus towards restoration and healing.[8] Specifically, it compelled sentencing judges to consider sanctions other than imprisonment where reasonable in the circumstances. The courts were to follow this directive for all offenders, 'with particular attention to the circumstances of Aboriginal offenders.'[9] The provision received limited judicial attention until 1999 when the Supreme Court of Canada released its decision in *R v. Gladue*. The case was historic in its consideration of section 718.2(e) and in articulating a framework on the sentencing of Aboriginal persons.

In *Gladue*, the court considered the appropriate sentence for an Aboriginal woman who fatally stabbed her common law partner and was convicted of manslaughter.[10] The lower courts determined that section 718.2(e) did not apply to her as she resided in an urban setting, not an Aboriginal community. The Supreme Court rejected this argument and used the opportunity to provide clarification on the section and on the approach lower courts should adopt when applying it. The court affirmed the remedial nature of section 718.2(e), stating in unequivocal terms that one of its central objectives was to address the predominance of Aboriginal people in the justice system. The decision confirmed the restorative aims of the provision and underscored the importance of incorporating Aboriginal viewpoints into the sentencing process. Specifically, the court stated:

> ... the point is that one of the unique circumstances of aboriginal offenders is that community-based sanctions coincide with the aboriginal concept of sentencing and the needs of aboriginal people and communities.[11]

It further observed that Aboriginal offenders and their communities are ill served by incarceration, particularly when the offence is minor and non-violent. The court argued for community-based alternatives, stating:

> Where these sanctions are reasonable in the circumstances, they should be implemented. In all instances, it is appropriate to attempt to craft the sentencing process and the sanctions imposed in accordance with the aboriginal perspective.[12]

In a lengthy review of incarceration rates for aboriginal persons, the court makes one reference to women's imprisonment. It cites a report that found that the rates of imprisonment were even 'more extreme' for treaty Indian women and Métis women in the Province of Saskatchewan.[13]

This chapter encourages a further review of the factors that the court commented on in one sentence. It is argued that the multiple oppressions encountered by Aboriginal women account for their conflicts with the criminal law. Stronger efforts should be made to apply section 718.2(e) to improve the criminal justice system's response to Aboriginal women when sanctions are imposed. This approach would ensure that a comprehensive view that incorporates 'the lived experience of discrimination' is adopted when sentences for Aboriginal women are determined.[14]

Aboriginal women and over-incarceration

For women, decisions about sentencing are particularly consequential. Even sanctions considered more minor, such as fines, challenge women due to their predominance among Canada's poor (Hadley, 2001: 3). Since women are concentrated in service sector employment where criminal record checks are common, a conviction for any level of offence can impose employment barriers. On more arduous sanctions, the research confirms that imprisonment for women is a particularly devastating and damaging experience.[15]

The negative aspects of incarceration are even more pronounced for Aboriginal women (Task Force on Federally Sentenced Women, 1990; Canadian Human Rights Commission, 2003). The reasons range from isolation from family to the challenges that surface when physical and emotional scars inflicted by a racist society emerge in confined and repressive quarters. Culturally appropriate programming is consistently identified as a pressing need (ibid.; and Sugar and Fox, 1989–90). Of further concern is the finding that Aboriginal women are more often classified as maximum security, resulting in further restrictions and confined quarters, sometimes in prisons for men (McIvor and Johnson, 2003: 9–10). Furthermore, women with a maximum-security designation cannot serve time at the sole institution specifically established to address the needs of Aboriginal women, namely the *Okimaw Ohci* Healing Lodge on the Nikaneet First Nation in southern Saskatchewan (McIvor and Johnson, 2003: 20).

Given the hardships that women encounter in prisons, it is alarming that sentences of incarceration are increasingly common.[16] While jail terms are more frequent, the conditions in women's prisons remain unacceptable, despite years of research and activism towards better environments. In 2003, the Canadian Human Rights Commission released *Protecting Their Rights: A Systematic Review of Human Rights in Correctional Services for Federally Sentenced Women*, a report on the Commission's investigation into federal women's prisons. One of the most disturbing findings is the 'disproportionate number' of Aboriginal women subject to a federal sentence of incarceration (Canadian Human Rights Commission, 2003: 6). According to *Protecting Their Rights,* Aboriginal women made up 29 per cent of the women in federal correctional facilities while they comprised only 3 per cent of the female population in Canada (Canadian Human Rights Commission, 2003).

Over-representation was more pronounced for Aboriginal women than it was for Aboriginal men. On this point, the report comments: 'From 1996–1997 to 2001–2002, the number of federally sentenced Aboriginal women increased by 36.7% compared with 5.5% for Aboriginal men' (Canadian Human Rights Commission, 2003: 6). These figures confirm that the numbers of Aboriginal women serving federal time were on the rise, even after the introduction of section 718.2(e) in 1996 and following the Supreme Court's directive that sentencing judges consider alternatives to incarceration.

Protecting Their Rights demonstrates the need for strong initiatives that address the over-incarceration of Aboriginal women. The next section of the chapter presents further arguments that sentencing should be approached with this goal in mind.

The particular circumstances of Aboriginal women

In *Gladue*, the Supreme Court authorised the lower courts to vary from typical sanctions for Aboriginal offenders where appropriate. The decision encourages sentences that strive to be holistic, in keeping with the nature of the offence and the circumstances of the offender. The court stated:

> The sentencing judge is required to take into account all of the surrounding circumstances regarding the offence, the offender, the victims and the community, including the unique circumstances of the offender as an aboriginal person. Sentencing must proceed with sensitivity to and understanding of the difficulties aboriginal people have faced with both the criminal justice system and society at large.[17]

Research on Aboriginal women offenders links their criminal involvement to historical and economic factors. First Nations and Métis women often occupy a lesser status in both mainstream and Aboriginal societies for reasons ranging from the undermining of traditional Aboriginal roles and values to the discriminatory provisions that were once found in the federal *Indian Act*. These factors cause tensions in male–female relationships resulting in the victimisation of women and leading to their involvement in criminality (La Prairie, 1987: 105–9).

Evidence that the 'particular circumstances' of Aboriginal women offenders differ from those of their male counterparts can also be found in *Protecting Their Rights: A Systemic Review of Human Rights in Correctional Services for Federally Sentenced Women*. The report confirmed the findings of earlier studies that documented the significant abuse that forms the backdrop for women's offending behaviour (Canadian Human Rights Commission, 2003: 5–7). In general, the research demonstrates that incarcerated women experience significant challenges: they may be mothers with primary child care responsibilities prior to incarceration; their educational attainment is low; and their employment history is extremely limited. Problems with alcohol and drugs are prominent. Substance addiction plays a direct role in women's involvement in property crime (Canadian Human Rights Commission, 2003: 5–8).

The disadvantages found among Aboriginal women in the federally sentenced population exceed that of other women subject to imprisonment. They are incarcerated at younger ages and have more extensive histories of childhood trauma and abuse.[18] Due to statistics like these, Margaret Shaw, a feminist criminologist, commented:

... there would appear to be considerable need for, and scope to develop alternative sentencing structures which place far more emphasis on constructively assessing the circumstances of the women involved, and far less on negative and largely punitive responses (Shaw, quoted in Arbour, 1996: 242–3).

In the *Gladue* decision, there is clear direction in support of the alternative sanctions that certain scholars recommend. Their reasoning has particular application to the Aboriginal women who are prominent in the incarcerated female population.

There are, however, few guarantees that gender considerations will, in fact, be included in post-*Gladue* sentencing processes. A review of recent cases leaves room for both doubt and cautious optimism. In general, the courts have demonstrated a limited ability to comprehend the lives of Aboriginal women. The tendency to ascribe negative qualities to Aboriginal women causes some to question the likelihood that they can receive a 'fair hearing.' One writer observes:

Canadian Native women in prisons, familiar with the denial and reverse onus claims of the dominant group, have wondered ... if Aboriginal women's stories of oppression are even 'translatable' for the court's benefit (Razack, 2001: 40).

Stereotypical notions about Aboriginal women preoccupy the legal imagination.[19] Notions of the 'promiscuous squaw' operate in broader society, infiltrating justice procedures (Razack, 2001: 68). These images serve to exonerate perpetrators of crimes against Aboriginal women while at the same time ensuring that Aboriginal women experience the law's full force as offenders. Examples of this unfold regularly and with little fanfare in Canadian courts.

The case of Lisa Neve

One more infamous example of the court's failures to adequately evaluate Aboriginal women is the case of Lisa Neve. In 1994, Lisa Neve, a 21-year-old Métis woman, became the third woman in Canada to be declared a dangerous offender. In making this determination, Queen's Bench Justice Alec Murray accepted the expert evidence of the Crown and held that Neve had a 'severe, anti-social personality disorder, which manifests itself in evil, violent and sadistic thoughts' (Canadian Press, 1999). He determined that there was scant likelihood that Neve would alter her offending behaviour (Canadian Press, 1999). Canadian Association of Elizabeth Fry Societies' Executive Director, Kim Pate, who met Lisa when she was 12 years old, describes Lisa as a confident leader, qualities that raised the ire of justice officials. Labelled a dangerous offender, Neve was institutionalised for six years, mostly in maximum-security institutions, before the Alberta Court of Appeal overturned the designation in 1999.[20]

In its ruling, the Court of Appeal noted that Neve's criminal record was short and that her involvement in prostitution was often a factor in her offences, along with her desire to redress the harm done to others (Canadian Association of Elizabeth Fry Societies, 1999: 2). The appeal court understood the inequalities based on race and sex that shaped Neve, although it refused to hear intervenors on this point (Canadian Association of Elizabeth Fry Societies, 1999). The outcome may serve as a precedent against the imposition of similar sanctions.

The severe punishment originally meted out to Neve may be reflective of an excessively punitive approach to Aboriginal women in conflict with the criminal justice system. As Pate states:

> (s)exism, racism, heterosexism and class biases intersect to provide an incredibly discriminatory lens through which women like Lisa are viewed and judged (Canadian Association of Elizabeth Fry Societies, 1999: 1).

Pate's observation supports the pressing need for greater cultural and gender sensitivity in sentencing determinations.

Examining the 'special circumstances' of Aboriginal women

In *Sentencing Within A Restorative Justice Paradigm*, Mary Ellen Turpel-Lafond outlines a framework for sentencing judges to apply when levying sanctions for Aboriginal offenders. She expresses optimism on the possibility for change in a post-*Gladue* climate, stating:

> The *Gladue* transition period will continue for some time as numerous matters are considered in a new light in various courts across the land. It is clear that society expects us to carefully consider the experiences of Aboriginal peoples and find creative responses which are appropriate to unique circumstances. The reasoning in this watershed decision will resonate throughout the criminal justice

system, and spill over into the correctional institutions and youth justice system (Turpel-Lafond, 1999: 8).

As a member of the Provincial Court of Saskatchewan, Judge Turpel-Lafond's words carry weight. Some scholars are doubtful, however, that the court is able to account for the unique factors that influence the criminality of Aboriginal women.[21] The next section of this chapter evaluates the likelihood for a gender-based analysis on sentencing. It summarises two decisions of the Ontario Superior Court of Justice in 2003, *R v. Hamilton and Mason*.[22] The cases involved black rather than Aboriginal women, a central difference that may have influenced the outcome. Nonetheless, the cases were a positive example of gender sensitive sentencing prior to a successful appeal by the Crown in 2004 (Makin, 2004).

R v. Hamilton and Mason (Ontario Superior Court of Justice)

In *R v. Hamilton and Mason*, Hill J. of the Ontario Superior Court of Justice granted a conditional sentence to two black women who were convicted of unlawfully importing cocaine. Although the charges would ordinarily have resulted in lengthy terms of imprisonment, this sanction was imposed due to the systemic discrimination faced by black women.[23] In the case, the intersections between sex, race and criminality were deliberately explored to foster a restorative outcome.

Judge Hill's comprehensive judgement in *R v. Hamilton and Mason* includes a detailed overview of the women's personal histories, noting that they both were impoverished, with limited education and work histories. They were both young mothers raising children with no financial support from the fathers. The judgment contains a lengthy review of the patterns of incarceration for women and the factors that lead to criminality, including women's economic and social marginalisation. The court acknowledged and cited the women-centred criminology generated in past decades, including *Creating Choices* (Task Force on Federally Sentenced Women, 1990) and the Arbour Report (1996).

In *Hamilton and Mason*, the *Gladue* judgment and section 718.2(e) provided the legal basis for the courts recognising the complex array of factors that converge in the lives of poor, black women. The crime of drug smuggling is located within the context of women's lives. They emerge as people, with histories, problems and strengths. From a feminist perspective, it is unfortunate that the Ontario Court of Appeal overturned the sentences in August 2004.[24] In its reasons, the appeal court dismissed

Judge Hill's finding that the social context of the offending behaviour could be considered on sentencing. The higher court stated that the sentencing process had a narrow focus. Its goal was to determine the penalty for a specific offender facing a particular charge. The court further stated:

> A sentencing proceeding is also not the forum in which to right perceived societal wrongs, allocate responsibility for criminal conduct as between the offender and society, or 'make up' for perceived social injustices by the imposition of sentences that do not reflect the seriousness of the crime.[25]

While the Court of Appeal acknowledged that ethnic and gender bias were part of the 'casual soup' that influences criminality, it emphasised individual responsibility as central to determinations of culpability.[26] This reasoning works against the expansion of the *Gladue* factors in the manner recommended in this chapter.

Further barriers to restorative sentencing

Aboriginal women's higher involvement in violent crimes also presents a significant barrier to the application of restorative justice.[27] In 1995, for example, Aboriginal women comprised 27 per cent of the federal inmate population serving time for crimes classified as violent.[28] They made up 19 per cent of women serving sentences for murder. In *R* v. *Wells*, the Supreme Court stated that the *Gladue* decision was not intended to mandate a lower sentence in every case.[29] In some instances, particularly those where violent offenses were committed, the court directed that it was appropriate to continue with the retributive focus of traditional sentencing. The *Wells* decision mutes positive aspects of *Gladue* by discouraging restorative-based sentences for the types of crimes that feature highly among Aboriginal women. As stated, there is need for a 'gender lens' that sees women's violent acts as a result of disempowerment rather than individual brutality. The research demonstrates that women's violent acts are often a defensive response to the danger posed by others. They are often motivated by self-protection rather than a desire to harm (Canadian Association of Elizabeth Fry Societies, 2003). Due to these findings, some claim that few women pose a risk to society, even those convicted of violent acts (Faith, 1993).

A case decided in the provincial court of Saskatchewan, *R* v. *Shore*, shows how the courts might apply a gender lens to homicide cases.[30]

R v. Shore (2002) Provincial Court of Saskatchewan

The case of *R* v. *Shore,* decided in the Provincial Court of Saskatchewan in 2002, demonstrates how the 'special circumstances' of women offenders might be taken into account on sentencing.[31] An Aboriginal woman, Tracey Ann Shore, was charged with operating a motor vehicle while impaired, causing the death of her common law partner, William McKay. After an evening of drinking, Shore fled her home in her car, fearing a violent confrontation. Mr McKay jumped on the hood of the vehicle, with the accused driving. Shortly after, he fell off the hood, hitting his head on the pavement. He later died from head injuries sustained in the fall.[32]

In its decision, the court made a careful study of the circumstances of the offence and of the offender, Tracey Shore. The court noted that the offence was a very serious one. It refused, however, to grant the Crown's request for a term of incarceration of 18 months to two years and imposed a conditional sentence of two years less a day. The court did not comment specifically on the accused's gender yet it highlighted life factors common among Aboriginal women. These included Ms Shore's history of substance abuse and the physical abuse she suffered as a child and in most of her adult relationships, including her relationship with the deceased. The decision also noted other aspects of her early home life: her father's incarceration at the time of her birth and her mother's unstable lifestyle that led to the accused's placement with an uncle and an aunt who was later murdered. Due to this turbulence, Ms Shore had limited education, completing only Grade 8. At the time of the offence, she was 24 years old and she was the mother of five children, three of whom resided with her. By the time of the sentencing, she had undergone addiction treatment, established a stable relationship and was looking to further schooling once her children were older.[33]

According to the court, these factors were of 'great significance in assessing her moral blameworthiness for the offence and in understanding why she committed the offence.'[34] Since the court carefully examined the context that informed the criminal event, it supported Tracey Shore's integration and involvement in society while serving a community-based sentence.

Implementing a restorative justice paradigm

Imposing appropriate sanctions for women has been identified as a key element in effective criminal justice reform. In *Habilitation: Sentencing of Female Offenders*, Graydon argues for a new paradigm that would promote women's empowerment and equality in society and in institutions like the criminal justice system (Graydon, 1992). She strongly recommends a shift away from the retributive model, where women are often punished for behaviour brought about by social inequities, including physical abuse and poverty. Graydon states:

> Criminal and sentencing law must incorporate women's definitions of crime and recognise women's experiences of crime. Sex inequality which underlies both crime against women and crime committed by women, must be recognised and addressed in reformulating the law. Issues relating to prostitution, abortion, incest, pornography, and physical and mental abuse must be discussed both in defining crime and in defining responses to criminal activity (Graydon, 1992: 17).

Section 718.2(e) and the *Gladue* decision provide strong motivations for courts to improve their success in meeting these objectives. As stated earlier in this chapter, the number of women being sentenced to federal institutions over the past years has increased. For *Gladue* to have an impact, this trend must be reversed. The imposition of community-based sanctions at the sentencing stage is particularly important for Aboriginal women. To fully achieve the remedial objectives articulated in *Gladue*, however, efforts must be made to improve the pre-offending, as well as post-offending, lives of Aboriginal women. Many acknowledge that restoration depends on the realisation of social justice policies and programmes that would address the inequalities that women experience. Graydon states:

> It must also be recognised that the female offender is not the sole responsibility of the criminal justice system. Legislators, other government agencies and the community as a whole must be prepared to seek a better life for all women in Canada. Equal economic opportunities, provision of adequate child care facilities for working parents, elimination of sexual abuse and violence against women, and allowing women to play an equal role in society are pre-requisites for the empowerment and enablement of all women, including the female offender (Graydon, 1992: 17).

For Aboriginal women, the need for more equitable social policy is even more urgent. Community justice initiatives geared towards fairness and equality are required both within and outside of the criminal justice system. In its submission to the Canadian Human Rights Commission, the Native Women's Association of Canada (NWAC) recommended the removal of Aboriginal women from Canadian prisons. NWAC stated that capacity building within native communities was a prerequisite to decarceration and reintegration. Job creation and training, economic development and enhanced social services including health were necessary components of a plan to remove women from institutional settings (McIvor and Johnson, 2003: 3). They argue for the creation of a special fund for the implementation of this plan (McIvor and Johnson, 2003: 4).

Conclusion

In this chapter, an argument has been made for gender sensitivity in sentencing that would locate Aboriginal women's offending within the context of their lives. It attempted to make a persuasive case that would see the Supreme Court of Canada's seminal decision, *R v. Gladue*, applied towards the restoration of those who most acutely experience the system's discriminatory effects – Aboriginal women.

The chapter has also explored the ways in which the *Gladue* decision could positively influence sentencing patterns in regard to Aboriginal women offenders. It has been argued that the special circumstances of Aboriginal women make them particularly appropriate subjects of sentencing reforms. The decision in *R v. Shore* and the Superior Court of Justice decision in *R v. Hamilton and Mason* illustrate the ways that gender analysis might influence the sentencing process. It has also been argued that restorative sentencing must take into account the 'special' circumstances of Aboriginal women to realise its claims as an alternative to traditional sanctioning.

Over a decade ago, Aboriginal women serving federal terms of imprisonment called for the justice system to respond to them in ways that addressed their need 'to heal and to walk in balance' (Sugar and Fox, 1989–90: 482). The women stated:

The solution is healing: healing through traditional ceremonies, support, understanding, and the compassion that will empower Aboriginal women to the betterment of ourselves, our families, and our communities (Sugar and Fox, 1989–90: 422).

Their words are a fitting end to this chapter for they underscore the urgent need for restorative alternatives. Attention to their 'special circumstances' in sentencing is essential to achieving the solutions called for by Aboriginal women.

Notes

1 The author acknowledges Trish Elliot, School of Journalism, University of Regina, for her comments on an earlier draft.

2 *R* v. *Gladue* [1999] 1 SCR 688 (SCC): 1–32; online at Supreme Court of Canada Lexum: http://www.lexum.umontreal.ca/csc-scc/en/pub/1999/vol1/html/1999scr1_0688.html.

3 Criminal Code, RSC, 1985, c. C-46, Part XXIII.

4 These debates are explored in a special edition of the *Saskatchewan Law Review*. See: (2002) 'Colloquy on Empty Promises: Parliament, The Supreme Court and the Sentencing of Aboriginal Offenders', *Saskatchewan Law Review*, 65(1), 3–105. The articles were prepared in response to Philip Stenning and Julian V. Roberts (2001) 'Empty Promises: Parliament, the Supreme Court and the Sentencing of Aboriginal Offenders', *Saskatchewan Law Review*, 64(1), 137–68.

5 In 'Of Fairness and Falkiner' (2002), law professor Mark Carter states at p. 74: 'Whatever s. 718(2)(e)'s contribution may be to the solutions that we are seeking, it can only be a small one, but it is a start'; *Saskatchewan Law Review*, 65(1), 63–74.

6 Chapter II: 'The Voices of Aboriginal People', in the Task Force on Federally Sentenced Women (1990) states, at p. 15:

> Our distinct experience as Aboriginal women must be recognized. We cannot be either women only or Aboriginal only. Our race and our gender are integrally linked. Our teachings as women flow from the teachings of our various Aboriginal nations.

7 Criminal Code, *supra* note 3.

8 Her Honour Mary-Ellen Turpel-Lafond, Provincial Court of Saskatchewan, wrote:

> The *Gladue* decision has brought the notion of healing into mainstream as a principle which a judge must weight in every case of an Aboriginal person, in order to build a bridge between their unique personal and community background experiences and criminal justice (Turpel-Lafond, 1999: 2).

9 Section 718.2(e), Criminal Code, *supra* note 3.

10 Tanis Gladue was originally sentenced to three years imprisonment. The Supreme Court upheld the sentence as Ms Gladue was granted day parole after six months and was living in the community at the time of the judgment.

11 *R* v. *Gladue*, *supra* note 2, at 30 of 32.

12 Ibid.

13 Ibid., at 21 of 32, quoting from Michael Jackson (1988–89) 'Locking Up Natives in Canada', *UBC Law Review*, 23, 215.

14 These factors are outlined in greater detail later in this chapter.

15 This finding is found in prominent Canadian studies on women's imprisonment including Task Force on Federally Sentenced Women (1990) and Arbour (1996).

16 *R* v. *Hamilton and Mason*, CRIMJ(F) 5789/01, Ontario Superior Court of Justice: 1–67; online at Canadian Legal Information Institute: http://www.canlii.org/on/cas/onsc/2003/2003onsc10227.html. Hill J. states at 14, para. 71: 'There has been a relatively steady increase in the population of federally sentenced women in prison.'

17 *R* v. *Gladue, supra* note 2, at 26 of 32.

18 Tanis Gladue might be said to typify female Aboriginal offenders. She was one of nine children, born to a Cree mother and a Métis father. She began her relationship with Reuben Beaver, the deceased, at the age of 17. At the time of his death, she was pregnant with the couple's second child. Physical abuse and alcohol abuse were factors in the relationship.

19 In 'Habilitation: Sentencing of Female Offenders', Charalee F. Graydon argues that the criminal justice system operates on notions of good and evil. Aboriginal women and minority women are cast as evil because they veer from the stereotypical 'good' woman, who is white, middle class and subservient (Graydon, 1992).

20 *R* v. *Neve*, 1999 ABCA 206; online at Canadian Legal Information Institute: http://www.canlii.org/ab/cas/abca/1999/19999abca206.html.

21 In *Looking White People in the Eye: Gender, Race and Culture in Courtrooms and Classrooms* (2001), feminist scholar Sharene Razack states that Aboriginal women are ignored in discussions on healing and restoration. The Report of the Manitoba Justice Inquiry criticised the excessive imprisonment of Aboriginal women yet it did not mention women in a chapter outlining a plan for reform. Razack doubts the ability of section 718. 2(e) to introduce meaningful reform for Aboriginal men and particularly for Aboriginal women. The provision leaves the 'colonial relation' intact. At 68, Razack observes the following on the judiciary and other criminal justice personnel:

> As benevolent patriarchs, they consider the special circumstances of the Aboriginal male offender, and sometimes his tragic history, but their gaze remains a colonial one in which the colonizers never consider colonization and their own complicity in it. Unlike Aboriginal women who consider colonization as it operates through gender, these judges and lawyers separate the systems of patriarchy and colonization, considering the former to be active and the latter to be over.

22 *R* v. *Hamilton and Mason*, CRIMJ(F) 5789/01, Ontario Superior Court of Justice; online at Canadian Legal Information Institute: http://www.canlii.org/on/cas/onsc/2003/2003onsc10227.html.

23 In a third decision, *R* v. *Spencer*, the decision in *R* v. *Hamilton and Mason* was relied on to grant a conditional sentence to a third offender, Tracy-Ann Spencer. She was convicted of drug smuggling. Ms Spencer was also a single mother and a landed immigrant who came to Canada from Jamaica.

24 The women were allowed to continue serving community-based sentence. The subject of a third case, Tracy Spencer, was ordered to serve her sentence in an institution.

25　*R* v. *Hamilton and Mason*, C39716/C39715, Court of Appeal for Ontario; online at Canadian Legal Information Institute: http://www.ontariocourts./on/ca/decisions/2004/august/C39716.html.

26　Ibid.

27　See Fran Sugar and Lana Fox (1989–90). The researchers interviewed 39 federally sentenced women.

28　*R* v. *Hamilton and Mason*, *supra* note 25, at 23.

29　*R* v. *Wells* [2000] 1 SCR 207; online at Supreme Court of Canada Lexum: http://www.lexum.umontreal.ca/csc-scc/en/pub/2000/vol1/html/2000scr1_0207.html.

30　(2002) SKPC 42 (Saskatchewan Provincial Court), Snell PCJ: 1–23; online at Law Society of Saskatchewan: http://www.lawsociety.sk.ca/.

31　Ibid.

32　Ibid., at 2–4 of 23.

33　Ibid. Details on Ms Shore appear throughout the case.

34　Ibid., at 7 of 23. See, for example, Saskatchewan Women's Secretariat (1999) and Amnesty International (2004).

References

Cases

R v. *Gladue* [1999] 1 SCR 688 (SCC); online at Supreme Court of Canada Lexum: http://www.lexum.umontreal.ca/csc-scc/en/pub/1999/vol1/html/1999scr1_0688.html.

R v. *Hamilton and Mason*, CRIMJ(F) 5789/01, Ontario Superior Court of Justice, per Hill J.; online at Canadian Legal Information Institute: http://www.canlii.org/on/cas/onsc/2003/2003onsc10227.html.

R v. *Hamilton and Mason*, C39716/C39715, Court of Appeal for Ontario; online at Canadian Legal Information Institute: http://www.ontariocourts./on/ca/decisions/2004/august/C39716.html.

R v. *Neve*, 1999 ABCA 206; online at Canadian Legal Information Institute: http://www.canlii.org/ab/cas/abca/1999/19999abca206.html.

R v. *Shore*, 2002 SKPC 42; online at Law Society of Saskatchewan: http://www.lawsociety.sk.ca/.

R v. *Wells* [2000] 1 SCR 207; online at Supreme Court of Canada Lexum: http://www.lexum.umontreal.ca/csc-scc/en/pub/2000/vol1/html/2000scr1_0207.html.

Statutes

Criminal Code, RSC, 1985, c. C-46, Part XXIII.

Articles and books

Amnesty International (2004) *Stolen Sisters: Discrimination and Violence Against Indigenous Women in Canda: A Summary of Amnesty International's Concerns*; online at Amnesty International: http://web.amnesty.org/library/Index/ENGAMR200012004.

Arbour, L. (1996) *Commission of Inquiry into Certain Events at the Prison for Women in Kingston*. Ottawa: Public Works and Government Services Canada; online at Justice Behind the Walls (1–351): http://www.justicebehindthewalls.net/resources/arbour_report/arbour_rpt.htm.

Canadian Association of Elizabeth Fry Societies Submission to the Canadian Human Rights Commission for the Special Report on the Discrimination on the Basis of Sex, Race and Disability Faced by Federally Sentenced Women (May 2003: 1–81): online at Canadian Association of Elizabeth Fry Societies: http://www.elizabethfry.ca/chrc/CAEFS_SUBMISSIO. . .

Canadian Association of Elizabeth Fry Societies (Fall 1999) *Opening the Doors*, Newsletter of the Council of Elizabeth Fry Societies of Ontario, accessed online.

Canadian Human Rights Commission (December 2003) *Protecting Their Rights: A Systemic Review of Human Rights in Correctional Services for Federally Sentenced Women*, accessed on line.

Canadian Press (1999) *Lisa Neve Eligible for Immediate Release*, Wednesday, 30 June; online at Walnet: http://www.walnet.org/csis/news/edmonton_99/cp-990630-2.html.

Carter, M. (2002) 'Of Fairness and Falkiner', *Saskatchewan Law Review*, 65(1), 63–74.

Faith, K. (1993) *Unruly Women: The Politics of Confinement and Resistance*. Vancouver: Press Gang Publishers.

Graydon, C. (1992) 'Habilitation: Sentencing of Female Offenders', *Canadian Journal of Law and Jurisprudence*, 5, 121–41; Quicklaw: 1–21.

Hadley, K. (2001) *And We Still Ain't Satisfied: Gender Equality in Canada, A Status Report for 2001*. Toronto: Centre for Social Justice.

La Prairie, C. (1987) 'Native Women and Crime in Canada: A Theoretical Model', in A. Ellen and C. Claudia (eds), *Too Few to Count: Canadian Women in Conflict With the Law*. Vancouver: Press Gang Publishers.

Makin, Kirk (2004) 'Judges blundered, appeal court told', *The Globe and Mail*, Tuesday, 10 February; accessed online at: http://www.globeandmail.com/servlet/ArticleNews/TPS; 23/92/04.

McIvor, Sharon D. and Johnson, Elisa C. *Detailed Position of the Native Women's Association of Canada on the Complaint Regarding the Discriminatory Treatment of Federally Sentenced Women by the Government of Canada filed by the Canadian Association of Elizabeth Fry Societies on May 5, 2003*; online: http://www.elizabethfry.ca/chrc/nwac_submission.html.

Monture-Angus, P. (2002) *The Lived Experience of Discrimination: Aboriginal Women Who Are Federally Sentenced*; online at Canadian Association of Elizabeth Fry Societies: http://www.Elizabethfry.ca/submissn/aborigin/1/html.

Razack, S. (2001) *Looking White People in the Eye: Gender, Race and Culture in Courtrooms and Classrooms*. Toronto: University of Toronto Press.

Saskatchewan Women's Secretariat (1999) *Profile of Aboriginal Women*. Saskatoon: Government of Saskatchewan.

Sugar, F. and Fox, L. (1989–90) 'Nistum Peyako Séht'wawin Iskwewak: Breaking Chains', *Canadian Journal of Women and Law*, 3, 465–82.

Task Force on Federally Sentenced Women (1990) *Creating Choices: Report of the Task Force on Federally Sentenced Women*. Ottawa: Solicitor General.

Turpel-Lafond, M.-E. (1999) 'Sentencing Within a Restorative Justice Paradigm', *Justice as Healing*, 4(3), 1–11; online at Native Law Centre, University of Saskatchewan: http://www.usask.ca/nativelaw/publications/jah/turpel-lafond.html.

Part 3

Victimisation and Restorative Justice

Chapter 8

A tale of two studies: restorative justice from a victim's perspective

Kathleen Daly

Abstract[1]

This chapter reviews two studies on restorative justice conducted in the past several years. One examines variability in the conference process and the second compares outcomes for court and conference cases. The studies show the strengths and weaknesses of restorative justice from a victim's perspective. The conference-only study demonstrates the limits of restorative justice in helping victims to recover from crime, and it suggests that some victims are more able to engage in a restorative justice process than others. The conference–court comparison demonstrates the limits of the court in attempting to adjudicate and sanction crime, and the court's failure to vindicate victims. Restorative justice advocates and critics must grasp the significance and 'truth' of both studies. Advocates should adopt more realistic expectations for victims in a restorative process while critics should be mindful of the court's limited ability to vindicate victims.

Introduction

This chapter offers a broad review of what is being learned about victims' experiences with court and conference processes, drawing from two major projects. The first is the South Australia Juvenile Justice (SAJJ) Research on

Conferencing Project, in which my research group and I observed 89 youth justice conferences and interviewed the victims and offenders associated with the conferences in 1998, and again, in 1999. The second is the Sexual Assault Archival Study (SAAS), in which my research group and I gathered documentation for all youth sexual offence cases finalised over a six and one half year period (1995–2001) in court and by conference and formal caution, a total of 387 cases. Together, these studies show the strengths and weaknesses of restorative justice (RJ) from a victim's perspective. The conference-only study identifies variability in the conference process, and it reveals the limits of RJ in assisting victims to recover from crime. The conference–court comparison reveals the limits of the court process in responding to sexual assault, especially from a victim's perspective. RJ advocates and critics must grasp the significance and 'truth' of both studies. Advocates should adopt more realistic expectations for victims in a restorative process, while critics should be mindful of the court's limited ability to vindicate victims.

Study I: South Australia Juvenile Justice (SAJJ) Research on Conferencing

SAJJ methodology

The SAJJ project involved two waves of data collection, in 1998 and 1999 (see Daly et al., 1998 and Daly, 2001a, for project overview, instruments used in 1998 and 1999, and the basis for instrument construction).[2] In 1998, the SAJJ group observed 89 conferences that were held during a 12-week period in the capital city (Adelaide) and in two country towns. The sample was selected by offence category: eligible offences were violent crimes and property offences having individual victims or community-organisational victims, such as schools or housing trusts. Excluded were shoplifting cases, drug cases and public order offences. The following are selected features of the 89 conferences and the primary victims:[3]

- 44 per cent dealt with violence (mainly assaults) and 56 per cent property offences (mainly breaking and entering, property damage, and theft of a motor vehicle).

- In 67 per cent, the victim was a person; 19 per cent of victims were organisations, and 14 per cent were persons victimised in their occupational role, or the incident victimised a person as well as his or her organisation.

- 74 per cent of conferences had a victim (or a family member representing the victim) present, and an additional 6 per cent had a representative from the Victim Support Service.

- In 28 per cent, the offence victims were under 18; 51 per cent of victims were male; 49 per cent, female.

- Of violence victims, 35 per cent needed to see a doctor.

- Of property victims, the total out-of-pocket expenses (that is, after insurance) ranged from none to $6,000; the mean was over $900 and the median was $400.

For each conference, the police officer and coordinator completed a self-administered survey, and a SAJJ researcher completed a detailed observation instrument. When a conference had more than one offender, the observations focused on a designated primary offender. Our aim was to interview all the offenders (N = 107) and primary victims associated with the conferences (N = 89). Of the 196 offenders and victims, we interviewed 172 (or 88 per cent) in 1998; of that group, 94 per cent were again interviewed in 1999. Both the victims who attended the conference ('conference victims') and those who did not ('non-conference victims') were interviewed. The interview had open- and close-ended items, although the findings presented here rely on the quantitative items. In addition to the observational and interview data, the project analysed official police data on the offending histories, pre- and post-conference for the 107 offenders.

Established SAJJ findings

In previous publications (Daly, 2001b, 2002a, 2003a, 2003b) analysing the SAJJ data, I have presented four key findings, which I highlight here.[4]

Procedural justice
The SAJJ observers, conference participants (offender and victim) and professionals (coordinator and police officer) judged conferences to be very high on all indicators of procedural justice. As measured by variables such as being treated fairly and with respect, having a say and partici-pating in the outcome, procedural justice was present in 80 to 95 per cent of conferences. Conference practices in this jurisdiction (and others studied in Australia and New Zealand) definitely conform to the ideals of procedural justice.

Restorativeness

Compared to the high levels of procedural justice, there was relatively less evidence of restorativeness (present in 30 to 60 per cent of conferences, depending on the variable). The variables tapping restorativeness included the degree to which the offender was remorseful, spontaneously apologised to the victim and understood the impact of the crime on the victim; the degree to which victims understood the offender's situation; and the extent of positive movement between the offender, victim or their supporters. Although conferences received high marks for procedural fairness and victim and offender participation, it was relatively more difficult for victims and offenders to resolve their differences or to find common ground, at least at the conference itself.

Capacities of victims and offenders

There were limits on offenders' interests to repair the harm and on victims' capacities to see offenders in a positive light. From the 1998 interviews, we learned that the conference process was novel for offenders and victims, and that some victims found it difficult to be generous to offenders. Just under half (47 per cent) of the offenders said they had given any degree of thought to what they would do or say to the victim at the conference, and half said that the victim's story had any degree of effect on them. More victims (66 per cent) had given thought to what they would say to offenders at the conference, but a minority (38 per cent) said that the offender's account of the offence had an impact on them.

In the 1999 interviews, the apology process was explored in detail. We found that while most victims thought the offender's apology was insincere, most offenders said they apologised because they really were sorry. For a subset of cases in 1999, in which the victims were present at the conference and the primary offender and victim were interviewed (N = 47), 61 per cent of offenders said they were really sorry, but just 27 per cent of victims thought that offenders were really sorry. I pursued this mismatch of perception by drawing on the conference observations, interview material, and police incident reports for the victims and primary offenders to make inferences about the apology process for all 89 conferences. The results reinforce the findings above, revealing that communication failure and mixed signals are present when apologies are made and received. Such communication gaps are overlaid by the variable degree to which offenders are in fact sorry for what they have done. In 34 per cent of cases, the offenders and victims agreed (or were in partial agreement) that the offender was sorry, and in 27 per cent the offenders and victims definitely agreed that the offender was not sorry. For 30 per cent, there was a perceptual mismatch: the offenders were not sorry, but the victims thought they were (12 per cent); or the offenders were sorry, but the victims did not think so (18 per cent). For the remaining 8 per cent, it was not possible to determine. This is but one example of the gaps that exist between the ideals of RJ and what actually occurs in a conference process in a high-volume jurisdiction (see Daly 2002a, 2003b).

High and low conferences

Does it matter if a conference is a 'good one' or not? The SAJJ data suggest it does.[5] To capture the varying degrees of restorativeness along with the differing interests and capacities of victims and offenders to see each other in positive and other-regarding ways, I devised a global conference measure. It combined the SAJJ observer's judgment of the degree to which a conference 'ended on a high, a positive note of repair and good will' with one that rated the conference on a 5-point scale ranging from poor to exceptional. The first measure depicted the degree of movement of victims and offenders (or their supporters) toward each other, and the second, elements of procedural justice and coordinator skill in managing the conference. This global conference measure had four levels: ended on a high and rated very highly (10 per cent), ended on a high and rated good (40 per cent), did not end on a high and a fair or good rating (20 per cent), and did not end on a high and a fair or poor rating (30 per cent). I collapsed these into two groups: high/good (N = 45) and low/mixed (N = 44). For ease of presentation, I term the conferences 'high' and 'low'.

Bivariate analyses showed no association of the global conference measure with characteristics of the offence (including the victim–offender relationship, type of offence, type of victim and number of offenders in the whole offence), or with other conference measures (such as the number of people attending), whether the victim was present or the degree of emotionality present such as participants crying. Although these characteristics of offences and conferences were unrelated to the high/low conference measure, the many indicators of procedural justice, restorativeness and coordinator skill were: all of the 'restorative' behaviours and movements one ideally hopes to see in conferences[6] occurred to a significantly greater degree in the high than the low conferences. The measure therefore has excellent construct validity (see Daly, 2003b: 29–36).

Does it matter, then, if a conference is high or low for how offenders and victims viewed the conference experience and its impact? The answer is yes, it does matter. For offenders interviewed in 1998, significantly higher proportions in the high conferences said that they felt sorry for the victim and that what happened in the conference would encourage them to obey the law. Significantly lower proportions of those in the high conferences reoffended during an 8–12 month period after the conference.[7] For victims interviewed in 1998, significantly higher proportions in high conferences were less frightened of offenders and held less negative attitudes toward them; they were more satisfied with how their case was handled and less likely to see the conference as a waste of time. In 1999, they were more likely to say the conference was worthwhile. These findings suggest that the theory of RJ is correct: when conferences proceed in optimal ways, they have more favourable results for victims and offenders.

Despite this, a puzzling set of findings emerged for victim recovery. In 1998, high conferences were more likely to be associated with victims saying that the conference was helpful in overcoming emotional or psychological effects of crime. But when we asked victims in 1999 if they had fully recovered from the incident or not, high conferences were not related to their recovery. One interpretation is that the conference process may have immediate, positive effects on victims, but over time other elements may make more of a difference.

In general, although high conferences are associated with increased levels of positive 'effects' for victims and offenders, I would caution against making causal claims about such effects. One reason is that conferences succeed or fail (or are high or low) because victims and offenders come to them with varied degrees of readiness to make the process work. Victims and offenders are not equally disposed to be restorative toward each other, to listen to each other or to be willing to repair harms. Some come to conferences with negative orientations and closed minds that cannot be changed, and others come with positive orientations and open minds.

New SAJJ findings: victim distress and offence recovery

The established SAJJ findings centred on the variable capacities and interests of offenders and victims to think and act restoratively in the conference process itself. However, a major element was missing: the differential effects of crimes on victims (e.g. how deeply the victimisation touches and distresses them) and how this may structure victims' orientations to offenders and the conference process. Further, it was unclear why victim recovery in 1999 was not related to the global conference measure. Was it because high conferences had temporary positive effects which were not enduring? Or was the process of victim recovery related to other phenomena? To address these questions, I carried out analyses of the degree of victim distress from the offence as indicated from their interviews in 1998,[8] their recovery as indicated from their interviews in 1999 and the relationship between the two.

Victim distress

In the 1998 interviews, we asked the conference victims if they had experienced any non-material harm as a result of the offence, and to key their answer to the period of time after the incident but before the conference.[9] We asked:

During that time, did you suffer from any of the following as a result of the offence:

- fear of being alone?
- sleeplessness or nightmares?
- general health problems (headaches, physical pain, trouble breathing or walking)?
- worry about the security of your property?
- general increase in suspicion or distrust?
- sensitivity to particular sounds or noises?
- loss of self-confidence?
- loss of self-esteem?
- other problems?

The respondent answered 'yes' or 'no' after each item was mentioned. A scale was constructed by assigning a one for each 'yes', and it initially ranged from zero to nine. The nine categories were then collapsed into four and included a companion 'distress' item asked of the victims who did not attend the conference.[10] Of the conference and non-conference victims interviewed in 1998, 28 per cent reported no distress, 12.5 per cent low distress, 36.5 per cent moderate distress and 23 per cent high distress. I collapsed the four categories in two, the no/low distress (40.5 per cent) and the moderate/high distress (59.5 per cent),[11] and then analysed the relationship of the two groups to other measures. For ease of presentation, I use the terms 'low' distress (or non-distressed) victims to refer to those in the no and low distress groups, and 'high' distress (or distressed) victims to refer to those in the moderate and high distress groups. Readers will appreciate that these terms are a shorthand way (albeit one-dimensional and infelicitous) to depict and compare victims' experiences in the aftermath of crime.

The high distress group was significantly more likely to be composed of female victims, personal crime victims (including those victimised in their occupational role or at their organisational workplace), violent offences, and victims and offenders who were family members or well known to each other.[12] Put another way, female victims were more likely to be distressed (69 per cent) than male (50 per cent), personal crime victims (70 per cent) more than organisational (19 per cent), victims of violence (72 per cent) more than property (49 per cent), and victims of family members or those well known (80 per cent) more than casual acquaintances or those known by sight (53 per cent) or strangers (also 53 per cent). The offences most likely to cause victims distress were assaults on family members or teachers (89 per cent), adolescent punch-ups (76 per cent), and breaking into, stealing or damaging personal property (75 per cent). By comparison, the offences least likely to cause victims distress were breaking into, stealing, or damaging organisational property (19 per cent) and stranger assault (33 per cent). Theft of bikes or cars was midway (55 per cent of victims indicated distress).[13]

For the global conference measure, high conferences were just as likely to be composed of low distress (51 per cent) as high distress (49 per cent) victims; but the low conferences were more likely to be composed of high distress victims (72 per cent). Put another way, whereas 45 per cent of high distress victims were in high conferences, nearly 70 per cent of low distress victims were. This finding is instructive: it suggests that the capacity of victims and offenders to engage in restorative behaviour is increased when victims are less distressed in the aftermath of victimisation. Additionally, I found that a higher proportion of distressed (27 per cent) than non-distressed (4 per cent) victims left the conference feeling upset by what the offender or supporters said, and a higher proportion of distressed (62 per cent) than non-distressed (17 per cent) victims were angry toward the offender after the conference. Remarkably, it was only the high distress victims who remained frightened of the offender after the conference: over 40 per cent were, compared to none of the low distress victims.

It is not surprising, then, that of the conference victims indicating any distress (N = 47 ranging from low, moderate to high), just under half (47 per cent) said the conference was not at all helpful in overcoming these difficulties, 19 per cent said the conference was helpful or very helpful, and 34 per cent said it was a little helpful. Depending on how one decides to interpret this finding (see Morris, 2002), we could say (less generously) that a conference was helpful for about 20 per cent of victims with any distress, or (more generously) that it was a little helpful or helpful for over half of these victims (53 per cent). Although most conference victims said they would recommend conferencing to other victims of crime (87 per cent), the per cent was greater for low distress (96 per cent) than high distress (81 per cent) victims. And although most victims (73 per cent) were satisfied with how their case was handled, satisfaction was greater for low distress (91 per cent) than high distress (62 per cent) victims.

Victims' distress was significantly linked to their attitude toward offenders and their interest to find common ground. For the 1998 conference victims, 43 per cent of high distress victims had negative attitudes toward the offender after the conference, but the corresponding per cent for low distress victims was just 8 per cent. And while 71 per cent of low distress victims had positive attitudes toward the offender after the conference, 49 per cent of high distress victims did. We asked the conference victims, 'When you look back at the conference and your feelings about what happened, can you tell me which was more important to you, that you be treated fairly or that you find common ground with the offender?' Most distressed victims said it was more important to them to be treated fairly (67 per cent) than to find common ground with offenders, whereas most non-distressed victims (71 per cent) said it was more important to them to find common ground.[14] This is a key finding. What crime victims hope to achieve from a conference, that is whether to seek mutual understanding with offenders (other-regarding victims) or to be treated well as individuals (self-regarding), is related to the character and 'experience' of their victimisation.[15]

The victims of the adolescent punch-ups and assaults on teachers and family members were split on their other-regarding interests: half were interested in finding common ground and half were not.[16] For the personal property crime victims (theft and damage, including cars and bikes), about one-fifth were interested in finding common ground. Two-thirds of the low distress organisational victims were interested to find common ground with the offender, but this orientation was absent for the small number of high distress organisational victims. All of the stranger assault victims were interested to find common ground. Thus victims' other- and self-regarding interests and orientations varied by the offence and the degree of distress the victim felt. Organisational and stranger assault victims were most likely to be other-regarding, that is, to want to find common ground, personal property crime victims were least likely, and adolescent, family and teacher assault victims fell in between.

When absorbing these results for the first time, they are simultaneously surprising and expected. They are surprising because RJ scholars have not discussed the differing effects of crime (and types of crimes) on victims and how this affects victims' abilities and interests to engage in an RJ process. I had not anticipated these results, but now see that they are a crucial area for further investigation. And although with the benefit of hindsight the results may seem obvious, they also challenge the RJ field in many ways. The SAJJ findings show, for example, that it is misleading to compare violent and property offences because some property victims (personal property) are more highly distressed than others (organisational property). Moreover, while assaults by adolescents on their peers, family members and teachers cause victims high distress, those on strangers are far less likely to do so.

It may be unwise to say that 'highly emotional' and 'serious' offences are best served by RJ practices. Surely, many are, and I would be the first to say that RJ processes are misspent on shoplifting cases. However, the SAJJ data show that in the context of youth justice, victims who are 'lightly touched' by a crime orient themselves more readily to the ideal RJ script.[17] Compared to the distressed victims, it is easier for this group to be other-regarding because the wrong has not affected them deeply. It is more difficult for the distressed victims to be empathetic and positive toward offenders, and therefore we should not expect restorativeness to emerge easily in conferences with these victims. A striking result from the SAJJ data was that after the conference ended, the high distress victims were far more likely to remain angry and fearful of offenders and to be negative toward them than the low distress victims. This result anticipates findings on victim recovery a year later when the victims were re-interviewed.

Victim recovery

In 1999, we asked victims, 'which of the following two statements better describes how you're feeling about the incident today? Would you say that it is all behind you, you are fully recovered from it; or it is partly behind you, there are still some things that bother you, you are not fully recovered from it.' Two-thirds said that they had recovered from the offence and it was all behind them.[18] Thus most victims had recovered from the offence a year later, but which victims? And did the conference process assist in their recovery?

An examination of victim distress in 1998 as compared with victim recovery in 1999 reveals dramatic and striking results. The greater the distress indicated in 1998, the less likely victims had recovered in 1999 (see Table 8.1).

Whereas 63 to 95 per cent of the moderate to no distress victims had recovered in 1999, 71 per cent of the high distress victims had not. For this latter group, an RJ process may be of little help for victim recovery. The

Table 8.1 Victim distress in 1998 and victim recovery in 1999

| | Per cent fully recovered | | | | | | |
	All	Male	Female		All	Male	Female
No distress	95	92	100	low	90	83	100
Low distress	78	67	100				
Moderate distress	63	71	54	high	50	68	36
High distress	29	60	17				

relationship between distress indicated in 1998 and recovery in 1999 was especially strong for the female victims: the majority of high distress female victims (64 per cent) said they had not recovered from the offence, whereas the majority of high distress male victims (68 per cent) said they had recovered. Personal crime victims were less likely to have recovered (58 per cent) than organisational victims (93 per cent), and again, the relationship was even stronger for female victims. These and other gender differences in the experience of victimisation and recovery from crime invite further analysis. In part, the differences are caused by a different mix of types of offending against the male and female victims in the sample, and in part by the ways in which gender and culture structure the 'experiences' of victimisation, vulnerability and recovery.

In 1999, we asked victims, 'Would you say that your ability to get the offence behind you was aided more by your participation in the justice process or things that only you could do for yourself?' Half (49 per cent) said their participation in the justice process, and 40 per cent only things they could do for themselves; 11 per cent said both were of equal importance. The recovered victims were more likely to say participation in the justice process (72 per cent) than the non-recovered victims (38 per cent).[19] Likewise, the low distress victims were more likely to say participation in the justice process (77 per cent) than the high distress victims (49 per cent). The conference process can have a constructive impact on distressed victims, but not in most cases. For example, of the distressed victims of adolescent punch-ups, assaults on family members or teachers, and theft or damage of personal property (including cars and bikes), one-third said their participation in the justice process was important in getting the offence behind them. When we asked all victims (both those who had recovered and those who did not) which things (from a long list of items) were most important in aiding their recovery, about 30 per cent cited a variety of conference-related elements, including participation in the conference, contact with the coordinator and police officer, and meeting the offender.

Non-recovered (or only partly recovered) victims held more negative views of the offender and how their case was handled compared to the recovered victims. They were significantly more likely to see the offender as a 'bad' person rather than a 'good' person who had done a bad thing, less satisfied by how their case was handled and more likely to say they wished their case had gone to court. When asked what was the most important thing hindering their recovery, 74 per cent cited financial losses, injuries and emotional harms arising from the offence.

The new SAJJ findings on victim distress and recovery pose significant challenges to the RJ field. They invite reflection on the variable effects of victimisation for the ways in which victims orient themselves to a restorative process. For the distressed victims in the SAJJ sample, it was harder to act restoratively at the conference, and it was more difficult to be generous to offenders. The effects of victimisation did not end with the conference but continued to linger for a long time. A process like RJ, and indeed any legal process (such as court), may do little to assist victims who have been deeply affected by crime. Improving practices by conference facilitators may help at the edges, but this too is unlikely to have a major impact. Victims who are affected negatively and deeply by crime need more than RJ (or court) to recover from their victimisation. And as we shall see, having one's case go to court is not without significant problems.

Study 2: The Sexual Assault Archival Study (SAAS)

Study 2 shifts the spotlight from variation in the conference process and how victims experience crime, to differences in how cases are handled in court and conference. The spotlight also shifts from a range of violent and property offences to an examination of sexual assault offences, although there is a good deal of variability within this category. With the shift from a conference-only study to a conference–court comparison, it becomes clear that despite the difficulties some victims (especially distressed victims) experience in the aftermath of crime, and the limits of conferencing to assist highly distressed victims' recovery, the formal court process also fails many victims.

A central question posed in the archival study was, from a victim's point of view, is it better for one's case to be dealt with by way of a RJ process (a conference) or to go to court? There is a good deal of controversy surrounding the use of RJ for cases of family and sexual violence. Critics cite the potential power imbalances in face-to-face encounters, threats to victim safety, pressure on victims to accept certain outcomes, mixed loyalties of family members toward victims and offenders, and the potential for too lenient penalties that may 'send the wrong message' to offenders (for debates, see Curtis-Fawley and Daly, 2005; Daly and Curtis-Fawley, forthcoming; Hudson, 2002). The many positions taken 'against' and 'for' RJ in these cases is matched by the dearth of empirical evidence. There are currently only two jurisdictions in the world, South Australia and New Zealand, which routinely use RJ to respond to youth sexual assault cases. In New Zealand, conferences are used when diverting cases from court and for pre-sentencing advice. In South Australia, conferences are currently used largely in the context of court diversion. No jurisdiction currently uses RJ routinely for cases of sexual assault involving adult offenders.[20] The archival study is the first to shed light on the potential and limits of court and conference processes from the perspective of sexual violence victims.

SAAS methodology

We gathered police documents, family conference files, court records and criminal histories for all youth sexual offences finalised from 1 January 1995 to 1 July 2001 in South Australia, which began with one or more sexual offences charged by the police. There were a total of 227 court cases, 119 conferences and 41 formal cautions. A detailed coding scheme containing over 200 variables was created, which described the offender's biography and orientation to the offence, the number of victims (with detailed information on the primary victim), the context and elements of the offence, how the offence was reported to the police and the time taken from police report to finalisation, the legal history of court cases from initial charges to finalisation (including whether an offence was proved or not), the features of conference cases and penalties imposed. In addition, the offenders' criminal histories (for all types of offending behaviour) were gathered and coded (see Daly et al., 2003a, 2003b, respectively, for summary findings and research methods). The study's strength lies in depicting the variable character of offending and in charting the legal journey of sexual offence cases finalised in court and by conference. Its limitation is that we could not interview victims retrospectively about their court and conference experiences. This would have been impossible for many reasons and inappropriate as a matter of ethical research practice.[21]

SAAS findings

When analysing the data with a focus on factors that matter to victims, we found that victims were better off if their case went to conference rather than court. The principal reason was that in conference cases, something happened, that is, there was an admission by the offender and a penalty (also termed an 'undertaking' or 'agreement'). If a case went to court, the chances of any sexual offence being proved was 51 per cent,[22] with the remaining cases being withdrawn or dismissed. From these results, we concluded that the potential problems of RJ in sexual assault cases (e.g. the potentially revictimising dynamics or power imbalances of a face-to-face encounter) may be less victimising than what occurs in a court process. So long as those accused of crime have the right to deny offending, a right enshrined in the adversarial legal process, the court can do little for victims of sexual assault. The potential of RJ is that it opens up a window of opportunity for those who have offended to admit to what they have done, without the potential risks associated with a court-imposed sentence.

Using several measures of seriousness (legal charges and offence elements), we found that the cases referred to court started out as more serious than those referred to conference. However, by the time the cases were finalised as proved (convicted),[23] the court and conference cases were of similar seriousness.[24] Cases that began with the most serious charge (rape) were the least likely to be proved of any sexual offence in court. While the more serious cases, and those with extra-familial victim–offender relations and non-admitting offenders, were more likely to be referred to court, the cases proved in court were less serious and involved intra-familial victim–offender relations. (Extra-familial relations included any non-family person such as a casual acquaintance, friend of the offender, or a stranger; intra-familial relations were typically siblings and step relations.)

Court cases took over twice as long to finalise as conference cases: using the mean, the time from a report to the police to case finalisation was 6.6 months for court and 3.2 months for conference cases. Victims would have had to attend court, on average, six times to follow their case to finalisation, and nearly 20 per cent would have had to attend ten or more hearings. If victims came to court on the day of finalisation, half would learn that their case had been dismissed or the charges withdrawn. On all our measures of the legal process from a victim's point of view, the court appeared to be less validating and more difficult for a victim to negotiate.

Contrary to Coker's (1999: 85) evocative notion that RJ may be a form of 'cheap justice', we found that conference penalties did more for victims than those imposed in court. A higher share of conference than court offenders apologised to victims, carried out community service, were ordered to stay away from the victim, and undertook an intensive counselling programme for adolescent sex offenders: the Mary Street Programme.[25] The court's greater power is its ability to impose a detention sentence. However, of the 116 proved court cases, 20 per cent of offenders received a detention sentence; in all but three, the sentence was suspended. A small number of court cases (18) was set for trial. Of these, six offenders eventually pleaded guilty and 12 entered no plea or a not guilty plea. Of the 12, eight were dismissed and three were found not guilty. One case was proved at trial.

The archival study found that conferences outperform court on measures that matter to victims: acknowledgment of the wrong (rather than offender denial or court dismissal), timely disposition and undertakings that are meaningful and reduce the chances of reoffending, especially when tied to a therapeutic intervention.[26]

Summary and discussion

The SAJJ study shows that conferences can have positive effects and outcomes for victims, but they can be modest and may not occur in most cases. The SAAS study shows that victims are better served when their case goes to conference rather than court for two reasons. First, something happens at a conference (that is, an offender admits responsibility for an offence and a penalty is agreed to), whereas about half of court cases are dismissed or withdrawn. Second, conference undertakings do more for victims than penalties imposed in court.

The conference-only study reveals the variable nature of restorative processes, which can be contingent on the offence, the kind of victim (individual or organisation) and the subjective impact of the victimisation. In general, an other-regarding and empathetic victim orientation is more likely to be present when victims are lightly touched by crime, a result that was especially apparent for the organisational victims. The conference process can have a positive influence on victim recovery a year later, but it is contingent on the degree of distress victims experienced after the offence and how often it continues to bother them.

A flaw with experimental study designs, which aim to compare court and conference cases, is that they ignore a crucial difference between the two legal sites.[27] Courts deal with the adjudication and penalty phase of the criminal justice process, whereas conferences deal only with the penalty phase. The adjudication phase is hard on victims, arguably even harder than the penalty phase. Courts fail victims when proceedings go on for a long time, when victims are not kept informed about the status of their cases and when prosecutors withdraw cases for reasons that victims may interpret as being on 'technical grounds'. Research comparing victims' experiences with court and conference, in which offenders have admitted offences to the police at an early stage of the legal process (e.g. Strang, 2002, analysing Re-Integrative Shaming Experiments (RISE) data) has merit. However, such research overlooks a broader failure of the court process from a victim's perspective. Offenders may not speak to the police or make admissions to offending at an early stage of the legal process, and prosecutors may not have sufficient evidence to ensure conviction at trial; these and other elements are major sources of case attrition prior to sentencing.[28] Of course, some youthful court offenders may have been wrongly or unfairly accused, but this alone cannot account for the high degree of attrition seen in SAAS.

We learn different things from the conference-only and the court–conference comparison. The conference-only study foregrounds the variable nature of victims' experiences with crime, the variable interests and capacities of victims to act and feel in restorative and other-regarding ways toward offenders, and the variable impact of the conference process. All of these elements have a bearing on the likelihood of victim recovery a year later. Some critics may interpret the SAJJ findings as proof that conferences do not assist victims, especially those distressed by crime. The evidence is mixed and equivocal. Conferences can benefit some victims, but there are limits on what the process can achieve for all victims. At the same time, and of equal importance, the court–conference comparison shows the drawbacks of the adversarial process from a victim's perspective. In the adjudication phase, a defendant is entitled to remain silent, the state must prove its case and a victim may be required to serve a role as witness if the case proceeds to trial. But, in this phase, the major activity for victims is waiting, and based on SAAS, half waited an average of six months to then learn that their case had been dismissed or withdrawn. Although many victims may believe otherwise, the court is not likely to be a site of their vindication, not a place where they will routinely 'get justice'.[29] Critics of conferencing often forget this limitation of the court process from a victim's perspective. Although both RJ critics and victims imagine that the court is a place where serious offences are treated seriously, actual court practices often suggest otherwise.

What lessons can be drawn from my tale of two studies? Imagine you were a victim of sexual assault and you could choose to have the case diverted to a conference or go to court. If the case goes to a conference, you know that the offender has already admitted to the offence, some penalty or outcome will be agreed to and you will have a say in deciding an outcome or penalty. If the case goes to court, you cannot be sure what will occur, but there is a 50–50 chance that it will be dismissed and no penalty will be imposed at all. In the real world, victims do not have this power. It rests instead with an offender, who, at a minimum, must make an admission to the police (or court) for a case to be referred to an RJ process. It also rests with police or judicial officers, who make referrals to conferences on other factors that they deem relevant (such as previous offending, the victim's wishes and case severity). If the sexual assault case does go to a conference, you as the victim run the risk of potentially experiencing revictimisation during a face-to-face encounter with the offender, but at least you know the offender has admitted the offence. Having all of this information before you, along with the power to make the decision, what would you decide to do?

Notes

1   My appreciation and thanks to Brigitte Bouhours and Sarah Curtis-Fawley for their assistance and comments in preparing this chapter. *Note*: The Sexual Assault Archival Study statistics given in this paper were correct as of November 2004 when this paper went to press. Subsequent analyses and data cleaning show that there were 385, not 387 cases in the total sample (one less court and conference case each). Three cases, not one, were proved at trial. Two, not three court youth, were sentenced to serve time in detention. These small N changes have a negligible effect on the results. Subsequent papers will present the data with these changes in N size.

2   Conferencing practices in Australia and New Zealand are varied (see Daly, 2001b; Daly and Hayes, 2001). Conferencing in South Australia (as in all other jurisdictions in the region) is 'New Zealand' style with two professionals (a police officer and coordinator) present. The Re-Integrative Shaming Experiments (RISE) in Canberra studied 'Wagga' style conferencing, where a police officer runs the conference.

3   These are conference-based percentages, not offender-based.

4   Unless otherwise noted, the percentages in 1998 are of 79 victims (including conference and non-conference victims), 61 conference victims and 93 offenders; and in 1999, they are of 73 victims (including conference and non-conference victims), 57 conference victims and 88 offenders. The analytical emphasis in this paper is on victims, but some of the variables discussed were constructed from interviews and observations of the offenders as well.

5   The following distils from Daly (2003a), which had many errors in the tables. Interested readers are encouraged to view the web version of the paper (www.griffith.edu.au/school/ccj/kdaly.html) or to write to Willan Publishing to obtain a detailed errata sheet.

6   The relevant variables for each of the three variables in the global conference measure were as follows: (1) *restorativeness variables* (offender was remorseful, actively involved, made spontaneous apology, assured the victim the offence wouldn't happen again and understood the impact of the crime on the victim; the victim was effective in describing the offence and its impact, the victim understood the offender's situation, there was positive movement between offender and victim, in words and symbolically, and positive movement between the offender's supporters and the victim or victim supporters); (2) *procedural fairness variables* (process of deciding the outcome was fair, police and coordinators treating offenders and victims with respect, coordinators permitting everyone to have their say, decision-maker neutrality, among many others); and (3) *coordinator conference management variables* (managed movement through stages and negotiated outcome well). Note that because observed procedural justice and coordinator skill were evident in a high share of conferences (80 to 95 per cent) whereas observed restorativeness was more varied and relatively less frequent (30 to 60 per cent of conferences), high conferences are those having a greater degree of restorativeness along with very high levels of procedural justice and coordinator skill.

7   See Hayes and Daly (2003) for an analysis of conferencing and reoffending using the SAJJ data.

8   I constructed the distress variable after exploring other ways to depict the effect of the crime on victims. The distress variable was a more powerful indicator than the type of legal charge or the property/violence dichotomy.

9   This question was taken from the victim interview instrument used in RISE, and I thank Heather Strang for providing me with a copy.

10 The non-conference victims were asked a reduced version of the distress question: 'Crime victims suffer other kinds of harm as a result of an incident, for example fear of being alone, sleeplessness, general health problems, concern about security of their property, loss of confidence, or other kinds of difficulties. To what degree did you experience any of these problems as a result of the incident?' The anchored responses were 'not at all', 'a little, but not much', 'to some degree' and 'to a high degree (a lot)'. The four categories for the conference and non-conference victims were no distress (none for the conference or non-conference victims), low distress (one item for the conference victims and 'a little' for the non-conference victims), moderate distress (two to four items for the conference victims and 'to some degree' for the non-conference), and high distress (five or more items for the conference victims and 'to a high degree' for the non-conference).

11 The non-conference victims were more likely to report 'no' or a 'high degree' of distress compared to the conference victims. However, when the four categories are collapsed into two (no/low and moderate/high distress), the distributions are similar (61 per cent and 56 per cent of conference and non-conference victims, respectively, reported moderate/high distress).

12 I have refrained from presenting all the results of the victim distress and recovery analyses in tabular form with the resulting tests of statistical significance. Rather, when I say that one group of victims is higher or lower, I report only those results that are statistically significant at the 0.10 error level or less.

13 These six categories of 'real offence' were constructed to reflect actual offending patterns and their contexts. Although often related to statutory charges, the two are not identical. For example, in the assault on family and teachers category, there were two cases with property damage charges.

14 There were four anchors for this variable: fair treatment, common ground, both equally and neither. In the results reported here, the four categories were collapsed into two: fair treatment and neither; and common ground and both.

15 By comparison, the self- and other-regarding orientations of offenders at conferences are unrelated to victim distress. The relevant items in the 1998 offender interview asked: 'In general, at the conference, was it more important for you to do or to say something to make the victim feel better or to make sure that you got what you wanted?' (72 per cent said to make victim feel better or both; 70 per cent and 75 per cent for high and low distress victims, respectively) and 'When you look back at the conference and your feelings about what happened, can you tell me which was more important to

you, that you be treated fairly or that you were able to do something for the victim?' (55 percent said to do something for the victim or both; 58 per cent and 50 per cent for high and low distress victims, respectively). The analysis is of a subset of 53 primary offenders at conferences where victims (or a family member representing the victim) were present.

16 For each of these offence categories, the low distress victims were more likely to say 'find common ground' than the high distress victims, although the number of cases in each cell is too small to make strong claims.

17 I use the term 'script' here to refer to behaviours and orientations that are optimally expected for victims in the conference process, not to a scripted model of conferencing.

18 Recovery was somewhat higher for non-conference (75 per cent) than conference (63 per cent) victims, but it was not statistically significant.

19 The victims who said 'both equally' were included in the 'participation in the justice process' group. No victim said 'neither'.

20 For exceptions, see Hopkins and Koss (2005) for the RESTORE project (RJ pilot project for adult sexual assault cases in Tucson, Arizona) and Lajeunesse (1996) for the Hollow Water healing circles in Canada.

21 It would have been impossible to locate victims for offences that had occurred many years before, but the more important consideration was ethical. To redress this problem, the research group followed 14 cases of sexual assault and family violence disposed during the second half of 2001, and we attempted to interview the victims in these cases (see Daly and Curtis-Fawley, forthcoming). We were able to carry out the in-depth study of conference cases while we were based in Adelaide, gathering data and documents for the archival study.

22 An additional 4 per cent were proved of a non-sexual offence. In an earlier study of sexual offence cases in court and conference using data from 1998, I reported that one-third of cases were proved in court (Daly, 2002b: 78). However, this figure excluded cases that were proved of a less serious offence (although it was not clear from the Office of Crime Statistics report what the charge was). Based on the archival study, I would say it is more accurate to include the less serious sexual offences. For example, in the SAAS dataset, 12 per cent of the rape cases filed were proved of rape, but another 28 per cent were proved of a less serious sexual offence.

23 In this Youth Court jurisdiction, a case can be proved 'with' or 'without conviction'. The latter is a legal device to protect a young person's criminal record. A 'proved' case means the same thing as a conviction or guilty plea in adult court.

24 This was caused by guilty pleas to less serious offences and by the more serious cases being dismissed or withdrawn.

25 The Mary Street Adolescent Sexual Abuse Prevention Programme 'promotes safety in families and communities by helping young people to stop sexual abuse and sexual harassment of others.' Young people charged with sexual offences can receive counselling before or after a conference or court sentencing. Without a treatment programme like Mary Street in place, I

would hesitate to support conferencing for sex offences. For a summary of the programme, see Daly et al. (2003b), p. 45, or visit the Mary Street website: http://www.wch.sa.gov.au/services/az/divisions/mentalhealth/asapp/index.html.

26 In analysing only those cases where any sex offence was proved (in court, N = 116) or admitted to (in conference, N = 112), the prevalence of reoffending (all types of offending, not just sexual offending) was higher for court offenders and for those who did not attend the Mary Street Programme. For conference cases, of those who attended Mary Street, 42 per cent reoffended; for those who did not, 60 per cent reoffended. For court cases, of those who attended Mary Street, 49 per cent reoffended; for those who did not, 75 per cent reoffended. These results are preliminary; further analyses will be carried out to correct for the different time periods that offenders were at risk to reoffend.

27 For example, in RISE, offenders were randomly assigned to court or to conference only after they had admitted the offence to the police. As an ethical matter, this is appropriate. As an empirical matter, it cuts out a large set of court cases that remain in the system for some time without guilty pleas or are eventually dismissed. A preferable research design when studying conferences as diversion from court (as compared to pre-sentencing advice to judicial officers) would be to compare conferences with two kinds of court cases, those in which the accused admitted early on and those in which admissions were made much later.

28 Case attrition is high for all offences, not just sexual assault. However, as Bryden and Lengnick (1997) argue in their comprehensive review and discussion of this question in adult cases, case attrition in sexual assault is unique because the prosecutor's burden of proof (that is, to prove victim non-consent) makes conviction difficult, especially in acquaintance cases (see also Kelly, 2001, on this point). This burden of proof is not relevant, however, to child or minor victims (age varies by jurisdiction, but it is under 17 for South Australia), for whom at law it is assumed that a victim cannot consent to sex. However, in an analysis of whether a court case was proved or not in court by victim–offender relation and age difference, I found that cases involving friends of a similar age were far less likely to be proved (23 per cent were) compared to friends for whom the age difference was more than two years (53 per cent proved) or those between strangers (59 per cent proved).

29 I would assume a good deal of variation in victims' knowledge of the legal process, especially in sexual assault cases, where victim support agencies can provide clients with a realistic assessment of how the police and courts are likely to respond.

References

Bryden, D. P. and Lengnick, S. (1997) 'Rape in the Criminal Justice System', *Journal of Criminal Law and Criminology*, 87, 1194–388.

Coker, D. (1999) 'Enhancing Autonomy for Battered Women: Lessons from Navajo Peacemaking', *UCLA Law Review*, 47, 1–111.

Curtis-Fawley, S. and Daly, K. (2005) 'Gendered Violence and Restorative Justice: The Views of Victim Advocates', *Violence Against Women*, 11(5), 603–38.

Daly, K. (2001a) *SAJJ Technical Report No. 2: Research Instruments in Year 2 (1999) and Background Notes*. Brisbane: School of Criminology and Criminal Justice, Griffith University; available at: www.aic.gov.au/rjustice/sajj/index.html.

Daly, K. (2001b) 'Conferencing in Australia and New Zealand: Variations, Research Findings, and Prospects', in A. Morris and G. Maxwell (eds), *Restoring Justice for Juveniles: Conferencing, Mediation, and Circles*. Oxford: Hart, pp. 59–83.

Daly, K. (2002a) 'Restorative Justice: The Real Story', *Punishment and Society*, 4(1), 55–79.

Daly, K. (2002b) 'Sexual Assault and Restorative Justice', in H. Strang and J. Braithwaite (eds), *Restorative Justice and Family Violence*. Cambridge: University of Cambridge Press, pp. 62–88.

Daly, K. (2003a) 'Making Variation a Virtue: Evaluating the Potential and Limits of Restorative Justice', in E. Weitekamp and H.-J. Kerner (eds), *Restorative Justice in Context: International Practice and Directions*. Cullompton: Willan Publishing, pp. 23–50.

Daly, K. (2003b) 'Mind the Gap: Restorative Justice in Theory and Practice', in A. Von Hirsch, J. Roberts, A. E. Bottoms, K. Roach and M. Schiff (eds), *Restorative Justice and Criminal Justice: Competing or Reconcilable Paradigms?* Oxford: Hart, pp. 221–36.

Daly, K. and Curtis-Fawley, S. (forthcoming) 'Restorative Justice for Victims of Sexual Assault', in K. Heimer and C. Kruttschnitt (eds), *Gender and Crime: Patterns of Victimization and Offending*. New York: New York University Press.

Daly, K. and Hayes, H. (2001) 'Restorative Justice and Conferencing in Australia', *Trends and Issues in Crime and Criminal Justice No. 186*. Canberra: Australian Institute of Criminology.

Daly, K., Curtis-Fawley, S. and Bouhours, B. (2003a) *Sexual Offence Cases Finalised in Court, by Conference, and by Formal Caution in South Australia for Young Offenders, 1995–2001: Final Report*. Brisbane: School of Criminology and Criminal Justice, Griffith University; available at: http://www.griffith.edu.au/school/ccj/kdaly.html.

Daly, K., Curtis-Fawley, S. and Bouhours, B. (2003b) *SAJJ-CJ Technical Report No. 3: Archival Study of Sexual Offence Cases Disposed of in Youth Court and by Conference and Formal Caution*. Brisbane: School of Criminology and Criminal Justice; available at: http://www.griffith.edu.au/school/ccj/kdaly.html.

Daly, K., Venables, M., Mumford, L., McKenna, M. and Christie-Johnston, J. (1998) *SAJJ Technical Report No. 1: Project Overview and Research Instruments in Year 1*. Brisbane: School of Criminology and Criminal Justice, Griffith University; available at: http://www.aic.gov.au/rjustice/sajj/index.html.

Hayes, H. and Daly, K. (2003) 'Youth Justice Conferencing and Re-Offending', *Justice Quarterly*, 20(4), 725–64.

Hopkins, Q. C. and Koss, M. (2005) 'Incorporating Feminist Theory and Insights into a Restorative Justice Response to Sex Offenses', *Violence Against Women*, 11 (5), 693–723.

Hudson, B. (2002) 'Restorative Justice and Gendered Violence: Diversion or Effective Justice?', *British Journal of Criminology*, 42, 616–34.

Kelly, L. (2001) *Routes to (In)justice: A Research Review on the Reporting, Investigation and Prosecution of Rape Cases*. London: Her Majesty Crown Prosecution Services Inspectorates (HMCPSI); available at: http://www.hmcpsi.gov.uk/reports/Rapelitrev.pdf.

Lajeunesse, T. (1996) 'Community Holistic Circle Healing, in Hollow Water Manitoba: An Evaluation'. Ottawa: Solicitor General Canada, Ministry Secretariat, unpublished report.

Morris, A. (2002) 'Critiquing the Critics: A Brief Response to Critics of Restorative Justice', *British Journal of Criminology*, 42, 596–615.

Strang, H. (2002) *Repair or Revenge: Victims and Restorative Justice*. London: Oxford University Press.

Chapter 9

Restorative justice: a healing approach to elder abuse

Arlene Groh

Abstract

Although many cases of elder abuse may be offences under the Criminal Code of Canada, relatively few come to the attention of the criminal justice system. Seniors may fear losing their relationships with abusive family members or friends if they identify mistreatment or seek assistance. In addition, allegations of abuse may be discounted by the police and by others. An innovative project in Waterloo, Ontario provides a safe environment in which to address the mistreatment of an older adult in a way that is fair and just for all concerned. Representatives from health, justice, cultural/faith and social services collaborate to provide an opportunity for change and healing to the affected people through the use of healing circles.

Introduction

Elder abuse is sometimes referred to as a 'hidden crime' (Wahl, 2000), and older abused adults may carry the secret of their mistreatment by others to their graves (Groh, 2003). Concern about this kind of tragedy led the individuals involved with the Restorative Justice Approaches to Elder Abuse Project to seek a safe, healing approach to elder abuse. The project grew from the practical experiences of the project's partners as well as a survey of the literature on elder mistreatment (e.g. Gallagher and Pittaway, 1995; Harbison, 1995; Pritchard, 1995, 1999). Experiences in practice frequently indicated cases that were believed to involve abuse or neglect, a reluctance to report the abuse or neglect on the part of both the affected seniors and service providers, a consequent failure to intervene in cases of abuse or neglect, and shared perceptions that the retributive criminal justice system failed to resolve abuse and neglect issues.

Although causing physical, financial or psychological harm to an older adult may be an offence under the Criminal Code of Canada, relatively few of these incidents come to the attention of the criminal justice system. The under-reporting of elder abuse and neglect is a common finding throughout the literature (see, for example, Health Canada, 2003; Groh, 2003). There are many reasons why seniors may not disclose abuse or neglect. Many older adults may be afraid of losing the relationship with the person who is harming them, ashamed that someone they trust has mistreated them, or believe that police and other agencies cannot help (Gordon and Verdun-Jones, 1992; Beaulieu and Spencer, 1999; Wahl, 2000). Professionals and other community members may also 'hide' the crimes. The reasons for such responses include ageist attitudes that disrespect the senior's perspective, disbelieving the older adult's story because of their supposed 'infirmity', a lack of knowledge about both what constitutes abuse and how to intervene, and a personal discomfort with the issue (Gallagher and Pittaway, 1995; Beaulieu and Spencer, 1999).

The Restorative Justice Approaches to Elder Abuse Project aims to decrease the fear among older victims of abuse and increase the community's ability to respond to abuse, by providing a safe environment within which to address abuse in a way that is fair and just for all concerned. The need to pursue alternatives to the traditional, retributive justice system is strengthened by comments like the following:

> Steps similar to those taken to combat domestic violence should be taken to combat different forms of elder abuse ... since the elderly are reluctant to use traditional legal recourse. [We recommend] full use of the provisions of Section 717 of the *Criminal Code* authorising alternative measures. If there is one area where these measures are appropriate and could be effective, it is elder abuse. Since, in most cases, older persons want not to punish their children, but rather to recover their property or reach an amicable understanding with their children, the use of these provisions, notably mediation, should be encouraged (Poirier and Poirier, 1999: 44).

About the Project

The Restorative Justice Approaches to Elder Abuse Project is a collaborative project involving several very diverse community agencies – health, justice, social services, ethno-cultural, faith and First Nations – in the Kitchener-Waterloo area of South Western Ontario.[1] This region has a large and diverse ethno-cultural community, is home to the first Victim Offender Reconciliation Program in the world, and is the home of the Waterloo Region Committee on Elder Abuse (WRCEA), a committee that, since 1992, has contributed greatly to the community's response to elder abuse.

The genesis of the Project

For over a decade, as a case manager and as a volunteer for the Waterloo Region Committee on Elder Abuse, the author has worked with older adults who are experiencing abuse. The author's experience is that seniors and family members are often reluctant to disclose abuse and are reluctant to access the available resource options, in particular the criminal justice system. The following case example is helpful in illustrating some of the issues associated with abuse cases.

Case example

Mrs Smith (pseudonym) is an 89-year-old widow who lives alone. The assistance of private and publicly funded services plus her family made it possible for her to live in her own home. One day, she disclosed that her son had taken $40,000 from her bank account. Mrs Smith was given information about various community resources including calling the police and reporting the theft. She refused these options. She said that her son was a good man. He probably needed the money more than her. Furthermore, she needed him to buy her groceries, to run errands, and to take her to church each Sunday. The relationship with her son and his family was more important to her than the $40,000.

As a case manager, the author had worked with Mrs Smith and her family for an extended period. Her son was always very attentive to his mother and the author trusted him. The disclosure of the abuse had a profound impact on those around Mrs Smith and became the impetus for the Project. A conversation with a friend who was coordinating a project using family group conferencing to address conflict and violence in local high schools planted the seed of what would become the Restorative Justice

Approaches to Elder Abuse Project. There appeared to be significant potential for a restorative justice approach for older adults experiencing abuse that would be a better way of addressing the needs of abused older adults than using the traditional criminal justice approach. However, significant questions remained unanswered. Would this holistic restorative approach that valued relationships be more acceptable to seniors? Would it remove the barriers to the identification of abuse cases? Would it be effective? Would the community be supportive? Through a community development process, a collaboration was formed with other groups and individuals and the participants applied for funding to design, implement and evaluate a restorative justice approach to elder abuse.

Theoretical framework

A broad community consultation was required to initiate and then move the project forward. This demanding first step of the consultation process was necessary to ensure that there was shared knowledge and understanding of elder abuse and restorative justice. The following sets out the mutual understandings in some core areas.

Defining elder abuse

Elder abuse was defined as the mistreatment of older adults by someone who they should be able to rely upon and trust such as a spouse, a child, another family member, a friend or a paid caregiver (WRCEA, 2000). According to Judith Wahl of the Advocacy Centre for the Elderly in Toronto (Wahl, 2000; Groh, 2003), examples of abuses that are Criminal Code offences include physical abuse such as pinching, slapping, pushing punching, and kicking; assault with a weapon; and forcible confinement (e.g. tying a person to a chair while the family is at work). Abuses that are offences also include sexual assault and financial abuses such as theft, fraud and forgery. Neglect may be a criminal offence if it involves deliberately failing to provide a dependent person with the necessities of life. Psychological or emotional abuses may include intimidation and other forms of verbal assault. Under some circumstances, mental cruelty could constitute a crime.

The causes of abuse

From a restorative justice perspective, it is important to consider why abuse happens. The root causes of abuse include a history of difficult family relationships including past abuse and a history of poor adjustment on the part of the abuser (e.g. emotional or psychiatric problems and substance abuse). Other factors may be an inability, on the part of the abuser, to sustain employment or to sustain relationships, and difficulty coping with the stress of caring for an elderly and dependent person. The social isolation of an older person may also be a factor in their abuse (WRCEA, 2000). The author's experience is that language and culture could be isolating factors for seniors.

Legal perspectives

In Canada, legislation at both the federal and the provincial levels is adequate for combating the various forms of elder abuse. However, Statistics Canada reports that it is 'suspected that only a small portion of the abuse of older adults ever comes to the attention of the justice system' (Beaulieu and Spencer, 1999: 70).

Some of the barriers to accessing the legal system that are cited in the literature (see, for example, Gordon and Verdun-Jones, 1992; Beaulieu and Spencer, 1999; Poirier and Poirier, 1999; Beaulieu et al., 2003) include the problem of 'ageism': laws that are designed specifically to protect the elderly treat older persons like children. An ageist perspective may result in the older adult being viewed as frail, dependent and incapable, and hence an unreliable witness. The difficulties involved in obtaining the evidence necessary to establish guilt beyond a reasonable doubt is another barrier. The older person may be unwilling or unable to complain to the police or to testify in court, resulting in a reluctance to prosecute. Complaints that the police are not interested in taking abuse cases to court may be related directly to the limited success of prosecutions.

Family values are another barrier to accessing the traditional criminal justice system (Gordon and Verdun-Jones, 1992; Beaulieu and Spencer, 1999; Poirier and Poirier, 1999; Health Canada, 2003). The elderly appear to refuse to report abuse to avoid hurting their abusive children. They do not sue their children because they feel it is improper, contrary to common sense and offensive to their family values. The elderly also express a desire to pass on money and property to their offspring so may not attempt to retrieve property that the latter may have stolen. Guilt and shame are other factors. The elderly person may feel guilt and shame about what has happened to them and may feel the misconduct is a reflection of their poor parenting. Fear is yet another key barrier. The older adult may be afraid that the relationship with the abuser, who may be a close family member, will be damaged if charges are laid. Finally, there is a lack of knowledge about abuse. The low incidence of reports to the police, by older adults or those who are in contact with older adults, may be because they do not realise that abuse is frequently a crime.

What is justice?

According to Dennis Cooley, '... justice means achieving a situation in which the conduct or action of individuals is considered to be fair, right and appropriate for the given circumstances' (Cooley, 1999: 17). Further, '... justice reflects our sense of right or wrong. It is called into question when our understanding of what is right is offended and is restored when wrongs are addressed' (Cooley, 1999: 17). How is justice realised with the traditional or adversarial approach to elder abuse? Consider what would have happened had Mrs Smith chosen to use the traditional criminal justice system. With the traditional or court-based approach, Mrs Smith's son would be seen as an individual who had violated a law. He stole $40,000 from his mother, which is an offence against the state. Her son would be charged with theft contrary to the Criminal Code, a Crown prosecutor would present the case to the court, which, if the son were found guilty, would impose punishment according to a set of prescribed standards. Mrs Smith could be required to testify against her son at both the preliminary hearing and the trial.

The focal point of this process is to establish whether the person who has done the harm is guilty or not guilty and to impose appropriate punishment on the guilty. Mr Smith is punished for his violation of the law, not his violation of his mother's trust. He does not have to take responsibility for his actions vis-à-vis his mother. Mrs Smith is only a witness in the process, which is focused more upon Mr Smith's violation of society's code of conduct than Mrs Smith's needs. The court has the discretionary power to order restitution. The court does not recognise that this offence is more multifaceted than the simple breaking of a rule. The root causes of the theft are complex and the ripple effect of the harm is profound because, at the end of the process, Mrs Smith and her son are estranged. He does not allow her grandchildren to visit her and other family members criticise the actions she took and ostracise her. Since she lacks the necessary supports she needs to live independently, she is forced to move out of her home and into a care facility.

Restorative justice and elder abuse

Restorative justice involves a fundamentally different approach to issues of justice and criminal justice. In *Changing Lenses*, Howard Zehr (1990) refers to the approach as a paradigm shift, while Susan Sharpe (1998), in *Restorative Justice: A Vision for Healing and Change*, sees the approach as a new philosophy or worldview. Restorative justice considers abuse primarily as a violation of people and relationships and secondarily as a violation of the law. Given restorative justice's focus on repairing the harm and restoring relationships, how might it be applied to cases of elder abuse? To help understand how a restorative approach can address elder abuse and mistreatment, key aspects of restorative justice – speaking the truth, healing and restoration, respect, the provision of equal voice and the prevention of further harm – are considered.

Speaking the truth focuses upon the ways in which abuse, and the lies and secrets that surround it, are a source of shame for those involved, perpetuate the abuse and block healing. Truth-telling about what has happened is essential, as is 'speaking from the heart' – speaking honestly about what has happened and its impact. Often secrecy is used to contain the victim's ability to speak and to act. Nils Christie in his paper 'Answers to Atrocities' writes, '... isolation of the victim is one of the major features in social systems where illegitimate violence is applied. There are no ends of attempts by oppressors to silence their victims', to which Wilma Derksen adds, '... and yet we need to have the truth known and spoken' (cited in Derksen, 2000: 135).

The healing and restoration of relationships involves the complex process of providing an opportunity for change and healing. When relationships of trust are fractured, individual counselling may be required to begin the process of healing, possibly before it is safe to bring the parties together for a circle or conference. Both the older adult and the person who has done the harm may need to gain an understanding of the dynamics around abuse, including power imbalances. The victim may require counselling to be able to identify and articulate what is needed for reparation. The person who has done the harm may require counselling to understand why he or she caused the harm and what needs to happen to change this pattern of behaviour. There needs to be an understanding of the context in which the abuse happened and insight into what may be required to transform those relationships so that each party has their 'rights to dignity, equal concern, and respect satisfied' (Lewellyn, and Howse, 1998: 39).

Respect for each participant is integral to the process and includes respect for cultural diversity, values and preferences, as well as respect for each participant's story and the choices participants make during the process. The provision of equal voice is also important. All participants in the process must have an equal voice because each voice brings a different and valued perspective to the complex issue of elder abuse. The prevention of further harm is another critical aspect. The restorative process looks to the future to determine what needs to be in place to prevent further harm and an interdisciplinary team is integral to a successful process. The cooperation of, and coordination among, professionals from several disciplines is required to support both the older adult and the person who has done the harm in their path toward healing and change.

The development of the Project

In the first months of the Project, a foundation was laid for using restorative justice with abused older adults. Restorative justice can be achieved through various practices including mediation, sentencing circles, healing circles and community conferencing. The Project team consulted with community partners, seniors, multicultural communities and faith communities to develop an appropriate approach. An extensive literature review was undertaken but no established model of restorative justice for abused older adults could be found. The Project team struggled to develop a model that would meet seniors' needs and, following consultation with key individuals in the restorative justice field (Groh, 2003),[2] the group decided that the tool or model for the restorative justice process needed to be incident driven.

In most situations, the tool used by the Project is a circle process;[3] however, it is not appropriate in all cases. In one case, 'shuttle diplomacy' was used to reach an agreement around the visiting rights for a long-time friend and neighbour of the older adult. The children had moved the older adult to a facility and had refused to allow visits. In another situation, the preparation for the circle process was sufficient to resolve the conflict and begin healing. In this case, a person with power of attorney for a capable older adult arranged for an estate sale without consulting the adult. The senior had moved to a retirement home as she required some assistance with her activities of daily living. The senior was outraged when she discovered what her attorney had done and, with the assistance of a lawyer, the estate sale was stopped. The circle facilitators worked with both the older adult and the person holding the power of attorney to prepare them for the circle. It was during this preparation that the issues were resolved and the participants decided that a circle was not required. Utilising a model that is incident driven has allowed the flexibility required to address the complex and varied needs of people affected by elder abuse.

For the restorative justice project to be an effective, safe practice it was essential for the members of the collaboration to reach a consensus on both the core values and principles that would guide the practice and on a clearly articulated mission statement. It should be noted that these principles were reviewed and supported by the Project's Seniors' Advisory Council. This Council reviews and makes recommendations regarding the activities of the Project. Council membership includes older adults from ethno-specific communities, health, business, academia, social work and community and other relevant services.

The following guiding principles have been adopted:

The Project upholds the belief that people have the right to:

- *Safety*: to live in safety and security. Parties need to be safe and need to feel safe before, during and after the restorative justice process.

- *Confidentiality*: to determine for themselves what personal information may be shared with others.

- *Dignity and respect*: to have personal values and preferences respected.

- *Autonomy*: to determine and control their own affairs.

- *Access to information*: to receive all the available information they need in order to make meaningful and informed decisions. Parties should understand the restorative justice process and the judicial process, and should be aware of community resources and how to access them, or be assisted to access them.

- *The use of the least restrictive form of intervention*: that is, least restrictive of the individual's rights, abilities and personal liberties and least disruptive of life-style (Gallagher and Pittaway, 1995: 55).

In practice, adherence to these principles includes but is not limited to the following considerations, which are framed as questions:

- *Safety*. What plan is in place to ensure that all participants are safe and feel safe before during and after the process? What measures are in place to balance power? Does the agreement include ways to prevent further abuse?

- *Confidentiality*. Have the participants determined for themselves what personal information may be shared with others? Do the participants understand the limits of confidentiality?

- *Dignity and respect*. Is there an understanding of ethno-cultural values and are these values respected? Are the participants' stories taken seriously and received without judgment by all participating in the process including police, health professionals, church workers, and court officials? Are the victim's needs for healing respected and addressed?

- *Autonomy.* Is participation in the process voluntary? Is the older adult allowed to make the maximum amount of choices/decisions possible?

- *Access to information.* Do all participants understand the restorative justice process? Do they understand the traditional judicial process? Are they aware of available community resources and how to access them?

- *Least restrictive interventions.* Has consideration been given to a solution that enables the older adult to remain in the home by providing support services? An older adult who receives support services may no longer be reliant on care from the person who has done the harm (Groh, 2003: 26–8).

The Project's mission is to provide an opportunity for change and healing to people affected by elder abuse. To illustrate how this is done, using a restorative justice process, it is useful to return to the case example of Mrs Smith.

The first step is 'intake'. A referral is made to Community Justice Initiatives (CJI), a non-profit organisation that provides services in conflict resolution in the Waterloo, Ontario, area. Trained volunteers facilitate the meetings of the people affected by the abuse of older adults.[4] Anyone affected by the abuse, including Mrs Smith, her son, health care professionals, police or community members, could initiate the referral. Screening takes place to determine whether all parties consider it safe to proceed, whether the person who caused the harm accepts responsibility for it, whether all parties are willing to participate and whether the older adult is capable of understanding and participating in the process. In the event that concerns emerge at this stage, a Screening Committee reviews the case before it proceeds.

Pre-circle

After the screening, two facilitators are assigned to the case. A facilitator contacts Mrs Smith to hear her story and to gain an understanding of the conflict. Mrs Smith might report that she is sad and angry that her son took the money because she thought that she could trust him. Lately her son has been edgy. He yells at her a lot. He seems to be drinking more. A facilitator then contacts Mr Smith to hear his side of the story. Mr Smith might say that he feels very badly about what he did. He really loves his Mom, but things have gotten out of hand. She is increasingly difficult to care for and flatly refuses to move into a retirement home. His mother, staying in her own home, is causing a fair bit of strain on his marriage. His business is also in a slump. To top it off, his own son has just moved back home because he could not find a job. All these stresses have caused him to start drinking again. He is not sure how to get things back on track.

With permission, the facilitators also contact supporters of both Mrs Smith and her son to gain a broader perspective on the situation. They may discover, for example, that Mrs Smith's minister does not know how to support the family, which has been active in the church for a long time. Mrs Smith's sister does not trust Mr Smith. Mrs Smith's daughter does not think her brother is a criminal while Mr Smith's wife did not know about the theft of money but is fed up with the hours he spends providing care to his mother.

In practice, such complexity is typical. For this reason, prior meetings with the various affected parties are essential. To prepare, the facilitators need to meet separately with the son and his supporters, as well as with Mrs Smith and her supporters. Together they decide who needs to come to the circle. For example, does the circle need a spiritual leader or a heath-care professional or someone with expertise in elder abuse? The son may need to resume attending Alcoholics Anonymous meetings, while his mother may need to find a support group that will empower her to speak about her situation. It may be weeks or months before everyone feels safe enough to come together and participate in a restorative justice circle.

The circle

Eventually, the facilitators bring everyone together. Each group of supporters sits close to the person whom they are supporting. The circle opens with a ceremony or prayer. Participants are instructed that they may speak only when holding the 'talking piece' (a feather or other symbolic object). They must speak truthfully and from the heart. Together they reach a consensus about why the situation happened, how to repair the harm and how to prevent further harm in the future. Mrs Smith may talk about her love for her son, and how sad she is that he has stolen money from her. She may admit that she is sometimes afraid of him. She speaks of prior abuse that she has suffered and of her husband having abused her son. She is sorry she was not able to prevent it. Mr Smith apologises to his mother. He knows that he has taken his frustration out on her but wants to get his life back on track. He will continue with Alcoholics Anonymous and agrees to a plan to repay the funds he misappropriated. Various supporters indicate ways in which they will be able to help. Church visitors, for example, may agree to provide caregiver relief hours for the son each Friday and the grandson each Saturday. The sister may agree to act as her mother's power of attorney in order to manage and protect her mother's financial affairs. The circle closes with a ceremony or prayer.

Post-circle

The participants are contacted three months after the circle and may report that the agreement is being followed. Mrs Smith is pleased. Her son has made regular payments to repay the money. She especially likes that her grandson comes weekly to help her. She enjoys her conversations with him. However, if Mrs Smith or other circle participants reported that the agreement was not being followed another circle might be called. In the alternative, a referral would be made to the appropriate community support service, including the traditional criminal justice system.

The role of the facilitator

Trained, skilled facilitators are the key to a successful restorative justice process. Facilitators need to be respectful of all participants, inspire trust and confidence in the process, and have the ability to create an environment of support and accountability. They also require interviewing, listening and negotiation skills. It is essential that facilitators understand and are sensitive to the complex issue of elder abuse. At the same time, they need to ensure that sensitivity does not express itself as an attempt to rescue the older adult. The facilitator cultivates humility, avoids thinking that he or she has all the answers, and avoids imposing solutions on the people affected by the abuse. Solutions that work best are the ones that the participants reach a consensus about in the circle process. The ability to prepare participants for the circle and the ability to trust the circle process are essential skills for circle facilitators and are key to an effective circle process. Facilitators contribute to a sensitive, responsive restorative justice approach when they help the group stay focused and productive by asking the right questions, ensuring that everyone present is heard and making sure that the final agreement addresses the relevant needs and is workable. They also help when they ensure that the individuals in the group, while denouncing the offending behaviour, show support of the person who offended and thus balance an ethic of care and an ethic of justice.

Project evaluation

An evaluation of the Project has been planned in order to provide feedback on whether the healing circle approach is achieving its objectives. The Project evaluation will assess the success of the Project in meeting its two main goals:

- to provide community education about the restorative justice approach to elder abuse that results in new learning and changes in attitude among participants;
- to provide intervention for clients that adheres to the principles of restorative justice and results in psychosocial benefit to the client and others.

The evaluators are using three approaches to assess the project's success: a process evaluation; evaluation of the community education initiatives; and an evaluation of client intervention outcomes (Groh, 2003). The project evaluation has experienced some difficulties. For example, it was not possible, as originally planned, to use the Minimum Data Set for Home Care screening tool to measure the victim's psychosocial status prior to intervention and any change in status post intervention. The introduction of a data collector before each circle process interfered with the process of bringing the participants to the circle.

Evaluation outcomes

Due to the changes required, evaluation outcomes are not yet available for publication, but the results of the formal evaluation will be posted on the Internet.[5] However, anecdotal feedback about the circle process is positive and encouraging. The following are examples of the comments made by participants about the circle process.

> The Restorative Justice Project for Elder Abuse has been a great resource that assists police in referring cases of elder abuse and neglect that are very personal and difficult to deal with. These cases are being dealt with in a manner that does not destroy their relationships and at the same time allows for a better understanding of the intertwining dynamics involved (Joanne Van Deursen, Domestic Violence Coordinator, Waterloo Region Police Services).

The circle process builds a powerful community that allows people to be honest with themselves and others. In an almost magical way it opens up possibilities that were never previously discussed in the family. It also helps people to recognize that there is support for them. I remember hearing one older woman tell her circle, 'I never knew that so many people loved me' (Circle facilitator).

In the circle everyone is valued. I was amazed how the circle got rid of barriers that are normally present in conflict situations. Also, very diverse comments came together at the end to create a unique and balanced perspective on the future. I found it very empowering (Circle participant).

According to Julie Friesen, former Program Coordinator of Mediation/ Conferencing Services at Community Justice Initiatives, there are many positive aspects to the model (Groh, 2003). It gets most, if not all, stakeholders involved in finding ways to move forward cooperatively. It gives a voice to the abused person; the presence of additional support persons, particularly for those individuals who have been seen as abusive, facilitates the hearing of the abused person's voice. The process can be individually tailored to different situations, cultures and preferences. The process gives dignity and respect to everyone, including the person accused of the abuse. It gives people a chance to fully explore the situation with facilitators who provide some structure and safety, an opportunity that is considered to be rare.

What is the future?

'Restorative justice is a response to conflict that brings victims, wrong-doers and the community together to collectively repair harm that has been done in a manner that satisfies their conception of justice' (Cooley, 1999: 25). As we look ahead, we continue to ask some basic questions. Is restorative justice a fair and just way to address elder abuse? Does it satisfy all participants' conceptions of justice? Does it provide an opportunity for change and healing to people affected by elder abuse?

Clearly, there are both benefits to this alternative to the formal criminal justice system and some limitations. Some of the benefits to this alternative process are as follows. The older adult has an effective voice in the process; they are able to tell their stories without interruption and these stories are listened to without passing judgment. Family values are respected; the family comes together to address the harm in a way that enables relationships to be healed. Older adults appear to be less fearful of the process when compared with the traditional criminal justice system; conflicts are addressed in the early stages, thus preventing an escalation to more serious harm. The process respects cultural diversity, values and preferences and this may be a factor in the strong interest and support from some ethno-cultural communities in the Waterloo area. There are no financial barriers to the service – it is free of charge. Requests for service are responded to within one working day and the process brings together legal, health and social services, as well as the faith and cultural communities, to provide support and to find solutions for the complex needs of people affected by elder abuse. Taken together, these benefits seem to address some of the barriers people experience with the formal criminal justice system.

With respect to the limitations, there is recognition that restorative justice is not a magic wand. Sometimes the gains seem limited and the path towards healing long and arduous. We need to be patient with the process. In addition, not all situations are appropriate for the restorative justice process. It is inappropriate to proceed when the alleged abuser is unwilling to participate or unwilling to accept responsibility for the harm done or when the older adult decides that it is not 'the right time' to proceed. Lack of cognitive capacity on the part of the victim has also been a factor in deciding that a case is inappropriate. Finally, if the people affected by the abuse do not feel safe to proceed, then the case is not appropriate for a restorative justice referral. For example, in a situation of domestic violence 'grown old', where the participants were unwilling to participate in the pre-circle work required for the process to be safe, the referral did not proceed. When cases are deemed inappropriate, they are either referred back to the traditional criminal justice system or referred to community support services.

Conclusion

The experience of the Project is that both traditional criminal justice and restorative justice have a role to play in addressing elder abuse. No single approach or service can meet the complex needs of people affected by elder abuse. The challenge is to find ways for legal, health and social services, and faith and cultural communities to work together with the people affected by elder abuse to find solutions. It is necessary to understand why older adults are abused and what is needed to repair the harm that results, to facilitate healing and to determine what must be put into place by families, communities and government to ensure the continued prevention and resolution of elder abuse. This is pivotal to building safe communities where seniors do not carry the awful secret of abuse to their graves.

The hope of the author is that the experiences of the Project will benefit other communities and be a catalyst for community specific responses. It should be noted, however, that Project model is not meant to be a blueprint for other communities. As Howard Zehr has noted:

> While the experiments, practices and customs from many communities and cultures are instructive, none can or should be copied and simply plugged into communities or societies. Rather, they should be viewed as examples of how different communities and societies found their own appropriate ways to express justice as a response to wrongdoing. These approaches may give us inspiration and a place to begin (Zehr, 2002: 62).

Notes

1   The collaboration is in the last quarter of a 4.5-year Ontario Trillium Foundation funded project to design, implement and evaluate a restorative justice approach to address elder abuse. Dr Michael Stones, Lakehead University, is directing the evaluation with Dr Rick Linden, University of Manitoba, providing consultation on restorative justice. Funding for the evaluation is from the Law Commission of Canada and Justice Canada, National Crime Prevention Centre.
2   Consultation and/or dialogue with Barry Stuart, Mark Wedge, Susan Sharpe, Rupert Ross and Mark Yantzi. A Healing Approach to Elder Abuse and Mistreatment: the Restorative Justice Approaches to Elder Abuse Project, available online: http://www.crnetwork.ca/about/elderabuse.asp p. 26.
3   Circles are a way of talking together where everyone is respected and has a chance to talk without interruption, where one can explain oneself by telling stories and where everyone is equal. No person is more important that anyone else. The circle is useful when two or more people have a disagreement, conflict or when there is a violation of a trusted relationship. The circle is a container strong enough to hold anger, frustration, joy, truth, conflict, opposite opinions and strong feelings. Everyone sits in chairs placed in a circle facing each other, without a table or other furniture between them. An object called a 'talking piece' is passed from person to person around the circle. Each person has a chance to speak when they have the talking piece. Everyone else listens without interruption until the person with the talking piece finishes and the talking piece is passed to the next person who then may speak. Respect is very important in the circle: speaking with respect and listening with respect. The circle allows us to balance ancient wisdom about being in community with

modern wisdom (Pranis et al., 2003; adapted by Eva E. Marsewski for Project facilitator training).

For a more detailed description of restorative justice practices and models, see: *A Healing River: An Invitation to Explore Restorative Justice Values and Principles* (Heartspeak Productions, 2004, DVD and CD-ROM; contact: www.heartspeakproductions.ca), Pranis et al. (2003), Sharpe (1998) and Zehr (2002).

4   For further information see Community Justice Initiatives at: http://www.cjiwr.com.

5   For further information see http://flash.lakeheadu.ca/~mstones/restorativejustice.html.

References

Beaulieu, M. and Spencer, C. (1999) *Older Adults' Personal Relationships and the Law in Canada – Legal, Psycho-Social and Ethical Aspects*. Ottawa: Law Commission of Canada.

Beaulieu, M., Gordon, R. M. and Spencer, C. (2002) *An Environmental Scan of Abuse and Neglect in Later Life in Canada: What's Working and Why?* Ottawa: Health Canada.

Cooley, D. (1999) *From Restorative Justice to Transformative Justice: A Discussion Paper*, No. JL2-6/1999. Ottawa: Law Commission of Canada.

Derksen, W. (2002) *Confronting the Horror: the Aftermath of Violence*. Winnipeg, Man.: Amity Publishers.

Gallagher, E. and Pittaway, E. (1995) *A Guide to Enhancing Services for Abused Older Canadians*. Victoria: Centre for Aging, University of Victoria.

Gordon, R. M. and Verdun-Jones, S. N. (1992) *Adult Guardianship Law in Canada*. Toronto: Thomson Carswell.

Groh, A. (2003) *A Healing Approach to Elder Abuse and Mistreatment: The Restorative Justice Approaches to Elder Abuse Project*. Waterloo, Ont.: Community Care Access Centre of Waterloo.

Harbison, J. (1999) 'Models of Intervention for 'Elder Abuse and Neglect': A Canadian Perspective on Ageism, Participation, and Empowerment', *Journal of Elder Abuse and Neglect*, 10(3/4), 1–17.

Health Canada (2003) *An Environmental Scan of Abuse and Neglect in Later Life in Canada: What's Working and Why?* Ottawa: Health Canada.

Lewellyn, J. and Howse, R. (1998) *Restorative Justice – A Conceptual Framework*. Ottawa: Law Commission of Canada.

Poirier, D. and Poirier, N. (1999) *Why Is It So Difficult to Combat Elder Abuse and, in Particular, Financial Exploitation of the Elderly*. Ottawa: Law Commission of Canada.

Pranis, K., Stuart, B. and Wedge, W. (2003) *Peacemaking Circles: From Crime to Community*. St Paul, MN: Living Justice Press.

Pritchard, J. (1995) *The Abuse of Older People: A Training Manual for Detection and Prevention*, 2nd edn. Philadelphia: Jessica Kingsley.

Pritchard, J. (1999) *Elder Abuse Work: Best Practice in Britain and Canada*. Philadelphia: Jessica Kingsley.

Sharpe, S. (1998) *Restorative Justice: A Vision for Healing and Change*. Edmonton, Alta: Victim Offender Mediation Society.

Wahl, J. (2000) *Elder Abuse: The Hidden Crime*. Toronto: Advocacy Centre for the Elderly and Community Legal Education, Ontario.

Waterloo Region Committee on Elder Abuse (2000) *Elder Abuse: What You Need to Know*. Waterloo, Ont. Available at: http://www.crnetwork.ca/about/elderabuse.asp.

Zehr, H. (1990) *Changing Lenses: A New Focus for Crime and Justice*. Waterloo, Ont.: Herald Press.

Zehr, H. (2002) *The Little Book of Restorative Justice*. Intercourse, PA: Good Books.

Chapter 10

Exploring treatment and trauma recovery implications of facilitating victim–offender encounters in crimes of severe violence: lessons from the Canadian experience

David L. Gustafson

Abstract[1]

Fraser Region Community Justice Initiatives Association (FRCJIA), a community-based non-profit organisation in Langley, British Columbia, operates a victim/offender mediation programme designed for use in crimes of severe violence. Of particular interest is the growing body of evidence demonstrating the therapeutic impact of victim–offender mediation upon the participants. Victims frequently report that this approach has contributed to their trauma recovery in profound ways, including a diminishing of severe symptoms of post-traumatic stress disorder. Offender participants also describe the process as deeply 'healing'. Therapists and prison programme facilitators have reported seeing significant increases in victim empathy and a commitment to relapse prevention in those who have participated. Other jurisdictions are implementing similar models, a number of them involving consultation, training and continuing mentoring provided by FRCJIA staff. If the results continue to be as auspicious as the first 15 years of empirical experience would indicate, these programmes will likely continue to proliferate, with significant implications for the fields of victimology, criminology and the related, rapidly developing, field of trauma studies.

Introduction

Fraser Region Community Justice Initiatives Association (FRCJIA), a community based non-profit organisation in Langley, British Columbia, operates what is believed to be the first government-authorised and funded Victim Offender Mediation Programme designed for use in crimes of severe violence. For many, the word 'mediation' suggests a dispute that can be settled, as in the term 'settlement-driven mediation'. With cases involving harms as grievous as those that are referred to this programme, 'settlement' is not usually what motivates participants to become involved. In lesser crimes, fiscal or other restitution might be sought or offered and make good sense but when the magnitude of the personal harms suffered makes it impossible to restore losses and balance the 'scales of justice', are there, nevertheless, symbolic and practical amends that can be made? Are there justice-making 'currencies' other than the amount of prison time served by which an offender's 'debt' can be paid? Are there justice-making processes that could maximise the opportunities for exchanges of information, participation, dialogue and mutual consent between victims and offenders (Zehr and Mika, 1998)? Might those same processes, coupled with an understanding of trauma recovery, enable healing and prove to be truly restorative for victims, offenders[2] and the families and communities from which they come? These are some of the questions that have been explored over the programme's history and for which this chapter may suggest some answers.

This chapter briefly describes research undertaken in 1989 with victims/survivors and prisoners that led to the development of the programme. A case study involving an adult male survivor of child sexual abuse and presented in his own voice will help illustrate the process as well as the healing outcomes for this crime trauma survivor, for the members of his family and for the offender. Some of the issues the case study raises will be explored, notably the nature of trauma and how facilitated dialogue can assist the journey to recovery. First, however, a review of the history of the programme is presented, beginning with the research findings upon which the 1990 programme proposal was based. The attitudes demonstrated and the views expressed by respondents in that study raise significant questions about commonly held myths about offenders and victims.

Debunking the myths

A number of unhelpful myths cling tenaciously to notions of face-to-face victim offender encounter in serious crime. Victims of serious personal crimes (we are led to believe) are satisfied to have the system apprehend, determine guilt, sentence and mete out punishment, and are content to have no active part in the process beyond that of appearing as the witnesses necessary to prove that the accused did indeed offend against the laws of the state in the matter before the court. This myth holds that victims would have no desire, need or interest in ever again meeting or speaking with the offender who caused them harm, except to do vengeance. Offenders (we are led to believe) are, similarly, 'of one stripe', except that they are usually characterised as remorseless, ravaging, animalistic and beyond redemption. Offenders, this view would hold, could only want to meet their victims in the hopes of avenging their convictions or gaining information and an opportunity for even greater mischief.

Given scenarios such as these, the state would have a clear responsibility to prevent further harm and, in attempting to do so, would have to ensure that victims and offenders are given no further opportunity to interact. But to what degree are these stereotypical notions actually held by these individuals and to what degree are they, instead, assumed and imposed upon them?

In the Fall of 1988, research was conducted into the attitudes of those most impacted by serious and violent crime concerning how they might feel about the need for an avenue of safe communication or interaction with the offender, including the need for a facilitated face-to-face meeting. It was decided to interview Canadian prisoners convicted of the most serious federal crimes and the survivors of those same offences to see how each might respond to the tenets of restorative justice and to the notion of participating in a facilitated victim–offender dialogue in cases involving harms of this magnitude. At the conclusion of the study, the findings were reported to the Ministry of the Solicitor General, Canada (Gustafson and Smidstra, 1989).

First, the researchers reviewed the files of all the prisoners placed in British Columbia, Lower Mainland federal institutions during the last six months of 1988 and listed those prisoners sentenced for serious crimes. Of the original 62 prisoners committed to federal prisons[3] during that period, 31 had committed violent personal crimes and, therefore, fit the criteria for the study. These individuals were available for interviewing and none refused to be interviewed.

The researchers then contacted the victims/survivors of these same crimes, beginning with a carefully worded letter and enclosure from the Ministry of the Solicitor General of Canada that made it clear that the study was authorised and genuine, and inviting their participation. The letter asked those interested to contact the researchers to arrange a personal interview. Child victims were not contacted, and two individuals were eliminated from the study because file information indicated that contact might cause undue stress. Of the 30 victims/survivors contacted, only two declined to be interviewed.

The primary goal of the study was to look at how crime trauma survivors, and those responsible for the harms they suffered, felt about the prospect of a face-to-face meeting convened by a skilled facilitator and conducted in a safe and secure setting such as a prison. If the subjects responded positively to the idea of such a meeting, they were invited to share the benefits they thought such a meeting would provide for the victim, the offender, the justice professionals working with them and the wider community. If the subjects responded negatively they were asked to expand upon their responses, sharing specific concerns that would preclude their own involvement and, more generally, listing the concerns they would want to see addressed if such a programme were to be developed.

Offender responses

Of the 31 prisoners interviewed, 27 indicated that they would choose to meet with the victims of their offences if such a programme were available. Of the four who would refuse a meeting, three indicated that they would do so having despaired of ever salvaging the familial relationship involved. Only one was philosophically opposed to the notion and would not meet a victim under any circumstances.

Often, prisoner respondents expressed an unanticipated sensitivity regarding the potential benefits to the victim of a facilitated face-to-face encounter. A number of prisoners felt that if they were the victim, they would find it extremely helpful to hear the offender say that he took responsibility for his offence, had no intention of trying to seek them out to 'punish' them for assisting in his conviction and felt a need to work at 'making it right' to the greatest possible degree.

Offenders indicated that, in the great majority of cases (27 out of 31, or 87 per cent), they felt the need for a personal encounter with their victims. To be seen by the victim as human rather than as the ravaging animal as portrayed by the courts was a commonly expressed need. Others felt the need to express remorse, to apologise and to ask the victim for forgiveness. One inmate had the insight to see that he could never pay the debt owed his victim if he simply and passively accepted his incarceration as 'paying his debt to society' and that more was required of him. He recognised that there was no way he could have escaped incarceration, but would have welcomed the opportunity to pay as much as possible of his debt to the one to whom it was due, by negotiating a consensual agreement, face to face, in the context of the prison, with his victim(s) and a facilitator trained for the purpose. A number of prisoners listed ways in which they felt they would derive benefit if the situation had been reversed, and they had been the victim of the crime they had committed. Many felt that such a meeting would help dispel fears about their intentions, especially towards the victim and the witnesses, upon release and would provide greater hope of their successful community reintegration.

Victim responses

In addition to feeling a good deal of anger, a number of victims felt considerable frustration at having no place in the criminal justice process to personally express their hurt and anger to the offender or to ask questions that continued to plague them, in some cases, for a number of years following the offence. While many felt a need to express their feelings to the offender, the researchers were struck by how few of the victims continued to feel vengeful. Most felt that neither personal vengeance nor the state's retribution would serve as a meaningful therapy for their grief or loss. The majority of victims (17 of 28), including those who had suffered severe personal trauma, indicated that they did, indeed, want to meet with their offenders, and considered such a meeting to be helpful, if not crucial, to their personal recovery and ability to bring an additional measure of 'closure'[4] to the offence.

The other 11 victims indicated that they would choose not to meet their offenders, but their reasons for declining were instructive. Two of the victims qualified their responses by saying that they agreed with the *concept* of a face-to-face meeting between victim and offender, but did not feel it necessary for themselves in the present circumstances. Four other victims who declined a meeting indicated that they would be willing to meet 'if the crime had been more serious' (two respondents), 'if the offender was young and remorseful' (one respondent) or if they were given 'more time to recover' (one respondent).

Of the 28 victims interviewed, only five (18 per cent) felt that they would derive no benefit from a facilitated face-to-face meeting with the offender in a crime as serious as the one recently committed against them, and would be unwilling to meet the perpetrator under any circumstances. The victim respondents, in the majority of cases (82 per cent), felt that there would be substantial benefit in developing what was then described as a 'victim–offender mediation programme' for addressing a victim's needs in serious crimes. At least three victims indicated that they would feel a need to participate in a face-to-face dialogue with the offender if the offence had been more serious and their experience of personal trauma greater.

The responses given by victims and offenders in this study ran counter to the following tenaciously held beliefs:

- the great majority of serious criminal offences are committed against victims by complete strangers; the research showed that almost one third of the offender respondents (15 out of 48) were well known to their victims;

- the belief that victims of serious crime could not possibly want to see or interact with the perpetrator(s) of the crimes except, perhaps, for the purposes of revenge;

- the belief that violent offenders are too addicted, too evil, or too lacking in empathy to be concerned about their victims or willing to be held to account for the harms suffered by them;

- the belief that the more serious the offence, the more essential it must be to ensure that victims and offenders are never provided an opportunity to interact in *any* forum;

- the belief that personal and public safety, as well as the safeguarding of prisoner rights and freedoms, necessitates the increase of the role of the state in the justice process, requiring that procedural and philosophical wedges be driven between victims and perpetrators even if it means denying them both a voice and agency if they express a desire for any role other than those scripted and provided for them in an adversarial system.

It was concluded that, from the viewpoint of the people most impacted by crimes – the victims and offenders – it would not only be *feasible* to create opportunities for therapeutic dialogue between trauma survivors and those responsible for the harms but that this could prove to be, as respondents anticipated, 'tremendously important', 'healing' and 'useful in a high percentage of cases'. FRCJIA set out, therefore, to develop a pilot project that would allow the use of a facilitated therapeutic dialogue model constructed specifically for cases of violent personal crime. The project was to include an independent evaluation that could help determine whether such programming should be made available on a wider and continuing basis.

Implementation of the model

Based, in large part, upon what had been heard during the research, a model programme was designed and funding obtained for a two-year pilot period. The programme was implemented throughout the Correctional Service of Canada Pacific Region (covering British Columbia and the Yukon Territory) in 1990. An independent evaluation conducted at the end of the pilot phase by a respected criminal justice programme researcher found 'unanimous support' for the programme's approach from both victim and offender participants. The evaluator concluded that

> ... it is clear that the Victim Offender Mediation Programme has had profound and positive impacts on the lives of both offenders and victims involved. It is an extraordinarily sensitive, complex and demanding process ... [which] has been valued extremely highly by all of the participants (Roberts, 1992: 35).

This evaluation, and another, larger, study that replicated the findings three years later (Roberts, 1995), supported the continuation of funding. From 1990 to the present almost 350 cases have been referred involving the most serious offences in the Canadian Criminal Code: those for which sentences range from two years to 'life'.

Referral sources

Victim/survivor referrals are received from victims/survivors themselves, from their therapists, from victim serving agencies and from victim liaison coordinators in prisons. Institutionally generated referrals are received on behalf of prisoners from staff working closely with them. Programme staff members screen the referrals and, if accepted, begin the, often lengthy, process of tailoring each case approach in keeping with the needs of the participants. Most cases in which participants go beyond the initial exploratory meetings with FRCJIA staff ultimately proceed to a facilitated face-to-face encounter. The same male-female staff team is responsible for all the work with participants from the initial meetings through the facilitated dialogues and the aftercare of participants.

Impacts and outcomes

Of particular interest, is the growing body of empirical evidence demonstrating the therapeutic impact of this approach upon both victims and offenders. A good deal of that impact is attested to by professionals working with the participants and, in some cases, accompanying them from start to finish through the process. Victims frequently report that the approach and its processes have contributed to their trauma recovery in profound ways, often manifesting in diminished symptoms of severe post-traumatic stress disorder (PTSD). Offender participants also describe the process as deeply 'healing'. Therapists and prison programme facilitators have reported seeing significant increases in victim empathy, increases in commitment to treatment and to relapse prevention in offenders who have participated in this programme and this appears to be supported by recidivism studies that are underway. Other jurisdictions in Canada, the United States and Europe are implementing similar models, a number of them involving consultation and training provided by FRCJIA. If results continue to be as auspicious as they have been in the first 15 years of empirical experience, these programmes will likely continue to proliferate, with significant implications for the fields of victimology, criminology and the related, rapidly developing, field of trauma studies.

Trauma

A premise from the author's 'conceptual baggage'[5]

Anthony's story, the case study that follows, illustrates within the space allowed in one chapter, how a case might proceed and some of the outcomes of the kind described above. At the outset, however, it is important to make explicit a premise that over 20 years of experience with trauma survivors demonstrates is critical. The premise is as follows:

> Until we have at least a working understanding of trauma and its impacts, we are stumbling in the dark in any attempt to bring about lasting healing, transformation and change in lives where harms have been as serious as these. It is clearly possible to see significant gains in the occasional case without such understanding, but victim–offender dialogue processes for crimes of severe violence are unlikely to accomplish what they might if facilitators had a thorough grounding in trauma and the post-traumatic syndromes.

It is not suggested that everyone who embarks upon work in this field as a dialogue facilitator must be a credentialled therapist. It is suggested, however, that virtually all survivors of severe trauma grapple with the following questions:

- 'What is it about traumatic experience that keeps me so *stuck* in painful memories?'

- 'Why do these memories so powerfully persevere, constantly reiterate, and bind me anew with each appearance?'

- 'Why is it so difficult to break free, to transcend that painful experience and begin to thrive again?'

- 'Why is it that I feel such responsibility, such enormous shame, when I am the innocent victim and all the shame ought to be on the shoulders of the perpetrator?'

- 'Is there reason to hope that I will ever be free of this bondage, and experience freedom and well-being once more?'

Facilitators who understand the dialectic of trauma start with a distinct advantage in helping address questions such as these, and more. Without taking responsibility, as professional therapists, for each client, a dialogue facilitator familiar with trauma and its manifestations can:

- help normalise the participant's experience of post-traumatic symptoms;

- knowledgeably explore with participants whether a victim–offender mediation process is suitable for them and, if so, how to tailor a process most likely to prove helpful in addressing their specific needs;

- insightfully engage with participants to assess when to move ahead and when to slow or halt the dialogue process in order to allow participants time to process and integrate new information;

- knowledgeably collaborate with counsellors or other treatment professionals (if they are involved) to ensure that the participant has the necessary supports and that the dialogue process itself proves to be empowering and healing for all involved parties rather than problematic and destructive;

- more ably 'companion' the trauma survivor in appropriate ways on this stage of their healing journey.

Offender participants can also have complex questions concerning their own behaviours. Answers may prove elusive, but an offender's sincere grappling with the questions can, in itself, be meaningful to victim/survivor participants. A sampling, gathered over years of practice, include the following:

- 'How did I allow my life to get so far out of control that I acted in the way I did, creating such painful consequences for my victims, for myself, for our families and loved ones?'

- 'How did I get power, shame, sexuality and rage so badly cross-wired?'

- 'Why did I purposefully select victims who share so many characteristics?'

- 'How did I get so 'bent' that I could believe that shaming and degrading someone else would rid me of my own sense of shame and degradation?'

- 'Is there any way back from crippling guilt to innocence? Back from Hell to Eden? I feel forever barred, and I'm desperately homesick for the Garden.'

Programme participants state that it is not therapeutic competence so much as the ethic of care, the values that undergird it and the relational bonds formed, that are fundamental to effectiveness in this work. Nevertheless, they highly value as well the fact that their facilitators are well informed and possess relevant education and experience in working with trauma survivors and violent offenders, alike. The dialogue facilitator can never become an expert in the lived experience of the participants any more than the finest therapist can, but facilitators can become expert, trusted, process guides. And the more knowledgeable the guide, the more likely it is that all will make a safe passage.

The 'pillars' of well-being

Psychologist Robert Johnson (1990) suggests that human 'well-being' rests on three primary pillars: 'safety', 'autonomy' and 'relatedness'. In the life of an adult who experiences well-being, these 'pillars' have been built, brick by brick, from childhood onwards. Such fortunate adults experience safety not only as freedom from negative things such as physical, emotional/ psychological or spiritual violence, but as a secure, grounded positive: the enjoyment of relative safety and freedom from serious threat to life or bodily integrity. Similarly, autonomy is not simply freedom from another's domination but, rather, the freedom and ability to exercise choices, power and agency as a free and independent being. The 'relatedness pillar' recognises the importance of relationships, of healthy mutual interdependencies and the degree to which we, as social beings, thrive when our primary relationships are healthy, caring ones and languish when they are not.

Well-being can be fragile, however. These pillars can be shaken and shattered in an instant by accidents, natural disasters, criminal violence or political aggression. Then, too, for those who have experienced significant abuse or chronic aversive experience through childhood and/or adolescence, for the desperately poor, the refugee, the sexual abuse survivor, for the victim of totalitarian subjugation in domestic life or religious cult, for the survivor of long exposure to war trauma – combatant or not – well-being may be an elusive dream. The pillars that would undergird it may never have been built in the first place.

Trauma can, and does, interfere with one's ability to successfully resolve and master the developmental challenges associated with maturation at each stage of the life cycle. In his book, *Childhood and Society*, Erik H. Erickson (1963) posited a set of eight primary challenges to be resolved through the successive stages of human development from infancy to old age, further suggesting that a successful resolution of each new challenge is predicated upon a resolution of the previous one. It takes little imagination to see what societal havoc might be wreaked if trauma caused substantial numbers of people in our communities to fail to resolve Erikson's eight challenges in favour of the positive character traits and assets mentioned in each set: (1) trust vs. mistrust; (2) autonomy vs. shame and doubt; (3) initiative vs. crippling guilt; (4) industry vs. inferiority; (5) confident, realistic self-identity vs. role and identity confusion; (6) intimacy, appropriate bonding and attachments vs. isolation and exclusivity; (7) generativity[6] and other directedness vs. selfishness and self-absorption; and (8) the integrity, wisdom and contentedness of mature old age vs. emptiness, disillusionment and despair.

The focus of this chapter is on crime-created trauma, but it is essential to recognise that the experience of both crime victims and criminal offenders is often replete with earlier layers of traumatic experience, complicating the recovery journey for both and, though this is never deterministic, often proving to be criminogenic across generations.

The impact of traumatic events

The 'pillars' metaphor discussed above is a simple, accessible one, but it is also profound in its implications. The safety, autonomy and relatedness themes find frequent expression in the best available trauma and recovery literature. Traumatic events shatter the integration of what trauma researcher and specialist Mardi Horowitz (1986) calls 'inner schemata': one's view of the self in relation to the outer world; and one's personal systems of self-preservation (safety), control (autonomy), connectedness (relatedness), meaning and belief. When escape is impossible, when action proves to be of no avail, helplessness and horror simply overwhelm all human self-defense mechanisms. When one is taken by surprise, trapped, physically harmed, sexually violated, threatened with death or witness to extreme violence and/or grotesque death, the entire complex system of self-defence strategies, actions and beliefs about one's self-preservation can become fragmented.

Despite having proven useless as self-defence at the moment of (or over the duration of) the trauma that has been suffered, each of the components of one's self-preservation strategies tend to become concretised. The survivor clings to those strategies, though in their now altered, highly exaggerated states, hyper-vigilant, instantly mobilised to fight or to flee for their life long after the immediate danger and cause of the traumatic symptoms is gone. Self-protective behaviours that might have been effective in less overpowering circumstances proved useless during the crushing, traumatic incident. Yet those strategies continue to be tested by the trauma survivor, for decades in extreme cases, in the hope that they will avail sometime soon. The very behaviours invoked to protect the self, to save life and preserve sanity, now appear to have joined forces with the enemy. They sap life energies in the desperate struggle to adapt to the trauma. Worse, given the apparent uselessness and inappropriateness of these behaviours in the face of what is no longer immanent, real danger but 'only' psychic and imagined danger, each new iteration of symptoms is experienced by the survivor, and often their supporters, as quite crazy-making.

Trauma knows no gender

In her landmark book, *Trauma and Recovery*, Judith Lewis Herman (1997) compares the post-trauma experience of female rape survivors and male combat veterans, providing powerful arguments for why we should end, forever, any notion that post-traumatic stress disorder is a female malady.[7] Male combat veterans, even the toughest, most courageous 'Rambos' among elite combat units, when exposed to prolonged combat exposure or traumatic incidents suffer the same symptoms as female rape survivors and are as likely to be diagnosed with PTSD. In fact, Herman points out, in the Henden and Haas study[8] of Vietnam veterans with post-traumatic stress disorder, 19 per cent had made suicide attempts and 15 per cent reported being 'constantly preoccupied with suicide': almost precisely the percentages reported for rape survivors. As Herman reported:

> The veterans suffered from unresolved guilt about their wartime experiences and from severe, unremitting anxiety, depression, and post-traumatic symptoms. Three of the men died by suicide before the study was completed (Herman, 1997: 50).

Trauma knows no gender. In fact, there is a suggestion that the 'Rambos' have been socialised into a type of masculinity that makes it difficult, if not almost impossible, for them to seek help and to talk about personal difficulties. There was a time, and not so long ago, when soldiers manifesting signs of 'shell shock' or 'combat neurosis' would have been discharged and their files stamped IMF ('Insufficient Moral Fibre'). Despite changes in such attitudes and advances in treatment methods the symptoms exhibited by many war trauma survivors tend to be highly resistant to treatment. We wonder how many combat veterans end up in prisons by virtue of unresolved trauma. Similarly, we wonder how many young male trauma survivors, with no combat training or experience but socialised into those same kinds of masculinities, end up warring against someone and something, creating a new generation of victims by virtue of their own unresolved trauma and their inability to talk about it.[9] Far too often, we meet the young 'Anthonys', the male survivor of child sexual abuse whose story appears below, not in a clinical counselling setting or as colleagues in the community, but in federal prisons, having committed enormous harms against another. Anthony is clear that it is only by fortune that his former high-risk behaviours, especially the need for the exhilaration of high speed, did not result in serious injury or death to himself and others before he began to understand, and take charge of, his own behaviours.

PTSD criteria and diagnostics

As Herman (1997) points out, traumatic incidents of the magnitude that cause PTSD '... usually involve threats to life or bodily integrity or a close personal encounter with violence and death ... evoking feelings of intense fear, helplessness, loss of control, and threat of annihilation' (ibid.: 50). No matter what the source of severe trauma, '... the very "threat of annihilation" that defined the traumatic moment may pursue the survivor long after the danger has passed. No wonder that Freud found, in the traumatic neurosis, signs of a "daemonic force at work." The terror, rage, and hatred of the traumatic moment live on in the dialectic of trauma' (ibid.).

As part of this discussion, two diagnostic instruments for post-traumatic stress disorder are included: one, the accepted instrument from the Diagnostic and Statistical Manual of Mental Disorders (DSM-IV)[10] (see Appendix 'A' to this chapter); the other, a diagnosis for Complex PTSD proposed by Herman (1997: 121) in *Trauma and Recovery* (see Appendix 'B' to this chapter). Herman's 'proposed diagnostic' is included because, due to the duration of exposure to the trauma, it has particular relevance to the case study included in this chapter. European readers will see important similarities between Herman's criteria and the World Health Organisation (WHO) PTSD diagnostic criteria that are used in Europe, both of which suggest important elements for possible future revisions to the DSM-IV criteria.

These instruments are not included here, however, to suggest that dialogue facilitators should use them to diagnose potential programme participants. Rather, these diagnostics provide criteria and language useful for the entire trauma discussion, and certainly for the remainder of the present one. They are also highly relevant for understanding the experience of most trauma survivors, on both sides of the prison's walls, and because, in a sense, there is an element of 'good news' about them, strange as that may seem.

The good news

Most of the diagnoses of 'mental disorders' in the DSM-IV describe what is 'wrong' with the sufferer. The PTSD diagnosis, on the other hand, normalises the trauma survivor's experience of these symptoms, suggesting that *any* normal person who had suffered a similar trauma would likely exhibit the cluster of symptoms. A PTSD diagnosis is not so much about what is 'wrong' with the trauma survivor as it is about *what happened to them*, and what continues to happen to them as they attempt to adapt to highly traumatic experiences. Put another way, the trauma survivor's behaviours are not so much about their pathology as about their history.[11]

As trauma therapist Joe Solanto points out, '… treatment begins with education.'[12] Imagine what it might mean to you if you had suffered a severe trauma just to have a relevant listener create sufficient safety to enable you to tell your story perhaps over and over again, understanding that you literally need to tell the story until you no longer need to tell the story. Imagine what it might mean to you to have a facilitator provide sufficient safety, choice and relational support to enable you to share even your secret anxieties concerning whether your symptoms indicate that you may be going insane; to have them respectfully listen, then normalise your behaviours on the basis of an accepted scientific instrument that assists you to see that not only are you not crazy, but that your symptoms are indicative of health and normalcy. That alone would have significance, but on the trauma recovery journey, it is only the beginning. Every process invoked, every intervention, must support the necessary recovery work of the survivor: 'establishing safety, reconstructing the trauma story and restoring the connection between survivors and their community' (Herman, 1997: 3).

Anthony's story[13]

'It was either, I kill myself, or I feel something.'

Anthony was six when his parents divorced. He was ten when his mother died in a car crash. The night after Anthony's mother died, Denny, the hired hand and trusted family friend who had been in the family since Anthony was born, began to sexually abuse him, beginning what Anthony once described as 'six years of sexual slavery'. Anthony's older sister became guardian to the children, 10-year-old Anthony and his three sisters, upon their mother's death. Bit by bit, Denny, the trusted hired hand, began to divide the sisters, convincing them that Anthony was a problem child who needed the discipline that he, the only father figure in this devastated family, could provide. At age 16, Anthony ended the abuse, suddenly aware that he had grown much taller and physically stronger than Denny. But the ramifications of that abuse did not end there. Anthony became aware that he had significant problems. Though longing to be a social person, he isolated himself. Though very bright, he languished and was chastised by teachers in his private school for being uninvolved, 'skimming along the surface'. They had no awareness of the reasons, nor was there safety, anywhere, for him to disclose. Anthony was in tremendous pain, but he suppressed it. He did not feel pain as others did.

Anthony shared his story and his experience of the Victim Offender Mediation Programme in a small conference setting during the International Alliance of Holistic Lawyers (IAHL) Conference in Vancouver a few years ago. The italicised sections below are verbatim comments taken from his story:

> *I remember knowing at the age of nineteen that something was very wrong because I walked up to a car windshield, leaned over and hit it as hard as I could without breaking my fist and not feeling pain. Seeing my knuckles red and raw and feeling no pain, and talking to a friend and going: 'I don't understand this; I don't get this ...' I used to be able to walk up to brick walls and just hammer on them and feel no pain and I never understood it.*

Anthony was diagnosed with four serious ulcers and decided it was time to get some help. He decided that making a police report and holding his abuser to account that way might be part of the answer. The police took his statement. The transcript ran to 54 pages. Of the scores of offences, the Crown decided to proceed on three, and the trial went ahead:

I felt, in some ways, vindicated ... that I'd been able to get up and tell my story and let the truth be known, and that my family was bonding together, but in some ways I felt very unsatisfied with what the court system had to offer ... I felt used ... unimportant ... the designated witness [despite the] judge's attempts to make me feel that this was about me.

Knowing that the sentence was entirely a matter for the judge to decide, Anthony, nevertheless, asked Crown counsel to request that the court sentence Denny to six years in prison: the equivalent of the number of years he had suffered abuse at Denny's hands. Instead, Denny was sentenced to three years and placed in a federal correctional institution where there was at least some hope of him getting appropriate treatment.

Meanwhile, Anthony also went into therapy although, with the exception of the first six months, entirely at his own expense. His first two highly priced helpers, Anthony reports, were of little help to him. About a year and a half after Denny's sentencing and incarceration, a psychologist who led sex offender treatment groups in the prison called the Victim Offender Mediation Programme office to explore the possibility of referring Denny. She had seen profound progress among a number of survivors of sexual assault referred to the programme. 'I don't know how Anthony will respond to this idea,' she said, 'but it may be that he would find it helpful to hear what Denny is saying, now that he has moved out of his denial, is taking responsibility for his offences, has some victim empathy and some sense of the damage he has inflicted on this young man.'

A letter and a programme brochure were sent to Anthony and he was asked to call the programme if he felt the approach might have something to offer him. Anthony was using his sister's mailing address at the time. His brother-in-law opened the letter, read it and discussed with Anthony's sister whether they should throw it in the garbage or give it to him. His sister gave it to him. Anthony understood his brother-in-law's motivation as protective, yet is very clear that well-intended attempts of this sort on the part of relatives to protect victims do anything *but* serve or protect them. On the contrary, Anthony says, such attempts can be another form of victimisation, keeping information and options from victims and, therefore, impinging on their autonomy. Anthony's choices had been denied through the abuse; he was not about to have that continue. Despite being somewhat concerned that the programme might prove to be staffed by 'religious nuts' with a message for him 'to simply forgive', Anthony invited the programme facilitators to attend one of his therapy sessions to explore, together with his counsellor, what participation in the programme might have to offer him:

I was initially sceptical. Dave and Eric came and met me. I was concerned that this was going to be about pressure to forgive. I'm not a violent person but I was not interested in forgiving at that point. I had had no opportunity to sit down and say, this is what you did to me, you son of a bitch; this is what happened, these are the effects. I was in no way given that opportunity. Sitting up on the witness stand, being able to look out over the courtroom and at the top of his head ... to be cross examined and have all the truths drawn out of me was relieving on a lot of levels because it was finally out, but it was not sitting one-on-one being able to say, this, or these, are the cause and effects. That was not the point of the trial at all. Rather it was about can you substantiate these things and are they relevant?

Meeting with Dave and Eric they suggested, 'you don't have to meet directly with him ... you can send us a letter, or a videotape, Denny will respond via videotape and we can take it from there'. So I said, sure. I drew up a letter of several questions and, in fact, the first question was, do you accept responsibility for sexually abusing me? Do you acknowledge that you sexually abused me for six years? If he replied to that and said, Yes, I do, then, that's fine; there were a series of other questions that were just little hurdles. I wanted to see where his mind was: if he was actually interested in being truthful about it or if it was just another attempt to be manipulative and get back in contact with me, as he had tried to do after I ended the abuse.

I wanted to know where his accountability lay in all of this. What did he feel he was responsible for? He was the adult; he should have known better. He made a conscious decision to get into this. I wanted him to accept responsibility for his actions. I wanted him to sit there and listen to me, and hear all the feelings, emotions that he put me through and for him to accept responsibility. I wanted to take all of that he had put on to me and give it back to him, and to say, I've carried this with me for so many years and this is yours now. You can deal with this.

This was obviously very important to me. I was in the middle of one of the most demanding parts of my school year, but when Dave and Eric brought Denny's video taped response back I determined to go through with the next step: a face-to-face meeting. I took a weekend off and flew to [an interior city] to meet with him. I remember that morning thinking, Holy... shit ... I am walking into a room with this person that has dominated so much of my life, that is almost this mythical figure because of the power that he had over me and the ways that he's affected my life ... and I'm going to sit down at a table with this creature, thing, person ... and ... attempt to communicate.

This brings us to the healing part of it. I really didn't want to get my hopes up too much because I wasn't really sure what would come out of it, but what I wanted to do, basically, is just cleanse myself ... it is a cleansing process ... to take what I had visualised as all the blackness that was under

209

the surface and I felt dominated my soul at that time…to purge it, get it out and just let my mind and body and soul be free of all of the damage that he had done and just be free: take it all out and throw it on the table and go, this belongs to you. This ugly piece of green, vinyl, tacky-ass luggage, full of crap, is yours. Take it home, it's a gift from me. Do with it what you will. So what I was able to do, sitting down, is just verbalise it, let everything out. I had let go of a lot of hate and anger at that point. I was able to let a lot of that go because that dominated my life for so long, manifesting itself in ways that – I played rugby for a lot of years which was probably a little bit of a godsend because it enabled me to get out so much aggression. It was probably the only thing that kept me sane for so long.

So what I did is, for 2½ hours that morning, I sat there and just laid everything out. Told him how he made me feel, about the shame he had brought upon me. How really the basis of what he had done was essentially rob me of my childhood. Take me and for six years make me a slave to him in terms of his sexual needs and in terms of dominating my life. I felt that is what I was for six years: a slave, to him. I had no identity of my own, I had no life of my own, I had no dreams of my own and I had no hopes of my own. I had to let him know that, what I went through. I was a ten-year-old kid who lost his mother, and the night after I lose my mother, you start preying upon me and after that my life was entirely changed. Childhood did not exist, bonding with friends was very difficult; basically, I withdrew from life.

He had pushed Anthony, the person, back so far, and had only left this physical shell that he had wanted to take pleasure in, and it was very hard for me to understand the person that I was and to bring that person into the foreground and say, this is who I am. Before that I was a shell; just a hollow shell walking around, making my way, stumbling my way through the dark trying to figure out what was going on, having no real idea what went on in life.

And, at the end of it I found that we had gone through so much that I was at a point where I could forgive him, and that was the one thing that surprised me beyond anything: that I had this ability in me, all of a sudden, to forgive this person and to say, I'm done with this. And that is where I got the closure from, and that is what was very important to me, to be able to get some closure. It was the sort of thing that dominated my life for so long, and will always be a part of my life, but at that point it was what everything else spread from. A lot of my problems came from it … and it was just at the core of my life at that point. And getting the closure was very important to me. It was finally being able to put this to rest and say I've dealt with it as fully as I can and to the best of my abilities and to be able to – let everything out, face-to-face, and give it to the person who is responsible for it. Not in the *separated way that happens in a court room: that follows procedures, laws, prosecutor and defense counsel calling each other my learned friend. It was the one-on-one dealing with each other that finally allowed me to get everything out, to pass it on, to say: this is how everything affected me, this is what you did to me, this is how it still affects me, this is what you did to my family.*

And that is another important point. My family was able to get a lot out of this as well. At one point, Dave brought the videotape that we had done of the face-to-face dialogue meeting – about four and a half hours – to my house. I was able to get my family together, three of my four sisters and we put the videotape on. It was about an eight-hour process, from three in the afternoon 'til eleven o'clock at night when everybody left. My family was able – because this affected them – my family was finally able to get some closure out of it. He was in my family since I was born, he was in my family while they were growing up. But it was also like a drop in a pool, the shock waves spread out. It affected my oldest sister because she was my guardian. The first thing he did was distance me from her … take down the walls of family. He befriended my second oldest sister so he could gain access to me, gain their trust so that they would send me to him because I was 'a problem child'. And they were young and inexperienced and couldn't deal with it … [One sister] needed to understand whether he was truly a friend to her or simply using her … [Another] needed to get rid of the guilt associated with it, to realise it's not hers to bear, so she could let that go, and my youngest sister just – I think just – had a sense of pride in me in what I'd gone through and overcome.

So, it was very good, and it continues on until this day, where the person I'm very much in love with, she wants to see the video to see what I've been through, to understand me more as a person. So, it keeps on going. For me it is just the ability to say it no longer dominates my life, and it no longer defines who I am … it will no longer be the sole definition of who I am. I am able, now, to move on; to move toward the understanding of what makes me happy, what defines my life, what creates me, what inspires me. It's become in perspective. It's become a chapter in my life. This is always very hard for me to say, but the thing that really struck me is afterward, E looked at me and said, 'You're no longer a victim; you're a survivor'. And that is what I am today, a survivor of the abuse, of the criminal justice process, and now I'm just able to move on, to gather up my family, and my friends, and move on with my life.

Anthony finished his post-secondary education, married the young woman he spoke about, and now works in a fast-paced, demanding industry. He is clearly a powerful and effective young man, without a vestige of the shame that once so weighed him down and diminished him.

Denny continues to live successfully in the community. He sees the entire victim–offender mediation process – the preparation meetings, the face-to-face dialogues and the debriefing and aftercare – as powerful and vitally important in both his life and in Anthony's. Denny had worked hard at his prison treatment programmes and had been particularly motivated in them when it became clear that Anthony had agreed to participate in victim–offender mediation once those programmes were completed. Denny believed he had done well and accomplished much in terms of understanding his own crime cycle, the 'risk factors' that would need to be monitored for the rest of his life and the harms suffered by Anthony from the time of his first intrusion into Anthony's life. Still, he spoke of the face-to-face dialogue as eclipsing the earlier treatment, as useful as that was. Denny claims he gave up the last vestiges of any rationalisation of his offending behaviours at that meeting. He had rationalised his offending in part on the basis of his homosexuality and his lack of courage to 'come out' in a very conservative community. Anthony had confronted any such notion in the first of their two meetings, saying:

> The issue, Denny, is not that you were gay and couldn't find an age appropriate partner or outlet for your sexual needs. I have many wonderful gay friends; none of them are pedophiles. The issue, Denny, is that you were a pedophile taking advantage of a child. I had you charged with offences against me partly because I couldn't stand the thought of you ever putting another child through what you put me through. I had to do what I could do to impact your thinking, and challenge you to make appropriate choices. This was as much about my concern for any future victims as it was for myself.

Denny acknowledged Anthony's challenge as true, and committed to use all that he had learned in prison, in treatment while on parole and in the facilitated dialogues to ensure that he never strays again from age appropriate relationships into acting out in ways that could create harms for another child. Only time will tell whether the impacts of this process on Denny's thinking, beliefs and behaviours prove as powerfully transformative as they have for Anthony.

The PTSD assessment scales on the following pages give additional indications of the degree to which this process was transformative, therapeutically, in Anthony's experience.

PTSD assessment scale

The 'assessment scale' included here is a simple inventory that is sometimes used with clients in the author's private, clinical practice and it is used with some victim–offender mediation participants as well. It is important to note that not everyone who has experience with the trauma symptoms listed here has a PTSD. Only when these symptoms appear in certain combinations according to the criteria listed in the diagnostic scheme below would anyone be diagnosed as suffering from the disorder. However, those who are diagnosed with the disorder inevitably do have a significant number of these symptoms, clustered in categories usually described as *intrusion, withdrawal,* and *arousal.*

Anthony has given permission to include his 'pre' and 'post' assessments in this chapter. Figure 10.1 represents Anthony's experience of those post-traumatic symptoms that had plagued him for years prior to his participation in victim–offender mediation. Figure 10.2 represents Anthony's experience of those same symptoms approximately three weeks following his face-to-face facilitated dialogue with Denny.

When examining the figures, note that the right-hand column is headed 'Never' indicating that the subject had not experienced that particular symptom from the time of the trauma, or was no longer experiencing its manifestation. The symptoms that were listed by Anthony, in Figure 10.1, as symptoms that he experienced frequently (and to such a degree that he had entered *two* 'X's, for 'Feelings of Shame and Embarrassment'), and which had plagued him for years, he later describes (in Figure 10.2) as simply not presenting any longer. Anthony's previous constant experience of shame and embarrassment, he reports, has been extinguished.

This phenomenon has been seen frequently over the duration of the Victim Offender Mediation Programme's operation (15 years, at the time of writing) although the staff have been cautious about making too much of it: things that appear too good to be true usually *are*. The therapeutic outcomes that Anthony experienced are, by no means, axiomatic; nor do all of the symptoms necessarily disappear completely for all time, even in cases as dramatic as Anthony's. But the frequency with which staff have observed the diminishing or extinguishing of post-trauma symptoms is instructive in itself. The phenomenon has now been observed dozens of times. Participants, and their therapists, when they have them, tell us that the difference, following their participation in the programme, is profound with respect to their experiences with the number, frequency and intensity of the symptoms.

POST-TRAUMATIC STRESS ASSESSMENT

Since the trauma, which of the following is being experienced and how frequently:

SYMPTOM	Frequent (3–5 ×/wk)	Occasional (1–2 ×/wk)	Seldom (1×/wk)	Never
INTRUSION				
• Intrusive thoughts and images				
• Recurring dreams – nightmares				
• Flashbacks				
Anxiety attacks		X		
Crying spells and tearfulness				
Feeling of shame, embarrassment	XX			
Guilt feelings ('If only …')				
WITHDRAWAL				
• Withdrawal	X			
• Depression – diminished interest	X			
• Feeling of detachment or estrangement	X			
• Inability to recall specific events of trauma		X		
• Disorientation, confusion	X			
• Restricted affect	X			
• Avoidance of thoughts of trauma	X			
Fear		X		
Job difficulties		X		
Sexual dysfunction		X		
Numbness – emotional/physical	X			
Helplessness, loss of control		X		
AROUSAL				
• Sleep disturbances	X			
• Anger/rage	X			
• Difficulty in concentrating	X			
• Hypervigilance		X		
• High startle response		X		
Headaches			X	
Muscle tension		X		
Nausea			X	
Eating disturbances			X	
Difficulty in breathing				X
Cold sweat			X	
Increased alcohol usage		X		
Increased drug usage	X			

Figure 10.1 Anthony's pre-victim–offender dialogue symptom assessment.

POST-TRAUMATIC STRESS ASSESSMENT

Since the trauma, which of the following is being experienced and how frequently:

SYMPTOM	Frequent (3–5 ×/wk)	Occasional (1–2 ×/wk)	Seldom (1×/wk)	Never
INTRUSION				
• Intrusive thoughts and images				
• Recurring dreams – nightmares				
• Flashbacks				
Anxiety attacks				X
Crying spells and tearfulness				
Feeling of shame, embarrassment			X	
Guilt feelings ('If only …')				
WITHDRAWAL				
• Withdrawal	X			
• Depression – diminished interest		X		
• Feeling of detachment or estrangement				X
• Inability to recall specific events of trauma				
• Disorientation, confusion				X
• Restricted affect				X
• Avoidance of thoughts of trauma		X		
Fear				X
Job difficulties		X		
Sexual dysfunction				X
Numbness – emotional/physical		X		
Helplessness, loss of control				X
AROUSAL				
• Sleep disturbances		X		
• Anger/rage				X
• Difficulty in concentrating		X		
• Hypervigilance				X
• High startle response				X
Headaches				X
Muscle tension		X		
Nausea				X
Eating disturbances				X
Difficulty in breathing				X
Cold sweat				X
Increased alcohol usage				X
Increased drug usage				X

Figure 10.2 Anthony's post-victim–offender dialogue assessment.

What makes it work?

The list of possible reasons (and their explications) for what makes this process 'work' would require volumes. Some of these reasons are clearly related to brain chemistry and neurology. Other reasons include the participants' experiences of being invited into what is virtually a therapeutic alliance, their relationships with the facilitators, how they experience the programme culture, climate, values, ethics, commitments and constancy being made real for them as they rebuild, sometimes over a period of many years. To separate these sets of reasons from one another is to miss a major point; they work *because* they are so closely tied. Herman goes so far as to assert that trauma '[r]ecovery can take place only within the context of relationships' (1997: 133). From among the reasons for the programme's effectiveness listed by participants, a number stand out as more frequently named than others:

1 The 'reality of the process' – it is not role play or some kind of psycho-drama therapy. Even if safe process requires a number of preliminary videotaped communications, the interchanges take place between the 'real' principals. And in those cases in which facilitated dialogues occur, 'the other' is in the room.

2 The degree of safety, respect and empowerment experienced at each stage of the process. One participant, a family survivor of her husband's homicide, described this as a 'cocoon' of safety.

3 The 'values commitments', 'professionalism', 'skills', personal traits and attributes of programme staff facilitators; such as 'humanness', 'warmth', 'care', 'honesty', 'trustworthiness', and 'tenacity'.

4 The trust relationships and therapeutic alliances formed between participants and facilitators.

5 The power of the process for discovering (or creating) empathy in offenders who demonstrated no empathy while committing their criminal offences.

6 The validation of the victim's perception of truth by the perpetrator.

Of these six reasons two – the first and the last – are of particular importance for what follows.

The reality of the process

Both Judith Herman (1997) and PTSD specialist Chris Brewen (2003) suggest that clinicians need to do therapy for survivors of criminal trauma with the perpetrator 'in the room'. The contexts, however, seem to make clear that both specialists mean this *metaphorically*. Victim Offender Mediation Programme staff are convinced that, with a process properly conceived, entirely volitional, extremely cautious, therapeutically informed, conducted in safe settings and with perpetrators who are prepared to take responsibility for the harms they have caused, it is not just feasible but highly efficacious therapeutically to have the *real* and not just a metaphorical perpetrator 'in the room'.

Conversely, offenders who undergo violent offender and violent sex offender treatment in Canadian prisons usually participate in a number of treatment modules focused upon the development of victim empathy. In the context of their treatment they write letters to their victims (which are never sent), then write letters to themselves as though those letters were from their victims. Towards the end of these programmes the offenders go through what are often gruelling role-plays in which they assume the part of their victims, attempting to approximate the feelings and experiences of their victims as they, their fellow group members and their treatment group leaders catalogue the horror and the harms suffered in the criminal incident and its aftermath.

Such treatment modalities are predicated on the now accepted notion that offender treatment must be done with the *victim* metaphorically 'in the room'. As useful as all of that might be, and given the caveats above concerning a 'process properly conceived', it is far more efficacious from a treatment point of view to have neither a metaphorical nor an imaginary victim 'in the room' but the real one. This is not to devalue other psychotherapies or treatment interventions. In fact, victim–offender dialogue almost always seems to work best when accompanied by other treatment modalities. But the power of properly prepared and facilitated victim–offender dialogue can, and often does, far transcend anything that can be experienced by either party in role-play or other therapies.

Validation of the victim's perception of truth by the perpetrator

As insane as this may initially sound, one trauma survivor after another has made mention of the importance of the 'validation of the perpetrator'. An example helps to illustrate this concept.

The following excerpts are from interviews with Diane,[14] an adult rape survivor, a newly married young professional at the time of her rape which was committed by a stranger in her own apartment. Diane had been diagnosed with PTSD and was suffering acutely. She had been under the care of various psychiatrists for over 20 years, with little respite. She was referred to the Victim Offender Mediation Programme, and while she knew little about the programme initially, came expressly for help in locating and communicating with the offender. He had been incarcerated for a subsequent offence in another province but was willing to meet with programme staff about the offence for which he had been exonerated. Twenty-two years after the rape, Diane finally heard what she had needed to hear since 1968. In a videotaped interview conducted following a therapy session almost ten years ago, Diane reflects on the importance of having the perpetrator validate her truth:

> *To have the one responsible for the harms acknowledge that you are a truth-teller, that you have been all along, while he was the liar – he pleaded not-guilty, and left me with the shame and degradation of a public trial in a small community, feeling responsible for my own violent rape by a stranger. He was acquitted: the system had told me he was not guilty, therefore, I must be. The community ostracised me, my husband left me. I had been pregnant at the time and bore a handicapped child ... even God seemed to have collaborated with my accusers.*
>
> *To have him finally take responsibility twenty-two years later, after being acquitted by the courts, and apologise for the way his lawyer had savaged me on the [witness] stand – that was beyond anything I dared dream. My dad died after years of trying to get this case re-opened, trying to clear his daughter's name ... It can't happen of course, you can't be tried again for the same offence once you're acquitted ...*
>
> *But to have him finally acknowledge that I'd been telling the truth all along, that was the beginning of my healing and return to normalcy. Of course therapists, my psychiatrists, loved ones, tell you, 'You're not responsible, it wasn't your fault'. But you never really internalise that ... I began to feel innocent the moment he declared himself 'guilty', despite what the courts had said. He declared himself 'guilty' and me 'innocent', and I felt the shame I had carried drop away ... I felt innocent for the very first time since the rape ... That was the beginning ... Since then, the nightmares have ended ... the fear is gone ... I can't even conjure up the terrifying images, any longer ... I'm finally free ...*

Diane's gains have continued. She reports being freer than at any time since the rape.

The neurophysiology

The literature of PTSD and trauma recovery is replete with references to the perserverative nature of traumatic 'memories': the ways in which these memories manifest, encoded as they are, not in the linear narrative of normal autobiography, but rather 'in the form of vivid sensations and images the trauma survivor experiences' (Herman, 1997: 38). In this section, as briefly as can be dared, that phenomenon is touched upon, and further explanation provided concerning how the facilitated therapeutic dialogue at the core of the Victim Offender Mediation Programme frequently assists in the diminishing or extinguishing of trauma survivors' symptoms.

The perseverative nature of the dreams, nightmares, waking intrusive thoughts, images, flashbacks or associations to trauma previously suffered can leave the trauma sufferer feeling as though all of their psychological defence gates have been breached, their senses flooded by the images and sensory overload of trauma's sights, sounds, smells, tastes and aversive or hostile touch. Diane reported that such flooding occurred 'daily, nightly ...' for 22 years following her rape, appearing unbidden, mercilessly, without warning and without respite, horribly complicating her work, professional and intimate relationships. As most trauma clinicians have witnessed, the helplessness and horror of the traumatic incident can live on and on. Diane needed something more than pharmaceuticals, she needed a safe way in which to revisit the trauma, as part of reconstructing the trauma narrative and gaining mastery.

Revisiting the trauma

As Diane and Anthony's experiences illustrate, participants in the Victim Offender Mediation Programme can revisit the trauma in many ways, exploring it, often, from a number of angles. As part of the preparation (even in considering *the concept* of dialogue with the 'other') participants approach the trauma experience again but, this time, with a difference. This time, at least the basic building blocks of recovery – safety, autonomy and relatedness to others significant in the recovery process – are being reconstructed and put in place.

Safety is paramount. Ensuring participant autonomy means the survivor assists in tailoring a process that suits their unique needs. They make the choices concerning which steps to include or omit, the direction of the journey, the stops along the way, the speed of the pace and (at their slightest suggestion) a complete 'about face' at any point. Programme staff strongly concur with Herman, who is adamant that '[n]o intervention that takes power away from the survivor can possibly foster her recovery' (1997: 133). The relatedness pillar is also a key component. This time, as the survivor approaches the trauma – its memory content, related feeling states and all that will entail for them – they are not alone, but accompanied by others who are no longer mere dialogue facilitators, but trusted companions.

Both victim and offender participants are empowered to revisit the trauma and its associations, once they are ready. Each is supported in integrating all that they 'see' as they approach and re-experience aspects of the trauma. For the survivor, this exercise in re-enactment will likely be accompanied by a reflooding of the sense gates. Once the associations begin, virtually nothing can stop the flow of the neuro-humoural transmitting substances (NHTS) as they link again, in fractions of seconds, to alert the organism to save itself: to flee for its life, fight for its life or, when too overwhelmed, to freeze, unable to do either. This time, though, rather than becoming completely overwhelmed by those associations, the survivor experiences, along with the fear states, a new degree of mastery.

Over time, this newer message, tested and stored in the more highly organised levels of the brain, begins to prevail over the earlier message, as the recovery journey continues and the threat to the life, health and integrity of the organism subsides, both in reality, and in the survivor's experience of the trauma symptoms and their 'triggers'.

Conclusion

It was once thought that victim–offender mediation or dialogue was appropriate in only relatively minor cases. However, the Victim Offender Mediation Programme involves the most serious offences imaginable: criminal negligence causing death; drunk or dangerous driving causing bodily harm or death; aggravated assault; armed robbery; kidnapping; sexual assault; attempted murder and homicide offences including manslaughter, first- and second-degree murder and multiple murder. Significantly, evaluations of the programme report profound and positive impacts on the lives of both victims/trauma survivors and offenders, and 'unanimous support for the programme from all victim and offender respondents' in just these sorts of offences (Roberts, 1992).

Part of the satisfaction, participants report, almost certainly has to do with the fact that other ostensible 'justice' processes with which they have been involved have delivered little of what they need. Their experience of respect, honour, care, constancy and other forms of 'responsiveness' at the hands of Victim Offender Mediation Programme staff appears remarkable by contrast. Yet both victim and offender participants are also adamant that they have experienced the Victim Offender Mediation Programme process as a healing intervention, eclipsing other attempts at remedy, enabling them to accomplish therapeutic goals that have eluded them in other processes. Trauma survivors have reported that post-traumatic symptoms have been greatly diminished, if not extinguished, by their participation and that even given exposure to associations that once would have 'triggered' their trauma to the point of crippling them, they no longer return to the same levels of fear.

If the results continue to be as auspicious as the first 15 years of empirical experience would indicate, these programmes will likely continue to proliferate, with significant implications for the fields of victimology, criminology and the related, rapidly developing, field of trauma studies. At the least, it is hoped that this article and others like it might precipitate additional dialogue between members of the trauma recovery, offender treatment and victim offender mediation communities, in the hopes of continued learning and the establishment of safe, efficacious practice. We have a lot to learn.

In the meantime, on the strength of over 15 years' experience and evidence of profound outcomes for participants, it is the programme's contention that well conceived victim–offender dialogue models, especially when informed by trauma recovery and offender treatment research, appear to have a good deal to offer in situations where the harms have been the greatest. Such models, the evidence would indicate, can be a key to unlocking traumatic experience and, in a significant percentage of cases, to greatly loosening the bonds of victim and offender 'captives', if not actually setting them free.

Appendix A: Diagnostic criteria for post-traumatic stress disorder (DSM-IV)

A. The person has been exposed to a traumatic event in which **both** of the following were present:

1. the person experienced, witnessed or was confronted with an event or events that involved actual or threatened death or serious injury, or a threat to the physical integrity of self or others;
2. the person's response involved intense fear, helplessness or horror.

B. The traumatic event is persistently re-experienced in **one or more** of the following ways:

1. Recurrent and intrusive distressing recollections of the event, including images, thoughts or perceptions.
2. Recurrent distressing dreams of the event.
3. Acting or feeling as if the traumatic event were recurring (includes a sense of reliving the experience, illusions, hallucinations and dissociative flashback episodes, including those that occur on awakening or when intoxicated).
4. Intense psychological distress at exposure to internal or external cues that symbolise or resemble an aspect of the traumatic event.
5. Physiological reactivity on exposure to internal or external cues that symbolise or resemble an aspect of the traumatic event.

C. Persistent avoidance of stimuli associated with the trauma and numbing of general responsiveness (not present before the trauma), as indicated by **three or more** of the following:

1. Efforts to avoid thoughts, feelings or conversations associated with the trauma.
2. Efforts to avoid activities, places or people that arouse recollections of the trauma.
3. Inability to recall an important aspect of the trauma.
4. Markedly diminished interest or participation in significant activities.
5. Feeling of detachment or estrangement from others.
6. Restricted range of affect (e.g. unable to have loving feelings).
7. Sense of a foreshortened future (e.g. does not expect to have a career, marriage, children or a normal life span).

D. Persistent symptoms of increased arousal (not present before the trauma), as indicated by **two or more** of the following:

1. Difficulty falling or staying asleep.
2. Irritability or outbursts of anger.
3. Difficulty concentrating.
4. Hyper vigilance.
5. Exaggerated startle response.

E. Duration of the disturbance (symptoms B, C and D) is more than one month.

F. The disturbance causes clinically significant distress or impairment in social, occupational or other important areas of functioning.

Appendix B: Complex post-traumatic stress disorder

Diagnostic criteria proposed by Judith Herman in *Trauma and Recovery* (1997):

---

1. A history of subjection to totalitarian control over a prolonged period (months to years). Examples include those subjected to totalitarian systems in sexual and domestic life, including hostages, prisoners of war, concentration-camp survivors and survivors of some religious cults. Examples also include survivors of domestic battering, childhood physical or sexual abuse and organised sexual exploitation.

2. Alterations in affect regulation, including:

   - persistent dysphoria
   - chronic suicidal preoccupation
   - self-injury
   - explosive or extremely inhibited anger (may alternate)
   - compulsive or extremely inhibited sexuality (may alternate).

3. Alterations in consciousness, including:

   - amnesia
   - transient dissociative episodes
   - depersonalisation/derealisation

- reliving experiences, either in the form of intrusive post-traumatic stress disorder symptoms or in the form of ruminative preoccupation.

4.   Alterations in self-perception, including:

- sense of helplessness or paralysis of initiative
- shame, guilt and self-blame
- sense of defilement or stigma
- sense of complete difference from others (may include sense of specialness, utter aloneness, belief that no other person can understand or non-human identity)

5.   Alterations in perception of perpetrator, including:

- preoccupation with relationship with perpetrator (includes preoccupation with revenge)
- unrealistic attribution of total power to perpetrator (caution: victim's assessment of power realities may be more realistic than clinician's)
- idealisation or paradoxical gratitude
- sense of special or supernatural relationship.

6.   Alterations in relations with others, including:

- isolation and withdrawal
- disruption in intimate relationships
- repeated search for rescuer (may alternate with isolation and withdrawal)
- persistent distrust
- repeated failures of self-protection.

7.   Alteration in systems of meaning, including:

- loss of sustaining faith
- sense of hopelessness and despair.

Notes

1   The chapter is based upon a workshop presented by Dave Gustafson and Sandra Bergen – Co-Directors of FRCJIA – at the 6th International Conference on Restorative Justice in Vancouver, Canada in June 2005.

2   As at note 4, below, language can be tricky. Terms such as 'victim' or 'offender' can be problematic. Both can certainly be pejorative terms. Participants in the VOMP programme quickly become known to FRCJIA staff facilitators by their first names. Prisoners, at least in Canada, usually prefer the term 'prisoner' to 'inmate' and will be glad to share just why; some victims prefer the term 'survivor' to 'victim', seeing 'victim' as disempowering. In Canadian legislation, 'victim' has precise definition, as does 'offender'. Because this article is directed to the criminal justice and trauma clinician communities, and to provide at least some clarity concerning which 'participant' I am referring to, I have used 'victim' and 'offender' where it seems necessary.

3   In Canada, anyone sentenced to a term of two years and more serves that time in a federal (as opposed to a provincial) institution. In the US, federal prisons are reserved for those who have committed crimes against federal, as opposed to state, law codes, including crimes such as mail fraud, treason and the like.

4   Language can be particularly tricky at points such as this. The word 'closure' here is in quotations because it was the word so often chosen by the respondents. Considerable controversy can be generated by such things, with strong opinions stated by victims/survivors, their advocates and helpers. Some, for instance, find it abhorrent that anyone could ever suggest that trauma survivors might find 'closure' in regard to rape or the violent death of a loved one; others – usually the survivors themselves – can be as adamant that new degrees of closure are among the many things they need. Our conviction is that the participants we are working with will choose language useful for them until it no longer serves them. They choose, we respectfully clarify, then try not to blunder once they have established the parameters of language meaningful to them.

5   'Conceptual baggage' is a term used to describe qualitative researchers' self-disclosures: it is 'the information about researchers that places [them] in relation to the research question and research process in an immediate and central way ... [enabling] their personal experiences, thoughts and feelings to enter into the research information on the same level as those of subsequent participants' (Kirby and McKenna, 1989: 21).

6   By 'generativity' Erickson meant not biological procreation (that would have been accomplished in the earlier stage) but the teaching, nurture and mentoring of others in the latter stages of one's own life: passing on the wisdom and values of a lifetime beyond the circles of one's own progeny.

7   Manifestation of trauma symptoms was once referred to as 'hysteria'. If the word hysteria is, literally, 'wandering womb', men, it could be presumed, lacked the prerequisites for the condition. The term began to be used of those suffering combat neurosis following the First World War, but was virtually always used, at least prior to 1941, as highly pejorative. Abram Kardiner, the American psychiatrist whose compassionate and pioneering work defined the clinical outlines of the traumatic syndrome in use today, described the term's earlier use thus: 'When the word "hysterical" ... is used, its social

meaning is that the subject is a predatory individual, trying to get something for nothing. The victim of such neurosis is, therefore, without sympathy in court, and … without sympathy from his physicians, who often take … "hysterical" to mean that the individual is suffering from some persistent form of wickedness, perversity, or weakness of will' (Kardiner and Spiegel, 1947: 406).

8   Hendin and Haas (1991).

9   See, for example, Kathleen M. Burke (1998) 'Take it Like a Man: The Silencing of Men's Experience of Sexual Abuse in Childhood'. Unpublished PhD Dissertation, Simon Fraser University School of Criminology, Burnaby, BC, Canada.

10 *Diagnostic and Statistical Manual of Mental Disorders*, 4th edn (DSM-IV), published by the American Psychiatric Association, Washington DC, 1994, the main diagnostic reference of mental health professionals in the United States of America.

11 Cathy Caruth, in her *Trauma: Explorations in Memory* (1995), asserts something similar: 'If PTSD must be understood as a pathological symptom, then it is not so much a symptom of the unconscious, as it is a symptom of history. The traumatized, we might say, carry an impossible history within them, or they become themselves the symptom of a history that they cannot entirely possess' (p. 5).

12 Trauma discussion led by Joseph Solanto, PhD, with prisoners and community members at Ferndale Insitution, Mission, BC, Canada, 19 March 2003, and sponsored by Heartspeak Productions. An extremely useful segment of the discussion held that day is included in *Healing River*, an educational video/DVD produced and distributed by Heartspeak Productions and available through http://www.heartspeakproductions.ca.

13 I have used a pseudonym here at the request of 'Anthony'. 'Anthony' chose this pseudonym for himself, and gave permission for the use of his story and the PTSD assessment scales in this article.

14 The use of Diane's real name is one of the rare exceptions to my usual use of pseudonyms to protect the confidentiality of my clients. Diane has used her full name to identify herself as a VOMP participant in the public media on a number of previous occasions as part of her own feminist concern that women – especially rape survivors – be made aware of every option available to them and able to find help with referrals to a wide range of services.

References

Brewen, C. R. (2003) *Post Traumatic Stress Disorder: Malady or Myth*. New Haven, CT and London: Yale University Press.

Butler, D. (2004) 'For Victims of Sexual Abuse, Finally Confronting Their Abusers Can Be an "Amazing, Freeing" Experience', *Ottawa Citizen*, 15 September, p. A6.

Caruth, C. (ed.) (1995) *Trauma: Explorations in Memory*. Baltimore, MD: Johns Hopkins University Press, p. 5.

Erickson, E. H. (1963) *Childhood and Society*. New York: Norton.

Gustafson, D. L. and Smidstra, H. (1989) 'Victim Offender Reconciliation in Serious Crime: A Report on the Feasibility Study Undertaken for the Ministry of the Solicitor General (Canada)'. Unpublished report.

Hendin, H. and Haas, A. P. (1991) 'Suicide and Guilt as Manifestations of PTSD in Vietnam Combat Veterans', *American Journal of Psychiatry*, 148, 586–91.

Herman, J. L. (1997) *Trauma and Recovery: The Aftermath of Violence – From Domestic Abuse to Political Terror*. New York: Basic Books.

Horowitz, M. (1986) *Stress Response Syndromes*. Northvale, NJ: Jason Aronson.

Janet, P. [1919] (1925) *Psychological Healing*, Vol. 1, trans. E. Paul and C. Paul. New York: Macmillan, pp. 661–3.

Johnson, R. M. (1990) *Death Work: A Study of the Modern Execution Process*. Pacific Grove, CA: Brooks/Coles Publishing.

Kardiner, A. and Spiegel, H. (1947) *War, Stress and Neurotic Illness* (rev. edn *The Traumatic Neuroses of War*). New York: Hoeber.

Kirby, S. and McKenna, K. (1989) *Experience, Research, Social Change: Methods from the Margins*. Toronto: Garamond Press.

Roberts, T. (1992) *Evaluation of the Victim Offender Mediation Pilot Project: Final Report for Fraser Region Community Justice Initiatives Association and Correctional Services Canada*. Report for the Uvic Institute for Dispute Resolution, 15 May.

Roberts, T. (1995) *Evaluation of the Victim Offender Mediation Project, Langley, B.C.* Final Report for Solicitor General Canada, March.

Zehr, H. and Mika, H. (1998) 'Fundamental Principles of Restorative Justice', *Contemporary Justice Review*, 1(1), 47–55.

Chapter 11

The involvement of insurance companies in restorative processes

Melissa Ouellette

Abstract

This chapter examines the implications of the involvement of insurance companies as stakeholders in restorative processes in order to determine whether there is a disjuncture between the practice of restorative justice and the principles that guide that practice. The chapter discusses incidents that involve both a direct victim and the payment of a claim by an insurance company for the damage caused by an offender. The questions that arise from these incidents are central to the practice of restorative justice, notably who are the relevant stakeholders and how should they be involved in a restorative process? More specifically, should a corporate entity such as an insurance company be considered a stakeholder and, if so, what should its role be in a restorative process?

Introduction

It is evident in both the new Canadian youth justice legislation, which is 'written in a language that echoes the teachings of a conventional brand of restorative justice' (Woolford and Ratner, 2003: 182), and in the growing number of restorative justice programmes that take referrals from the criminal justice system, that restorative justice is experiencing mounting acceptance by the Canadian government and the mainstream criminal justice system. In order to maintain its integrity as it evolves, however, the restorative justice movement will need to contemplate whether its practices are consistent with its philosophical foundations.

The purpose of this chapter is to examine the implications of the involvement of insurance companies as stakeholders in restorative processes in order to consider whether there is disjuncture between the practice of restorative justice and the principles that guide that practice. This chapter will discuss incidents that involve both a direct victim *and* the payment of a claim by an insurance company for the damage caused by an offender. The questions that arise from these incidents are central to the practice of restorative justice. Who are the relevant stakeholders? How should stakeholders be involved in a restorative process? More specifically, should a corporate entity such as an insurance company be considered a stakeholder and, if so, what is their proper role in a restorative process? This chapter will likely raise more questions than provide answers; the intent is simply to raise this issue for discussion.

Restorative justice

The philosophy of restorative justice is by no means new; it is rooted in ancient forms of justice and reflected in the traditional practices of many indigenous peoples throughout the world (Weitekamp, 2002; Umbreit, 1999). Historically, in many non-state societies '[r]e-establishing peace in the community was of utmost interest' (Walgrave and Bazemore, 1999: 364). As a result, instead of punishing the offender, restoration to the victim or the victim's family was the 'dominant way of reacting' (ibid.).

Despite its long history, the incorporation of restorative justice into our present adversarial criminal justice system is a relatively recent development. In a number of different countries, programmes based upon restorative philosophies are now available at various stages of the criminal justice process, and are inextricably connected to the systems that are currently in place. As Walgrave and Bazemore (1999) suggest:

> [W]hile the idea of restoring harm caused by a crime is not new, the cultural and structural context in which it has to be implemented today is completely different. The restorative justice ideal can no longer rely on the assumption of strong communities, and it must 'compete' with other, now well-established, criminal justice models (p. 365).

The existence, in contemporary society, of corporate entities such as insurance companies is an additional element that must be taken into account by those involved in restorative justice programmes.

The theory and practice of restorative justice offers an understanding of crime and justice that differs significantly from that of the adversarial criminal justice system. Rather than responding to crime as a violation of laws that requires the use of formal court proceedings to dispense punishment,

> restorative justice treats crime as fundamentally a violation of people and interpersonal relationships, the impact of crime as violations of people that create needs, obligations and liabilities, and the appropriate (restorative) justice response to engage victims, offenders and their communities to put right the wrongs (Mika and Zehr, 2003: 140).

The focus, in a restorative response, shifts from an adversarial process of determining guilt and assigning blame to finding out who has been affected and how. As a result, instead of asking who deserves to be punished and for how long, seeing justice served becomes a question of repairing the harm and preventing a similar event from happening in the future. As Zehr (2002) puts it:

> [T]he criminal justice system centres around offenders and deserts – making sure offenders get what they *deserve*. Restorative justice is more focussed on *needs*: the victims, the needs of communities, the needs of offenders (p. 18, emphasis in original).

Restorative processes, which emphasise dialogue, reparation and the active involvement of the people directly affected by an offence, have the potential for creating positive changes in the ways crime and conflict are handled in our communities.

The stakeholders in restorative processes

When a crime occurs, a restorative response compels us to ask: 'who are the affected stake-holders and how shall they be represented?' (McCold, 2000: 363). As Bazemore (2000) suggests, '[t]he stakeholders must assume prominence, precisely because harm cannot be understood in a vacuum and, therefore, repair cannot be achieved in the absence of those most affected by crime' (p. 465). The offender, the victim and the community are all affected by crime and, therefore, ought to be given an opportunity to play a role in addressing the harm caused. Before discussing the specific issue at hand, however, the terms 'offender', 'victim' and 'community' require a brief examination.

Arguably, the least controversial of these concepts is the first: the 'offender' is the person who caused the harm.[1] *Primary* offenders are those 'who accept primary responsibility for the offence' while *secondary* offenders 'accept some responsibility for contributing to the offence' (McCold, 2000: 364). McCold (2000: 365) categorises victims as either *direct* (i.e., 'those against whom the crime was committed and who suffered physical injury, monetary loss and/or emotional suffering as a consequence of the offence') or *indirect* (i.e. 'those who suffered indirect financial loss because of their relationship to the victim or offender').[2] Various models and situations call for the involvement of the primary offender and direct victim or a combination of primary and secondary offenders, and direct and indirect victims.

The last concept – 'community' – is the most contentious of the three. McCold (2000) makes a distinction between micro-communities, which include secondary victims and communities of support, and macro-communities, which consist of 'local residents who are not personally connected to victims or offenders, and the local government which represents them', as well as 'the totality of society and the agents of government responsible for justice policy, including state and federal authorities' (p. 365). Van Ness and Strong (1997b) suggest the term 'community' can have a geographic connotation (for example, the neighbourhood in which we live) as well as non-geographic interpretation that they call 'communit[ies] of interest' and which are characterised by a 'fundamental sense of duty, reciprocity and belonging' (p. 32–33).

One of the challenges faced by restorative justice practitioners is how to include the 'community' in a restorative process without compromising the values of restorative justice, most notably the principle that advocates that those most directly affected by an offence are given the opportunity to be most actively involved in finding a resolution. McCold and Wachtel (1998) caution against 'a geographic definition of community' as it may result in restorative processes coming 'dangerously close to the traditional justice system view that offenders must pay their debt to society … Christie's (1977) principle of ownership reminds us of the danger that conflict is easily "stolen" from the victim by defining the society as the victim' (p. 78). Instead, restorative justice practitioners should look towards involving non-geographic communities that take into account the people affected by the offence.

There is an opportunity to involve the community in the restorative resolution of one class of offences. Offences such as auto theft, vehicle break-ins and vandalism of vehicles are quite prevalent[3] and cause great inconvenience and financial cost[4] to many members of communities. These types of offences can be, and often are, referred to restorative programmes for a conference or mediation meeting to take place between the owner of the vehicle and the person or persons responsible for the theft or damage. The impact of the offence on the owner, both personally and financially, may be the subject of a discussion at these meetings, and an agreement that includes reparation or restitution to provide redress for the inconvenience and expense caused to the owner may be drawn up. Participation in such a process may result in a high level of satisfaction for the owner of the vehicle and may also encourage the person responsible to consider the human consequence of his or her actions, thus impacting his or her future behaviour.[5] This process, however, does not address the wider impact of the offence.

In cases where there is damage to an insured vehicle and a claim is made, the insurance company pays for the repairs made to the vehicle and passes this cost on to its customers. Consequently, the insurance company could be considered a stakeholder in the restorative process and their inclusion could be a way of indirectly including those who would be affected by an increase in insurance rates (i.e. all customers) in the process. Directly including the wider community in a conference or mediation meeting itself is not desirable or feasible but involving insurance companies may be a way of addressing the concerns of the community. When a crime occurs the persons beyond the direct and indirect victims may need reassurance that what happened was wrong, that something is being done about it and that steps are being taken to prevent its re-occurrence. As well, community members often want to be assured that an offender is taking responsibility for his or her actions, is being held accountable and is taking steps to repair the harm caused. These concerns can be addressed through restorative processes.

At this time, it does not appear that insurance companies are formally involved in programmes in the Lower Mainland of British Columbia.[6] Concern has been expressed regarding the involvement of insurance companies *after* a pre-charge restorative conference has been held between the owner of the vehicle and the youth responsible for its theft or damage. Anecdotal evidence suggests that the Insurance Corporation of British Columbia (ICBC)[7] has issued letters to youth in the Lower Mainland who have participated in restorative justice programmes demanding that the youth repay ICBC for the cost of the claim.

Options for involving insurance companies in restorative processes

Not including insurance companies in restorative processes is one option for programmes that accept offences involving insurance claims. Restorative conferences or mediation meetings would only include the victim and the offender and their support networks; the insurance company would not be invited to attend and would not provide input into an agreement but would, of course, continue to be free to pursue a financial settlement against the offender in other ways, such as through civil litigation. The offender would have to contend with that situation, if it arose, without the involvement of the restorative programme. There are, however, difficulties with this course of action.

Restorative justice has been criticised for its failure to see beyond the personal harm created to the direct victim, to the social implications caused by wrongdoing (see Bussman, 1992).[8] There is concern that the need for a public component to the sanctioning of wrongdoing will not be addressed by allowing the victim and the offender to come up with a resolution to the offence. By limiting the participants in a restorative resolution to the direct victim and the offender, programmes may not address the impact on the wider community.

Furthermore, a core standard for restorative practice is that participation in a restorative process should not cause further harm to victims, offenders or the community. Involving an offender in a process that could have the unintended consequence of opening them up to a claim of civil liability could be seen as causing harm to the offender. Of particular concern are those cases referred to community-based restorative programmes prior to a charge being laid. Rather than pleading guilty (because there is no charge before the courts to plead guilty to) an offender 'accepts responsibility' for the offence in order to participate in a restorative process. The 'acceptance of responsibility' by the offender may be sufficient for an insurance company to pursue the offender for damages without the legal protections afforded to an offender when a case is dealt with through the criminal courts. In addition, if the insurance company sends a demand letter to the offender following the restorative process and after the offender has already made amends with the direct victim it could be viewed by the offender as unfair if the offender perceives the matter as having been resolved, particularly if the possibility of this happening has not been discussed with him or her beforehand. Therefore this alternative does not address the full impact of the offence on the community *or* the full impact of the offence on the person responsible and, as a result, is not a fully restorative choice.

A second option may be that restorative justice programmes refuse to accept referrals in which an insurance claim is a possibility and, as a result, these cases would be processed through criminal courts. The outcome of this alternative would be that the people who are impacted by these types of offences would lose the opportunity to participate in a restorative process and, accordingly, this option is not in keeping with the values of restorative justice.

A third way of addressing this issue may be that as part of the intake process, restorative programmes would advise the offender of his or her right to access legal advice[9] and discuss with the offender the role of the insurance company, specifically the fact that the insurance company could be considered a stakeholder in the restorative process. Taking full responsibility for the harm caused may include paying restitution to the insurance company in addition to making amends to the direct victim. If the offender agrees, the restorative justice programme would then arrange and facilitate a conference or mediation session with the offender and the insurance company.[10]

The benefit of this option is that it would ensure that the perspective of a more diverse group of stakeholders is included in the restorative process. The insurance company could communicate to the person responsible the financial impact of the offence on the wider community and if restitution to the insurance company were negotiated this could be considered to be tangible recompense to the community (providing, of course, that the restitution paid by the offender results in lower insurance rates for consumers and not higher profit margins for insurance companies). Accordingly, this would add a structural dimension to the process. There are a number of positive aspects to this proposal.

This suggestion satisfies the principle of inclusion that is so important to restorative justice. Bazemore (2000) suggests '[t]he argument for inclusion … is … based on the hope that, by applying restorative principles, practitioners can continue to create options that meet multiple and emerging stake-holder needs' (p. 469). Many types of offences affect several stakeholders simultaneously; restorative pro-grammes need to ask themselves who the stakeholders are in a given situation and how they can be invited to be involved in the process. Insurance companies have an interest in a number of different types of criminal offences and this is a strong argument for their inclusion in restorative processes. The inclusion of a representative from an insurance company may assist the offender to not only appreciate the wider impact of their offence but also to humanise a corporate entity such as an insurance company. Involving insurance companies in restorative processes may also satisfy the public that something meaningful is being done about auto crime in a way that only involving the direct victim may not.

However, before implementing this suggestion, restorative justice programmes would need to create policies and practices to ensure that the involvement of insurance companies does not have a negative impact on the restorative process. Programmes must thoroughly assess the possible consequences of this course of action, being particularly careful that insurance companies do not receive preferential treatment.[11] If they chose to involve insurance companies, programmes must ensure that their practice is congruent with the principles and goals of restorative justice.

Restorative justice processes produce high levels of satisfaction for participants, in part because they provide a venue to address the emotional issues that arise when harm has been caused. Restorative justice provides opportunities for dialogue, healing and emotional restoration, for both victims and offenders. Victims may choose to participate in a restorative process in order to receive answers to questions such as, 'why me?', 'who are you?', 'what really happened?', 'what are you thinking and feeling now?' and 'what are you going to do with your life now?' (Ross, 2001). Victims may also wish to receive a personal apology and may decide to participate in a restorative process because they want to be heard and vindicated. They may also want acknowledgment from the offender that he or she understands the impact of the offence and will not behave in the same manner in the future.

For offenders, restorative processes provide an opportunity to understand the direct and personal impact of their actions and to take responsibility for their behaviour in an active, positive way in order to repair the harm done. They may choose to participate in order to apologise to the person they have harmed and to be forgiven. Through dialogue, restorative processes encourage participants to see each other as complex human beings rather than as 'offenders' or 'victims'. Offenders are encouraged to repair the harm they have caused and consequently be reintegrated into the community as a whole, contributing person.

Restorative programmes 'aim to increase contact between victims and offenders as a means of "humanizing" the justice system' (Schiff, 1999: 328). Johnstone (2002) suggests that their principal function is not to come up with an agreement or to reconcile the parties but to foster moral growth. Restorative processes, which cultivate in the offender an awareness of the human consequences of his or her behaviour, break through his or her rationalisations and expose the offender to the disapproval of ordinary members of the community.[12] They can cause an offender to truly feel remorse for his or her behaviour and commit to change (Johnstone, 2002).

While insurance companies may wish to see a decrease in recidivism and consequently may be willing to become involved in a discussion with a specific offender regarding the impact of his or her behaviour, it is likely that, as a business with no personal connection to the offence or the offender, their principal motivation for participating in a restorative process would be to receive financial restitution. The result may be a more punitive attitude when compared with participants who have been personally affected by the offence. As McCold (2000) states, '[t]he closer people are to the situation, the less punitive they tend to be – personalised justice tends to be more restorative' (p. 361). Whenever a corporate stakeholder is included, whether it is a representative from an insurance company or the manager of a major supermarket, questions can be raised regarding power balances and fairness (Pate and Peachey, 1988).

A restorative resolution encompasses more than simply the payment of restitution. Dialogue and negotiation are also important. One of the cornerstones of restorative practice is flexibility; responses can and should be tailored to meet the needs and wishes of the individual participants. An offender may enter into a restorative process in good faith and genuinely wish to make amends but may suffer undue hardship if held responsible for the entire cost of the damages he or she caused. If the insurance company required standardised agreements, practitioners would have to question the value of their involvement in restorative processes. Restorative programmes do not want to 'run the risk of becoming debt collection schemes for corporate and commercial entities, as opposed to providing negotiation or mediation opportunities for individual victims and young persons' (Pate and Peachey, 1988: 115).

'Restorative justice cannot be done *to* the offender, or *for* the offender, but must be done *with* the offender' (McCold, 2000: 392). The benefits of restorative justice are often gained through participation in a restorative process.[13] It has been found that young offenders who meet with the victims of their offences are more likely to perceive the process as fair, and increased feelings of fair treatment have been shown to have a positive impact on the willingness of young offenders to pay restitution (Schiff, 1999). Further research would need to be carried out to determine if this holds true with regard to the participation of corporate stakeholders in restorative processes.

Another concern would be that, as motor vehicle offences happen with relative frequency, insurance companies may not have the resources (or the desire) to be directly involved in a dialogue with each offender referred to a restorative programme. Dialogue is one of the core processes that Presser and Van Voorhis (2002) suggest 'distinguish[es] ... restorative justice interventions … from other correctional responses to crime' (p. 167). In the context of restorative responses they suggest that 'dialogues are exchanges of information about what happened, psychological and material harms, moral values, and just courses of action' that are 'expected to change people and communities such as by arousing offender empathy' (ibid.). If insurance companies choose not to be involved in the process but request restitution, restorative programmes would have to evaluate the impact of this to assess whether this results in an outcome that is truly restorative.

The involvement of insurance companies may result in other unintended consequences for restorative programmes and their partici-pants. Participation in restorative programmes is generally voluntary.[14] If there is a possibility that the person responsible may suffer more onerous consequences as a result of participating in a restorative programme, they may choose *not* to participate but, instead, may choose to take their chances in court. This possibility would need to be monitored and the effects evaluated. Alternatively, the offender may request that a lawyer assist them through the restorative process. The involvement of lawyers in restorative processes is generally discouraged due to fears that their presence will 'introduce confrontation' (Wright, 2002: 665) or 'create barriers for a smooth mediation process' (Levrant et al., 1999: 7).

One issue that remains is the uncertainty regarding the role of a restorative justice programme if the offender chooses *not* to involve the insurance company. Could the offender still participate in a restorative process with the direct victim or would the case have to proceed to court?

Conclusion

The involvement of insurance companies in restorative processes is a controversial and possibly unpopular suggestion; however, it is hoped that raising the issue will result in restorative justice practitioners asking themselves questions about who the stakeholders in restorative processes are and how they should be involved. In addition, practitioners need to be aware of the unintended consequences of their actions. For example, accepting cases in which an insurance claim could be filed may result in civil claims against their clients. Practitioners need to ask themselves how this possibility can best be dealt with in a way that is congruent with the principles of restorative justice. These are not easy questions to answer, particularly in situations in which the diverse and not necessarily compatible interests of the offender, the direct victim, the community and a corporate entity must be taken into account.

Enlisting insurance companies to represent the needs of the 'community' in restorative processes is not without its dangers. The consequences of any changes to programme policy such as those suggested in this chapter would have to be monitored by examining statistics regarding the number of cases dealt with and their outcomes, as well as by evaluating the more intangible effects on the satisfaction of the participants with the process.

Notes

1 Many restorative programmes prefer not to use the label 'offender', preferring instead to use 'the person who caused the harm'.

2 It is interesting to note that he does not include emotional suffering in this category. McCold (2000) also includes as *secondary victims* 'those who suffer because they have a personal relationship of responsibility with a victim or offender, including family members of offenders and victims' (p. 365).

3 Insurance Corporation of British Columbia (ICBC) statistics state that there were 22,100 claims for auto theft, 56,022 claims for vehicle break-ins and 52,662 claims for vandalism in BC in 2001 (ICBC, 2003a).

4 ICBC statistics state that 130,784 claims for theft, break-in and vandalism in BC in 2001 resulted in a total cost of $167.1 million (ICBC, 2003a).

5 See Umbreit (1996) for research regarding the impact of participating in victim offender mediation on both victims and offenders. See also Immarigeon (1999) for a review of the literature on this point.

6 The Insurance Council of Canada is involved in attempts to reduce auto theft through crime prevention and technical measures by making vehicles harder to steal and more difficult and less profitable to resell (Pfeifer and Skakum, 2002). Insurance companies are involved in local programmes in other provinces: the Regina Auto Theft Strategy identifies, and provides programmes to respond to, four categories of offenders: youth at risk, first-time offenders, repeat offenders and high-risk repeat offenders (Pfeifer and Skakum, 2002). Help Eliminate Auto Theft (HEAT) is an alternative measures programme in place to respond to first-time auto theft offenders as part of this strategy. Offenders who complete the programme 'will not have a criminal record and may be excused from future litigation for damages enacted by SGI [Saskatchewan Government Insurance]' (Pfeifer and Skakum, 2002: 23).

7 A provincial crown corporation, ICBC was 'established in 1973 to provide universal auto insurance to BC motorists. All motorists in BC are required to buy a basic package of ICBC Autoplan insurance that provides coverage for third-party legal liability protection, accident benefits, underinsured motorist protection, hit-and-run and uninsured motorists protection and inverse liability' (ICBC, 2003b).

8   Restorative justice has also been criticised for perpetuating an individualistic construction of crime while ignoring the structural inequality (see Roche, 2003).

9   Advising offenders of their right to consult counsel is currently part of the intake process for most if not all restorative justice programmes.

10 Restorative programmes would have to decide whether separate conferences would take place to address the concerns of the direct victim and the insurance company or if it would be beneficial to bring everyone together at one time.

11 See Kruttschnitt (1985) and Hagan (1982) for a comparison of how individual victims and corporate victims are treated in the courtroom. Kruttschnitt (1985) found that businesses are in fact treated differently from individuals in the criminal courtroom – she found that offences in which there is a corporate victim result in longer probation sentences. Hagan (1982) found that, due to the fact the criminal justice system and corporate entities are both bureaucracies and thus have similar modes of operation, the criminal justice system serves the interest of the corporate entities better than it serves individual victims.

12 Johnstone (2002) specifies community in this instance as the offender's micro-community, not the macro-community.

13 There is disagreement within the field about whether parties need to come together in order for a process to be truly restorative (see McCold, 2000; Bazemore and Walgrave, 1999).

14 See Bazemore (2000), McCold (2000) and Walgrave (2003) for discussions of the use of coercion in restorative processes.

References

Bazemore, G. (2000) 'Rock and Roll, Restorative Justice and the Continuum of the Real World: A Response to 'Purism' in Operationalizing Restorative Justice', *Contemporary Justice Review*, 3(4): 459–77.

Bazemore, G. and Leip, L. (2000) 'Victim Participation in the New Juvenile Court: Tracking Judicial Attitudes Toward Restorative Justice', *Justice System Journal*, 21(2): 199–226.

Bazemore, G. and Walgrave, L. (1999) 'Restorative Juvenile Justice: In Search of Fundamentals and an Outline for Systemic Reform', in G. Bazemore and L. Walgrave (eds), *Restorative Juvenile Justice: Repairing the Harm of Youth Crime*. Monsey, NY: Criminal Justice Press.

Bussman, K. D. (1992) 'Morality, Symbolism and Criminal Law: Chances and Limits of Mediation Programs', in H. Messmer and H. Otto (eds), *Restorative Justice on Trial: Pitfalls and Potentials of Victim Offender Mediation*. Dordrecht: Kluwer Academic.

Christie, N. (1977) 'Conflicts as Property', *British Journal of Criminology*, 17(1): 1–15.

Hagan, J. (1982) 'The Corporate Advantage: A Study of Involvement of Corporate and Individual Victims in a Criminal Justice System', *Social Forces*, 60(4): 993–1022.

Immarigeon, R. (1999) 'Restorative Justice, Juvenile Offenders and Crime Victims: A Review of the Literature', in G. Bazemore and L. Walgrave (eds), *Restorative Juvenile Justice: Repairing the Harm of Youth Crime*. Monsey, NY: Criminal Justice Press.

Insurance Corporation of British Columbia (2003a) 'Auto Crime Incidents Reported to ICBC – 2000–2001. Comparison for Regions and Selected Cities'; accessed 29 April 2003 from ICBC at: http://www.icbc.com/Crime-Fraud/index.html.

Insurance Corporation of British Columbia (2003b) 'Corporate Information'; accessed 29 March 2003 from ICBC at: http://www.icbc.com/Inside_ICBC/corpinfo.html.

Johnstone, G. (2002) *Restorative Justice: Ideals, Values and Debates*. Portland, OR: Willan Publishing.

Kruttschnitt, C. (1985) 'Are Businesses Treated Differently? A Comparison of the Individual Victim and the Corporate Victim in the Criminal Courtroom', *Sociological Inquiry*, 55(3): 225–38.

Levrant, S., Cullen, F., Fulton, B. and Wozniak, J. (1999) 'Reconsidering Restorative Justice: The Corruption of Benevolence Revisited?', *Crime and Delinquency*, 45(1): 3–27.

McCold, P. (2000) 'Toward a Holistic Vision of Restorative Juvenile Justice: A Reply to the Maximalist Model', *Contemporary Justice Review*, 3(4): 357–414.

McCold, P. and Wachtel, B. (1998) 'Community Is Not a Place: A New Look at Community Justice Initiatives', *Contemporary Justice Review*, 1: 71–85.

Messmer, H. and Otto, H.-U. (1992) *Restorative Justice on Trial: Pitfalls and Potentials of Victim–Offender Mediation – International Research Perspectives*. Dordrecht: Kluwer.

Mika, H. and Zehr, H. (2003) 'A Restorative Framework for Community Justice Practice', in K. McEvoy and T. Newburn (eds), *Criminology, Conflict Resolution and Restorative Justice*. New York: Palgrave Macmillan.

Pate, K. J. and Peachey, D. E. (1988) 'Face-to-Face: Victim–Offender Mediation under the Young Offenders Act', in J. Hudson, J. P. Hornick and B. A. Burrows (eds), *Justice and the Young Offender in Canada*. Toronto: Wall and Thompson.

Pfeifer, J. and Skakum, K. (2002) *Regina Auto Theft Strategy: Process Evaluation*; accessed 21 June 2004 from: http://www.cps.gov.sk.ca/Publications/PfeiferProcessEvaluation.pdf.

Presser, L. and Van Voorhis, P. (2002) 'Values and Evaluation: Assessing Processes and Outcomes of Restorative Justice Programs', *Crime and Delinquency*, 48(1): 162–88.

Roche, D. (2003) *Accountability in Restorative Justice*. New York: Oxford University Press.

Ross, R. (2001) *Victims and Criminal Justice: Exploring the Disconnect*. A discussion paper prepared for presentation at the 27th Annual Conference of the National

Organization for Victim Assistance, 22 August 2001, at Edmonton, Alberta, Canada.

Schiff, M. (1999) 'The Impact of Restorative Interventions on Juvenile Offenders', in G. Bazemore and L. Walgrave (eds), *Restorative Juvenile Justice: Repairing the Harm of Youth Crime*. Monsey, NY: Criminal Justice Press.

Sharpe, S. (1998) *Restorative Justice: A Vision for Healing and Change*. Edmonton Victim Offender Mediation Society.

Umbreit, M. (1996) 'Restorative Justice Through Mediation: The Impact of Programs in Four Canadian Provinces', in B. Galaway and J. Hudson (eds), *Restorative Justice: International Perspectives*. Monsey, NY: Criminal Justice Press.

Umbreit, M. (1999) 'Avoiding the Marginalization and "McDonaldization" of Victim–Offender Mediation: A Case Study in Moving Toward the Mainstream', in Bazemore, G. and Walgrave, L. (eds), *Restorative Juvenile Justice: Repairing the Harm of Youth Crime*. Monsey, NY: Criminal Justice Press.

Van Ness, D. and Strong, K. H. (1997a) *Restorative Justice Practice* (monograph). Washington, DC: Justice Fellowship.

Van Ness, D. and Strong, K.H. (1997b) *Restoring Justice*. Cincinnati, OH: Anderson.

Walgrave, L. (2003) 'Imposing Restoration Instead of Inflicting Pain: Reflections on the Judicial Reaction to Crime', in A. Von Hirsch, J. V. Roberts and A. Bottoms (eds), *Restorative Justice and Criminal Justice: Competing or Reconcilable Paradigms?* Portland, OR: Hart Publishing.

Walgrave, L. and Bazemore, G. (1999) 'Reflections on the Future of Restorative Justice for Juveniles', in G. Bazemore and L. Walgrave (eds), *Restorative Juvenile Justice: Repairing the Harm of Youth Crime*. Monsey, NY: Criminal Justice Press.

Weitekamp, E. (1999) 'The History of Restorative Justice', in G. Bazemore and L. Walgrave (eds), *Restorative Juvenile Justice: Repairing the Harm of Youth Crime*. Monsey, NY: Criminal Justice Press.

Weitekamp, E. G. M. (2002) 'Restorative Justice: Present Prospects and Future Direction', in E. G. M. Weitekamp and H.-J. Kerner (eds), *Restorative Justice: Theoretical Foundations*. Portland, OR: Willan Publishing.

Woolford, A. and Ratner, R. S. (2003) 'Nomadic Justice? Restorative Justice on the Margins of the Law', *Social Justice*, 30(1): 177–94.

Wright, M. (2002) 'The Court as Last Resort: Victim-Sensitive, Community-Based Responses to Crime', *British Journal of Criminology*, 42: 654–67.

Zehr, H. (1997) 'Restorative Justice: the Concept', *Corrections Today*, December: 68–70.

Zehr, H. (2002) *The Little Book of Restorative Justice*. Intercourse, PA: Good Books.

Part 4

Evaluating Restorative Justice

Chapter 12

Penetrating the walls: implementing a system-wide restorative justice approach in the justice system

Don Clairmont

Abstract

In November 1999, after several years of pre-implementation planning and extensive discussions among both non-profit agencies delivering alternative measures and leaders at all levels of the justice system, Nova Scotia launched its ambitious restorative justice initiative. The central objective was to have the restorative justice approach operationalised in different strategic ways, phased in by offender status and by region, and applicable to all offences and all offenders throughout the province. Compared with other Canadian restorative justice initiatives, the Nova Scotia model is unusual not only in its scope but also in its mixture of core paid staff and volunteers, and its province-wide coordination. Initial research indicated that however well funded, prepared and institutionalised, the restorative justice initiative would have to deal with two major 'walls' limiting and marginalising its impact on the justice system. These 'walls' were the uncertain engagement of post-charge, post-police, criminal justice system role-players, and the hesitant support and participation of victims and community leaders advocating on behalf of victims. This chapter examines the processes and outcomes associated with implementation to date, especially highlighting process issues and the successes and challenges in penetrating these 'walls'. The chapter draws upon an extensive and in-depth evaluation that the author has been conducting of the Nova Scotia initiative.

The central challenges for Nova Scotia restorative justice

There is an incorrect view of the [restorative justice] agencies as diversion services. What they offer within the criminal justice system is a different way of looking at crime, with an opportunity to work out effective outcomes in complex conflicts (Foundation Day Discussion, Nova Scotia Restorative Justice, January 2003).

The Nova Scotia Restorative Justice Initiative (NSRJI) was implemented in November 1999. It was preceded by almost two years of discussions throughout the criminal justice system in Nova Scotia, protocol development, strengthening the capacity of the service providers (non-profit agencies which had delivered alternative measures for youth for over a decade) and other preparatory planning. It is now a thoroughly institutionalised programme, coordinated and entirely funded by the Department of Justice, Nova Scotia. The thrust of the NSRJI, as cited above, has been, in principle, to implement the restorative justice approach for all offenders and offences, albeit in stages and utilising strategic interventions appropriate to the different circumstances.

As indicated in three major evaluation monographs written by this author (Clairmont, 2001, 2002, 2003), the programme has been quite successful in most respects and has made significant progress with regard to all its objectives. Not surprisingly, NSRJI has to date largely depended on police referrals (with significant low-end crown prosecutor referrals in the Halifax area) and could be said to have been largely a diversion programme for low-end offences. There are clear indications that such a characterisation is increasingly less valid as new collaborative arrangements have been developed to secure referrals beyond the police level, and most especially at the prosecutions and corrections entry point (i.e. custody and probation). As these changes impact on the NSRJI, they yield a more penetrating implementation of the restorative justice approach and, in these respects, make the NSRJI a potential world leader in the restorative justice movement. Diversion, healing, reintegration, complex cases and serious offenders, all increasingly become 'grist' for the NSRJI 'mill'.

While much is known about extra-judicial measures, alternative and restorative justice at the front-end of the criminal justice system, little is known about how these approaches impact at higher levels. Clearly, some re-specification might be required here; for example, the concept of 'an agreement' associated with success at a 'diversion' restorative justice session probably differs profoundly (would lack of such an 'agreement' represent failure?) in the post-sentence restorative justice session given that the offender has already completed his or her sentence. This uncertainty and ambiguity concerning the operationalisation of the restorative justice approach is largely the consequence of restorative justice programmes either failing to penetrate the criminal justice system (i.e. remaining rather marginal) or being of limited scope (i.e. not being part of a comprehensive system-wide programme). Implementation that purports to be system-wide takes time to penetrate more fully. The NSRJI, after several years, has only just begun to penetrate deeply.

The context for restorative justice

Restorative justice as a social movement within the criminal justice system has had both a long history and a chequered past (Viano, 2000). The criminal justice system in its present guise (i.e. structures and processes) has developed over the past two centuries, at least in part in reaction to practices advocated in restorative justice (e.g. direct participation by offenders and victims, informalism or popular justice). The alternative justice movement of the 1970s, less theoretically elaborated than the current restorative justice movement and more focused on diversion and 'community' mediation, was largely discredited by academic research and criminal justice system practitioners as being ineffective, inefficient and of limited value for larger goals of justice. A major circumstance associated with this judgment was that alternative justice practices, such as diversion and community panels, were of limited scope (e.g. minor offences, restricted to special population segments) and largely marginalised by system-equilibrating forces within the criminal justice system.

For a number of reasons (continuing push factors associated with the costs and alleged rehabilitative ineffectiveness of the criminal justice system, and pull factors associated with the victims' movement, Aboriginal justice movement and the revitalised moral entrepreneurship of progressives and/or religiously committed advocates) the restorative justice movement has become very influential over the past decade. Restorative justice philosophy and practices have explicitly assumed the mantle of alternative justice, building upon the past approaches. It remains to be seen what impact they will have on the criminal justice system. There are some reasons to think that the impact will be substantial this time. The restorative justice movement appears to be more theoretically firmed up now, more internationally rooted, more focused on holistic, system-level change, and to have much stronger support among senior governmental officials and justice personnel. There is a widespread appreciation that 'entering the mainstream' requires the recognition of restorative justice as a basic premise of how the criminal justice system is to function (Clairmont, 2000). Most restorative justice initiatives have been primarily directed at young offenders and low-end offences and, at that level, have established a solid basis for optimism among advocates (Latimer et al., 2001). Still, it is often contended that only when restorative justice emerges as an important factor in how serious offences and adults are treated will it trump the marginalisation of the alternative justice experience and realise its promise, even in how restorative justice would apply to young offenders.

The social constructions of restorative justice (RJ) and the criminal justice system (CJS) that have accompanied RJ's recent revitalisation, despite the greater grounding and realism of its advocates, remain largely edenic and binary in character. RJ is depicted in positive ideal-type terms and contrasted to the CJS, which is depicted also ideal-typically but with much emphasis on its negative features. In this regard – sharply contrasting themes and images to the conventional approach – the RJ social constructionism has striking similarities to those social constructions associated with the community-based policing movement (which was presented as a radically new paradigm but subsequently became absorbed and compartmentalised in policing), and to the Aboriginal justice movement (which has sharply contrasted themes and images of Aboriginal and mainstream justice but which, thus far anyway, has made very modest inroads in how natives receive justice). Moreover, there is neither much discussion of the appropriateness of diverse RJ strategies for different kinds of offences and offender-victim situations nor studies of how the dynamics of the 'black box' of the RJ session/intervention actually work. Other areas of shortcoming include the lack of discussion or analysis concerning strategies to effect a system-wide usage of RJ principles in the CJS (e.g. how to get RJ used more at CJS levels subsequent to the laying of charges) and to convince victims and victims' advocates of the appropriateness of the RJ approach.

If RJ is not to experience the same fate as alternative justice approaches did in the 1960s and 1970s, there has to be more sophisticated, empirically based conceptualisation, more strategic reflection and more vigorous effort to have the RJ approach permeate all levels of the justice system. It should be recognised, too, that there are credible alternatives to RJ, certainly in dealing with young offenders, which have to be taken into consideration. Intensive supervision, whether of a rehabilitative, supportive or a punitive, monitoring sort, is advocated by many researchers and CJS practitioners. In these models, most young offenders – low-end offenders – presumably can be dealt with through letters of caution or low investment strategies, while the intense supervision would be directed at the serious and repeat offenders. It is not clear where the RJ approach would fit in these models. It may well be that the restorative justice movement would carve out a middle ground of applicability for offenders and offences, between minimal intervention strategies for the 'low end' and intensive supervision for the 'high end.' It may also be that restorative justice strategies or practices will become a component of a larger, more thorough intervention. Clearly, issues of process (i.e. how RJ is implemented and meshes with other philosophies and practices in the CJS) and outcomes (i.e. how well RJ achieves its objectives of participation and reconciliation/reintegration of all parties to an offence) are important and intertwined.

There seems little doubt, though, that one key to a major impact of RJ on the justice system will be getting past the police gatekeepers. Judges, crown prosecutors and correctional officials have often been the moral entrepreneurs behind RJ movements in Canada and some exerted a significant presence in the NSRJ initiative being examined in this chapter. Still, the RJ literature indicates that, in both Europe and North America, prosecutors and judges have generally been reluctant to engage in RJ and to see it as more than a fall-back (Archibald, 2001; Green, 1999). A leading RJ scholar has contended that

> ... the strongest opposition has come from lawyers, including some judges, under the influence of well-known critiques of the justice of informal crime processing (Braithwaite, 1997: 3).

In his appraisal of prosecutors' viewpoints internationally, Archibald found

> ... a uniform tendency for prosecutors to see their role as one of presenting evidence in court to get convictions, rather than promoting problem-solving restorative options (Archibald, 2001: 38).

Notwithstanding the dramatic and international development of problem-solving courts (e.g. mental health courts and drug treatment courts) over the past decade, the corrections level may well be the level of the CJS where the most significant implementation of the RJ philosophy will occur in the near future.

The challenge and the opportunity

The NSRJ could well be said to be on the cusp of breaking through the 'walls' or barriers that have prevented earlier penetration of RJ into the mainstream of the CJS. It is starting to get significant referrals from beyond the police level, especially from the corrections/probation level. There is now a presumption that RJ could apply to all correctional files. Three significant developments here have been: (1) a new protocol which permits RJ agency staff to review probation files on a monthly basis and suggest cases for RJ intervention; (2) a community reintegration project to develop protocols for RJ processing in cases where the institutionalised offender is about to return to the community; and (3) a pre-probation breach charge project where, possibly in lieu of laying charges, probation officers refer cases to RJ agencies for possible RJ intervention. The new Canadian Youth Criminal Justice Act 2003 (YCJA) has, of course, stimulated some of these developments, which to a lesser extent are also occurring at the Crown and judicial levels. There seems to be little doubt that RJ agencies will be receiving more complex cases and that the value of the RJ approach is increasingly subject to a more rigorous test. This trend has been developing quickly, as indicated in the NSRJ evaluation cited in the references for this chapter (e.g. Clairmont, 2003).

There has been some progress dealing with the other main 'wall' to a more thoroughly implemented RJ, namely victim/victim advocate resistance. The evaluation literature indicates that RJ programmes usually provide more services for victims and more opportunities for the airing of their views as well as some direct restitution (Clairmont, 2003). Still, victim participation has been modest even for the minor offences typically dealt with in RJ programmes and there appears to a widespread reluctance among victims and victim advocacy groups such as seniors, women's organisations and business leaders to see RJ extend much beyond cases involving minor property crime and young offenders. RJ programmes, such as the NSRJ initiative, typically have been introduced from the top down from within the CJS system and without significant community involvement, and have been implemented through organisations with a legacy of being offender-oriented service agencies. It is not surprising, then, that quite apart from the controversial issues of the merits of the RJ approach in dealing with complex matters and serious harms, there is considerable reluctance and suspicion in the victim 'community'. Clearly, if the RJ philosophy is to become more widespread in dealing with offences as projected in the NSRJ objectives, there will have to be more partnering with salient community organisations, more strategic planning concerning how RJ is to be implemented for different more serious offences, more training for the staff and volunteers to effect RJ in such situations, and extensions of the programming to adults.

An overview of the processes and outcomes of the NSRJ initiative to date

The author has recently completed two assessments of the NSRJ initiative dealing, respectively, with outcomes and with processes (Clairmont, 2002, 2003). Each report begins with an overview of the NSRJ programme, focusing upon, in sequence, the project challenge and background, project outcomes/processes and indicators, the key partners and major project elements, interim process evaluations, interim outcomes evaluations and lessons learned. The NSRJ programme has basically been implemented, as planned, as a system-level innovation bringing the restorative justice (RJ) philosophy and practices to bear on almost all youth offences everywhere in the province. A continuing moratorium on sexual assault and spousal/partner violence (put in place in 2000 in response to criticisms from female-oriented victims' advocates several months after the NSRJ initiative was launched) and the restriction of NSRJ to young offenders (there has been a delay in extending the RJ programme to adult offenders) limit its system-wide implementation at present.

The NSRJ programme has been thoroughly institutionalised within the Nova Scotia Department of Justice and is no longer a project marginal to justice planning and strategising. It is argued that the NSRJ has been a successful initiative in substance as well. It has made significant progress on all objectives delineated in its originating proposal. The path of change has been in the desired and anticipated direction on all relevant issues – recidivism, participant involvement and satisfaction, the utilisation of the RJ session format, agency capacity, provincial coordination and the presumption of restorative justice among police and corrections – capturing, respectively, perhaps, the diversion and healing dimensions of restorative justice. Still, the 'value-added', in comparison to its alternative measures predecessor, has been modest, and unless there is much greater collaboration and use of the RJ agencies by crown prosecutors, judges and correctional staff, it will likely remain so. Difficult challenges for the NSRJ programme will come if it has to deal more with serious offenders and offences, with adults and with family violence of all sorts. Then the adequacies of the RJ strategies, the agencies' capacities and their collaborative linkages with other community service providers will be more severely tested. There remains widespread scepticism among field-level criminal justice system personnel and community leaders that the NSRJ and the non-profit RJ agencies could meet these challenges, but, at the same time, there is much support for the programme as it is presently implemented.

Outcomes

The outcomes report (Clairmont, 2002) deals with core outcomes analyses, that is case processing under restorative justice and its impact on the major NSRJ objectives for offenders, victims, the community and the criminal justice system. Analyses are also provided, in order to assess these outcome impacts more fully, on court-processed youth cases and more serious offenders and offences. Analyses of court-processed youth charges and cases for 2001 indicated that the NSRJ programme and police cautioning did have a modest effect in reducing the court load, continuing a trend observed in the 2000 data when the restorative justice programme compared favourably on this measure vis-a-vis the alternative measures programme it replaced. Still, more than one-third of all charges and cases dealt with in court involved minor, or level one, offences (four levels of offences were delineated in the original NSRJ protocol). Youth aged 16 or 17 were the chief young offenders in terms of both numbers of offences and serious offences. The minor level offences handled in court typically result in probation, fines or court costs, singly or in combination. Even in the limited time-frame of the data set and the absence of data on criminal record information prior to November 1999 or in adult court for those who reached 18 years of age, the court data indicated there was significant recidivism. Shortfalls in the provincial court data management system (JOIS) included the absence of measures of ethnicity and socio-economic status, and the limited time-span of the data.

Formal police cautions have increased with the duration of the Nova Scotia restorative justice initiative, and have been very largely restricted to level one offences and first-time offenders. In these respects, perhaps as anticipated in the NSRJ programme, the police caution system virtually reproduces the earlier alternative measures programme in Nova Scotia that focused on level one offences and first-time offenders. There was some interesting variation in the issuing of cautions by police service and by region. There was some modest variation by age, gender and ethnicity (e.g. females virtually always were cautioned for shoplifting while males received letters of caution more often for less minor offences).

The data also indicate that cautions and restorative justice referrals have gained a modestly larger share of the total youth charges or cases since 1999. Nova Scotia courts are dealing with fewer level one or minor youth offences. Both police cautions and police RJ referrals increased significantly in 2001 while crown prosecutor and other RJ referrals remained essentially at their 2000 levels. Police cautions and police referrals essentially focus on level one or minor (i.e. the 'alternative measures template') offences and there has been little change in that regard over the first 25 months of the NSRJ programme. Crown prosecutor and higher CJS entry level RJ referrals have moved decidedly in the direction of involving more serious youth charges but that benefit, from the NSRJ perspective, has been somewhat mitigated by the lack of growth in the number of 'crown prosecutor and other' RJ referrals. The data also point to the diversity of discretion in cautioning and restorative justice referral; there are clearly some police services and some police officers more likely than others to exercise the discretion to caution or to refer youth cases to restorative justice agencies.

The Restorative Justice Information System (RJIS) – a data management system created for the NSRJ initiative – yielded some useful comparisons between cautions and referrals to restorative justice and underlined the significance of post-charge restorative justice referrals. While police cautions were quite evenly distributed among female and male youths, it is clear that restorative justice referrals were given more to males who, of course, were considerably more likely to have committed eligible offences. Post-charge RJ referrals were the most likely to be directed at male youths (i.e. 67 per cent). The age category 14 to 15 received the most referrals but the distribution of referrals was more skewed to older youths than was the distribution of police cautions. Whether discussing charges or cases, post-charge referrals were modestly more likely than police referrals to be directed at males, older youths and incidents where the accused faced more than one charge (presumably a weak indicator of seriousness).

The RJIS data gathered through the NSRJ programme indicates that males and older youths are proportionately more likely than females and younger youths to receive a restorative justice referral than a caution. Post-charge RJ referrals enhance that difference, not surprisingly given that these types of referrals are less likely to focus on level one or minor offences. Recidivism in terms of repeat RJ referrals has been quite modest. Recidivism in general terms (i.e. repeat offence incidents) was shown in this data set to be less likely if one's first case processed was done as either a caution or restorative justice referral rather than through the courts. And while there are many caveats to acknowledge concerning these findings, at the very least they are consistent with restorative justice objectives.

Overall, then, analyses of the processing of youth cases in Nova Scotia have found that cautions and RJ referrals have reduced the court load each year by some 6 per cent compared to the alternative measures era but that about one-third of the court load still involves minor or level one offences. Recidivism is high among those going to court and those going to court are especially likely to be males and aged 16 or 17. Both cautions and restorative justice referrals have increased significantly since 1999 and together now account for between 20 per cent and 25 per cent of all youth charges or cases. Cautions and police referrals have remained focused primarily (over 80 per cent) on minor, level one offences where the offender is a first-time offender. Still, there was significant variation in the police use of discretion in this regard. Crown prosecutors and other RJ referrals typically involved more serious offences and repeat offenders but the numbers here have shown little increase over the first two years of the NSRJ programme. There is some evidence that cautioning and restorative justice referral reduce recidivism compared to court processing, but it is difficult to draw firm conclusions given the limitations of the data sets and lack of random assignment in the NSRJ programme. Detailed analyses of the Halifax Regional Police Service's processing of youth crime underlined the point that police cautions and RJ referrals were basically given to first-time offenders for level one offences. That combination has accounted for more than 90 per cent of all Halifax police cautions and referrals since November 1999. The Halifax police data also point to significant differences by gender and by ethnicity. In particular, the high level of accused among Afro-Canadian youths, in both alternative justice and court venues, merits serious attention and underlines the need for creative and perhaps more macro-level strategies to supplement the NSRJ initiative.

The impact, from the participants' perspective, has also been quite positive. The RJ session exit data for 2001 (year two) reveal a strong, pervasive positive consensus about the experience among all types of participants and over the different types of sessions and offences. The patterns found strongly echo those found in the year-one data. Where there is variation, the factors producing it are the participant's role (e.g. whether the person is an offender, a victim or a supporter) and, to a lesser extent, the type of session participated in (e.g. accountability or victim–offender conference). The interpretation of the variation advanced in the outcomes report suggests that, where differences exist, these differences support the premises and objectives of the restorative justice initiative.

As for the follow-up interviews, the interviewee sample appeared to be representative of the participants attending the RJ sessions in the first-phase agencies. Roughly half of those in each role category who agreed to be interviewed were interviewed, though only some 43 per cent of the offending youths were. The description and analyses of the follow-up interviews represented a 'first cut', pending the examination of interviewee comments and potentially more sophisticated statistical analysis. The follow-up data dealt with participants' assessments of pre-conference issues, the conference itself, the agreement or disposition reached, reintegration and closure issues, and overall assessment of the RJ experience.

The RJ participants indicated that for the most part they had little knowledge of restorative justice approaches prior to the incident being considered. The reasons for participating varied by role, with offenders and their parents/supporters emphasising the avoidance of court and a criminal record, while victims and their parents/supporters stressed that they liked the idea of RJ, as it was explained to them. Evidence suggests that few participants needed much persuasion and certainly most considered their participation to be totally voluntary. The majority of RJ session participants indicated that they had significant contact with agency staff prior to the session and that this contact involved both telephone calls and face-to-face meetings. As for the conference itself, the perceived 'most important thing about it' varied by role, with young offenders emphasising the 'good resolution' of the process and the avoidance of court, while their parents/supporters pointed to the opportunity for the youth to show remorse and apologise. On the victim 'side', the opportunity to talk about the offence was highlighted. Few participants reported surprises happening at the conference but when surprises were noted, the positive surprises were more common than the negative ones, especially on the part of the young offenders themselves.

The large majority of participants in all role categories could find nothing negative about the conference and, on the positive side, it was commonly noted that they had an opportunity to discuss the incident and present their views about it and what should be done. Virtually all participants considered that the conference was fair to all parties and most interviewees were emphatic about this feature; the least positive were the victims but even 50 per cent of them considered the conference to be 'very much' fair. Both offenders and victims were equally likely to report (and with equal emphasis) that they understood what was happening at the session, were treated with respect, had adequate support there, and liked the conference set-up. On both the offender and the victim 'sides', a large percentage of respondents emphasised that they had had their say. Most neutral participants reported that they witnessed a frank and in-depth exchange among offenders, their parents, their supporters and the victims and victims' supporters.

The participants, especially the offenders and their parents/supporters, indicated that in retrospect they were satisfied with the conference outcomes at the time of the session. The large majority reported themselves also to be happy with how the agreement had worked out for them, although there was some modest drop-off in enthusiasm on the victims' parts. Offenders reported significant closure in 'being able to put it all behind now', while their parents/supporters reported themselves better able to cope with the youth. Roughly 40 per cent of the victims reported positive closure but a large minority indicated that they were unsure on this score. Most neutral participants considered that the conference had probably helped to reintegrate the offender into the community.

In assessing the RJ experience as a whole, few participants could identify anything when asked about 'the worst thing' but they were quick to cite various facets as 'the best thing'. Offenders and their supporters emphasised avoiding court and the fairness and friendliness of the sessions, while victims and their supporters highlighted having their say and the direct communication between the offender and the victim. Few suggested that in retrospect the matter should have gone through the court process. Most respondents considered that, if the latter had happened, there would have been significant differences, primarily that the court experience would have been more intimidating and yielded more severe sanctions. The participants overwhelmingly believed that, for offences such as the ones featured in their incidents, restorative justice was the desirable option. However, there was much less enthusiasm among all role types, save the neutral participants, for utilising restorative justice in the case of more serious offences; this restrictive position was especially taken by the victims and their parents or supporters. In conclusion, the participants generally considered the RJ experience to be quite positive and felt that no changes were required concerning its structure and processes.

The outcomes report also examined more deeply serious offences and offenders, where the former involved level three and four offences, and the latter multiple repeat offenders within a one-year time span. Here all data were drawn from the metropolitan Halifax area serviced by the Halifax Regional Police Service. Overall, robbery accounted for 75 per cent of the more serious offences committed by youth in 2001, those offences ineligible for police cautions or RJ referrals. Afro-Canadian youths and multiple repeat offenders were prominent among this group of offenders charged by Halifax police officers. If restorative justice programming were to impact on these youths it would have to be from referrals beyond the police level. Similarly, youths arrested on two or more occasions by Halifax police officers in 2000 typically continued to reoffend and get arrested in 2001, and in that year rarely received a caution or police RJ referral. They, too, were essentially outside the RJ system at the police level. Repeat offenders arrested by Halifax police in 2001 who did not have a record in 2000 were also disproportionately Afro-Canadian youth, and youths in this repeater grouping as a whole, typically (80 per cent), did not receive a police caution or RJ referral on any of their offences. Data can be (and will be) obtained to determine whether these repeat offenders and others involved in serious offences did receive subsequent RJ referrals at the crown prosecutor and corrections levels. Clearly, unless it is to be considered the case that these youths are beyond the scope of restorative justice (and that the focus in RJ programming has to be entirely on much more effective early intervention), there must be much more RJ activity at the crown prosecutor, judicial and corrections levels.

Turning to follow-up interviews conducted with those involved in court-processed cases, the offenders, supporters and victims in these court-directed cases reported that they were not presented with an RJ option, but many would have been interested in considering it. The total court processing experience was perceived in more positive terms by the youth than by either the parents/guardians or the victims. Youth appeared to more surprised by, and appreciative of, their treatment while the parents and the victims, perhaps focusing more on the substance of the experience, were more critical. Youth were more reticent but many presented a self-image of indifference and 'coolness'. Parents were more emotional and engaged in discussions of the experience. Victims, in turn, conveyed a sense of marginality in virtually all aspects of the process subsequent to the police investigation. Both youth supporters and victims reported less reintegration and closure than the youths did. While the plurality response in all three groupings was that the experience had not altered their views about the justice system, the youths were more likely than the parents or the victims to indicate that this court case experience had increased their confidence in and respect for the justice system.

Future evaluation of the NSRJ outcomes will continue to focus on the four major objectives of the initiative, dealing with the offenders (e.g. recidivism, behaviour and attitudes, etc.), the victims (e.g. participation and satisfaction), community (e.g. involvement and respect for the justice system) and the CJS itself (e.g. court load and collaboration with other justice players). In examining these concerns, there will be comparisons over time within the RJ case processing system (e.g. offences and offenders dealt with and victim participation), rural–urban comparisons in RJ processes and outcomes, and comparisons regarding the impact of RJ intervention at the police and crown prosecutor and corrections levels. The latter comparisons will be especially important given the lack of a random assignment of cases in the RJ programme. Referrals at the prosecutor and corrections levels are by definition more similar to cases processed through the courts involving more serious offenders and offences and effecting other aspects of restorative justice (i.e. more healing than diversion). The comparison of RJ and court-processed cases remains a main evaluation objective and new strategies are being devised to obtain larger, more representative, court samples.

Processes

The process report (Clairmont, 2003), deals with (1) the context for the NSRJ initiative and development; (2) the special features, value-added measures and central operational issues of the RJ agencies; (3) patterns of discretionary decision-making and perspectives on RJ and referrals held by police officers and crown prosecutors (the two major referral sources); and (4) the standpoints of CJS and community panel members whose assessments of RJ and the NSRJ are regularly monitored. In addition, there is a brief section on concluding observations and recommendations.

In examining the process dimension of the NSRJ initiative, the initial focus has been on 'placing' NSRJ and the RJ agencies with reference to restorative justice elsewhere in Canada, other related programming in Nova Scotia, the other constituents of the CJS and the earlier alternative measures service. It has been contended that NSRJ is unique in its hybrid character (e.g. significant core paid staff and large volunteer base) and in its system-wide objective. Within Nova Scotia, the linkages with other related programmes – the Royal Canadian Mounted Police's community justice forum, the Mi'kmaq's Young Offenders Program, the Public Prosecution Service's Cautioning Project and Corrections' Adult Diversion – were examined and the overall argument made that there is a positive symbiosis operating to the benefit of all programmes. The fiscal year 2001/2002, it was observed, has seen the institutionalisation of NSRJ and the implications of the programme having a place at the CJS table were discussed. Finally, several features of the RJ agencies were discussed, particularly those wherein the transformation from alternative measures to restorative justice was quite meaningful. The features discussed were resources (e.g. the resources implications for core staff, for volunteers and for different agencies), procedures (e.g. how the programme works and responding to victims), training and the scope of RJ activity (training was considered adequate only for the present and near-future scope of the RJ activity but some shortfalls were identified), networking and the active organisation (i.e. the push and pull factors that have profoundly changed the organisational style of the RJ agencies), and perceptions of the added value on the part of agency personnel (e.g. confidence that the transformation has yielded added value, an assessment that RJ is efficient and efficacious, and high intrinsic work satisfaction).

In terms of the three major criteria for determining the added value vis-a-vis alternative measures of the agencies' involvement in the NSRJ initiative, there is little doubt that progress has been made. According to both the restorative justice information system (RJIS) and the agencies' monthly reports, the RJ agencies received more referrals in 2001 than in

2000 and now handle more cases than in the alternative measures era. While police referrals accounted for most of the increase, there were modest gains in securing RJ referrals from the Crown prosecutor and corrections levels. The cases that the agencies dealt with in 2001 were, on average, more complex than those dealt with in 2000 and substantially more complex than those handled in the alternative measures era. The accountability session, analogous to the alternative measures conference, remained the most common type of session in 2001 but less so than in 2000, testimony to the increasing complexity of the agencies' interventions (i.e. involving victims and others much more in the agencies' contacts, services and conferencing). There were some interesting variations by agency in growth patterns, offences dealt with and types of sessions held.

The value-added measures were considered in the context of other important objectives such as the 'turnaround time' in the agencies' processing of RJ referrals and their multi-faceted response to victims. Through discussions with agency personnel and other sources, a number of key issues were identified as especially pertinent to the success of the agencies in meeting the NSRJ objectives. In large measure the issue of resources cut across almost all the areas of concern raised. There appeared to be a strong consensus that if the resources could be there for the training, the co-learning and the proactivity, then the challenges of getting and responding effectively to more serious referrals could be met. There was no apparent lack of confidence in the efficacy of the restorative justice alternative but there were frequent nagging doubts about whether the agencies, for the most part, were instead involved primarily in a 'downsizing and offloading' of justice responsibilities.

Virtually all referrals to the RJ agencies, thus far, have come from the police and crown prosecutors so much attention was paid to their perspectives on RJ and the patterns of their discretion in deciding whether to send a case to RJ or to proceed through the court process. A variety of samples were analysed. The findings from the several police samples were quite consistent. In deciding not to refer youth cases, police officers highlighted legally relevant variables (e.g. criminal record and the seriousness of the offence), or 'bad attitudes', or 'not taking responsibility' on the part of the offenders. The blending of the latter two factors was evident. The wishes of the victims were also heeded, especially where the victim was seen by police as supportive and in an authority relationship with the youth. The need to bring more sanctions than RJ presumably could to bear on problem youth acting up was also highlighted by police as a consideration for taking the incident to court. Police tended to see letters of caution and RJ referrals as 'a break' and limited in their interventionist efficacy.

Comparison of police and crown prosecutor discretionary decision-making revealed that police officers were focused more on the context and relationships entailed by the youth's actions or offence while the crown attorney focused on the offence itself. Police, with their more detailed knowledge of the youth, his or her social milieu, the criminal context and the victims, quite reasonably considering their role in the CJS, took all these factors into account in deciding whether to lay charges or divert. The prosecutor lacked that rich detail and had inadequate access to information but, perhaps more importantly, focused more on the fact that what was being considered were often 'minor offences by young kids', a focus that was probably due to the individual's professional training and a sense of what is legally relevant for a successful prosecution. Where police and prosecutor disagreed on a case – whether or not it was appropriate for RJ – police explained their decision to charge in terms of this larger context. Perhaps only a counter-argument based upon different or reconsidered contextual factors could have changed their minds; clearly, arguments solely on the act and the value of extra-judicial measures were not effective in doing so.

Each year, the evaluation re-interviews roughly 150 CJS and community leaders to ascertain their experiences with, and assessments of, the RJ initiative. The viewpoints and actual experiences of CJS panel members in 2001/2002 were marked more by continuity than by change vis-à-vis 2000/2001. At all levels, though, there was some detection by the panel members of modest changes, whether it be police officers' perceptions that more referrals involving more serious offending were being made at subsequent CJS levels, prosecutors' and judges' sense that fewer minor cases were being court-processed, defence counsel's belief that the RJ option was being acknowledged more in open court, victim services staff 'beginning to see some post-charge cases' going to RJ, or correctional officers' sense that 'natural minimums' were vanishing from their caseload partly because of the RJ initiative and that collaborating with the RJ agencies was increasingly incorporated into their case management. 'Other' CJS panel members, leaders in the RJ initiative, referred both to significant accomplishments and to significant challenges for the NSRJ programme. There was a widespread recognition that the RJ programme was now an established part of the CJS and could figure substantially in future CJS strategising, particularly if the results demonstrated efficacy and efficiency. There was evidence of RJ becoming more of a factor in the strategic planning of police, crown prosecutors, correctional staff and victim services officials. And this development was expected by many panel members to be enhanced due to the imperatives of the YCJA which emphasizes conferencing and reintegrative programming for young offenders.

Generally, CJS panel members readily identified the potential benefits of the RJ approach for all parties but especially for offenders and for the CJS as a whole. There was more ambivalence concerning the impact of RJ for victims, especially among panel members from victim services but also among the crown prosecutors and judges. With few exceptions, the panel members thought that the RJ programming should be extended to adults for minor, non-violent crimes at least. There was much divergence of views about whether the RJ programming should extend to more serious offending than it does now and to the moratorium offences, whatever their level of seriousness. Panel members from policing and victim services were quite wary of a lifting of the moratorium and of extending the reach of RJ. Defence counsel encouraged a broader implementation of the RJ approach. Crown prosecutors, judges and correctional panel members generally supported a broader implementation of RJ but their viewpoints were quite nuanced.

The different role-players raised different issues concerning the RJ initiative, ranging from police concerns about what to discuss at the RJ sessions to the concern of other panellists for inspiration and 'champions' from all segments of the CJS. Panel members usually emphasized the need for timely feedback on referrals made and for some evidence concerning the impact of the RJ intervention for both offenders and victims. For some role-players (e.g. police and victim services), RJ was seen as appropriate for a limited range of offending, and for most of the remainder (e.g. crown prosecutors and judges) RJ was seen as largely falling outside their initiative. In the case of defence counsel and correctional officers, there was uncertainty about how extensive their engagement might become. The 'wall' referred to in the year-one report (Clairmont, 2001), was still standing, its bricks clearly discernible, but there were many cracks and openings showing.

Information and knowledge were crucial factors for RJ referrals, operating in different ways at different levels of the CJS. For police, knowledge of the victims, the family background and the milieu was important to the exercise of their discretion. For crown prosecutors, their lack of such detailed background knowledge was central in their standpoint that RJ referrals should be left to the police save in special circumstances (e.g. defence counsel initiative, etc.). And judges, in turn, emphasized that they did not have sufficient relevant knowledge of the cases and offenders to exercise their initiative without requests from either the prosecution or the defence. Of course, other factors were found to be important and to interact with the knowledge factor, especially important here being the panel members' view of their role vis-à-vis other role-players. Clearly, if the objective is to obtain more and higher end referrals, then a strategy has to be developed for each CJS level: for example, some guidelines for prosecutorial or judicial referrals that transcend mere designation of eligible offences.

The 2001/2002 re-interviews of community panels found considerable continuity in their viewpoints and experiences with respect to NSRJ and RJ programmes. There continued to be sharp differences in enthusiasm with respect to both support and anticipation of benefits between the offender-oriented service panellists and those identified as representing victims' concerns (i.e. female-oriented victim advocates, seniors and family services representatives) and other community interests (e.g. school officials). Still, the common themes identified in 2000/2001 continued to undergird the different perspectives or standpoints. These include an emphasis on the macro social factors in the causation and prevention of youth crime, a general belief that dealing with minor youth property crime via the RJ approach is a good strategy, a caution about too quickly implementing a more elaborate RJ approach, and a sense that the RJ agencies have limited capacity and that the RJ intervention itself, as presently designed, is limited in its efficacy for dealing with offenders. Other perspectives included the contention that the NSRJ initiative has been top-down, CJS-exclusive and largely driven by downloading and cost considerations, and scepticism about the adequacy of the resources that government is prepared to invest in the initiative.

The offender-oriented individuals were knowledgeable about the NSRJ initiative and often quite engaged with it. They were very positive about the RJ approach and saw lots of potential benefit in it not only for offenders but also for victims, the community at large and the CJS. There was consensus among the panellists with respect to both the benefits and the possible extension of the RJ approach to more serious youth offending and to adult crimes. On offences of sexual assault and family violence, the panel members' views were quite varied but all exhibited some concerns about the utilisation of RJ without guidelines, more agency resources and some evidence of RJ's effectiveness. Three issues associated with the impact of the NSRJ initiative were highlighted by panel members: implementation resources, fairness (equity) concerns in terms of accessing RJ and the need to get the public on side.

Among the panellists chosen to represent the interests of victims and the community at large, there was much less enthusiasm for the RJ approach but, nevertheless, a widespread sense that it could be appropriate, at least for a narrow range of youth offending. Even the panellists most engaged in RJ programming, while clearly more enthused about its achievements and potential, were wary about any significant elaboration of the programme. Three factors appeared to account for this viewpoint on the RJ approach: the panellists' views of crime and justice, of the nature of the RJ intervention and of the resources available to the RJ agencies (for training, in-depth session preparation, etc.). These panellists typically did not think that more serious youth offending, adult offences, and sexual assault or family violence cases, should be referred to RJ, certainly not at the pre-court level, if at all.

There was virtually no change in standpoint reported by the victim-oriented panellists nor had their involvement in actual RJ programming increased. The female-oriented victims' advocates were much more exposed, over 2001/2002, to literature and debates on the RJ approach via research carried out by their provincial organisations. They had considerable knowledge about the RJ philosophy and its implementation in various contexts, though not in Nova Scotia (their research might well be filling that gap). The other panellists, with a few exceptions, had a limited awareness of the RJ approach and equally limited familiarity with NSRJ and the local RJ agencies. The victim-oriented panellists, on the whole, perceived the RJ programming as benefiting offenders and also possibly having some benefits for victims, the community and the CJS. At the same time, they thought there was a 'downside' in RJ for victims, and expressed scepticism that the potential benefits for the community and the CJS would be realised. The panellists raised a number of general issues, such as the importance of maintaining the moratorium against the use of RJ for certain offences, the burden that downloading what might have been probation responsibilities has produced for women and parents, the dangers of inequity in access to RJ, the need for a more holistic, inclusive approach to youth and other crime problems, and the need for public discussion fuelled by appropriate statistical and other evidence.

Business and other community leaders generally expressed views most congruent with the victim-oriented panel members. They were not well informed about RJ, either as a philosophy or as operationalised in Nova Scotia, and they acknowledged their marginality. They supported the RJ approach for a limited range of youth offending but were concerned about any, more elaborate, implementation. The main issue advanced by these panellists was the need for more information on the programme and evidence concerning its impact.

The concluding observations and recommendations in the process report advance several themes: (1) that progress continues to be made with respect to the primary objectives of the NSRJ initiative; (2) that RJ is now established in the CJS and is an increasingly relevant player in CJS strategising; (3) that there are certain dilemmas or tough choices now facing the RJ agencies that will have to be considered carefully; (4) that there is a need for more strategic planning concerning where NSRJ and the RJ agencies are going in their continuing development of RJ in Nova

Scotia's CJS, balancing NSRJ programme objectives, resource requirements and the standpoints of agency personnel, CJS officials, and
community leaders in related service provision and mobilisation; and
(5) that more strategic thinking should also be directed at developing
protocols and guidelines for the sessions, for feedback and experience
sharing among staff/volunteers and among the agencies, for identifying
more specifically expectations and operational guidelines for RJ referrals
from beyond the police level, and for responding to special referrals (e.g.
flagging cases involving family violence and dealing with repeat and
serious offenders).

Conclusion

The NSRJ initiative, through the RJ agencies, has added value to the
former alternative measures programming. The contribution is continuing
and much fine-tuning can be done to enhance it further, for example,
providing modest resources to stabilise core staff by increasing their
compensation, especially fringe benefits, resolving the liability concerns of
the local boards and centralising training oversight under NSRJ for staff
and volunteers. Strategic planning, though, appears to be necessary before
significant new challenges are engaged (e.g. extensions of the programme
to adults and 'serious' offenders) or major new resources allocated.
Special, well-conceived pilot projects could explore new challenges while
the RJ initiative remains focused on stabilising and fine-tuning what has
already been put into place.

References

Archibald, B. (2000) 'Democracy and Restorative Justice: Comparative Reflections
    on Criminal Prosecutions, the Role of Law and Reflexive Law'. Unpublished
    paper, 5th International Conference on Restorative Justice, Leuven, Belgium.
Braithwaite, J. (1997) *Restorative Justice and a Better Future*. The Dorothy Killam
    Memorial Lecture, Dalhousie University, Halifax, Nova Scotia.
Clairmont, D. (1999) *Restorative Justice in Nova Scotia: A Pre-Implementation Report*.
    Halifax: Nova Scotia Department of Justice.
Clairmont, D. (2000) 'Restorative Justice', *Suma*, 1, 1–5.
Clairmont, D. (2001) *The Nova Scotia Restorative Justice Initiative: Year One Report*.
    Ottawa: Crime Prevention Centre, Department of Justice.
Clairmont, D. (2002) *The Nova Scotia Restorative Justice Initiative: Year Two, 2001 Core
    Outcomes Report*. Ottawa: Crime Prevention Centre, Department of Justice.
Clairmont, D. (2003) *The Nova Scotia Restorative Justice Initiative, Year Two, Core
    Process Report*. Ottawa: Crime Prevention Centre, Department of Justice.

Green, G. (1999) 'Community Sentencing and Mediation in Aboriginal Communities', *Manitoba Law Journal*, XXI.

Latimer, J., Dowden, C. and Muise, D. (2001) *The Effectiveness of Restorative Justice Practices: A Meta-Analysis*. Ottawa: Research and Statistics Division, Methodological Series, Department of Justice.

McCold, P. (2000) 'A Survey of Assessment Research on Mediation and Conferencing'. Unpublished paper, 5th International Conference on Restorative Justice, Leuven, Belgium.

Nova Scotia Department of Justice (1998) *Restorative Justice: A Program for Nova Scotia*. Halifax, NS: Nova Scotia Department of Justice.

Viano, E. (2000) 'Restorative Justice: A Return to American Traditions', *Corrections Today*, July, 132–5.

Chapter 13

Restorative justice in cases of serious crime: an evaluation

Tanya Rugge and Robert Cormier

Abstract

This chapter focuses upon the evaluation results of the Collaborative Justice Project (CJP), a demonstration project running in the Ottawa, Ontario area. Whereas many restorative justice programmes (such as mediation and family group conferencing) focus on relatively minor offences, the CJP employs a restorative justice approach in cases of serious crime. The goal of the research is to expand the empirical base regarding restorative justice by determining whether programmes like the CJP are successful. The research evaluates the CJP by examining satisfaction levels of victims, offenders and participating community members; by determining whether participation with the CJP meets the needs of clients; and by assessing the reaction of clients and key criminal justice personnel to the CJP. Several outcome measures are examined through a pre- and post-measure design. The sample consists of CJP clients and matched comparison groups of offenders and victims. Results assessing whether the CJP served as an alternative to incarceration and whether participation by offenders reduced their likelihood of reoffending, are also addressed. The implications of the research are discussed from a restorative justice perspective.

Introduction

This chapter reports on the preliminary results of an evaluation of a restorative justice programme called the Collaborative Justice Project, which has operated as a demonstration project in Ottawa, Canada for the past three and a half years. Before discussing the project and the findings of the evaluation, it may be useful to begin with a brief introduction to restorative justice. There is no single, universally accepted definition of restorative justice, although a central feature of any definition would include some notion of repairing the harm caused by crime and restoring the parties to a state of wellness or wholeness which was disturbed by the criminal act. For our purposes we adopted the following working definition of restorative justice:

> Restorative justice is an approach to justice that focuses on repairing the harm caused by crime while holding the offender responsible for his or her actions, by providing an opportunity for the parties directly affected by a crime – victim(s), offender and community – to identify and address their needs in the aftermath of a crime, and seek a resolution that affords healing, reparation and reintegration, and prevents future harm (Cormier, 2002: 1).

When we say that restorative justice is an 'approach' to justice rather than a programme or a set of programmes, we are speaking of the philosophy and values that underpin restorative justice. The values, as reflected in the above definition, include responsibility, inclusiveness, openness, trust, hope and healing. Since restorative justice is an approach to justice, it has a potentially broad application to the field. It can be applied to prevent crime; for example, mediation can be used to resolve conflicts before they escalate and reach the threshold of criminal behaviour. As a response to crime, restorative justice can be applied at every stage of the criminal justice system, from police diversion to the post-sentence (incarceration and parole) stage. In Canada, the most extensive application of restorative justice in the criminal justice system has been court-based victim–offender mediation programmes and police-led Community Justice Forums. Community Justice Forums are based on the family group conferencing model, which has been widely applied in New Zealand and Australia. Both of these applications in Canada, however, have focused on minor or less serious crimes.

What about the application of restorative justice in cases of serious crimes? One could argue that the potential benefits of restorative justice are greater in cases of serious crime because healing and reparation are especially important where the amount of harm done has been significant. On the other hand, there are concerns expressed by some victims' advocates (Canada, House of Commons, 1998) and academics (Roberts, 2002) that the pre-sentence application of restorative justice, with its emphasis on repairing harm, may fail to adequately punish offenders who have committed serious crimes. Accordingly, the application of restorative justice in cases of serious crimes has been largely restricted to the post-sentence stage.

In 1995, a programme in Canada involving the use of victim–offender mediation post-sentence in cases of serious crime, such as aggravated sexual assault, murder and armed robbery, was the subject of a preliminary evaluation (Roberts, 1995). This Victim–Offender Mediation Programme, operated by Community Justice Initiatives in Langley, British Columbia, conducts extensive screening and provides therapeutic preparation for victims and offenders before a face-to-face meeting is arranged. For the evaluation, interviews were conducted with victim and offender participants as well as the practitioners involved in the programme. The major finding of this study was that there was strong support for the programme from all victim and offender respondents. Specifically, participants appreciated the 'reality of the experience', the flexibility and absence of pressure and the caring, supportive staff. The results also showed that the motivation for victims' participation was twofold: first, to know why the perpetrator committed the offence, and second, to communicate the harmful impacts. For the offenders, the motivation was most often that it was 'the right thing to do', both for themselves and for the victim. A very high percentage (91 per cent) of the criminal justice practitioner respondents indicated strong support for the programme (Roberts, 1995).

Despite these findings, the problem of how to apply restorative justice in cases of serious crime at the pre-sentence stage, in a manner that would not be viewed as interfering with sentencing and the imposition of appropriate punishment, remains unresolved. One strategy that could be used to address this issue is to introduce a process that would operate in parallel with the current system (after a plea of guilty but prior to sentencing) and provide an opportunity for healing and reparation for victims and offenders within the context of the existing judicial process. The restorative justice process would complement and enhance the current system, rather than replace the court process and sentencing by a judge. This strategy was developed for the Collaborative Justice Project (CJP).

The Collaborative Justice Project

The CJP is an innovative pilot project that was developed and supported through a joint effort by representatives of the Church Council on Justice and Corrections and the Ottawa Crown Attorney's office in collaboration with our Department, the Correctional Service of Canada, and the Department of Justice Canada, as well as the National Crime Prevention Centre and the Trillium Foundation. It is a multi-disciplinary approach that works towards helping offenders, victims and community members to cope with the effects of the behaviour that led to criminal charges.

The rationale behind the CJP is to provide an alternative to the traditional criminal justice system that offers support to victims and assists accused persons in taking responsibility for their criminal behaviour. The CJP draws on a wide spectrum of community services to meet partici-pants' needs. The CJP approach is also flexible in that trained staff may facilitate a victim–offender meeting or circle conference, or assist in other more indirect interchanges between the victim and the offender. These meetings or interchanges may result in a collaborative resolution proposal which is presented before the court at sentencing. The CJP accepts a variety of cases that meet the following criteria: the crime is serious in nature (i.e. the offender is facing imprisonment of two years or more); at least one victim is interested in receiving assistance from the CJP; the accused has accepted responsibility (i.e. a plea of guilty has been entered); and the accused has indicated a desire to make amends for the harm caused by his or her actions.

Evaluation design

The research team began its data collection for the evaluation of the CJP in the fall of 1999 and is currently in the final evaluation stages. The evaluation design incorporated pre- and post-test measures as well as control groups. The evaluation procedure was slightly different for victims than for offenders. For victims, three measures were administered: the pre-measure questionnaire, the pre-meeting questionnaire in cases where a meeting was expected and the post-programme interview. The pre-measure questionnaire is a two-page general opinion survey asking respondents about their opinions regarding the traditional justice system. The pre-meeting questionnaire is a two-page survey that asks respondents about their feelings towards the offender prior to the meeting, their current needs and the goals they hope to accomplish during the meeting. The post-programme interview is a 30-minute interview that focuses on a number of areas. Respondents are questioned regarding: their attitudes and perceptions (e.g. about the restorative justice process, the traditional justice process, etc.); their experience with the CJP programme and its processes (e.g. whether their needs were met, their opinions about the offender's reparative efforts, etc.); their perceptions of fairness and satisfaction (e.g. most satisfying aspects, most difficult aspects, etc.); their perceptions of fear (e.g. life changes since the crime, thoughts about likelihood of offender reoffending, etc.); information about the offence (e.g. injury, loss, etc.); and past victimisation incidents.

For offenders, four measures were administered: the pre-measure questionnaire, the Level of Service Inventory – Revised (LSI-R),[1] the pre-meeting questionnaire (if applicable) and the post-programme interview. Case completion interviews were also conducted with the CJP facilitators. These interviews asked the CJP staff about the challenges and difficulties with each case, and their thoughts on the benefits of the process for each case participant.

In addition, the CJP facilitators completed assessments, at three different intervals, for each client. The assessment instruments asked the CJP staff to record demographic information, the situational context, offence information, the CJP process goals, the client's needs, the client's support system, the client's perception of the offender's accountability, and his or her attitudes at various stages throughout the process. Research staff conducted extensive file reviews for each client at the completion of each case. Demographic information was recorded, as well as information concerning the particulars of the CJP process (e.g. number of contacts, meetings, whether there was a victim–offender mediation or circle, reparation activities, disposition, etc.). In addition, a one-year follow-up review of criminal histories will be conducted to determine whether or not offenders reoffended following completion of the CJP.

Although an attempt was made to complete all measures for each and every client, this was not always possible. Since participation in the CJP and the evaluation was voluntary, some victims chose not to participate in the programme, and some who became involved with the CJP chose not to participate in the evaluation. Two comparison groups were constructed in order to address a variety of questions. The first comparison group consisted of victims and offenders who met the criteria for inclusion in the CJP but declined participation in the CJP. This group will permit an assessment of whether persons who agree to participate are different in certain aspects from those who do not. The second comparison group consisted of victims and offenders who were not approached by the CJP staff. These cases were processed through the traditional criminal justice system. Offenders within this comparison group pled guilty, and were matched on age, gender, offence type and risk level.

Results

As noted earlier, the evaluation of the CJP is ongoing; however, an examination of data to date shows promising results. As of March 2003, 173 participants had voluntarily participated in at least one aspect of the evaluation of the CJP. The current sample consists of 66 offenders (58 male, 8 female) and 107 victims (59 males, 48 females). Of the 66 offenders, 57 are adult offenders and 9 are young offenders (under the age of 18).

Preliminary results indicate that, based on the offence type, the majority of offenders who participate in the CJP have committed serious offences, indicating that the CJP goal of dealing with offenders who have committed serious crimes is being met. Of the 66 offenders, 30 per cent were charged with assault or assault causing bodily harm, 30 per cent were charged with robbery, 23 per cent were charged with dangerous driving or impaired driving causing bodily harm or death and 15 per cent were charged with a property crime (break and enter, and fraud). In cases where offenders were charged with more than one crime, the researchers recorded the most serious crime. Additional evidence regarding the seriousness of cases came from discussions with the Crown Attorney. In almost all cases, the Crown Attorney intended to seek imprisonment. Whether or not a judge would have imposed a term of imprisonment, irrespective of the CJP process, cannot be addressed at this time; however, the incorporation of the comparison groups will aid in addressing this issue.

Evidence suggested that the CJP was adhering to its mandate to target cases of serious crime; however, the next step was to determine whether the CJP was dealing with *serious offenders*, those who are at a high risk to reoffend. A person who commits a serious *offence* may not necessarily be a serious *offender*. Results indicated that 51 per cent of offenders were first-time offenders, 20 per cent had three to six prior convictions, and 10 per cent had more than 10 prior convictions. LSI-R scores were also examined to provide a standardised risk-assessment level on each offender. LSI-R scores can range from zero to 54, with lower scores indicating low risk to reoffend and higher scores indicating high risk to reoffend. The median LSI-R score was 12.0, with an average score of 15.0 and a range of 2 to 36. Only four offenders scored above 20. Based on the established norms for the LSI-R, these results indicate that these offenders were 'low' to 'low-medium' risk offenders. This illustrates an important point: a serious offence does not necessarily mean the perpetrator is a serious offender.

These findings have important implications for the CJP, and other programmes like it, which are applying restorative justice practices to cases of serious crime.

The evaluation also examined whether participation in the CJP reduced the likelihood that an offender would receive a term of imprisonment. Although reducing the use of incarceration is not an explicit goal of the CJP, one might expect that a process that focuses on repairing harm might lead to proposals that would reduce the imposition of punishment. To determine whether the CJP served as an alternative to incarceration, the number of offenders who received a term of imprisonment was examined. It is important to remember that, according to the Crown, these offenders were most likely facing imprisonment prior to their participation in the CJP. The results indicated that only 16 per cent of offenders received a custodial sentence. The remainder received a variety of non-custodial sanctions (e.g. probation, community service, conditional sentence, restitution, suspended sentence). These results suggest that offenders who participate in the CJP are less likely to receive a term of imprisonment, notwithstanding the prosecutor's intention to seek a prison sentence. Comparisons with the group of matched offenders who did not participate in the CJP will provide further evidence on this point.

In order to assess whether this restorative justice programme is a 'best practice' model, several areas were examined. Since an explicit goal of the CJP is to address the needs of victims and offenders in the aftermath of a serious crime, it is important to examine whether clients were satisfied with the process and how well their needs were met. An examination of post-programme interviews yielded the following results. Of the 173 evaluation participants, 114 participants have completed post-programme interviews, consisting of 40 offenders (35 male, 5 female) and 74 victims (38 male, 36 female). Results presented below are based solely on these post-programme interviews. Pre- and post-test analysis will be conducted upon the conclusion of data collection. However, to date, preliminary results suggest that the programme is effective from the clients' perspectives.

Victim–offender communication can occur directly or indirectly (through the facilitator) in the CJP design. As of March 2003, 58 per cent of cases resulted in a face-to-face victim–offender meeting or circle. In these cases, over 50 per cent of participants cited 'getting together' as one of the important strengths and most satisfying aspects of the programme. These participants stated that bringing everyone together to talk about the situation and having the opportunity to share experiences, perspectives and personal stories was extremely beneficial. For victims specifically, they had the opportunity to describe to their offender how the crime affected them. Meeting also allowed victims to obtain information from the offender and other parties, and learn facts about the case to assist in understanding the 'larger context surrounding the crime'. Both victims and offenders felt that the meeting helped them come to terms with the crime and initiated feelings of closure. Again, both victims and offenders highlighted their personal involvement in the process where they were able to play an active role in the decision-making process. Victims had an opportunity to be heard and offenders had a chance to actively participate in the outcome of their case and attempt to repair the harm caused, an activity that is not usually available in our traditional justice system.

Another positive aspect that was cited, by 52 per cent of participants (both victims and offenders), was offender rehabilitation. Although this target is incorporated throughout the CJP process, victims felt that it was important to address offender rehabilitation, and in some cases build it into a reparation plan. Victims frequently stated that they wanted to make sure the offender's behaviour 'did not happen again'.

Evaluation participants were also asked about the most difficult and unsatisfying aspect of the programme. Some individuals (39 per cent) stated that they did not experience anything 'unsatisfying' and 14 per cent did not have any difficulties with the programme. However, those who did cited anxiety about the meeting and the overall process. In terms of the overall process, participants expressed that not knowing what to expect was one of the most difficult aspects. In addition, participants also expressed that participating in the CJP was an extremely emotional process. Both victims and offenders found it difficult to talk about the offence and their feelings surrounding it.

Evaluation participants were also asked explicitly about their needs, and whether the programme met those needs. The majority of clients felt that the CJP met their needs – 89 per cent of victims and 77 per cent of offenders stated that the programme met their needs. Although the needs of individuals varied, there were common trends. Briefly, the most frequent responses included: the victims' needs to obtain information about the incident and the offender; both parties' needs to move towards a feeling of closure and resolution; the victims' needs to address and participate in plans for the rehabilitation of the offender; the victims' needs to express their feelings to the offender, whether it was through CJP facilitators or in person, and make certain that the offender heard how the crime affected them; in cases of financial loss, the victims' requested financial reparation; and the victims' needs to ensure that the offender made reparations to the community as a whole, through actions such as community service work.

For the victims specifically, there appears to be overall satisfaction (89 per cent), mainly due to the fact that someone in the system attended to their needs, they had an active role in the criminal justice process and there was an attempt to repair the harm they experienced. However, it is important to note that only 58 per cent of cases resulted in a victim–offender meeting, suggesting that a face-to-face meeting is not necessarily needed to meet the needs of victims.

Offenders' needs were not as diverse or individualised. By far, offenders evidenced three predominant themes. First, offenders felt a need to apologise to the victim(s). Second, they felt a need to provide an explanation for their actions. Third, offenders felt a need to have the opportunity to repair, or to attempt to repair, the harm they caused. Reparation was offered in such forms as financial reparation, community service, public speaking and, in some cases, an offer to do 'anything' the victims asked.

Some of the more frequently used forms of reparation included apologies (in person or by letter), financial restitution, community service work and the offenders' demonstrated willingness to participate in counselling or treatment. Some victims felt that the offender's willingness to meet the victim(s) and to repair the harm they caused were also forms of reparation. Satisfaction levels regarding the various forms of reparation were examined, which found that, generally, victims were satisfied. It should be noted, however, that 8 per cent of victims were not satisfied with the apology that the offender provided, 14 per cent of victims felt that the offender was not held adequately accountable for his or her crimes, 14 per cent of victims felt that the offender's efforts to make reparation were insufficient, and 23 per cent felt that the offender could have done more to repair the harm that he or she caused.

Participants' perceptions of the programme were also investigated. Post-programme interviews were examined separately for victims and offenders. Victims were asked about their perceptions regarding the programme, the process, fairness, satisfaction and fear levels. A review of the post-programme interviews indicated that the majority of victims (91 per cent) felt that their opinions regarding the crime and the offender were adequately considered. Ninety-five per cent of victims indicated that they would choose the restorative approach over traditional criminal justice processes in the future. Of the victims who met their offender, 97 per cent found the meeting helpful. Ninety-four per cent of victims indicated that they were treated fairly at the meeting and 97 per cent of victims found the resolution agreement to be fair. Eighty-eight per cent of victims felt that justice was adequately served in their case, and only 5 per cent felt that the outcome would have been more satisfying if they had pursued the case solely in the traditional justice system, while 16 per cent felt that the sentence imposed by the judge did not satisfy justice. However, 91 per cent of victims indicated that they felt that a restorative approach was a fair approach to criminal justice.

Victims were also asked questions about their levels of fear of victimisation in the post-programme interview. On a scale of zero to 10, with 10 being extremely afraid, victims, on average, placed their current level of fear of crime at 5.0. Four per cent of victims were afraid that the offender would commit another crime against them and 22 per cent of victims felt that the offender would reoffend against someone else. As expected, 27 per cent of victims stated that they were more afraid of crime as a result of the offender's crime against them and had implemented protective strategies in their daily lives.

Offenders were also asked about their perceptions of the programme, the process, fairness and satisfaction. Post-programme interview results revealed that 98 per cent of offenders felt that they were held adequately accountable for their crimes and only one offender felt that he did not make sufficient reparation to the victim(s). Although the CJP process was challenging, and perhaps more difficult than the offender's role in the traditional system, 88 per cent of offenders stated that they would choose a restorative justice approach over a traditional one in the future. Critics may argue that the offenders' preference for the restorative approach may hinge upon the fact that they may have received a more lenient sentence. Responding to this criticism will be addressed when comparisons are made with the offenders in the control groups.

Participants arrived at an all-party agreement in 91 per cent of the cases that included a victim–offender meeting or circle. Participants were asked if they felt justice had been served through the restorative process, and 90 per cent of offenders felt that it had been, while only 8 per cent of offenders felt that the outcome would have been more satisfying if pursued in the traditional criminal justice system (2 per cent of offenders indicated 'no opinion'). The majority of offenders (82 per cent) felt that the sentence imposed by the judge satisfied justice. Only one offender expressed the belief that a restorative approach was not a fair approach to criminal justice. All but one of the offenders (98 per cent) interviewed stated that they would recommend a restorative justice process to other offenders.

Overall, this preliminary review of the post-programme interviews indicated that, for the most part, CJP participants felt the offender was held adequately accountable, were satisfied with the process and programming of the CJP and felt they were treated fairly. Based upon these data, the CJP seems to working well in providing an alternative process that meets the needs of both victims and offenders. Despite this, there are other outcome measures of the CJP process that need to be examined, such as whether offenders re-offend after completion of the programme. A concrete answer to this question is not currently available, as the one-year follow-up to examine recidivism has not yet been conducted; however, based upon the results of the LSI-R assessment, the likelihood that many of these offenders would reoffend, even in the absence of any specific interventions, is low.

Conclusion

The results of the evaluation of the CJP to date indicate the CJP is satisfying the needs of their clients. The CJP is also meeting its goal of focusing upon serious crimes. However, an important finding of this preliminary evaluation is that offenders participating in the CJP are *not* serious, high-risk offenders. This may be a consequence of the project's selection criteria, which stipulate that an offender must take responsibility for his or her behaviour and have a desire to make amends. Perhaps it is not surprising that higher-risk offenders, those with extensive criminal histories, anti-social personalities, anti-social attitudes, criminal associates and minimal participation in pro-social activities, would not volunteer to participate in such a programme.

Although the CJP is not designed to divert offenders from prison, it is possible that a reduction in the imposition of prison sentences will emerge as a by-product of the restorative process. Whether the CJP serves to reduce the use of imprisonment must await further analyses. Similarly, comparisons with matched offenders who did not participate in the CJP have yet to be done in order to determine whether participation in the CJP reduces the likelihood of recidivism.

The results presented in this chapter are preliminary; however, initial findings suggest that clients are satisfied with the CJP process and that the strategy the CJP utilises can operate effectively in parallel with the traditional criminal justice system. Further analyses will examine outcomes of the CJP through comparisons of participants with matched offenders and victims who did not participate in the programme, with a view to furthering our knowledge about the impacts of restorative justice.

Note

1   The Level of Service Inventory – Revised (LSI-R) is a validated, structured risk assessment instrument designed for use with adult offenders (Andrews and Bonta, 1995).

References

Andrews, D. A. and Bonta, J. (1995) *The Level of Service Inventory – Revised*. Toronto: Multi-Health Systems, Inc.

Cormier, R. B. (2002) *Restorative Justice: Directions and Principles – Developments in Canada*. Ottawa: Solicitor General Canada.

Canada, House of Commons (1998) *Taking Responsibility: Report of the Standing Committee on Justice and Solicitor General on its Review of Sentencing, Conditional Release and Related Aspects of Corrections*. Ottawa: Supply and Services Canada.

Roberts, T. (1995) Evaluation of the Victim–Offender Mediation Project, Langley, B.C. Ottawa: Solicitor General Canada.

Roberts, J. V. (2002) 'Restorative Justice: Some Caveats', *Justice Report* (Canadian Criminal Justice Association), 17, 1–3.

Chapter 14

Evaluating conferencing for serious juvenile offenders

Inge Vanfraechem

Abstract

This chapter examines a conferencing project in Belgium for juvenile offenders who have committed either serious crimes or a series of crimes. The model and the procedure of conferencing are outlined and the research methods used to conduct the evaluation are examined. Some quantitative and qualitative results of the research are presented. These include information about the numbers of referrals over a two- to three-year period, the interactions among criminal justice practitioners involved in the process, the satisfaction levels of the participants, the involvement of the youths' and victims' support networks and the rates of recidivism.

Introduction

Action-research was undertaken on a pilot project on conferencing for serious juvenile offenders in Flanders, Belgium between 2001 and 2003 with funding from the Flemish government's Department of Welfare. The project is situated at the level of the youth court and is used for juveniles who have committed either serious crimes or a series of crimes. A referral procedure was worked out to implement conferencing within the existing juvenile justice system and the general aim of the research was to find out whether the New Zealand model of conferencing could work within a Belgian context. Different research methods were used and the main results of the project focus on the satisfaction of the parties, how the project worked within the criminal justice system, the rights of the participants and the provision of support people for victims and offenders.

The conferencing model

The New Zealand model[1] of conferencing was used in the project. This involves a neutral facilitator, the presence of the police and the possibility of private time for the juvenile offenders and their support networks. The police have a specific role, namely pointing out the seriousness of the crimes and their social consequences. The presence of the police is also meant to enhance the victims' feelings of safety and broaden the applicability of conferencing to serious crimes. The presence of the police reflects the importance that the authorities attach to the cases and to the need to handle the cases correctly.

The private time for the offender and his or her network also offers advantages since, eventually, any underlying problems can be identified and addressed by the offender's family and friends. Since conferences involve a significant investment of time and energy for all participants (Hokwerda, 2004), they are reserved for the more serious cases. Moreover, the practice of victim–offender mediation is developed in almost every judicial district in Belgium and deals effectively with the less serious cases.[2]

What follows is a brief outline of the procedure for referring juveniles, as well as the procedures used at conferences.[3] Since the project is situated at the level of the youth court, the youth judge assesses whether a case is appropriate for a conference.[4] The two main criteria are that the juvenile does not deny the facts and that the crime is of a serious nature. In practice, judges take the total circumstances of juveniles into consideration, including the availability of support networks, schooling and the capacities of the juvenile. This may be one of the reasons why referrals are rather slow. In the pilot phase of the project and in the absence of legislation, judges are not obliged to consider using a conference.

If the juvenile denies the facts, a conference cannot take place and the case goes through the normal proceedings at the youth court. If, on the other hand, the juvenile does not deny the facts, the youth judge can refer the youngster to a mediation service if this is recommended by social services.[5] A facilitator[6] contacts the parties, namely the offender, the victim and their respective networks. Offenders are contacted first to provide them with information about the process and to determine who they can bring to the conference for support. The facilitator ensures that the juvenile does not deny the facts. If the young offender does deny the facts, the case is sent back to the youth judge. When the youngster is willing to participate, the facilitator contacts the victim to see whether he or she is also willing to attend. Even when the victim does not want to be present, the conference can still take place. Victims can have their views represented, for example, in a letter or by friends or relatives presenting the victim's views. When victims decide to attend a conference, they can also bring individuals to support them during the process.

At the conference, all parties are introduced and their respective roles are outlined. This way, everybody knows what their role in the conference will be (e.g. to support either the offender or the victim). The police officer reads out the facts and checks to see whether the offender agrees with them. If the offender denies the facts, the conference cannot take place. Since the recognition of responsibility by the juvenile is checked several times in the process, it is rare for a denial to occur at the conference. The recognition of the facts by juvenile offenders is an important starting point for victims because, by doing so, the juveniles show their willingness to take responsibility for their actions.

After the reading of the facts by the police, the victim and his supporters, and the offender and his supporters, explain what effect the offence has had upon them. This phase can be seen as the core of the conference (Retzinger and Scheff, 1996) in which all thoughts and feelings can be shared and where a participant can come to an understanding of the harm that has been caused by the offence. The offender and his supporters can then have private time during which they discuss possible solutions to the offence, taking the needs and wishes of the victim into account. The underlying causes of the juvenile's criminal behaviour, such as drug use or problems at home, can be addressed. The proposed solution is then presented to the victim and discussed until an agreement is reached, if possible.

The aim of the agreement is threefold: repairing the harm to the victim; repairing the harm to society; and making sure that the agreement can be carried out by addressing any underlying issues. The individuals involved in either implementing the agreement or providing follow-up, as well as the victim, sign the 'declaration of intention', that is the intent of the juvenile with respect to making up for his or her conduct. Once the judge confirms this declaration, it becomes an 'agreement'. However, if no agreement can be reached in the conference, this outcome is reported to the judge. If there is partial disagreement with some element of the juvenile's declaration of intention, this can be noted. The judge then decides what the outcome should be.

The declaration of intention (or report of non-agreement) is brought before the judge, who decides whether or not to accept it. In principle, youth judges accept the intentions but still evaluate whether they are appropriate, and they retain the final decision-making power. The judges usually agree with what the parties have developed. The judge ensures the protection of all procedural safeguards and keeps an overall eye on the proceedings. This is an important safeguard; an often heard criticism of restorative justice is that it may lead to disproportional agreements and that legal safeguards are not considered (Eliaerts and Dumortier, 2002).

Once the agreement is accepted by the judge, it can be put into practice. An agreement can include various elements: writing an apology letter to the victim, working for the victim, community service, counselling and/or agreements about the juvenile's daily activities (e.g. regularly attending school and respecting rules at home). The agreement includes a means of follow-up (e.g. who will make sure that the juvenile carries out the agreed upon tasks) and the period within which the agreement should be executed. Following the implementation period, during which time the agreement is carried out, the judge evaluates its impact.

Research methods

Action-research entails a double role for the researchers. On the one hand, there is a strong involvement in the project with the researchers coordinating the project and being in contact with all the professionals and others involved. On the other hand, the project is being evaluated by a researcher who may also be involved in the project and, therefore, interested in making the project work. In this research, every effort was made to set aside any subjective biases that may have influenced the research results.

Data were drawn from the judicial dossiers for the crimes, which contained general information such as the date of birth of the parties, the date and kind of crime, the date of the judicial decision and any previous offences. The dossiers of 58 juveniles who participated in conferences were examined. In addition, the conference facilitators filled out questionnaires on the preparations for the conferences. The literature (see, for example, Mirsky, 2003) indicates that the preparation phase is very important so that people know what and what not to expect. The preparation questionnaire provides an idea of the degree of resistance among the parties with respect to participation, the information given by the facilitator and the parties' involvement in inviting support people to attend.

All the conferences were observed using a standardised observation scheme. At the beginning of the conference general information was recorded, such as the time and place of the conference and the people present. During the conference, the general proceedings were recorded (in writing) and a report of almost every conference is available.[7] Right after the conference, the observer recorded information about the fairness of the proceedings and the role of the facilitator. The victims (present: N = 27, not present: N = 21), the juveniles (N = 38) and their parents (N = 37) were interviewed a couple of weeks after the conference. The questionnaires included various topics, such as procedural justice (Tyler, 1988), the consequences of the crime, the amount of preparation by the facilitator, the events at the conference and the experience of shaming and other emotions.

Various professionals were asked about their opinions of the project. About one-third of the lawyers who participated in a conference were interviewed (N = 16), as well as most of the judges (N = 9) and police officers (N = 7). All the social services personnel (N = 4) and all the mediation services personnel (N = 5) were interviewed, as well as one representative of the victims' assistance service. These interviews offered additional perspectives on the project, particularly with respect to its advantages and its difficulties.

The research results

Conferencing for serious juvenile crimes

Over the course of approximately 30 months, 53 conferences were organised for 58 juveniles (co-offenders can have one conference). Ninety-eight juveniles were referred to the project, but conferences could not occur for a variety of reasons: the juvenile and/or his parents were not willing to participate; the crimes were not serious; there was some dispute about the involvement of the juvenile in the crime; the victims were not identified; or there were too many problems in the juvenile's life.

When examining these reasons for cancelling the conference, various points stand out. The willingness of the juvenile to cooperate is deemed essential. When the youth did not want to participate, the conference was of no use because this could lead to a secondary victimisation of the victim, especially when he or she notices that the juvenile is not willing to take responsibility for his or her actions. Some juveniles considered the conference to be too challenging: they did not want to be confronted with and by so many people. Also, some juveniles would rather have the judge decide what should happen in the case. As one juvenile stated, '... it is easier to go to the judge once, without everybody there.' Another juvenile felt that '… participating in a conference takes too much effort.'

When the victim does not want to attend, the conference can still go ahead. Victims can feel pushed into attending when they know the conference will occur anyway whether they agree with it or not. It is important to inform victims of their rights and to ensure that their participation is voluntary. In the research, victims were present in about 50 per cent of the conferences while in another 20 per cent they are represented by a relative or by their partner (e.g. their spouse). In the other conferences, the co-facilitator[8] conveyed the victim's story so that victims' views are always presented, whether they are physically present or not.

The juvenile's underlying problems can prevent the conference from proceeding. When these problems are significant, they have to be resolved before the issue of restoration for the victim can be addressed. These problems have included drug problems, problems at home and psychiatric problems.

The conferences usually took place at the mediation service or in a local cultural centre, and took between 45 minutes and about seven hours (split into two meetings) to complete, with a mean of 2 hours and 15 minutes. The juveniles' ages ranged from 13 to 18, with the majority being about 16 years of age. Only one juvenile was female. The victims could be either individuals or the representatives of businesses.

In all conferences, a 'declaration of intention' was reached and the youth judges confirmed these declarations in an official judgment. The judges usually stated that they wanted to confirm the input and investment of the parties but sometimes thought the agreement was a bit too 'light'. While the focus on the needs and interests of the victim was usually considered by the parties to be extensive and satisfying, the 'social consequences' of a crime were not always considered. Facilitators and police officers have noted this shortcoming and now bring this element into conference discussions. The issue does not necessarily have to be included in the agreement, but the social consequences should at least be discussed.[9]

Working with the criminal justice system

Since the project is situated at the level of the youth court, judges refer cases for conferencing. The project is only a pilot project, so no legislation that compels referral is in place. A referral procedure was worked out with the assistance of lawyers and judges to enhance the referrals. From the beginning of the project, all the judicial actors were informed of all the steps being taken. This has proven to be crucial in receiving referrals.

Lawyers attend the conference to support the juvenile but stay in the background during the communications between the participants. The presence of the lawyer ensures the protection of the juvenile's rights and the lawyer can help the juvenile to formulate his or her ideas and intentions thereby ensuring the young person's involvement in the conference. The lawyers of the victims may be present but seldom are. In addition, social services personnel provide follow-up for juveniles who appear before the youth court and are in a position to address any problems that may surface.

The role of the prosecutors is fairly limited within the procedure, since they do not attend the conference. In theory, the police cannot represent the society in the conference since this is considered to be the role of the prosecutor (Vanfraechem, 2003a). The symbolic aspect of having a police officer present is important because this may underscore the seriousness of the crime. Discussion is still ongoing with regard to the judicial consequences of a police officer's attendance, but the added value of his or her presence is certainly recognised.

Participants' rights

The presence of the lawyer and the judicial oversight provided by the youth judge are important in ensuring the protection of the participants' rights. Although it is not always clear to participants what exactly their rights are, they felt that their rights were protected at the conference. Participants were also content with regard to the issue of procedural justice, as can be seen from the data in Table 14.1.[10] Tyler (1988) found that people are more satisfied with the process when they perceived it to be procedurally just. This includes being able to have your say and having your opinion taken into account.

Satisfaction

Restorative justice puts the conference participants at the centre of the response to a crime, and especially the victims and the offenders (Christie, 1977; Zehr, 1990); their satisfaction with the process thus becomes important. The various stages of the conference were evaluated with an eye to answering the following questions: were the participants satisfied with the preparation? were the participants satisfied with the conference itself? and were the participants satisfied with the outcome of the conference?

It was clear that the preparation phase is crucial in order for victims and offenders to know what to expect from the conference and, as the data in Table 14.2 indicate, the conference preparation was thorough and

Table 14.1 Procedural justice for participants

	Juveniles	Parents	Victims
Did you understand what was going on?	97.4%	–	100%
Did you have the opportunity to express your views in the conference?	71%	100%	92.6%
Did all sides get a fair chance to talk about the facts?	100%	97.3%	100%
Was your opinion taken into account?	81.6%	89.2%	92.3%
If, at the conference, the facts were described wrongly, did you feel able to get this corrected?	75.8%	–	84%
Mean (1 not at all – 5 a lot)	**3.84**	**4.7**	**3.99**

Table 14.2 Preparation for the conference

	Juveniles	Parents	Victims present	Victims not present
Were you told what would happen at the conference?	94.7%	81.7%	77.7%	63.6%
Did you feel well prepared for the conference?	–	75.6%	61.5%	–
Were you able to decide whom you wanted to invite?	97.4%	91.4%	72%	–
Were you consulted about the time and venue of the FGC?	–	94.5%	85.2%	75%

effective. Offenders and victims are contacted and receive information on the process during an initial home-visit by the facilitator. Victims, offenders, and their parents have a say at the time and venue of the conference. For the offenders and their parents, the involvement of support people appears to be a difficult issue because they often do not want to have others find out what has happened.

The juveniles decided to participate either to make amends with the victim (63 per cent) or because it would help them (58 per cent). For example, one juvenile felt that by participating in a conference he would get another chance, while another wanted to explain to the victim why it happened. Another juvenile wanted to make up with his parents, while another participated in order to avoid placement in a closed institution.

Victims often do not know what to expect from the conference. This insecurity is not due to the preparation, per se, but to the fact that they are not familiar with the idea of conferencing. Most victims participated so that the offender could take responsibility for his or her actions (70 per cent) or to let the juvenile know how they felt about the crime (59 per cent). When the victim chooses not to attend the conference, it is mostly because the crimes are not serious enough (when the juvenile was referred for a series of crimes) or because they are still too scared to meet the offender.

Most people were satisfied with and felt involved in the conference. At the start of the project, some juveniles did not feel involved in the decision-making process. This has been subsequently addressed by the conference facilitators and no longer poses a problem.[11] One, possible, negative side-effect of conferencing is that involvement on the part of the offender's extended family can lead to the parents and others taking over the process, leaving little or no time for the juvenile to have his or her say (Weijers, 2003b). In this regard, participants indicated that having the opportunity to talk and discuss the crimes is an extremely important element. Juveniles considered that the process of pointing out that they had done something wrong was the most important aspect of the conference.

Almost all the parties to a conference agreed with the decisions that were made and thought the agreement was fair. About 33 per cent of the juveniles considered the agreement to be very severe, but all of them thought the agreement was fair. Victims were generally satisfied with the agreement, but awaited its actual implementation. Some victims thought that it was important that the juvenile took responsibility for their actions by working in order to provide financial reparations.

Table 14.3 Satisfaction with the outcome of the conference

	Juveniles	Parents	Victims present	Victims not present
Conferencing should be offered, on a voluntary basis, to all offenders/victims.	75.7%	–	61.5%	91.7%
If you had to do it all over again, you would choose to participate in a conference.	86.8%	88.6%	92.3%	58.3%
The damage is repaired.	–	–	48.1%	50%

Offenders and victims think conferencing should be offered to all victims and/or offenders. Non-present victims considered this to be important and even though they chose not to take part in the conference they still valued the offer to participate. Juveniles, parents and victims who were present would take part in a conference again, rather than having their cases handled by the courts in the conventional way. Some victims who were *not* present at the conference also indicated that they would take part in the process again.

Only a small number of victims thought that the damage done to them was 'repaired'; however, for many victims, the actual implementation of the agreement had not taken place. Some victims interpreted the damage to them solely as material or financial damage, and a complete restoration or reparation was not, therefore, possible. Victims stated that other elements were more important to them such as the opportunity to ask questions or to receive an apology (Strang, 2002). Nevertheless, financial compensation can be important to the victims and can have an immense symbolic value. A small number of victims were not satisfied because they wanted the judge to impose a punishment. The issue of punishment is a difficult one[12] and should be addressed further, particularly since the feelings of the victims have to be dovetailed with the need for the juvenile to take responsibility for his or her actions in a constructive manner.

The involvement of support people for the juvenile

All juveniles brought at least one parent to their conference, and in almost all cases a lawyer was present to support the juvenile. The lawyers are always invited to attend the conference but in some cases did not attend. Nevertheless, the facilitators thought that it was desirable to continue with the conference since all the other participants were present. On average, a juvenile brought along four or five support people. It was not always easy to involve such people, since the juveniles and especially their parents wanted to keep the crime a private matter. When support people did attend, their presence was important for the juvenile.

In principle, the juvenile can invite anyone he or she would like to be present at the conference but it is important that the facilitator monitors who is going to be present. Two categories of supporters require special attention: co-offenders and the juvenile's parents.

Co-offenders can be sent to a conference by the judge;[13] if this happens, the facilitator will then decide whether to involve them in one conference or in separate conferences. Conferences involving both options have been observed and the advantages and disadvantages of each have become apparent (Vanfraechem, 2003b). One advantage to a single conference is that agreements can be attuned to one another; for example, if financial compensation is to be paid to the victim it is easier to determine who will pay what part of the damages. The offenders may still have their own private time with their respective families to ensure that the agreement is geared towards the specific situation of the young offender so this valuable element is not lost. Another advantage is that the separate offenders cannot deny or minimise their role when confronted with the perspective of their co-offender. In one case encountered in the research, for example, two juveniles had separate conferences. In the first, the juvenile downplayed his role but gave a full account of what had happened. A week later, the co-offender, during his conference, basically put the blame on the first offender and claimed that he was pressured to co-operate in the crime. Although this might have been the case, it was felt that the juveniles might have been more honest about their involvement had they been participating in a single conference. One disadvantage of having a single conference with multiple offenders present is that such conferences might well intimidate, and therefore revictimise, the victim (Weijers, 2003b). In one conference, for example, the two co-offenders were seen talking to each other and laughing and did not seem to take the conference seriously. This spectacle could well demoralise and frighten a victim who would likely find the conference process profoundly unsatisfying.[14]

From the beginning of the project, it was thought that the presence of the parents was a necessary pre-condition for the conference to take place. Parents play an important role in the lives of juveniles, including juvenile offenders, and in the subsequent handling of cases (Prichard, 2003). Furthermore, in Belgium parents are legally responsible for any damage caused by their children. The research indicated that some conferences could not proceed because the parents of the juveniles involved were not willing to participate. This raised the question of whether, in some cases, it would be desirable to proceed with the conference despite the absence of the parents. As Weijers notes (2003a: 3), parents are not always the reference people for juveniles and some juvenile offenders do not have a good relationship with their parents. It might, therefore, be necessary to involve other support people in the conference.

People may be involved in a conference to support the juvenile, but it is not easy to keep them involved afterwards. One goal of a conference is to strengthen the juvenile's network, but it is necessary to keep in mind that a conference is just one moment in time and that various things can occur outside the scope of the conference (Maxwell, 2003). Facilitators should take this into account, not only during the preparation phase, but also when writing up agreements. The juvenile's network can be involved in the follow-up so that they actively assume responsibility for supporting the juvenile and his or her parents.

The involvement of support people for the victim

Unlike the juvenile offenders, most victims come to conferences alone or have only one support person present. In New Zealand, research has shown that victims showed up in a minority of the cases because they could not bring support (Maxwell and Morris, 1996); therefore, special attention was paid to this issue in the pilot project. Victims noted that at the beginning of the conference they felt uneasy when the juvenile had a lot of support people present, but once the conference started this imbalance ceased to be of importance. Facilitators ensured that both parties could have their say and that there was balance between the parties. The presence of the police can be important, especially for the victims of violent crimes, as this provides considerable reassurance that the conference is occurring in a safe setting. Only one victim, representing a youth residence that was vandalised, came to the conference alone. In the other conferences, the victims either brought support or felt supported by other victims who were present. Only four victims would have liked more support people present.

In Belgium, the police are legally obliged to refer a victim to victims' assistance services in cases of serious crimes or where there is a direct contact with the offender. Considering the kind of crimes being dealt with in the conferences (e.g. armed robbery and assaults), it was expected that the victims would have been supported by, or at least have heard of, victims' assistance.[15] This was not the case, however, and only a small number of the victims were aware of the service. Although these victims stated that they did not need victim support, the deficiency should be addressed by facilitators who can refer victims to services when necessary.

Only two victims brought a lawyer to their conferences, while the juvenile almost always had a lawyer present. This kind of situation can create an imbalance between the parties and an argument can be made for victims to be able to seek legal advice in order to properly evaluate the conference agreement. The juvenile has the right to a legal aid lawyer (free of charge) while the victim does not, although if a victim is a minor this problem is addressed in some judicial districts. Victims' assistance can offer legal aid, which is another reason to refer victims to these services.

Recidivism

The recidivism of the juveniles involved in the conferences was assessed through an examination of the court files six to 18 months after either the referral to the conference or the actual conference. This method of studying recidivism has certain limitations. First, no control group is available. We only know whether new offences are recorded for the juveniles who were referred to a conference and no recidivism rates are available for a matched group of juvenile offenders who are dealt with through the conventional court procedure. Second, only crimes that are recorded by the justice system are looked at. Research indicates that, in practice, there is a large dark figure of crime (see, for example, De Witte et al., 2000). An 'at random' project was not possible; that is, it was not possible to ask judges to randomly assign juveniles to the conference project since that would infringe upon their freedom of decision. It is also possible that the juveniles involved in the project were positively screened for participation and thus would have had lower recidivism rates anyway when compared with other juveniles going through the criminal justice system. One prosecutor stated that the juveniles referred to conferencing were unknown to him, which may suggest that repeat offenders did not get the chance to participate. Given all these sources of potential bias, the results set out in Table 14.4, using data from the public prosecutor's offices in Antwerp and Leuven, need to be interpreted with caution.

Table 14.4 Recidivism rates: juveniles involved/not involved in conferences

	No conference	Conference	Total
Recidivism	11 juveniles (58%)	8 juveniles (22%)	19 juveniles
No recidivism	8 juveniles (42%)	28 juveniles (78%)	36 juveniles
Total	19 juveniles (100%)	36 juveniles (100%)	55 juveniles

New crimes were recorded in the judicial files of 22 per cent of the juveniles who took part in a conference. Most of these juveniles did not commit new crimes for several months and, when they did, the crimes were of a less serious nature than the crime(s) for which they were referred to a conference. These results are consistent with the findings of a more extensive research project in New Zealand, where about 25 per cent of the juveniles had committed new crimes post conference (Maxwell and Morris, 1999, 2002). In the Netherlands, research has shown that the effect on recidivism seems to be most pronounced in cases of serious crimes (Hokwerda, 2004).[16]

Conferencing and closed institutions

Youngsters are referred to a conference for serious crimes or a series of crimes; consequently, the research examined the possible relationship between conferencing and placement in closed institutions since these institutions deal with similar juveniles. It was found that conferencing can influence a juvenile's intake to, as well as release from, a closed institution. With regard to the intake, a conference can be an alternative to a placement. The juvenile takes responsibility for his/her actions by going to a conference and setting out how he/she will restore the damage he/she has done to the victim. A juvenile can also leave a closed institution to take part in a conference or to implement the conference agreement. A conference then facilitates the juvenile's transition from the closed institution to his/her home and ensures the victim's needs receive attention.

Some specific concerns have to be taken into account. Firstly, the juvenile's motivation to participate in a conference may be dominated by trying to avoid the placement or a longer stay in the institution. Voluntariness is important in restorative practices, but can such a rather negative motivation (participating to avoid placement in a closed institution) be avoided altogether? Although the victim should not be confronted with a juvenile who is unwilling to take responsibility for his or her actions, the motivation of the juvenile offender can change while he or she is taking part in the conference. It is often only when the juvenile is confronted with the consequences of his or her crimes that he or she becomes motivated to compensate the victim for the damage caused (Harris et al., 2004).

The needs of the victim should always be taken into account. One conference took place within an institution and none of the victims attended. The setting of the institution can be threatening for victims who should always have a say in where the conference takes place.

At the start of the placement, a 'proposal of orientation' is worked out in which the institution reports back to the judge on possible measures with regard to the specific juvenile. A conference could then be suggested as a suitable measure for the juvenile. Once the pedagogical programme for the juvenile in the institution has started, it may be important to first conclude that programme, before a conference can take place.

In some institutions, the duration of the stay is rather short (15 days to three months); consequently, it is not always possible to organise a conference within such a short time-frame. A conference should not just be added to a placement, since that would constitute a 'double punishment'; attending a conference is an investment of time and effort on the part of all the parties and, for juvenile offenders, the conference experience can be difficult.

Juveniles and their parents find conferences to be a more positive approach than being sent to a closed institution. Juveniles claim that closed institutions are not a good idea because they lead to more crime, and they participate in conferences in order to avoid being placed in institutions where no solutions to their problems are offered. The parents of offenders note that taking part in a conference means that their child may avoid an undesirable and unproductive placement in a closed institution.

Conclusion

This chapter has examined the outcomes of some research conducted on a conferencing project for juveniles who have committed either serious crimes or a series of crimes. The New Zealand conferencing model is used as a basis for the project but adaptations have been made to the procedure in order to implement it in a Belgian context. The results, so far, look promising although there are still some points of contention, such as the specific role of the police, the need for the ongoing training of facilitators, extending the practice throughout Belgium and ensuring a central role for victims in the process.

Discussions have been continuing with regard to reforming the existing youth protection law in Belgium, which dates back to 1965. The current Minister of Justice has written a new proposal (March 2004) which would add restorative practices such as mediation and conferencing to the existing law. Although a more integrated approach to restorative justice in youth law would offer advantages, it is gratifying that at least the pilot project described in this chapter is to receive a clearer legal foundation that may lead to an expansion of the practice throughout Belgium.

Notes

1 Conferencing was introduced in New Zealand in 1989 in the Children, Young Persons and Their Families Act. The Wagga model originated in Wagga Wagga, Australia and differs from the New Zealand model in that a police officer facilitates the meeting and there is no private time for the youngster. Usually, practices adopt one of these two models and adapt it to their own context. Discussion thus arises whether one can speak of 'two models' or whether there is just the 'conferencing model' which is adapted to the local circumstances. See, for instance, Vanfraechem (2004).
2 Mediation can also be used for more serious cases (see for, example, Umbreit, 2001).
3 For a more detailed account, see Vanfraechem (2003a).
4 In Dutch: 'Herstelgericht Groepsoverleg', or in short: 'Hergo'.
5 Social services are attached to the youth court to ensure follow-up for the youth. They examine the youth's environment and living circumstances so the judge has an idea about the person and environment of the offender.

Belgium still has a youth protection law under which decisions are taken for the benefit of the youth.

6   Mediators from five mediation services (ADAM and Elegast in Antwerp, BAS! in Brussels, BAAL in Hasselt/Tongeren and BAL in Leuven) were trained in May 2000 by Allan MacRae, then a Youth Justice Coordinator in New Zealand, with the financial help of the King Boudewijn Foundation.

7   In order to respect participants' privacy it was decided not to tape the conferences, even though that would offer more qualitative material and would register the actual wording of people.

8   Often the facilitators work in pairs during the conference, sometimes also during the preparation. The facilitator takes up the main role; the co-facilitator can intervene or add things when needed. This way, facilitators build up more experience during the pilot project with a low number of referrals. Furthermore, facilitators find it offers practical advantages such as being able to structure the communication process more easily.

9   There is an ongoing discussion about what the content of the social consequences would or could be. Also, bringing these consequences into the picture could overshadow the needs of the victim and the active participation of the offender, while involving the parties is central in restorative justice (Christie, 1977).

10 The results reflect answers on a scale from 1 (not at all) to 5 (a lot). The percentages point out extremes (four and five). The mean answers are thus excluded.

11 The action research has proven to be useful in this regard: the researcher reported the results from the interviews with participants to the facilitators, who could then improve their practice.

12 See, for example, Daly (1999), Duff (2003), Walgrave (2004) and Willemsens (2003).

13 Since, under the youth protection system, measures are taken on the basis of the person, one offender might be referred to a conference while the co-offender might get a community service or another measure while being involved in the exact same crime.

14 This was, happily, not the case in the conference at hand.

15 Police are legally obliged to inform victims of serious offences of the existence and availability of victims' assistance.

16 The researcher is cautious about generalising the results due to the small number of subjects and other methodological problems.

References

Christie, N. (1977) 'Conflicts as Property', *British Journal of Criminology*, 17, 1, 1–14.

Daly, K. (1999) 'Restorative Justice and Punishment: The Views of Young People'. Unpublished paper presented at the American Society of Criminology Annual Meeting, Toronto, November 1999; available at: www.gu.edu.au/school/ccj/kdaly_docs/kdpaper9.pdf.

De Witte, H., Hooge, J. and Walgrave, L. (eds) (2000) *Jongeren in Vlaanderen: gemeten en geteld. 12 tot 18-jarigen over hun leefwereld en toekomst.* Leuven: Universitaire Pers Leuven.

Duff, R. A. (2003) 'Restorative Punishments and Punitive Restoration', in L. Walgrave (ed.), *Restorative Justice and the Law.* Cullompton: Willan Publishing, pp. 82–100.

Eliaerts, C. and Dumortier, E. (2002) 'Restorative Justice for Children: In Need of Procedural Safeguards and Standards', in E. Weitekamp and H.-J. Kerner (eds), *Restorative Justice. Theoretical Foundations.* Cullompton: Willan Publishing, pp. 204–23.

Harris, N., Walgrave, L. and Braithwaite, J. (2004) 'Emotional Dynamics in Restorative Conferences', *Theoretical Criminology*, 8, 2, 191–210.

Hokwerda, Y. M. (2004) *Herstelrecht in jeugdstrafzaken. Een evaluatieonderzoek van zeven experimenten in Nederland.* Den Haag: Boom Juridische Uitgevers.

Maxwell, G. (2003) *Achieving Effective Outcomes in Youth Justice: Implications of New Research for Principles, Policy and Practice.* Paper presented at the 6th International Conference on Research on Restorative Justice for Juveniles, Vancouver, Canada, June 2003; available at: http://www.sfu.ca/cfrj/fulltext/maxwell.pdf.

Maxwell, G. and Morris, A. (1996) 'Research on Family Group Conferences with Young Offenders in New Zealand', in J. Hudson, A. Morris, G. Maxwell and B. Galaway (eds), *Family Group Conferences: Perspectives on Policy and Practice.* Monsey, NY: Federation Press and Criminal Justice Press, pp. 88–110.

Maxwell, G. and Morris, A. (1999) 'Understanding Re-offending', unpublished report. Wellington: Institute of Criminology, Victoria University of Wellington.

Maxwell, G. and Morris, A. (2002) 'Restorative Justice and Reconviction', *Contemporary Justice Review*, 5, 133–46.

Mirsky, L. (2003) *Family Group Conferencing Worldwide: Part One in a Series.* Available at: http://www.restorativepractices.org.

Prichard, J. (2003) 'Juvenile Conferencing and Restorative Justice in Tasmania'. Unpublished PhD thesis, University of Tasmania, Faculty of Law.

Retzinger, S. M. and Scheff, T. J. (1996) 'Strategy for Community Conferences: Emotions and Social Bonds', in B. Galaway and J. Hudson (eds), *Restorative Justice: International Perspectives.* Monsey, NY: Criminal Justice Press, pp. 315–36.

Strang, H. (2002) *Repair or Revenge: Victims and Restorative Justice.* Oxford: Clarendon Press.

Tyler, T. R. (1988) 'What is Procedural Justice?: Criteria Used by Citizens to Assess the Fairness of Legal Procedures', *Law and Society Review*, 22, 1, 103–35.

Umbreit, M. (2001) *The Handbook of Victim–Offender Mediation. An Essential Guide to Practice and Research.* San Francisco: Jossey-Bass.

Vanfraechem, I. (2003a) 'Implementing Family Group Conferences in a Legalistic System. The Example of Belgium', in L. Walgrave (ed.), *Repositioning Restorative Justice. Restorative Justice, Criminal Justice and Social Context.* Cullompton: Willan Publishing, pp. 313–27.

Vanfraechem, I. (2003b) *Herstelgericht Groepsoverleg in Vlaanderen, Verslag van een wetenschappelijk begeleid pilootproject*, unpublished research report. Leuven: Research Group on Juvenile Criminology.

Vanfraechem, I. (2004) 'Kritische reflecties over conferencing in Nederland en Vlaanderen', *Tijdschrift voor Herstelrecht*, 4, 4, 6–19.

Walgrave, L. (2004) 'Has Restorative Justice Appropriately Responded to Retribution Theory and Impulses?', in H. Zehr and B. Toews (eds), *Critical Issues in Restorative Justice*. Monsey, NY: Criminal Justice Press, pp. 47–60.

Weijers, I. (2003a) 'Groups and Restorative Dialogues'. Unpublished paper presented at the 6th International Conference on Research on Restorative Justice for Juveniles, Vancouver, Canada, June 2003; available at: http://www.sfu.ca/cfrj/fulltext/weijers.pdf.

Weijers, I. (2003b) 'Het herstelgesprek: overwegingen en aanbevelingen naar aanleiding van een studiereis', *Proces*, 3, 166–88.

Willemsens, J. (2003) 'Restorative Justice: A Discussion of Punishment', in L. Walgrave (ed.), *Repositioning Restorative Justice*. Cullompton: Willan Publishing, pp. 24–42.

Zehr, H. (1990) *Changing Lenses*. New York: Herald Press.

Chapter 15

Evaluation and restorative justice principles

Howard Zehr

Abstract

In this chapter, the author raises some issues that point to the importance of evaluations and suggest some approaches to these issues that have implications for both practice and evaluations of practice and pro- grammes. These include questions about whether restorative justice is as victim-oriented as it claims (or are victims being 'used') and whether the needs of offenders are being adequately addressed. Are the ethnic and cultural dimensions of restorative justice being addressed? How well is restorative justice doing in societies dominated by a culture of punish- ment? Evaluations have to be multi-method and multi-focused activities that address processes and outcomes and that ensure we are clear about our principles and philosophies – that ensure we are engaged in principled practice.

Introduction

I am going to begin with a disclaimer. I am not an evaluator, but I am an advocate of evaluation. I see myself as having two goals in this chapter: to raise some issues that make evaluations essential, then to suggest approaches to these issues that have implications for both practice and evaluation. The context of my comments is a deepening concern for what I call 'critical issues' in the restorative justice field. Toews and I have published a book – *Critical Issues in Restorative Justice* – in which we define critical issues in the following way:

> Critical issues are questions, forces or directions that affect the integrity or overall direction of the field – including gaps in theory or practice and ways that restorative justice is in danger of going astray or failing to live up to its promise. The term 'critical' suggests that these issues are crucial to the field, but also implies a critical stance toward the field (Zehr and Toews, 2004: ix).

These critical issues have been a longstanding concern of mine, starting when I first began in this field of work in the late 1970s. Unfortunately, though, our field has not always been very comfortable with such issues. In the early 1980s, for example, I presented to a group of practitioners in what I think was the forerunner of the Victim Offender Mediation Association. After raising some critical issues I received a hostile reaction from the audience. 'Why are you raising these kinds of questions?' they asked. 'What a downer.'

More recently, during the fall of 2002, I took a kind of international road trip, helping to facilitate a series of palavers – or as they say in New Zealand, 'hui' – around critical issues. We brought together various sectors – academics, policy makers, and practitioners – to identify and discuss some key concerns. The trip took me to England, to South Africa and to New Zealand, as well as places in North America. The following is a discussion of a few of the issues that have arisen in these dialogues.[1]

Some general issues and concerns

One of the issues with which people have been wrestling is whether we have been too focused, in restorative justice, on conferences and on individuals. In London, practitioners were asking, 'are we in danger of seeing the conference as a whole thing, not realising that many of these individuals have many other needs, other things going on in their lives that needed to be addressed? What do we do when other issues get unearthed in a conference? How do we provide the resources we need?' On a related note, are we individualising forms of wrongdoing that have a wider scope or context? Much like the criminal justice system, are we taking harms that have larger social, economic, political dimensions and treating them as individual wrongs, thereby helping to ignore underlying structural problems? Mamdani has offered a similar critique of the South African Truth and Reconciliation Commission – which claimed a restorative framework – arguing that individualising wrongdoing tended to gloss over economic and social apartheid (Mamdani, 2000).

One of my chief concerns is whether we are being as victim-orientated as we claim. Are we really delivering justice for victims or are we using victims for our own purposes? Despite efforts to include victims over the past several decades, the criminal justice system remains predominately offender-oriented: cases are defined and tracked through the system by offenders' identities, the primary focus is on what happens to offenders and most job descriptions in the system are oriented toward offenders. Moreover, many of us come to the restorative justice field from offender-related backgrounds. All this means that it is difficult, in practice, for restorative justice to be truly balanced. In theory, restorative justice offers a more central place to victims than probably any previous effort to correct the system. On the other hand, this claim could turn out to be primarily rhetorical. Many victims and victim service providers are deeply sceptical, and with good reason.

On the flip side, are we adequately addressing offender needs? We talk a lot about offender accountability but what about their other needs? And what about needs language itself? In a recent conversation Don Evans, a rehabilitation specialist in Canada, raised serious concerns about the impact of risk assessment in Canada and the United States. In restorative justice we often talk in terms of needs. What happens, Evans asked, when those needs began to be seen as criminogenic needs and become part of risk assessment? Moreover, are we thinking enough about the dynamics of offender transformation? For example, how do we deal with their narratives of victimisation? I am convinced that much offending grows of a sense of victimisation. As Gilligan (1996) has argued, violence can be seen as an effort to do justice or undo an injustice. Are we addressing this in our practices and theories? Or what about the processes offenders must go through to re-narrate their lives? I have recently read Maruna's (2001) book *Making Good* and I am trying to fully comprehend the implications. He interviewed offenders who have ceased to be involved in crime and found that those who successfully stop may have different understandings of their responsibilities than restorative justice advocates might prefer. Offenders turn their lives around, in part, by 're-storying' their lives. In that process, they have to incorporate the bad things they have done while still preserving their sense of identity and self-worth. To do that, they may not take responsibility as fully as we might like. How do we incorporate that into our work?

What about prisoners' worldviews? How does that affect their understandings of restorative justice? While sitting with some lifer friends several years ago, I suddenly realised that although we have spent much time articulating restorative justice from the standpoint of victims and the community, we have done little to articulate it from an offender or prisoner perspective. What would that involve?

There are also a whole set of questions around whether we are adequately addressing the ethnic and cultural dimensions of restorative justice. Although much more research is needed, some attention is being given to cultural biases and assumptions in our models of practice; however, what about our understandings of victimisation and offending? To what extent are they culturally shaped, and what are the implications for practice? What about the way we conceptualise restorative justice itself? What does it say when so many of the spokespeople for this field are old white guys like me?

There are significant issues associated with indigenous justice, particularly the ways in which mainstream society or governmental structures may be appropriating these traditions and even using them as a means to recolonise people. In our Conflict Transformation Programme at Eastern Mennonite University, where practitioners come from 50 countries to learn together, participants often find that restorative justice serves as a way to legitimate and activate their own traditions. But are we giving adequate attention to the retributive and restorative elements that are in all our traditions? Are we talking enough about the fact that when restorative justice builds upon indigenous values, it often cannot be a simple resurrection of traditional approaches but rather a mix of traditional and modern human rights values? Are we giving adequate concern to how those traditions can be appropriated by others, to how they are being distorted and misused?

There are large issues associated with the role of the community. For instance, to what extent is community taking the place of victims? Are communities healthy enough to be doing the job that we are asking them to do? What do we mean by community? As one woman in New Zealand recently asked, as we rely heavily on volunteers are we feminising justice since, in many societies, women are the people who typically volunteer? What are the implications of that?

The use of shame has raised serious concerns for many. I am intrigued with honour and humiliation as keys to understanding offending behaviour, understanding victim behaviour and understanding the way people are experiencing justice. There are many concerns about the way we may be misinterpreting and misusing shame, however. We may be trying to shame people rather than learning that the focus ought to be on processes for removing and transforming shame. One day I am going to make a bumper sticker that says, 'Shame Happens'. The question is not how do we shame people, but what do we do about the shame that is there already?

In New Zealand, someone asked, 'what are people going to say, 200 years from now, about restorative justice? Was it an opportunity lost, or was it an opportunity misused?' How this movement turns out will hinge in part, I believe, on how we handle the following four areas.

Four critical issues

We need evaluation, and we need to pay attention to the results. Those of us who are restorative justice advocates and practitioners naturally believe we are doing a beautiful thing. How could anyone question it? We tell the good stories and ignore the bad; we engage in butterfly collecting, as some critics have charged. As a result of this mentality, we tend not to want evaluation. When we are evaluated, we do not want to listen to the results.

We desperately need evaluation, and evaluation has to be multi-method and multi-focus. We need to evaluate processes and outcomes, and we also need to evaluate the goals and functioning of our organisations. We need to evaluate what we are doing and how it compares to what we think we are doing. It is very interesting to evaluate a restorative justice programme by asking all the stakeholders and actors what they think they are doing and why. If you do this, you may find everybody is playing a different game and that they are not at all on the same page. The implications can be quite serious.

We also need to think carefully about how we do evaluation, what yardsticks we use, and what values – implicit and explicit – underlie our approach to evaluation. In a recently published chapter – 'Ways of Knowing for a Restorative Worldview' – Toews and I have argued that too often our assumptions and approaches to evaluation mirror those of the 'retributive' worldview (Zehr and Toews, 2003). We have advocated, instead, for a set of 'transformative guidelines' that call for a more restorative stance toward knowledge, our subjects and our roles.

A second essential is conscious and structured accountability. We need to make ourselves deliberately accountable to various sectors in society including, and especially, those we claim to serve. For example, to help guard against the biases and distortions noted above, we need victims looking over our shoulders, auditing our programmes. We need to have them on our boards and on our start-up committees. That goes for other players as well. Restorative justice advocates for accountability for offenders but accountability applies to service providers as well.

Third, we need to encourage dialogue between the various sectors involved. A number of us recently completed a 'listening project' with victims and victim services. We sent listening teams out to seven US states where we knew there were tensions between victim services and restorative justice. The listening teams were made up of one victim advocate and one prominent restorative justice advocate. We asked the teams to sit down with groups of victims and victim service providers, ask a series of open-ended questions and to just listen to what they said. A lot of very difficult but important things were heard in this important dialogue. We have published the results and are hoping that a similar dialogue will now go on locally in various communities (Mika et al., 2002).

The fourth imperative is to be clear about our principles, values and philosophies and having accomplished that, to do what I have come to call 'principled practice'. When observing New Zealand practitioners who are really getting it right, I realised that they were doing principled practice. The law in New Zealand sets down seven principles and seven goals for restorative practice (MacRae and Zehr, 2004). These practitioners were virtually carrying those principles and goals in their back pocket and for every decision they made, they were referring to those principles. In our Conflict Transformation Programme at Eastern Mennonite University, we have a practice sector called the Institute for Justice and Peacebuilding. As we assess the requests and opportunities for practice that come to us from around the world, our decisions are guided by a series of ten principles that we have agreed should shape our practice. When a request comes in, we literally do a written analysis using those ten principles. That is, in part, what I mean by principled practice. It requires clarity about our principles and values, and a commitment to be guided by them on a daily basis.

I recently completed a book that involved interviews with victims who had been through very severe violence (Zehr, 2001). The conversations confirmed the importance of metaphors in trauma and trauma healing. In fact, some people say that the process to transcend the trauma of severe violence is a process of changing metaphors. Victims used metaphors of trauma such as bricks on their chests, 'trauma bubbles', and pots of grief being carried on one's head. The metaphors were diverse and often individual. However, one metaphor used by almost everyone is the metaphor of a journey. They are on a journey, and it is a journey that never quite ends.

We in the restorative justice field are on a journey as well. It is a journey that is circuitous. It is a journey whose destination is unclear. I think it is also important to remember we are at a very early stage in that journey and that we will encounter many forks in the road. We need to make sure we do not take the wrong road but, if we do, we need to get back on the right track. To stay on the right road, or to get back on it, we need to be deliberate about four things: we need to be evaluated and to take the results seriously; we need to make ourselves accountable in conscious ways; we need to encourage open dialogues among the various sectors that are impacted by our work; and we need to not only articulate our principles but also let our practices be guided by those principles.

Conclusion

Restorative justice claims to be responsive to the needs of various individuals and stakeholders, including victims, offenders and communities. At its best, it creates an arena in which people can sort out, within limits, what justice means in their situations. Restorative justice is postmodern in its realisation that our truths about justice are contextual and that justice needs to be shaped from the community up. I close, then, with what has become my mantra: that restorative justice is above all about respect for all, and that such respect requires humility. In the meaning of humility I include the common understanding of not taking undue credit but, more importantly, I also include a deep appreciation for the limits of what we know: a recognition that what I 'know' is at best only part of reality, that what I 'know' is inevitably shaped by my biography and identity, that what I 'know' might not be generalisable to others. Central to restorative justice is a commitment to listen to other voices, including the dissonant ones. Only if we are grounded in respect and humility can we prevent the restorative approach to justice that seems so liberating to us from becoming a burden or even a weapon to be used against others, as has happened so often with the reforms of the past.

Note

1   Proceedings of the New Zealand hui are available in Juelich (2003).

References

Gilligan, J. (1996) *Violence: Reflections on a National Epidemic*. New York: Random House.

Juelich, S. (ed.) (2003) *Critical Issues in Restorative Justice: Advancing the Agenda in Aotearoa, New Zealand*. Auckland: Massey University Centre for Justice and Peace Development.

MacRae, A. and Zehr, H. (2004) *The Little Book of Family Group Conferencing, New Zealand Style*. Intercourse, PA: Good Books.

Mamdani, M. (2002) 'The Truth According to the TRC', in I. Amadiume and A. An-Na'Im (eds), *The Politics of Memory*. London: Zed Books.

Maruna, S. (2001) *Making Good: How Ex-Convicts Reform and Rebuild Their Lives*. Washington, DC: American Psychological Association.

Mika, H., Achilles, M., Halbert, E., Stutzman-Amstutz, L. and Zehr, H. (2002) *Taking Victims and Their Advocates Seriously: A Listening Project*. Akron, PA: Mennonite Central Committee.

Zehr, H. (2001) *Transcending: Reflections of Crime Victims*. Intercourse, PA: Good Books.

Zehr, H. and Toews, B. (2003) 'Ways of Knowing for a Restorative Worldview', in E. Weitekamp and H.-J. Kerner (eds), *Restorative Justice in Context: International Practice and Directions*. Portland, OR: Willan Publishing.

Zehr, H. and Toews, B. (eds) (2004) *Critical Issues in Restorative Justice*. Monsey, NY and Portland, OR: Criminal Justice Press and Willan Publishing.

Index